ALSO BY BOB WOODWARD

Obama's Wars

The War Within: A Secret White House History, 2006–2008

State of Denial

The Secret Man
(*with a Reporter's Assessment by Carl Bernstein*)

Plan of Attack

Bush at War

Maestro: Greenspan's Fed and the American Boom

Shadow: Five Presidents and the Legacy of Watergate

The Choice

The Agenda: Inside the Clinton White House

The Commanders

Veil: The Secret Wars of the CIA, 1981–1987

Wired: The Short Life and Fast Times of John Belushi

The Brethren
(*with Scott Armstrong*)

The Final Days
(*with Carl Bernstein*)

All the President's Men
(*with Carl Bernstein*)

# THE PRICE

SIMON & SCHUSTER PAPERBACKS

# OF POLITICS

## Bob Woodward

NEW YORK · LONDON · TORONTO · SYDNEY · NEW DELHI

*To Benjamin C. Bradlee*

---

 Simon & Schuster Paperbacks
Division of Simon & Schuster, Inc.
1230 Avenue of the Americas
New York, NY 10020

First Simon & Schuster paperback edition September 2013

SIMON & SCHUSTER PAPERBACKS and colophon are registered trademarks
of Simon & Schuster, Inc.

For information about special discounts for bulk purchases,
please contact Simon & Schuster Special Sales at 1-866-506-1949
or business@simonandschuster.com.

The Simon & Schuster Speakers Bureau can bring authors to your
live event. For more information or to book an event, contact the
Simon & Schuster Speakers Bureau at 1-866-248-3049 or visit our
website at www.simonspeakers.com.

Designed by Joy O'Meara

Manufactured in the United States of America

10  9  8  7  6  5  4  3  2  1

The Library of Congress has cataloged the hardcover edition as follows:

Woodward, Bob.
The price of politics / Bob Woodward.
    p. cm.
Includes bibliographical references and index.
1. Obama, Barack. 2. United States—Economic policy—2009–.
3. United States—Economic conditions—2009– 4. Budget—United States.
5. Budget deficits—United States. 6. Government spending policy—United States.
7. United States—Politics and government—2009– 8. Fiscal policy—United
States. I. Title.
    HC106.84.W664 2012
    973.932092—dc23               2012037733

ISBN 978-1-4516-5110-2
ISBN 978-1-4516-5111-9 (pbk)
ISBN 978-1-4516-5112-6 (ebook)

# CONTENTS

# AUTHOR'S PERSONAL NOTE

I had two terrific people assist me full-time on this book: Rob Garver, a 20-year veteran reporter and editor, spent just six months on this project, coming to work for me in February 2012. I call him the workhorse who energized and focused me. Determined and fair-minded, he did at least two days' work in each single day. He never wasted a minute as best I can tell. His mature insights, skills and willingness to tell me "no" when it was needed kept us on track. Rob, 43, is one of the best natural editors and reporters I have ever worked with. He graduated from the University of Vermont and has a master's degree from the Georgetown Public Policy Institute. His sophisticated understanding of business, banking and policymaking guided me at every step. He quickly grasped the story we were trying to get and went after it. He is a delight in every way, enduring a long commute each day to and from Springfield, Virginia, where he lives with his two sons, Ryan and Andrew. Several mornings each week, he arrived at work by 6:30 a.m., before the newspapers. Without Rob, this book never would have been completed—not even close.

Evelyn M. Duffy, who worked with me on two previous books, *The War Within* and *Obama's Wars*, continued on this third book. I will say it again, Thank God. Now 27, she is a lady of balance and levelheadedness. She again transcribed hundreds of hours of digitally recorded interviews with President Obama and top White House and congressional officials. Her editing skills have grown immensely. What seems a decent draft will come back to me covered in countless marks as she identifies inconsistencies, factual errors and grammatical problems. She can find any person and almost any information. Evelyn graduated from George Washington University in 2007 with a degree in English and creative writing. Her work and presence are marked by grace, kindness and integrity. She is smart, practical and knows how to enjoy a good laugh. No one I have ever worked with of any age has more common sense. I thank her with gratitude. Without her efforts and wisdom we would never have finished.

# NOTE TO READERS

Nearly all the information in this book comes from interviews with key White House and congressional officials. Some provided documents, contemporaneous meeting notes, working papers, diaries, emails, transcripts and chronologies. Democrats and Republicans cooperated in about equal amounts.

This book examines the struggle between President Obama and the United States Congress to manage federal spending and tax policy for the three and one half years between 2009 and the summer of 2012. More than half the book focuses on the intense 44-day crisis in June and July 2011 when the United States came to the brink of a potentially catastrophic default on its debt.

Most interviews were conducted on "background," meaning the information could be used in the book but none of the sources would be identified by name. Many sources were interviewed multiple times, and nearly all allowed me to digitally record our interviews. These recordings produced transcripts that run to thousands of pages. In all, more than 100 people were interviewed for this project.

Three key figures spoke to me on the record. I interviewed President Barack Obama for 1 hour and 25 minutes in the Oval Office on July 11, 2012; House Speaker John Boehner in his Capitol office on June 8, 2012, for 1 hour and 25 minutes; and Senate Minority Leader Mitch McConnell at his Capitol office for an hour on July 12, 2012.

As much as possible, I have tried to preserve the language of the main participants by quoting them directly or using their words to reflect their speech and attitudes. Verbal exchanges were checked and rechecked with participants as much as possible. No reporting can provide the equivalent of a perfect engineer's drawing of events. This is the best obtainable version, and it is impossible to do this work and not realize—and be humbled by—what you have not discovered and do not know.

Any attribution of thoughts, conclusions or feelings to a person comes from that person directly, from notes, or from a colleague whom the person told.

In the course of such an in-depth immersion in the decision making during such a crisis, the attitudes of the players become clear. Occasionally, a person said something was "off the record," meaning it could not be used unless the information is obtained elsewhere. In many cases, I was able to get the information from others so it could be put in this book. Some people think they can lock up and prevent publication of information by declaring it "off the record" or by saying that they don't want to see it in the book. But in the White House and Congress, nearly everyone's business and attitudes become known to others. And in the course of extensive interviews with firsthand sources about key decisions, the role and goals of the major players become clear.

*Bob Woodward*
*July 14, 2012*
*Washington, D.C.*

# CAST OF CHARACTERS

**THE PRESIDENT OF THE UNITED STATES**
Barack H. Obama

**VICE PRESIDENT OF THE UNITED STATES**
Joseph R. Biden
    Ron Klain, chief of staff (to January 14, 2011)
    Bruce Reed, chief of staff (January 14, 2011–present)

**SECRETARY OF THE TREASURY**
Timothy Geithner (January 26, 2009–present)

**WHITE HOUSE ECONOMIC TEAM**

**Director, National Economic Council**
Larry Summers (January 20, 2009–December 31, 2010)
Gene Sperling (January 20, 2011–present)

**Director, Office of Management and Budget**
Peter Orszag (January 20, 2009–July 30, 2010)
Jack Lew (November 18, 2010–January 27, 2012)

## WHITE HOUSE STAFF

**Chief of staff**
Rahm Emanuel (January 20, 2009–October 1, 2010)
William Daley (January 13, 2011–January 27, 2012)
Jack Lew (January 27, 2012–present)

**Senior adviser to the president**
David Plouffe

**Director of legislative affairs**
Rob Nabors

**Director of communications**
Dan Pfeiffer

**Press secretary**
Jay Carney

## THE SENATE

**Majority Leader**
Harry Reid, Democrat of Nevada
　　David Krone, chief of staff

**Minority Leader**
Mitch McConnell, Republican of Kentucky
　　Rohit Kumar, domestic policy director and deputy chief of staff

**Senators**
Max Baucus, Democrat of Montana, chairman, Finance Committee
Kent Conrad, Democrat of North Dakota, chairman, Budget Committee
Dick Durbin, Democrat of Illinois, Majority Whip
Jon Kyl, Republican of Arizona, Minority Whip
Patty Murray, Democrat of Washington State, supercommittee co-chair

## THE HOUSE OF REPRESENTATIVES

**Speaker of the House (to January 2011)**

Nancy Pelosi, Democrat of California

**Speaker of the House (January 2011–present)**

John Boehner, Republican of Ohio

    Barry Jackson, chief of staff

    Brett Loper, policy director

    Kevin Smith, communications director

    Michael Steel, press secretary

**Majority leader**

Steny Hoyer, Democrat of Maryland (to January 2011)

Eric Cantor, Republican of Virginia (January 2011–present)

    Steven Stombres, chief of staff

    Neil Bradley, policy director

    Brad Dayspring, communications director

**Members of the House**

Dave Camp, Republican of Michigan, chairman, Ways and Means Committee (January 3, 2011–present)

Jeb Hensarling, Republican of Texas, supercommittee co–chair

Kevin McCarthy, Republican of California, Majority Whip (January 2011–present)

Paul Ryan, Republican of Wisconsin, chairman, House Budget Committee (January 3, 2011–present)

Chris Van Hollen, Democrat of Maryland, ranking member, House Budget Committee (January 3, 2011–present)


## NATIONAL COMMISSION ON FISCAL RESPONSIBILITY AND REFORM

**Co–chairmen**

Alan Simpson, former Republican senator from Wyoming

Erskine Bowles, Democrat, former chief of staff to President Bill Clinton

# PROLOGUE

The lavish dinner at the Capital Hilton Hotel in downtown Washington on the evening of Saturday, March 11, 2006, was about the last place you would expect to find him. But there was Barack Obama, age 44, the junior senator from Illinois for only the last 14 months, in formal white-tie with tails and very much at ease in the crowd of 600. His trademark smile, broad and infectious, dominated his face as I met him for the first time.

We were at the annual Gridiron Club dinner—a rite of passage for national political figures such as Obama. The crowd included President George W. Bush and most of the major politicians in Washington. It was one of Senator Obama's maiden voyages into the unsavory belly of the Washington beast. Bush was to speak for the Republicans, and Obama had been selected to speak for the Democrats.

Founded in 1885, the Gridiron—named because its motto was to "singe but not burn"—had the reputation of being an old-school event of in-jokes, skits and music that seemed more fitted to a bygone era.

"You're from Wheaton, Illinois," Obama said to me, referring, unprompted, to the small town where I was raised in the late 1940s and '50s. Wheaton, 25 miles west of Chicago, is home to Wheaton College, best known for its alumnus evangelist Billy Graham, whose influence permeated the town.

"I'll bet you didn't carry Wheaton," I said confidently, referring to his Senate race 16 months earlier. A bastion of Midwestern conservatism and country-club Republicans, Wheaton was the most Republican town in the country in the 1950s, or at least regarded itself that way.

"I carried DuPage County by 60 percent!" Obama responded, beaming that incandescent smile. Wheaton is the county seat of DuPage.

I said that seemed utterly impossible. That couldn't be the Wheaton or DuPage I had known.

Obama continued to smile me down. The certainty on his face was deep, giving me pause. Suddenly, I remembered that Obama's opponent for the Senate seat had been Alan Keyes, the conservative black Republican gadfly. Keyes had substituted at the last minute for the first Republican nominee, who withdrew from the race when divorce and child custody records revealed that he had taken his wife to sex clubs in New York, New Orleans and Paris.

"Well, everyone who runs for office should have Alan Keyes as their opponent," I said, trying to hold my ground.

Obama smiled some more—almost mirthful, yet unrevealing. The conversation turned to Illinois politics, and Obama ticked off the areas where he had strong support—Chicago, the labor unions—and weak support, downstate and the farm areas. He defined the categories skillfully, expanding on the state's interest groups and voting blocs. He made it clear he knew where he had work to do.

He sounded like a graceful old-fashioned pol. Though he had carried DuPage by 60 percent, he had won 70 percent of the statewide vote.

His wife, Michelle, stood by his side in a stunning gown. But the focus and the questions from people crowded around were all directed at the dazzling new star.

When he appeared at the podium several hours later, Obama stood perfectly erect, projecting radiant confidence.

"This is a true story," he said. "A friend sent me a clip about a new study by a psychologist at the University of Scotland who says sex before a public speaking engagement actually enhances your oratorical power. I showed this clip to Michelle, before we arrived here tonight. She looked it over, handed it back and said, 'Do the best you can!' "

The laughter ignited instantly.

"This appearance is really the capstone of an incredible 18 months," he said, citing the keynote speech at the Democratic National Convention in 2004, cover of *Newsweek*, a best-selling autobiography, *Dreams from My Father*, a Grammy award for reading the audiobook. "Really what else is there to do? Well, I guess . . . I could pass a law or something."

The self-deprecation played well.

Referring to Senator John McCain's positive treatment by the press up to that point, Obama said, "Some of my colleagues call John a prima donna. Me? I call him a role model. Think of it as affirmative action. Why should the white guys be the only ones who are overhyped?"

The self-awareness played smooth.

Noting the speculation that the 2008 presidential campaign could come down to McCain, a maverick Republican, versus Senator Hillary Clinton, he said, "People don't realize how much John and Hillary have in common. They're both very smart. Both very hardworking. And they're both hated by the Republicans!"

This played bipartisan.

Obama turned toward President Bush, who was on the stage nearby. "The president was so excited about Tom Friedman's book *The World Is Flat*. As soon as he saw the title, he said, 'You see, I was right!' "

The joke played confident.

"I want to thank you for all the generous advance coverage you've given me in anticipation of a successful career. When I actually do something, we'll let you know."

The audience clapped and hooted in delight.

After dinner the buzz was like a chain reaction. Not only could this young Obama tell a joke on himself, with the required self-effacement, but he had remarkable communications skills. An editor at *The Washington Post* once said that journalists only write two stories: Oh, the horror of it all, and Oh, the wonder of it all. Obama was the wonder of it all that night and he basked in the attention he had captured. Rarely have I seen anyone manage the moment so well. He had frankly and forthrightly trumpeted his lack of accomplishment, and the roomful of egos ate it up. But if he had done nothing much so far, why was he there? Why the buzz? The approbation? What exactly was being measured?

It was the dramatic impact he was having on his audience. The triumph was the effect.

Twenty-five years earlier in 1981, I had attended a Gridiron dinner where the speaker for the Democrats was Senator Daniel Patrick Moynihan, the bookish intellectual who had served in prominent posts in both Republican and Democratic administrations. Moynihan, then 53, made some good jokes, but his theme was serious: what it means to be a Democrat. The soul of the party was to fight for equality and the little guy, he said. The party cared for the underdogs in America, the voiceless, powerless and those who got stepped on. It was a defining speech, and the buzz afterward was that Moynihan was going to be president. He wasn't, of course. That was then, this was now.

Obama had not once mentioned the party or high purpose. His speech, instead, was about Obama, his inexperience, and, in the full paradox of the moment, what he had not done.

Two and a half years later, he was president-elect of the United States.

# 1

Two weeks before their inauguration, President-elect Barack Obama and Vice President–elect Joe Biden headed to Capitol Hill to meet with the Democratic and Republican leaders of the House and Senate. It was 3:15 p.m. on Monday, January 5, 2009, and Obama was fresh from a 12-day Hawaiian vacation.

The leaders gathered in the ornate LBJ Room of the Senate decorated with a painting celebrating the laying of the first transatlantic cable. In it, the allegorical figures of Europe and America joined hands in friendship across the ocean.

As if in that spirit, Obama called on the group to work together across the partisan divide to address the looming economic crisis.

"Action on our part is urgent," he told them. Unemployment was at 7.2 percent and rising, and the economic situation was threatening to get worse with the financial system in full-blown crisis. He wanted the Congress to quickly pass an economic stimulus package in the range of "$800 billion to $1.3 trillion."

It would include some tax cuts—sweet music to the Republicans—and some investment, such as spending on roads, buildings and other job-creating projects. In addition, he said, they had to "build in medium- and long-term fiscal discipline" to tame the growing federal deficit.

Looking at the four Republican leaders—the GOP was in the minority in both houses of Congress—Obama reached out.

"I want everyone's ideas," he said. "But we can't get into political games."

Nancy Pelosi, the California Democrat and speaker of the House, interjected, "I come to Washington to work in a bipartisan manner."

Both Republicans and Democrats stifled chuckles. Pelosi, a 12-term veteran of Congress and the first female speaker, was notably partisan in her leadership of the 257 House Democrats. She had been born into Democratic politics. Her father was a congressman from Maryland and both her father and brother served as mayor of Baltimore.

"We're in a unique situation," said Harry Reid, the soft-spoken but combative Senate majority leader. The son of a miner, Reid had grown up in the tiny town of Searchlight, Nevada, without electricity or indoor plumbing. A former amateur boxer who had faced down organized crime bosses while chair of the Nevada Gaming Commission, Reid avoided declarations about bipartisanship, adding simply, "I want to work."

The Senate Republican Minority Leader Mitch McConnell spoke next. At 66, a veteran of five terms representing Kentucky in the Senate, McConnell was known for the ruthlessness with which he ruled the Senate Republican minority. He cut straight to his suggestions.

I like the idea of tax cuts, he said. But we should also take a look at the money the federal government pays to the states for programs like Medicaid, the health insurance program for the poor. Beloved by the Democrats, Medicaid cost the federal government more than $250 billion a year. Perhaps, he suggested, we should treat that money as loans instead of outright grants. Having to pay the money back would make the states more judicious in spending it, he said.

Obama seemed receptive. "If it works, we don't care whose idea it is," he said evenly.

John Boehner, the leader of the House Republican minority, came next.

Tanned from many hours on the golf course, Boehner (pronounced

BAY-ner) spoke in a casual Midwestern baritone roughened by years of incessant cigarette smoking. At age 59, he was beginning his 10th term as congressman from his largely suburban district in southwestern Ohio. The second of 12 children, Boehner had grown up working in a bar owned by his grandfather, and was the first person in his family to attend college, working his way through Xavier University in Cincinnati to earn a degree in business administration. The minority leader was a conservative and ardently pro-business, but not an ideologue. A force for moderation, who had forged agreements with Democratic icon Ted Kennedy on education, Boehner understood that the secret to getting anything done in Washington was the ability and willingness to cut deals.

Boehner knew how to tend to personal relationships and, unlike many of his colleagues, was not a workaholic. Informal and on the surface accessible to colleagues and press, he liked to tease fellow congressmen and staff, and enjoyed a glass or two of red wine at the Republican Capitol Hill Club in the evening.

A stimulus package would have to go through the congressional committees to ensure transparency, Boehner said, but he agreed they could not tolerate unnecessary delay. "The economy is in unprecedented turmoil."

No one needed to spell out the political risks of passing a new stimulus bill, but Obama said he thought there was a lesson to be learned from TARP, the Troubled Asset Relief Program, which had passed in the last months of the Bush presidency. TARP was controversial and dauntingly complex, a $700 billion temporary bailout for the banks—money that was supposed to be paid back. "If the public doesn't know what the money is for," the president-elect said, citing TARP, "it's a big problem."

He pledged to personally sell the stimulus package to the American people as something that would help everyone. At the moment, Barack Obama, president-elect, was the most famous and possibly the most admired political figure in the world. The Republicans were a dispirited lot. Political writers were speculating that the GOP might devolve into a regional party representing mainly Southern whites as the Democrats ascended to permanent majority status. Obama held all the cards. How would he play his first hand?

"There will be times," he said cordially, "when we will want to bull-doze each other."

True, all knew.

"This isn't one of those times," he said.

"Time frame?" asked Boehner.

"Have to get it done before Presidents Day recess," Obama said, re-ferring to a four-day break in the congressional schedule that was to begin in six weeks.

"We understand the gravity," added Vice President–elect Biden, suggesting that they could work seven days a week on the stimulus package.

Senators McConnell and Dick Durbin, the Democratic whip, joked that they would not work weekends.

What about the thousands of homeowners who owed more on their mortgages than their homes were worth? asked Durbin.

"We will not roll out an aggressive housing plan," Obama said, and it would not be part of the stimulus bill. The housing problem was massive and baffling, and none of them had solid ideas for fixing it.

Then Virginia Representative Eric Cantor spoke up. Cantor was the minority whip, and the title suited him—thin and taut, he was quick with stinging partisan sound bites and was a fast-rising figure in Republican national politics. He had trained as an attorney and worked in his family's real estate firm in Richmond for a decade before entering politics in the early 1990s. Now he was the House Republicans' vote counter and disciplinarian. He made it his business to be closely tied in to all the GOP House members and had especially strong links to the ultraconservative wing of the party.

"Fear is grasping the country," Cantor said, giving voice to something everyone in the room already knew. People were worried that they might lose their jobs. But there was a parallel concern that affected them all, "A fear of Washington." It was a familiar Republican talking point.

"We need to do something bold that says we are not wasting their money," Cantor urged. There was little public confidence in government, so the only solution would be "full transparency."

After the meeting, Obama approached the Republican House leaders, Boehner and Cantor. "I'm serious about this," he told them. "Come with your ideas."

Steven Stombres, Cantor's chief of staff, left the meeting with conflicting emotions. A former Army Reserve intelligence officer with a shaved head and a military bearing, Stombres was impressed. If this really was a bipartisan "coming together" it was precisely what the country needed at such a critical time, and as a citizen he found it genuinely inspirational. As a Republican, though, he was worried: If Obama followed through on this promise of political togetherness, Republicans would be in bad shape.

"Phew," Cantor said afterward, "we may be in this minority for a while."

After the meeting, Senator McConnell told reporters, "I thought the atmosphere for bipartisan cooperation was sincere on all sides." The Republican leader said of Obama, "I think he's already been listening to the suggestions we've made."

Reid and Pelosi seemed almost giddy. Pelosi announced that it was "a new day in the capital."

Obama's stimulus package, meant to jump-start the failing economy, had been in the works for weeks. His chief economic advisers had been working on it since the election.

Larry Summers, the incoming head of the National Economic Council, which coordinates all administration economic policy, supported instant additional spending of hundreds of billions of dollars.

A former treasury secretary in Bill Clinton's administration, the brusque Summers was better known for his brainpower than his people skills. He had hesitated to take the job as Obama's NEC head, viewing it at first as a step down from his previous job running the Treasury Department. In the end, he had relented under the combina-

tion of pressure from Obama and the urging of friends, including former Federal Reserve Board Chairman Alan Greenspan, who assured
him that the job could offer him more influence than he realized.

In Summers's view, the economic problem was lack of demand: Not
enough people were spending money on goods and services. The administration had to stimulate consumer spending. He later described
it to others in simple terms: "We didn't have jobs because we didn't
have demand. And if we didn't get more demand, we weren't going
to get more jobs. And if we did get more demand, we would get more
jobs."

Worried about the cost of a stimulus package, Obama wondered what else could be done. What about accelerating job training,
strengthening employment services, and reforming unemployment insurance?

Demand is the big elephant in the room, Summers insisted.

Obama didn't like that answer, but finally came to accept it.

In the weeks before the election, Obama was interviewing candidates
for the all-important post of treasury secretary. While in New York, he
met with Timothy Geithner, the head of the Federal Reserve Bank of
New York, who had been a key figure in stabilizing the U.S. economy
after the 2008 financial crisis.

The two had not met before. Geithner, who was 47 but looked a decade younger, launched immediately into a well-rehearsed, five-point
argument on why he should not be picked.

One, I promised my kids I wouldn't move them again. Two, we're at
a moment of national crisis. I'm not a public figure. You need to have
a public figure people have seen before in this context, because it matters hugely. Three, there are better-qualified people than me for this.
Four, at some point the U.S. will have solved the financial crisis, and
you'll be left with a whole set of other challenges that I've not spent
my life thinking about. And fifth, he said, I'm up to my neck in this
crisis, as you know. And I'm going to carry with me all those decisions.
And you may need to have some separation from those decisions. It's

harder for you if you choose me. Because I'm not going to walk away from them.

It was a brilliant case against himself—precisely the kind of analytical power that appealed to Obama. After the election, he picked Geithner.

Obama selected Peter Orszag as director of the White House Office of Management and Budget. Just a few weeks past his 40th birthday, Orszag was a summa cum laude graduate of Princeton with a Ph.D. in economics from the London School of Economics. He was tall, gangly and brilliant. Obama had plucked him from his position as head of the powerful and independent Congressional Budget Office, which Orszag had held for nearly two years.

Unlike Summers, Orszag and Geithner did not believe the need to increase demand trumped all other policy priorities. Both recognized the need for a stimulus, but resisted the idea of a package that might last for more than two years. They were facing contradictory policy requirements: spend more quickly, but address the long-term deficit of hundreds of billions of dollars per year.

In one early memo, the team advised Obama that there was no danger of too much stimulus, or spending too much money in the first year. The question was: How do you make it politically salable?

Once he accepted the need for a huge infusion of public spending, Obama began to see it as an opportunity—a chance to invest in projects like high-speed rail, visionary environmentalism and innovation-related projects.

"A lot of that is going to take seven years to happen," Summers pointed out, splashing cold water on Obama's big dreams. "Big visionary things just take a long time."

The Hoover Dam, which had employed thousands of workers during the Great Depression, had taken five years to build, Biden reminded them.

Obama wanted to pull the Band-Aid off fast, as he put it. "Let's do whatever needs to be done, but let's not keep at this for five years."

He made it clear he wanted to pivot as soon as possible from rescue to a broad kind of economic renewal. He thought and spoke in terms of FDR, and some in the White House wondered if he had Roosevelt envy.

Comprehensive health care reform, though, remained his priority. The world knew that from his campaign. What the world didn't know was that his top advisers, led by incoming chief of staff Rahm Emanuel, disagreed, arguing that it would require too much effort. Survival had to come first.

But to Obama, health insurance for everyone as a new entitlement was the major unfulfilled task of the political movement of which he was a part and now led.

It was now or never, he said. So it would be now.

Later, Cantor approached Emanuel, who had been No. 3 in the House Democratic leadership before joining the incoming administration. Is this bipartisanship stuff for real? he wanted to know.

Wiry and intense, Emanuel was seen as something of a political bodyguard for the relatively inexperienced Obama. A veteran of the Clinton White House before his own election to Congress in 2000, he had a varied background. He had been a serious ballet dancer as a young man, and served as a civilian volunteer with the Israel Defense Forces during the Gulf War in 1991. Above all, he was known for his quick-draw temper, foul mouth, and killer political instincts.

"We want to work with you," Emanuel said. "We're serious."

Cantor, the only Jewish Republican in Congress, and Emanuel, also Jewish, had a history of working together on Israel.

"There are some things we're going to disagree on," Emanuel explained, "but I think there's a lot we can work on together."

Cantor considered the incoming administration's offer to work with Republicans sincere, but finding common ground on how to jump-start the economy would be tricky.

Obama and his economic advisers were economic Keynesians— they believed that government spending could create jobs and grow the economy. It was a philosophy Cantor and many young House Republicans rejected. Instead, Cantor believed that entrepreneurs—small-businessmen and risk takers—were the engine that would drive the economy. Cantor realized that his 10 years in the family real estate business made him the only former small-businessman in the group that Obama had met with.

The 45-year-old Cantor, a workaholic even by Washington standards, quickly set up what he called the House Republican Economic Recovery Working Group, made up of 33 conservative members of Congress, to map out an alternative to a traditional stimulus package.

The group insisted on what Cantor called "three ironclad criteria": Proposals had to be limited in scope and spending; they had to result in real, long-lasting jobs; and small businesses had to be put first. They solicited input from former eBay CEO Meg Whitman, former Massachusetts Governor Mitt Romney, and anti-tax leader Grover Norquist of Americans for Tax Reform.

Three days after his inauguration, Obama summoned the congressional leadership to the White House Cabinet Room to discuss the stimulus package.

Protocol dictated that the president control the agenda and discussion, but Cantor spoke up immediately.

"Mr. President, with your permission I'd like to hand something out."

Obama nodded, and Cantor passed out copies of a one-page document entitled "House Republican Economic Recovery Plan." It listed five unambiguously conservative proposals:

- Immediate reduction in the two lowest individual income tax rates. Because all taxpayers pay some of their income at these initial rates, taxes would go down on more than 100 million tax returns, saving families between $500 and $3,200 in taxes each year.

- A tax deduction of 20 percent on the income of all small businesses.

- No tax increases to pay for stimulus spending.

- Make unemployment benefits tax-free.

- A homebuyer's credit of $7,500 for those who make a down payment of at least 5 percent of their home's value.

Obama glanced at his copy, looked at Cantor, and said amiably, "Eric, there's nothing too crazy in here."

But Orszag, the budget director, noticed that Cantor's proposals were all tax cuts.

And Cantor's document declared that, furthermore, "any stimulus spending should be paid for by reducing other government spending."

Absurd, thought Orszag. The whole point of the stimulus was to inject extra money into the economy. The requirement that all stimulus spending be offset by cuts elsewhere would defeat the purpose. Meeting Cantor's goal would be impossible, Orszag concluded instantly. But no one asked him, so he didn't say anything.

Obama said his plan would include tax cuts, but not only tax cuts. He seemed inclined to compromise.

"Mr. President," Cantor offered, "I understand that we have a difference in philosophy on tax policy." But a massive stimulus package would be too much like "old Washington," he said.

"I can go it alone," the president said, "but I want to come together. Look at the polls. The polls are pretty good for me right now."

Cantor chuckled and nodded. The polls certainly looked good for Obama now. To Cantor, that meant there would be no easier time to compromise and to disappoint some on the left. As he listened, Obama's tone seemed to change.

"Elections have consequences," the president said. "And Eric, I won."

On the table, some copies of the one-page document called "House Republican Economic Recovery Plan" lay where Cantor had put them.

"So on that, I think I trump you," Obama said.

•        •        •

In his short tenure as a senator, Obama had dealt with South Carolina Senator Lindsey Graham several times. Now, in his early days as president, he had Graham, a moderate conservative Republican, to the White House to talk.

"Barack," Graham said, dispensing with the formal "Mr. President" when they were alone in the Oval Office, "can you believe this has happened to you?"

"No," the new president replied. "I mean, this is kind of one of these things you think about, but it really doesn't happen to you."

"The power of this office is amazing," Graham said. "Your worst critic is going to be like a schoolboy coming into this office. Just the power of it. They may shit on you when the meeting's over, out in front, but people are going to listen to you unlike any other setting in any other time in your life. Don't ever let that be lost upon you."

# 2

---

The $800 billion stimulus bill of new spending and additional tax cuts, introduced on January 26, was the first bill of the new Congress and the Obama administration. It was called, appropriately, H.R. 1, and it contained not one proposal from Eric Cantor and his conservative Republican group.

The bill was drafted by the Democrats and whenever any Republican tried to make changes, Emanuel's response was, more often than not, "We have the votes. Fuck 'em."

This was the bulldozing that Obama had promised to avoid. Cantor reached for the phone and his BlackBerry and launched a full-court press. He was the Republican whip, and he was whipping his members against H.R. 1.

The stimulus bill will not get a single Republican vote, he declared.

"Oh, man," Stombres, Cantor's chief of staff, said. "What are you doing?" Cantor's staff was horrified. It was a promise he would almost certainly not be able to keep.

On January 27, Obama again came to the Capitol, this time to meet just with the House Republicans.

He excoriated Boehner and Cantor for already being against the bill.

"How is it that we could be for your bill," Cantor replied, "if we weren't a part of any of this?" It looked like a Democratic spending wish list.

"It's a bipartisan bill," the president insisted, listing elements he assumed Cantor's caucus would support. "Republicans like business expensing. They like bonus depreciation."

Cantor resented Obama's presumption that he knew what Republicans wanted, and what their priorities were, without consulting them. Cantor had served in the Virginia state legislature for years when Democrat Douglas Wilder had been governor. Wilder, the nation's first African American governor, had taken the time to develop personal relationships with Republicans and find common ground.

Rahm Emanuel told Cantor flat out that his pledge of zero Republican votes for H.R. 1 was delusional. "Eric, don't embarrass yourself."

Despite Cantor's promise, the White House exuded confidence. They had won the election. They were winners. Ray LaHood, a Republican and former member of Congress whom Obama had picked as his transportation secretary, assured the White House that they could confidently count on 30 Republican votes because of money allocated for projects and contracts in Republican districts.

But as details of the bill emerged, it turned out there was less money than expected, and support began to evaporate.

Soon, there were just a few House Republicans saying they would vote with Obama.

Then there was only one.

The holdout was first-term representative Joseph Cao, Republican of Louisiana and the only Vietnamese American in Congress. He planned to vote yes on H.R. 1.

Cantor knew every member in his conference, and he judged that changing Cao's mind would be nearly impossible. Cao was an idealistic 41-year-old attorney whose 2008 victory was a fluke. Some 70 percent of registered voters in his New Orleans district were Democrats, 19 percent were independents, and only 11 percent were Republican. Representative William Jefferson, the Democratic incumbent, effectively handed Cao the win when FBI agents investigating charges of corruption and bribery found $90,000 in cash in Jefferson's freezer. He was indicted on 16 felony counts, and Cao became the first Republican to serve the district since 1891.

Emanuel and the White House worked hard on Cao, reminding him that his congressional district was heavily minority—65 percent African American—and Obama had carried the 2nd District by 75 percent in 2008.

Emanuel still worked out in the House gym, where he got up close with Cao, and he got personal on the phone. According to Cao, Emanuel "insinuated" that if he voted for the stimulus bill, he would be owed a big favor—even help in a reelection campaign.

Meanwhile, Cantor also pressed Cao, making the standard Republican pitch. Federal spending would not revive the economy, but it would contribute to the soaring deficit. The Republican Party was about small business, which created jobs. They had to put incentives in place for the private sector. Small business first.

The mantra rang true to Cao, whose district was dominated by small businesses that served the vast New Orleans tourism industry.

"Look," he revealed candidly, "the White House is going to help me with my reelection." Obama's endorsement—or even his neutrality—could be critical in 2010.

Cantor was skeptical. "Why don't you get it down in writing?" he said, urging Cao not to believe any promises White House staff weren't willing to put on paper.

Cao never asked for anything in writing. He was still inclined to support the bill, even if he were the only Republican to vote for it.


Meanwhile, the White House was dealing with a bigger problem.

The day before the stimulus was to come up for a vote in the House, the phone rang in Emanuel's office.

It was Baron Hill, a second-term Democratic congressman from Indiana who served as co-chair of the House Blue Dog coalition. The 52-member coalition had met at 11 a.m., and they were pissed.

Founded in 1995, the Blue Dogs were Democrats who defined

themselves as fiscal conservatives. Most came from politically split congressional districts closely divided between Republicans and Democrats. Many were freshmen who had won traditionally Republican seats by touting their passion for spending constraints and deficit reduction.

The Blue Dogs held mandatory weekly meetings, whipped their votes intensely to ensure that they voted as a bloc, and were not shy about bucking the Democratic leadership on fiscal issues. Obama's stimulus package cut against the grain of their anti-spending beliefs, and they didn't think they were getting anything in return.

As one member, Louisiana Representative Charlie Melancon, put it, "We felt like we were getting pushed into a corner and we were damned if we were going to stay there."

On the phone with Emanuel, Hill said, "Look, we've got a problem here." The majority of the Blue Dog coalition planned to vote against Obama's stimulus package—more than enough to kill the bill.

And this from Obama's own party.

Emanuel erupted into a profanity-spiced tirade. "This is the first piece of legislation that our administration is going to be voting on and you guys are going to kill it?"

Hill waited out the storm of F-bombs—anyone who had worked with Emanuel knew his technique—and said, "Look, I'm just delivering the message. I'm trying to make this thing work. I don't want to embarrass the president. And I'm telling you that these guys are going to vote against it."

Emanuel asked Hill to arrange a meeting with the Blue Dog leadership for later that day.

Hill had reason to hope that the White House would accommodate the Blue Dogs. An early endorser of Obama during the election campaign, Hill had spent time with him on the campaign trail.

More than once, in conversations about economic and fiscal policy, Obama had told him, "I feel like I am a Blue Dog, Baron."

For their part, White House senior staff recognized that the Blue Dogs had some leverage—just not as much as the coalition believed. The sense in the White House was that with aggressive arm-twisting, enough Blue Dogs would vote to push the legislation through the House. But just winning wasn't enough. Emanuel wanted to win big.

"Win big" was a mantra he and Phil Schiliro, the White House's chief lobbyist and congressional liaison, kept repeating: Success breeds success, one legislative victory leads to future legislative victories. This vote needed to set the Big Win tone for the new administration. And the Big Win had to come fast. Delay would break the positive momentum.

The focus on "win big" was more a product of Emanuel and Schiliro's legislative strategy than the president's. Orszag could see the president was focused on getting the deal done. He was in implementation mode.

The stimulus package found the president in a position similar to that of the Blue Dogs—torn between competing priorities. Wanting to tame the federal deficit, he nonetheless believed that, with unemployment on the rise, the economy needed aggressive government support.

Later that day Emanuel, accompanied by Summers and Orszag, met with the Blue Dog leadership in Majority Leader Steny Hoyer's private conference room just outside the House chamber. Things didn't begin well.

"You guys can't do this," Emanuel lectured. "You can't embarrass the president right out of the gate."

His tone grated. Yelling broke out on both sides until Allen Boyd, an influential Blue Dog from Florida, stepped in. A burly fifth-generation farmer with a shock of white hair and a Southern drawl, Boyd tried to calm everyone down.

Look, we want to try to get to resolution on this, he said. But we can't vote for the stimulus package because, first of all, we think it's too big. Secondly, there are things in there that we don't feel are stimulative. And thirdly, we want a commitment on PAYGO.

PAYGO was an enforcement mechanism previous Congresses had imposed on themselves. The rule required that all new federal spending be offset by cuts or new revenue.

Despite his anger, Emanuel understood the Blue Dogs. During his tenure as head of the Democratic Congressional Campaign Committee from 2005 to 2007, he had focused intensely on defeating Republicans in swing districts, typically by recruiting and supporting candidates who were moderate and fiscally conservative. He had personally persuaded many of them to run.

Emanuel made them a threefold promise. The administration would support cutting some of the nonstimulative items from the package, Orszag would put the administration's commitment to reinstating PAYGO in writing, and the president himself would meet with the entire coalition after the vote so that they could make their case personally.

Hill looked around the room and hoped that would be enough.


On January 28, the day of the first House stimulus vote, the White House sent Congress a copy of the projected stimulus spending in each of the congressional districts. Since the bill now contained some $767 billion, Cao calculated that the average district would get about $1.7 billion—a welcome windfall for New Orleans, still recovering from an estimated $81 billion in damage from Hurricane Katrina in 2005.

But when he reviewed the White House report, Cao discovered that his own 2nd District would get only $330 million, about 20 percent of the average. He was astonished. Given the billions the district residents paid in taxes each year, he concluded the deal was no longer a good one for his constituents.

On the House floor, Cao voted no.

Cantor almost couldn't believe the good news. The House vote was 244–188. All 177 Republicans had voted against it.

"Not even one?" Emanuel said to Cantor. "What's going on?"

"You really could've gotten some of our support," Cantor said. "You just refused to listen to what we were saying."

Cantor might have admired Obama's self-assuredness—the confidence, the smooth articulation and eloquence—but the president had taken it too far, to the point of "arrogance," he said.

Obama had demonstrated that he believed he didn't need any other input. The Republicans were outsiders, outcasts. The president and the Democratic majorities in the House and Senate would go it alone. There was no compromise.

What really surprised Cantor, though, was how badly the White House had played what should have been a winning hand. Though Obama won the vote, he had unified and energized the losers. Not only had he missed the opportunity to get the Republicans into the boat with him, he had actually pushed them away. The failure was one of human relations. There had been no sincere contact, no inclusiveness, no real listening.

Soon after the vote, Cantor attended a White House reception and met Michelle Obama for the first time. The first lady was gracious. But there was a coolness toward him among White House staff that he would remember for years.

Despite their reservations about government spending, the Blue Dogs largely supported the stimulus bill. Of the 52 members of the coalition, 43 cast critical yes votes. Without them, the stimulus would not have made it out of the House.

Walking through the tunnels beneath the Capitol after the vote, John Tanner, a Blue Dog from Tennessee, playfully jumped on the back of coalition co-chair Baron Hill.

"What the hell did we just do, Baron?" he asked.

"I don't know," admitted Hill.

At the White House senior staff meeting the next morning Schiliro and Orszag received a loud round of applause. The bill had, at least, passed by a comfortable margin, giving the new administration its first legislative victory and the staff a huge sense of relief.

Emanuel was upbeat. Victory begets victory.

Obama, however, was surprised that no Republicans voted for the measure. Emanuel had voiced utter confidence that they would get a substantial number. His chief of staff was supposed to be an expert in these matters, the practiced veteran.

But Rahm had been wrong. What was going on?

Summers, Obama's chief White House economic adviser, was also stunned. To win public support, the White House and the Democrats needed to look like the reasonable people in the room, willing to compromise. But the zero votes made them look the opposite— unreasonable and partisan. Not a single moderate Republican would join the new, popular president in a big spending program to save the economy? Odd, he concluded, though in his view the massive stimulus had been absolutely necessary in the effort to improve the U.S. economy.

But, Summers rationalized, if you were a Republican and Obama was successful in reviving the economy, nothing good was going to happen to you. On the other hand, if the economy stayed down despite the stimulus, as a Republican you would not want to be implicated in anything Obama had done, especially his stimulus and economic recovery program. Had it come to that so early in the term?

# 3

---

On Capitol Hill, the final version of the stimulus package was being hammered out, and negotiations were getting intense. In early February, Reid and Pelosi summoned Emanuel and Orszag to the speaker's office in the Capitol.

Emanuel and others had been urging Obama to get involved, to weigh in, engage with Congress. Yes, the final bill was going to be written on the Hill—because legislation written on the Hill by the majority will pass—but the tension was so high that it could unravel. The president needed to show his commitment.

The president's advisers arrived in Pelosi's office, with its breathtaking view of the National Mall and the towering Washington Monument, to find Reid and Pelosi in full deal-making mode. The economy was falling off the cliff and the Republicans were not cooperating, so the Democrats at least had to come together.

Reid and Pelosi knew they needed to cut a deal on the actual numbers that would avoid a Republican filibuster in the Senate while retaining Democratic support in the House. It was the 11th hour, and they were down to the details. Numbers were flying around the office. How about $4.1 billion for school renovation? A little more? A little less?

At this moment, Obama called into the speaker's office and Pelosi put him on the speakerphone near the window so everyone could hear.

He delivered a high-minded message. They were going to save the economy with this bill, everything was at stake, unity of action, unity of purpose.

Thank you, Mr. President, thank you, said Reid.

Pelosi thanked Obama. We understand. We get that.

But the president wasn't finished. Warming to his subject, he continued with an uplifting speech.

Pelosi reached over and pressed the mute button on her phone. They could hear Obama, but now he couldn't hear them. The president continued speaking, his disembodied voice filling the room, and the two leaders got back to the hard numbers.

It took days more, but on February 13, both the House and Senate passed the final $787 billion stimulus bill. All 177 House Republicans again voted against it.* It included $288 billion in tax cuts, $224 billion more for entitlement programs, such as extending unemployment benefits, and $275 billion for contracts, grants and loans. The bill was 1,100 pages long.

At a signing ceremony in Denver three days later, Obama said, "Today does not mark the end of our economic troubles. . . . But it does mark the beginning of the end." The plan "will create or save 3.5 million jobs"—squishy language, as it would be difficult to identify specific jobs that had been saved.

"Absolutely, we need earmark reform," candidate Obama had said in the first debate of the presidential campaign in 2008.

A typical feature of most spending bills, earmarks are provisions added by individual senators and congressmen directing specific

---

* In the 2010 House election for the Louisiana 2nd District, Obama did an ad for Democrat Cedric Richmond, who beat Cao 65 percent to 33 percent.

amounts of money to specific projects in their states or congressional districts.

"And when I'm president, I will go line by line to make sure that we are not spending money unwisely."

Less than a month after he signed the stimulus bill into law, Obama was staring at a massive appropriations bill that had passed Congress and was awaiting his signature.

Reid wanted the president to sign it, but the bill had 8,570 earmarks adding up to $7.7 billion in spending, much of it on easily ridiculed hometown pork and pet projects.

The president balked. He wanted to take a stand.

Republican leaders in Congress were howling for a veto and claimed anything less would be a violation of Obama's campaign promise.

House Minority Leader John Boehner's spokesman reminded reporters, "The president has made some very specific promises when it comes to earmarks, and in order to keep them he is going to have to stand up to Democratic leaders on Capitol Hill."

Reid was incensed. Members saw that spending as key to serving the needs of their constituents, and Congress actually had reduced the number of earmarks compared to previous years. Politically, a veto of the bill would blow up months of painful negotiations, opening previously settled issues to another round of debate.

In a meeting with Obama, Reid said, Look, this is our prerogative. I understand you don't like earmarks, but they serve an important purpose, and if you get rid of them all, you're not going to get anything else done.

Reid's threat left the president tense and frustrated. In public, he tried to make the best of it.

He signed the bill, in private, on March 11, 2009. At the same time, he issued a statement proposing increased safeguards against abuse in the future.

Republicans hammered him for breaking his word. And the president's erstwhile allies, congressional Democrats, fumed over what they saw as White House overreach.

House Majority Leader Steny Hoyer, a Maryland Democrat, all but dared Obama to try reforming the process, telling the press, "I don't think the White House has the ability to tell us what to do."

For the Obama true believers, those who saw him as a reformer, it was, perhaps, the first hint of disillusionment. He had promised things would be different.

To those members of the administration new to the executive branch, it was an early indication that the inside game of governing was very different from the outside game of campaigning.

On Tuesday, November 24, 2009, just before Thanksgiving, Senator Kent Conrad headed down Pennsylvania Avenue for a private meeting at the White House with his former colleague, now the president. It was another step in a career-long effort of what could be called "The Project," or "The Mission." Conrad, the head of the Senate Budget Committee, believed the country was heading off a fiscal cliff. He could prove it, and he was going to fix it.

His intense, scholarly look inspired one Senate colleague to refer to him as "The Auditor." But the 61-year-old North Dakotan also had an honorary tribal name given by the Sioux Indians in his home state: It translated as "Never-Turns-Back."

From his five years as state tax commissioner to his 23 years in the Senate, Conrad was the quintessential fiscal hawk. He had been the second senator to endorse Obama for president, and the two had a friendly, though not close, relationship.

In the Oval Office with Obama and his economic troika, Geithner, Summers and Orszag, Conrad warned that federal debt and spending posed a long-term threat, more now than ever. The country's present course was not sustainable. And that's not just my view, he said. It's the view of your budget director, Orszag. It's the view of the head of the Congressional Budget Office. It's the view of the Federal Reserve.

"Kent," Obama said, "I've seen your charts."

Everyone laughed. Conrad's charts were notorious. He used so many on the Senate floor and in committee hearings—more than all the other senators combined—that he had earned his own printing equipment. He could wear out even the most dedicated green eyeshade with his presentations of the nation's finances and their descent into oblivion.

"You convinced me long ago that we're on an unsustainable course," Obama said.

The reasons to rein in the deficit were abundant and obvious. The public debt was now approaching $12 trillion, about 85 percent of the Gross Domestic Product (GDP), the sum of all goods and services in the American economy. Just paying the interest on the debt cost the country hundreds of billions of dollars per year. The question, the president said, was how to do it? How to get the Republicans involved? And what is the timing, since the short-term economic problems are hardly over?

Conrad didn't want to impose fiscal austerity in the midst of a downturn. That would only lead to a bigger downturn, more deficits, more debt. The trick, he said, was to take steps to strengthen consumer demand, as they had with the stimulus bill, and to improve job creation and economic growth.

Standing in the way was a legislative process that, Conrad was convinced, had completely failed. The Senate had been squabbling over the federal budget for six months with no result, and government funding was now dependent on stopgap, short-term continuing resolutions. It was chaos.

"I believe so strongly in what you're saying," the president said, "I'd be willing to be a one-term president over this."

It was a stark private declaration that Orszag had heard from the president before. But the president's assurances weren't enough for Conrad.

About a dozen senators, Conrad warned, felt strongly enough about the issue that they were going to take it to the next level by insisting that Congress create a commission to tackle the problem. Until the commission was in place, they would block any increase of the debt ceiling.

It was a clear threat. The debt ceiling placed a limit on how much the Treasury could borrow, and failure to increase it could lead to a catastrophic default on U.S. debt. Raising the debt ceiling was normally a routine matter, but Conrad was determined to change that. "Unless we get a commission we're just not" raising it, he said flatly.

"I agree with you so strongly," Obama repeated, "I'm prepared to be a one-term president. But we've got to deal with some practical situations—of timing, of how we construct such a commission."

The president and his senior staff had good reasons not to resist Conrad's pressure to create a fiscal commission. First, there was the possibility that a commission might actually produce something. Second was the president's promise to set the country on a fiscal path leading to deficits of less than 3 percent of GDP. The economic team couldn't agree on how to get there, and a commission would buy them valuable time.

*4*

---

Nearly a year into Obama's presidency, the nation was not on the strong path to recovery the president's advisers had anticipated—and that Obama had pretty much promised.

The economy had been in much worse shape than they realized when Obama took office. Revised economic growth numbers for the last three months of 2008—the end of the Bush administration—were now showing negative economic growth of nearly 9 percent. A decline in real growth of 10 percent is often considered an economic depression. Now, in late 2009, the unemployment rate had risen to 10.2 percent, the highest level in 25 years. Republicans were beating hard on the administration, repeating their slogan, "Where are the jobs?"

Whatever bump the president's stimulus package had given the economy had been inadequate.

Geithner, Orszag and Summers went to work on a strategy for the next year's presidential budget request, which was due to Congress in early February 2010. They had to produce something that would show Obama was equally serious about deficit reduction and job creation. Back and forth they went, debating, defining and calculating. It was dizzying.

"Let's sort of just gimmick it up," Larry Summers said to Orszag at one point.

In a memo to the president dated December 20, 2009, they grimly set the scene for the president. Economic deterioration was so much worse than anyone realized that since Obama took office the "unfavorable economic and technical re-estimates have worsened the deficit outlook by a total of $2.2 trillion" over the next 10 years—a whopping number. The memo ran to eight pages, and included several ideas for achieving federal budget savings.

Their first proposal for deficit reduction was to "impose a three-year freeze" on the budgets of departments like Transportation, Agriculture, Interior, Labor, and Housing and Urban Development. The freeze would also hit smaller agencies, like the Environmental Protection Agency.

This was practically nothing—savings of $20 billion each year.

Orszag realized it was insignificant. It was a symbolic gesture that would give the deficit hawks in the Democratic Party, like Conrad, something to talk about without actually taking much money out of the economy. It was one of the "gimmicks" Summers had proposed.

Summers thought it was a worthy gesture, if only that. In the end, whatever the Congress decided could be undone by a future Congress anyhow.

The president approved it, putting a check mark next to the proposal in the memo.

Item two was "reduce the allowance for disaster costs to $5 billion per year." That would save $19 billion in 2015 "based on the statistical probability of a major disaster requiring federal assistance for relief and reconstruction." In 2005, Hurricane Katrina had cost the federal government $108 billion. The Obama team was now acting as a weather forecaster.

"Pure gimmick," Orszag declared. But they put it in the memo anyway, and the president put a check mark beside it.

Item three was "assume a deficit neutral extension" of keeping Medicare payments to doctors at current levels. The Balanced Budget Act of 1997 had established the Medicare Sustainable Growth Rate (SGR) formula, which was supposed to reduce government payments to doctors who saw Medicare patients—"a blunt tool," as the memo said. It had been an ambitious cost-cutting proposal—overly so. Medicare reimbursement rates were already low compared to private insurance, and the SGR cuts turned out to be so draconian that Congress had intervened every year to avoid implementing them—a practice that had come to be known as the "Doc Fix."

The Doc Fix would continue, but it would be "unpaid for" and "without offsets." On paper, it reduced the deficit by $25 billion, but it left future administrations to find the offsetting cuts or revenue.

It was another gimmick, and it received a presidential check mark. But this check mark had a distinctly unsteady wobble on the upsweep.

What did the president actually think about all of this?

"He's come to the view," Orszag later remarked to others, "that this whole exercise is kind of silly anyway, so sure, let's play the game."

On the Doc Fix, the memo noted that the White House had at least some political cover. Senator Conrad, it read, "has expressed the possibility that the Senate could move toward a five-year unpaid-for-fix" on the Medicare payments to doctors.

Orszag explained: "It's almost like we're saying, well they're [the Senate] cheating too, so we will. So we can follow their lead. Welcome to sausage making."

In all, the memo proposed deficit reductions totaling $85 billion. A pittance. The Treasury had borrowed more than $1.8 trillion to finance deficit spending in 2009 alone. Geithner was a near absolutist on the need to reduce the deficit to an average of only 3 percent of the GDP. The deficit was currently running at 10 percent of GDP and by their own forecasts, included in a Budget Summary Table given to Obama, would rise to 10.6 percent in 2010. Full-scale calamity was on the horizon.

There was a hole in the budget proposal where a serious deficit reduction plan should have been and they needed a filler—a plug in the budget to show there would be more cuts to reduce the deficit.

This was where the fiscal commission pushed by Senator Conrad would come in.

The memo described a commission made up of members of Congress and outside experts that would be charged with creating a plan to achieve "deficits of about 3 percent of Gross Domestic Product by 2015." It was a version of what David Stockman, Ronald Reagan's first budget director, called the "magic asterisk"—an undefined solution to constrain the budget without providing specifics. Instead of doing the hard work of budget cutting within the administration, they would outsource it to a commission.

"Identifying a goal of about 3 percent of GDP," they wrote, "would make the commission appear more credible by sending a signal about the amount of deficit reduction that it is expected to recommend."

The meetings on this went on for hours.

Orszag thought the commission was a fig leaf. Without it, the administration's lack of a solution to the deficit problem would be exposed. The truth was their proposal did not put the deficit on a path to that 3 percent level. Orszag suggested including exact numbers the commission might contribute to deficit reduction.

Geithner vacillated. He wanted to get to 3 percent but he wasn't really convinced an outside commission would work, so he didn't want to put too much weight on it.

"Fucking figure it out," Rahm Emanuel finally told them. Define what you expect—or don't expect—from the commission.

Despite their misgivings, they finally took the debate to the Oval Office. Orszag argued for the 3 percent target—it would put more pressure on the commission to be meaningful, give it teeth, and boost Obama's credibility.

The president looked at his budget director, who was supposed to figure this stuff out, and said it was ridiculous that a question like that should come to him.

In the end, the economic team punted. They put a large box in the Budget Summary Table that mentioned the 3 percent but didn't do anything specific to get there. A commission "is charged with stabilizing the debt-to-GDP ratio at an acceptable level once the economy recovers. Under current Administration projections, that would require achieving deficits of about 3 percent of GDP by 2015. The magnitude and timing of the policy measures necessary to achieve this goal are subject to considerable uncertainty and will depend on the evolution of the economy. In addition, the Commission will examine policies to meaningfully improve the long-run fiscal outlook, including changes to address the growth of entitlement spending and the gap between the projected revenues and expenditures of the Federal Government."

Summers had proposed gimmicks, but this was a model of obfuscation. The mouthful of budget jargon promised to practice some tough love. But certainly not on any timetable, and certainly not now.

The box would come back to haunt Geithner when the House Ways and Means Committee held hearings on the president's budget request a few months later. Given his three minutes to question the treasury secretary, a relatively unknown young Republican congressman from Wisconsin named Paul Ryan pointed out that while the budget explicitly said it was essential to get the deficit down to 3 percent of GDP, it failed to do so.

"So you've got this warning under here; it's like the warning on a cigarette pack," Ryan said. "You've got this little magic box underneath your budget totals that says we're going to have a commission to do it."

Ryan demanded an explanation. "If you're going to solve our fiscal situation, why don't you do that? Why don't you give us a budget that actually gets the deficit to a sustainable level?"


Orszag, the numbers and budget expert, saw a ticking time bomb in the budget. Massive tax cuts enacted during the Bush administration were scheduled to expire at the end of 2010, and the president was committed to not extending them for the two upper-income brackets. This affected only about 2 percent of those who filed income tax returns but would increase tax revenue by up to $800 billion over the next ten years. Obama was determined to extend the cuts for the middle- and lower-income brackets. The cost would be $3.2 trillion over 10 years. Orszag argued that by making the middle-class tax cuts permanent the administration would be handcuffing itself. The federal revenue base would be too low, and there would be no plausible way of raising it. If they did make them permanent, he predicted, "we would

have a fiscal crisis at some point over the next decade with very high—
I don't say 100 percent—but very high probability."

Was it possible that these middle- and lower-income tax cuts could
be ended?

Phil Schiliro proposed that they do exactly that—a daring suggestion. They came up with a modified version that Orszag liked. Obama
would declare that the tax cuts should only be extended if they were
paid for. There was no way, of course, given the deficit problem, that
they could possibly be paid for. So that would end them, Orszag
believed.

In one scenario imagined by the team, the president would say
something like, "I'm in favor of the tax cuts but they just can't add to
the deficits. So if people can come up with offsets, I'll sign that bill. If
not, I won't."

Obama seemed open to that idea for a while. But like many politically risky propositions, when no one stood up as its champion, it
faded away.


Summers saw the budget exercise on future deficits as pointless.
There might be political benefits to proposing deficit reduction for
years such as 2015, but Congress could easily unwind the cuts.

Orszag was less pessimistic. Looking back at past budget deals
with delayed implementations—the Social Security fix in 1983, and
the budget negotiations of 1993 and 1997—it was clear that the vast
majority of spending caps and cuts had stuck.

He was worried less about Congress than the judgment of history.
There was an opportunity for the president to do something about the
long-term deficit. It would be economically and politically painful. But
if he didn't do something, and the country plunged into fiscal crisis
later in the decade, Orszag told others, "I think he gets blamed by history for not acting."

# 5

"Outrageous," said Senator Max Baucus, 68, the Montana Democrat, when he heard about plans for the fiscal commission. Baucus chaired the Senate Finance Committee, which had jurisdiction over taxation. Taxes had been his business since he first came to the Senate more than 30 years before, and he saw it as an end run around his committee.

Handing over a basic function of Congress to a commission that would include business and union leaders who would never have to answer to voters? Unacceptable. Even with some members of Congress on the commission, likely including Baucus himself, it would be like hiring a bunch of mercenary generals to lead the U.S. Army.

Baucus considered Conrad's debt limit brinkmanship deeply irresponsible. The extension of the debt limit was supposed to be routine. This "vanity exercise" by Conrad to extend his role was a dangerous game. It was no less than "hostage taking."

The selection of someone to coordinate with Congress on the fiscal commission came down to Biden and Emanuel. Obama decided to tap the vice president.

Thank goodness, Orszag thought. This was pure Senate deal

making, and nobody was better at that than Biden, a 36-year Senate veteran.

Conrad had been pushing Harry Reid very hard on the issue of the debt and the need for a commission that would work outside the regular order. For Reid, in charge of the Senate process, this was difficult to accept, but Conrad pressed, and the president's backing seemed to tip the balance.

"I'm a convert to your cause," Reid finally told Conrad.

Biden brought Senate Democrats to his residence for breakfast. He brought them for lunch. He visited them on Capitol Hill and worked with them over weekends.

At one point, he asked Orszag to take notes during a speakerphone call with Conrad. During the call, Biden and Conrad debated the structure of the commission and how to manage the debt limit vote.

The vice president hadn't told Conrad that Orszag was listening in. After a while, Biden realized that Conrad thought it was a private talk, but it was time for Orszag to enter the discussion directly because Biden needed an expert voice.

"Oh, hold on a second," said Biden into the speakerphone. "Peter Orszag is just right outside the door. I think I could call him in. Would that be okay? Please hold."

Orszag went along with the ruse. Conrad was put on hold, and Orszag made his "entrance" into the discussion.


Senator Conrad, meanwhile, remained more than a distraction for the White House. As the debt limit vote approached, he kept pecking away, demanding special favors for North Dakota. He knew that no one was going to look out for his small state, with its population of less than 700,000, unless he did.

He was talking with staff at the highest levels of the White House about payments for North Dakota hospitals. He wanted to negotiate on Medicare provider reimbursements. And on education funding.

Obama's team knew Conrad had them in a vise and they had to deal with him. But it was nonstop, and it was starting to get to Emanuel.

In a flurry of nine terse emails on January 14, Orszag and Emanuel went back and forth over one of Conrad's issues. The senator thought the White House had agreed to support indexing Medicare and Medicaid reimbursements in North Dakota to rates in its higher-cost neighbor, Minnesota.

Orszag: "I need to talk with you. Conrad believes you already promised him the wage index."

Emanuel: "What?"

Orszag: "Conrad believes that you already promised that North Dakota hospitals would get the Minnesota wage index in addition to the demo project, so he's not willing to accept that in return for dropping Frontier [another payment plan for North Dakota hospitals]. He believes you already made a clear commitment . . ."

Emanuel: "I do not do details on that level."

Orszag: "What do you want me to do?"

An hour and a half went by without an answer.

Orszag: "What do you want me to do on Conrad? They're expecting some response."

Emanuel: "I have no idea."

Orszag: "At this point, my calling back will probably backfire. So when you're free maybe you, me, [deputy chief of staff Jim] Messina, Phil [Schiliro] should regroup on this quickly. We'll have commission language in a bit."

But the Conrad issues wouldn't go away, and days later an exasperated Emanuel sent Orszag a stern directive:

"You fix this now."

Orszag did not. Soon Emanuel was emailing Orszag because Conrad was threatening to change an important budget measurement on education. He ordered in reinforcements, including Biden, who was close to Conrad. He emailed Orszag, "Conrad is intending to switch. Get the VP on this ASAP."

On Thursday evening, January 14, 2010, the president loaded the Cabinet Room with the key congressional Democrats for continuing negotiations on health care reform. Included were Reid, Pelosi, their deputies, committee chairmen wrestling with health care reform, and senior White House and congressional aides. All shared essentially the same view about the need for large-scale, transformational legislation that would provide coverage to the nation's more than 45 million uninsured. This was the president's big move. But the Senate and the House had passed different bills. They needed to make them into one, and they needed to do it quickly. Obama attempted to preside as House members demanded more spending on prevention and extra subsidies while senators pressed for Medicaid subsidies for states like New York. It would go on for an hour or two, then the House people would break and go into one room, and Senate people into another. They would then come back for more, making little or even no progress.

"That's it," Obama said around midnight. "Stop this bullshit." We're all Democrats, and we've all agreed to do this. "But you won't come to an agreement. I'm happy to stay here all night to help you, but none of you are listening." He was close to losing his temper. "It's very clear that there's nothing I can do to help you. So I'm leaving. You can call an end to this or you can figure out how to do this. I'm going upstairs and going to bed." He stood up and walked out.

Pelosi stood and began to gather her papers, as did the others.

"Nancy, sit down for a minute," Emanuel said. "Let's go through these numbers one more time." The real differences, as always, were about money, in this case a difference of about $26 billion between what the House and Senate wanted. Everyone returned to their seats.

"Humor me," Emanuel said. "You have this number two here," he said, referring to one House item for $2 billion. "You have this number four," he continued for the Senate, which wanted $4 billion. "What's the number between two and four?"

"Three," somebody said, falling for his question.

"Okay, three," he said.

"I'm not going to do three!" someone shouted. Others protested.

"I didn't say you were going to do three," Emanuel said. "I didn't say that at all. I just wanted to know what was between two and four. It's three. Okay, we all agree. Three."

It was juvenile and insulting, but they were all tired.

Emanuel found another number where the middle ground was eight. "Now," he continued, "what's three plus eight?"

Another explosion. "I never said we'd do eight!" More protests and head shaking all around.

"I didn't say you'd do eight," Emanuel said. "But I just want to know, what's three plus eight? It's 11." He continued through the list amid growing protests and derisive comments. "This is not an attempt to forge an agreement," he said. "I'm just playing with numbers here. Just humor me. No one's bound by this. I'm not even saying anyone should do it."

By about 1 a.m. he had gone through the list and found the middle.

Everyone pretty much said they had not agreed at all, not to any of these arbitrary numbers or alleged compromises.

"I didn't say you did," Emanuel replied. "But come back tomorrow morning and we'll talk about it."

The next morning the president was back in the chairman's seat.

"Okay," said Pelosi, "we can do those numbers Rahm wrote down last night."

"We can do that," Reid said.


The Democrats' filibuster-proof 60-vote hold on the Senate was in jeopardy as a result of the death of Ted Kennedy the previous August. Under Senate rules, 60 votes were required to end debates, so a 41-vote minority could block almost any legislation. Kennedy had been replaced by a temporary Democratic appointee, but Republican Massachusetts State Senator Scott Brown was campaigning for the seat. Brown promised that he would become the GOP's critical 41st vote, making it possible to sustain a filibuster of Democratic initiatives, especially the health care plan. He often signed his autograph "Scott 41."

On January 19, 2010, he won 52 percent of the vote to become the first Republican senator from Massachusetts in 36 years. Brown was sworn in on February 4. Even with the agreement over money, there was no way Democrats had time to get a new version of the 2,700-page health care reform law through the Senate before he was sworn in.

For weeks, Biden had been slowly building consensus on how to structure Conrad's fiscal commission. By late January, a plan had emerged with support from Democrats and Republicans. The proposed commission had been granted extraordinary power—so much power that Biden worried the White House might lose control of the process.

He failed to persuade Max Baucus, the Senate Finance Committee chairman, but he did get Harry Reid to bring the commission up for a vote in the Senate on January 26. It needed 60 votes to overcome a potential filibuster, but just before the vote, six Republican co-sponsors withdrew their support and it failed 53–46.

What a wonderful late Christmas present, Biden thought. Whew.

See? he told Conrad. The Republicans screwed you. You can't trust them. They talk tough about deficit reduction, but then vote against any real effort to fix the problem.

In an interview, President Obama later recalled the Republican decision to abandon the fiscal commission.

"At that point we'd already got a hint of things to come when the sponsors of that commission, including Mitch McConnell and John McCain, as soon as I say this is a great idea and we should do it, decide to vote against it."

But Conrad and his group would not go away. They wanted the president to appoint a deficit commission through an executive order. Biden promised to keep working.

Obama unveiled his budget proposal in a speech at the White House on February 1, 2010. He called for $3.8 trillion in spending, which would add about $1.3 trillion to the deficit. He said he hoped to save more than $1 trillion, chiefly through revenue brought in by ending the Bush tax cuts for the top two tax brackets.

He blamed the meagerness of the effort on decisions made during the former administration. "We're at war," he said. "Our economy has lost 7 million jobs over the last two years. And our government is deeply in debt after what can only be described as a decade of profligacy.

"Previous Congresses created an expensive new drug program [for seniors], passed massive tax cuts for the wealthy, and funded two wars without paying for any of it." He presented a laundry list of modest proposals—tax cuts for investors in small businesses, clean energy, some commonsense cuts and efficiencies, new fees on big banks. He also formally laid out his plan for a bipartisan fiscal commission, which he would set up with an executive order.

As a measure of the problem, he opened the national suggestion box, saying, "I welcome any idea, from Democrats and Republicans."

Few were impressed. The president had put off anything that would seriously address the problem. Senator Orrin Hatch, 75, the Utah Republican who had served 32 years in the Senate and made many deals with Democrats, scoffed publicly, "They are sending a toy fire truck to combat a five-alarm fire."


A fiscal commission set up by executive order would not have the force of law, but it would be symbolically important. Biden was assigned the task of recruiting a Republican co-chairman for the fiscal commission. They needed a rare bird—a Republican who would go along with tax increases in some form. Biden went after the rarest bird of all, former Wyoming Senator Alan Simpson.

Colorful and outspoken at 78 years old, Simpson was a natural showman who routinely shocked whatever audience he faced. He liked to call others—senators, friends, reporters—"rascals." But he was the genuine rascal, albeit a good-government rascal, who would not and could not hold his tongue. A critic was a "banjo-ass."

Simpson had served in the Senate for 18 years with Biden. They didn't agree on much, but as full-fledged members of the Senate club, they knew how to live in that chummy world, where even the starkest policy differences were not to be taken personally.

"We've got a tough one here," Biden said in a call to Simpson. After explaining that the commission would be tasked with essentially fixing the federal budget, Biden offered him the co-chairmanship.

"Boy," Simpson replied, chuckling, "that doesn't sound like anything I want to do."

"The president wants you," Biden said, knowing that left Simpson little choice. He explained that Congress had been expected to set up the commission itself, giving its recommendations the full force of law, but a group of Republicans revoked their support, joining to scuttle the effort.

Yeah, Simpson knew. "It was just 'let's stick it to Obama' day."

So a presidential commission, Biden said, is the only option left. Simpson knew a commission appointed by the president would not have the legal heft of one created by Congress—so Obama's personal commitment would be key to its success.

"I'd sure want to visit with the president first," Simpson said. "Everything has to be on the table, or it's just a feckless cause."

Okay, Biden agreed.

Simpson talked with Erskine Bowles, the former Clinton White House chief of staff, who would serve as the Democratic co-chair.

He met with Obama's economic brain trust, Summers and Orszag. "You know this is a suicide mission," Simpson reminded them. He would be pilloried by his fellow Republicans for supporting Obama's effort. "Everything has to be on the table including Obamacare, as they call it. I say you can call it anything you want. Call it Elvis Presley–care, call it care-care. It's totally unsustainable." Obamacare can't work, he said, even though it had not yet passed.

Simpson dropped in on his former colleague Senate Minority Leader Mitch McConnell. Simpson knew too well that the dour McConnell wasn't one for heart-to-heart talks, but he wanted to sound him out. He didn't ask for McConnell's support, because at this point the commission was so nebulous that no one could know what sacred cows it was going to hit.

"Good luck," McConnell said. "It's a tough one."

Three senators from McConnell's side of the aisle would sit on the commission.

"I'll tell you one thing, Mitch," Simpson said. "I know you pretty well. You know how to keep your troops together. And that's the awesome strength of your leadership. I don't know how you do it, what various methods you use, but you're a remarkable leader because you've got them together."

Of course, Simpson did know how McConnell managed his caucus. He made threats and promises, used fear and cajoling. Take one tough vote for me, he'd say, take two, and we'll eventually win the majority and I'll get you a committee chairmanship.

"So," Simpson said, "we know that whatever happens here, you're going to call the shots and that'll be the way that is."

McConnell didn't agree or disagree.

These machinations did not meet Rahm Emanuel's standards. There was no agility in the White House, no ability to get organized and move fast on critical issues like the fiscal commission. He emailed Summers and others on February 8, 2010:

"This does piss me off that we have debated this internally for months ad nauseam and we are a day and a half before the announcement and just now reaching out to a Republican senator." Emanuel did not see the appeal of Simpson. "He's going to be a headache. Our internal process is a fucking debating society."

Obama had Simpson and Bowles to the Oval Office on February 18, the day he would sign the order creating the National Commission on Fiscal Responsibility and Reform.

Simpson sat down in the front chair, which was normally reserved for the vice president, who hadn't arrived yet. When he realized, he apologized and started to move.

No, no, Obama said, you stay there.

After some preliminaries, Simpson stretched out his 6-foot-7 frame and turned to Obama. "Mr. President, I want to make sure you're serious about this, because my Republican friends are going to take my head off." The commission would have to consider everything, all spending, all taxes. "Everything has to be on the table, including all health care spending and reforms."

Everyone knew this would include Obamacare.

"Is it all on the table?" Simpson asked.

"Yes," the president said.

"Rush Limbaugh, he's just going to say I'm sleeping with the enemy," Simpson added. "Mr. President," he continued, "that reminds me of a joke. A guy goes and buys a really expensive car, but takes it back to the dealer and says, 'God damn it, I just spent $300,000 on this car and the radio doesn't even work.' And the dealer says, 'No, no, you have to understand, you bought such an advanced car that your radio is the newest. Just say what you want to hear and it comes on the radio. You say jazz, and on comes jazz. You say country, and on comes the country station.' The guy, once again really proud of his new purchase, drives off the lot and gets cut off by another driver. 'Asshole!' he yells, and Rush Limbaugh comes on the radio."

The Obamaites were used to profanity—they worked with Rahm Emanuel—but this was new. An extremely tall Republican was telling Rush Limbaugh jokes in the Oval Office. And they had worked hard to get him there.

Bowles said it wasn't good enough that he and Simpson knew that no policy or program was off-limits. Everyone on the commission needed to hear it, and they needed to hear it from the president.

In April, before the 18-member committee held its first meeting, the members gathered in the Roosevelt Room in the White House, and Obama obliged. He came into the meeting and said, "Everything is on the table. Wish you well."

Later, in the public signing ceremony, Obama introduced Simpson and Bowles, saying they "are taking on the impossible. They're going to try to restore reason to the fiscal debate."

# 6

---

Stymied on the health care bill by the loss of their 60-vote Senate majority, the Democrats set out to exploit the Senate's arcane reconciliation process, which allows certain budget-related bills to be brought to the floor for a vote without the possibility of a filibuster.

On March 21, the House held a series of votes that ended with the passage of a bill identical to the Senate's original legislation, followed immediately by a reconciliation bill making the changes to it that the Democrats had negotiated among themselves. No Republicans voted for either bill.

It would take another four days for the House and Senate to finalize the changes in the reconciliation bill, but with the Senate version having finally passed both houses, Obama had something to sign.

At a ceremony in the East Room of the White House on March 23, the president signed the Patient Protection and Affordable Care Act into law.

Vice President Biden introduced Obama, and before relinquishing the podium, leaned over to whisper something to him. The microphones caught his words and broadcast them live:

"This is a big fucking deal."

• • •

"I know you guys are Republicans," Obama told a small group of lead-ing chief executive officers at a White House dinner in early 2010.

"How do you know that?" asked Ivan Seidenberg, the CEO of Veri-zon and currently the longest-serving CEO of a Fortune 500 company. He considered himself a progressive independent among executives and was surprised by the stereotype.

Seidenberg was also head of the Business Roundtable, the fore-most CEO association in the country, whose member companies had $6 trillion in annual revenue and 13 million employees.

There are natural and inevitable tensions between the business community and a Democratic president. Both sides knew it, and it was to the benefit of both sides to find channels of communication and mutual interest. President Obama was an affable, sports-loving politi-cal hero who promised hope and change. The powerful CEOs of Amer-ica were no longer isolated barons, but were themselves public figures, subject to polls, the media scorecard, and even personal star treatment when things went right or opprobrium when they didn't.

Seidenberg worried that Obama did not appreciate the importance of business. Sure, he understood it intellectually, but did he really admire the guts and instincts that made corporations succeed, hire workers, and grow America?

The White House invited Seidenberg and two other CEOs to the pres-ident's Super Bowl party on Sunday, February 7, 2010. Seidenberg felt courted. Neither Clinton nor Bush had invited him to the White House. There was a blizzard that day, which made travel unappeal-ing, but there was no way he was going to snub the president. At the White House, Obama chatted with Seidenberg for about 15 seconds before the game. But then he went down to the front row to watch the game with his buddies. That was it. Fifteen seconds. Seidenberg felt he had been used as window dressing.

He complained to Valerie Jarrett, a close Obama aide and longtime family friend from Chicago, whose duties included managing relations with business executives and the White House. Her response: Hey, you're in the room with him. You should be happy.

Seidenberg was not.

On May 4, 2010, Obama addressed the Business Council, another CEO group, at a meeting in Washington. He used a TelePrompTer and took no questions. Again, the CEOs were dissatisfied. It wasn't communication—he was just going through the motions. Orszag later responded by suggesting the Business Council compile a wish list in writing. What was it, precisely, they wanted?

The Business Roundtable and the Business Council on June 21, 2010, sent in a 47-page report called "Policy Burdens Inhibiting Economic Growth" that listed hundreds of complaints about regulations, taxes, the new health care reform law, the federal deficit and massive debt. Immigration policy is broken and corporate tax rates are too high, the report said. The list of specific burdens ranged from Mexican trucking tariffs "placing U.S. Businesses at a competitive disadvantage" to a new credit card law that would require "millions of gift cards currently in the stream of commerce" to be replaced.

Nine days later, on June 30, Seidenberg had a two-hour meeting with Jarrett in the West Wing to receive the administration's response to the report.

Jarrett was furious.

This is total bullshit, she said, carpet-bombing the White House with a 47-page inventory of complaints without singling out what was really important. This was unfair, done without warning, not in the spirit of collaboration.

Seidenberg was astonished at the reaction. After all, Orszag had asked them to be specific.

•　　•　　•

Greg Brown, the president and CEO of Motorola Solutions, took a seat on the couch in the Oval Office on Tuesday, October 12, 2010. Obama's outreach program had by now extended to seven lunches, each with a trio of CEOs; attendance at key business group gatherings; and several one-on-one sit-downs like this one.

Brown, 50, a cerebral executive, had at first found Obama personable, bright and articulate in a previous meeting. Yet underneath the surface polish, he sensed remoteness. Obama talked, then seemed to listen—but Brown got the feeling that he was really just waiting to talk again, to make his points, to win the argument.

Brown wanted to help close the widening divide between Obama and America's business leaders, so he was determined to be forthright. After discussing the state of the economy—not bad, not good—they turned to the question of how the president might improve relations with CEO America.

Trust is low, Brown said. You come to meetings with us, use a TelePrompTer, take no questions—or only prearranged questions—and the media is in the room. Those are three things that are not conducive to an open exchange. It would be viewed more favorably if the media wasn't there, you lost the TelePrompTer, and we just talked. Take questions, give some short remarks, and follow them with a genuine, unprogrammed discussion—both ways.

Obama didn't say anything, just sat with his hand on his chin.

Second, Brown said, the rhetoric is inflammatory. It is not constructive.

Give me an example, Obama said.

"Fat-cat bankers"—something the president had said on the CBS program *60 Minutes* a year earlier. That was offensive to me, Brown said. I'm not a banker or on Wall Street. Using that language is polarizing. I'm not defending financial services or the banking CEOs. I'm on a different point: It is not appropriate, it is not presidential.

"I'm surprised that you have such thin skin," Obama replied.

I don't, Brown said. It is not presidential, he repeated. We can agree to disagree, and you can have a strong point of view, but I didn't think that was a presidential comment.

Okay, the president said.

Let's assume you don't change even one policy—nothing bipartisan or Republican. No common ground with the business community. The atmospherics are critical. If you changed the way you talk about business, the way you talk with business—no TelePrompTer, more casual, less performance, no photo op—you would generate better feelings.

Then there was Larry Summers.

Larry Summers, I'm sure, is brilliant, Brown said. No question. In fact I think he's probably an economic savant. But he's a pain in the ass to deal with. He's an obstacle. And nothing ever comes out the other end.

"Greg," Obama said, "he's leaving." The administration had announced in late September that Summers would leave at the end of the year.

But he's still here for a while, Brown continued. Summers was a big issue with the CEOs. When they had questions about administration policy or plans, they were told to see Summers. When I call, I don't get answers. I get cross-examined for even asking questions. And it's not a fun experience. So while he's an economic savant, nothing gets done.

The president burst into laughter. "Larry's leaving," he repeated.

Brown felt he had at least achieved his goal of being frank with the president. But would anything change? The president did not have to agree with the CEOs, and since he was a progressive Democrat, there was no reason to believe he would. But he had to show he was listening, find ways to accommodate them, and demonstrate some empathy for those running businesses in a down economy.

The abuse had to stop. It wasn't just Summers, it was also Rahm Emanuel, the chief of staff and the eyes, ears—and some would say tentacles—of the White House.

Emanuel was in regular contact with Sam Palmisano, the CEO of IBM. It was an opportunity for Palmisano, a major business leader, to offer his thoughts on the reduction of government spending, stimulating investment, creating jobs, pressing for free trade, reforming the corporate tax code, and working harder to help businesses be more competitive.

Often Emanuel didn't like what he heard because it seemed to be the standard business agenda.

Palmisano voiced his objection on one administration health care proposal to Emanuel, saying it would cost IBM about $700 million over 10 years. "You got to understand how we work," he explained. "My role is to maximize profits. Yours is to get your guy reelected." The $700 million in increased cost would mean he would have to lay off some 20,000 employees out of his workforce of 426,000 to offset the new costs and keep profits steady.

"What the fuck!" Emanuel shouted. That's not going to happen. Jobs were a sensitive subject. What the fuck are you talking about? He continued to drop F-bombs over the phone.

"It's just math," Palmisano replied. "Don't get yourself crazy. Economics is not politics."

The phone call then ended abruptly.

Reports quickly circulated among CEOs that Emanuel had hung up on Palmisano. But the IBM chief later said that he thought Emanuel just had to leave the call in a hurry.

Palmisano, nonetheless, believed the Obama White House had a bigger problem. Obama had no chief operating officer, no COO to implement his decisions. He had people like Emanuel whose primary focus was Congress. And Obama had Valerie Jarrett and David Axelrod but they were advisers, and in Palmisano's view "political hacks" and "B or C players" who did not know how to get serious about fixing problems and following through. There was no implementer. Thus the country was adrift and was not serious about its most fixable problem—becoming and staying competitive.

Whatever the analysis, however, it was clear the Obama business outreach program needed work.

On December 8, 2010, Ivan Seidenberg released another Business Roundtable manifesto called "Roadmap for Growth." It covered "the deep recession and weak economic recovery," high unemployment, the federal deficit and "unprecedented" debt.

Seidenberg said publicly, "I think the president has shown a willingness to learn."

Jarrett immediately phoned Greg Brown of Motorola.

"The president is learning?" she asked. "Is Ivan the teacher and he's the student? This is offensive."

She emailed Seidenberg directly just one word: "Learning?" Then she called him and expanded on her outrage.

Valerie, Seidenberg wrote back, that was an extreme compliment. Wasn't everyone, the president and the CEOs, always supposed to be learning?

Unappeased, Jarrett continued contacting other members of the Business Roundtable to say that Seidenberg had insulted the president of the United States.

The bottom line for Obama, as best Seidenberg could tell, was that the president did not trust that anything he did with the business leaders would ever work out for him. If he cut a deal with business, he was going to look bad. Business's interests were not his. And whenever Obama was cornered, out would tumble the "fat cat" language.

Seidenberg felt that the president just didn't think it was important to address the complaints of the business leaders. That was a mistake, he told Jarrett. He had been the CEO of Verizon throughout the entire Clinton and George W. Bush presidencies.

"With all due respect," he said, "we will be here when you're gone. I'm a perfect example of that. So you have to realize that this very progressive agenda, and this once-in-a-lifetime moment for this man in this world can be lost because guys like me can hunker down and wait you out."

So, the theory of the business case shifted. If Obama was going to be a pain in the ass, Seidenberg calculated that maybe they should turn to the GOP. "The best way to check them is McConnell and Boehner."

Word of this soon reached the House minority leader, and it was not long before Ivan Seidenberg's phone rang.

"I'd like you to do a fundraiser for me," Boehner said.

Seidenberg said he'd be delighted.

Two weeks later, at an event in New York City, the business community raised $1.5 million for Obama's main Republican opposition. It was only the beginning.

After 16 months on the job as OMB director, Peter Orszag wanted out. Obama and the other senior staff—Emanuel in particular—agreed it was time for him to go. Emanuel thought Orszag was leaking to the media and said he had too cozy a relationship with congressional Democrats.

Orszag delivered his final speech as a cabinet member at the Brookings Institution on July 28, 2010. Responding to a question, he affirmed that it was the administration's policy to push for extension of the Bush administration's tax cuts for middle- and lower-income taxpayers, but to allow the cuts for the wealthy to expire.

"That's the administration's position, period," he said.

But privately, Orszag was increasingly concerned that the administration was going to move to make the Bush tax cuts permanent. "A disastrous course," he warned, because the Treasury needed more revenue.

His last day as OMB director was to be July 30, and with his time in the cabinet waning, Orszag had his good-bye session with Obama. His kids had their photo taken with the president, and Obama made one last request of Orszag.

"Can you write me another one of those memos?" the president asked. He wanted a private recommendation, which Orszag had provided before. Obama wanted no one else to see it. Independent, out-of-channel communications could be more honest.

Why not, Orszag said. Yes, sir.

He began a fellowship at the Council on Foreign Relations, and from there he went to work. The country was facing an unsustainable budget deficit over the next 10 years and beyond. It just did not add up. Tax cuts simply were not affordable. Yes, raising taxes in the recession would impact consumer spending—the necessary driver of a recovery. But the United States would not solve its long-term budget problem unless revenue—meaning tax increases—was part of the equation.

In a draft of his memo for the president, Orszag made his case for additional revenue, but noted that "Even with substantial fiscal pressure, Republicans are extremely unlikely to affirmatively vote for revenue increases."

He proposed what he called "the best alternative among admittedly very unattractive options." The administration should move to extend the Bush tax cuts for a year without offsetting them, and then demand that the cost of any further extensions be fully offset.

Ideally, only the lower- and middle-class tax cuts should be continued, but Republicans, of course, would want to extend them for the high-income brackets as well. Reaching a deal on extending them all would be worth it, but just for a year or two.

Orszag sent these thoughts in his memo to Obama, back-channeled through the president's personal secretary, Katie Johnson. He heard nothing back.

By late August, Orszag had branched out. He was preparing for his debut as a columnist on the op-ed page of *The New York Times*, some of the most valuable and high-visibility opinion real estate in journalism. He sent Katie Johnson an email saying that in a week he was planning to write a column on taxes, and he planned to make the same arguments he had made in his private memo to the president. Please, make sure you tell the president about what I am going to do.

I have told the president, thank you, Johnson emailed back.

It was a delicate path, Orszag was aware. He wanted to alert the president, but not give him veto power. Johnson's response and thank-you was all he needed. He took parts of the Obama memo and cut and pasted them into his column, which ran in the *Times* on September 6. It proposed a compromise: "Extend tax cuts for two years and then end them altogether."

At his press briefing the following afternoon, White House spokesman Robert Gibbs attempted to distance the administration from Orszag's column. "We certainly didn't see Peter's column before it appeared today," he said, adding, "nobody that I'm aware of saw the column before."

It's not true that no one in the White House was notified about the coming column, Orszag wrote in an email to Rahm Emanuel.

Are you saying you told me? Rahm emailed back.

No, I'm saying I told your boss.

The former budget director was slightly surprised that Obama would hoard information, but Orszag often said that it was a mistake to think you've got someone figured out.

Orszag continued his star turn in the op-ed spotlight and a month later drafted a column to appear October 20, 2010, on the sensitive subject of Obamacare. He wanted to focus on one of its weaknesses. The health care legislation "does many things right," he wrote. "But it does almost nothing to reform medical malpractice laws." The president himself, Orszag said, had urged, at the American Medical Association in June 2009, that there should be "broader use of evidence-based guidelines" for doctors treating a specific illness or condition. Orszag proposed that any doctor who could demonstrate he had followed these guidelines should not be held liable for malpractice.

Orszag later described the plan to others as a sort of Nixon-goes-to-China moment. By proposing its own version of malpractice reform, the Democratic administration could blunt one of the Republicans' most common attacks: the claim that Democrats were in the pocket of the trial lawyers, who benefited immensely from medical malpractice cases.

Should he alert the White House? he wondered. Better not to surprise them. With some discomfort, because a columnist is supposed to speak for himself, not his former employer, Orszag sent his draft to Valerie Jarrett. It was about three days before the column was scheduled to run. Here's a draft, he wrote in an email to her. Let me know if you have any comments.

Thanks, Jarrett wrote back. She offered no comments on the draft.

The column ran as scheduled, unchanged from the draft Orszag had provided the White House.

Orszag was in an airport when he got Jarrett's email. How could you have done this? It's ridiculous. You're so disloyal.

You have got to realize the health care bill is wildly unpopular, Orszag replied. Every single speech I give, if I lead with this reflection on its imperfections, the dynamic changes. People will then listen. You can't hold this law out as perfect. It won't sell. People think it's a piece of crap. The weaknesses must be acknowledged. Then it's credible to say, here's why it is good and why it is the only thing that will work.

Jarrett's answer was delivered with Politburo finality: You have burned your bridges.

# 7

On election night, November 2, 2010, the Republicans seized control of the House, winning an astonishing 63 seats—the largest swing in 62 years.

Protocol dictated that the president make a congratulatory call to Boehner, the presumptive incoming speaker of the House. The trouble was, nobody in the White House had thought to get a phone number.

Staff began to scramble. Who would know how to reach Boehner?

Finally, someone remembered that Brad Woodhouse, communications director for the Democratic National Committee, was a fishing buddy of somebody who worked for Boehner.

Someone called Woodhouse. Could he help?

Woodhouse called his friend Nick Schaper, new media director for Boehner, and relayed a number back to the White House.

At midnight, the phone rang in the Grand Hyatt in Washington, where Boehner and his staff were celebrating.

Congratulations, John, the president said.

Thank you, he replied. Mr. President, he added, I've always been straightforward and honest with you in the past and that's the way I'll be with you in the future. I'm looking forward to working together to create jobs and cut spending.

The conversation lasted only a few moments.

Thanks for the call, the speaker said.


The president had to reassess.

In the next Congress, the Republicans would have a majority of 242–193. But it wasn't just control of the House that had changed. The election had altered the character of the Republican Party in Congress. Dozens of incoming freshman Republicans identified closely with the anti-tax, anti-government-spending Tea Party movement, shifting an already conservative Republican conference further to the right.

In the days immediately following the election, White House staff saw a different president from the man they had worked with the past two years.

Obama had kept his cool through the auto industry bailout and the struggle to pass the Affordable Care Act. But in the immediate aftermath of the election, he chaired meetings in which he allowed staffers to ramble on as he sat there, very quietly, very introspectively. He seemed to be trying to absorb it all and figure it all out. He looked down and withdrawn in a way the staff had never seen him. He'd been rocked by the election. Gut-punched.

The "why?" of what happened was left to the pundits, columnists and analysts—the talking heads. The economy was better but still not in full recovery. Reports showed that GDP growth in the second quarter of the year had fallen to 1.7 percent from 3.7 percent in the previous quarter, and unemployment, though down from its peak, was holding stubbornly at 9.6 percent.

The $787 billion stimulus had helped, but not as much as the administration had implied it would. Obamacare was misunderstood and unpopular, and the same, perhaps, could be said of the president.

One thing was plain. Obama had an immediate operational problem. After largely ignoring the Republicans for nearly two years, he would need to open up.

•     •     •

For nearly nine months, Alan Simpson had been flying back and forth between Wyoming and Washington to work out of the nondescript office space the fiscal commission had rented on F Street. Tall, and with an artificial knee, he couldn't cram himself into the coach seats that the commission's frugal spending rules required. He estimated that he had spent upward of $25,000 of his own money upgrading to first class.

The 18-member commission had met five times between April and September, but Simpson and co-chair Erskine Bowles were frustrated by the lack of agreement among members. The president had set a December 1 deadline for them to vote on a proposal, so on November 10, Simpson and Bowles took the unexpected step of issuing a plan of their own.

The 50-page draft outlined measures to cut $4 trillion from the federal deficit over 10 years through a combination of spending cuts and increased tax revenue. The proposal included $200 billion in cuts equally distributed between Defense and non-Defense spending in its first three years. It offered several options for tax reform. The proposal that received top billing was the so-called zero option, which dramatically simplified the tax code by streamlining income brackets, eliminating all deductions (including the popular exemptions for charitable donations, mortgage interest and employer-sponsored health care), and by taxing income from investments, capital gains and dividends at the same rate as wages. The savings would be used to lower individual rates and reduce the deficit.

The proposal cut payments to doctors under Medicare and increased beneficiaries' premiums. It left Obama's Affordable Care Act in place, and actually strengthened the authority of the controversial Independent Payment Advisory Board, which was supposed to control costs by identifying which treatments were effective and which were not. The proposal also advocated the creation of a government-run health insurance plan that would compete with private insurers on the law's health care exchanges.

All payments from entitlement programs that were indexed to inflation were reduced by changing the way the Consumer Price Index was calculated. The shift to the more accurate measure, called "Chained CPI," had been resisted for years because over time it would dramatically reduce the growth of entitlement payments.

Finally, the proposal reformed Social Security by gradually raising the retirement age to 67, making the benefit formula more progressive, and increasing the amount of an individual's wages subject to the Social Security tax.

There was something in the plan for everyone to hate.

"Simply unacceptable," outgoing House Speaker Nancy Pelosi said in a statement, citing proposed cuts in entitlement spending.

Americans for Tax Reform, the conservative lobbying group headed by anti-tax activist Grover Norquist, warned the more than 275 members of Congress who had signed its Taxpayer Protection Pledge that support for the plan would be considered a violation of their oath to never raise taxes.

Simpson and Bowles had exactly three weeks before the scheduled vote. Under the terms of the executive order creating the commission, their proposal needed the support of 14 of the panel's 18 members for the president to send it to Congress.

They began meeting with commission members individually in an effort to gather enough votes. Among the six senators on the commission, two Democrats and three Republicans were on board. Of the four outside experts, three supported it. But only one of the six House members, South Carolina Democrat John Spratt, who had recently lost his reelection bid, said he would vote for the plan. Counting Simpson and Bowles themselves, that left them with 11—three votes shy of the number needed to require the president to send it to Congress.


As part of his new effort to engage with House Republicans, Obama called Boehner on November 17.

Happy Birthday! the president said. Boehner was turning 61 that day.

In a second gesture, Obama asked the Senate and House leaders of both parties—eight in all, including Boehner and Cantor—to meet with him and Biden for a summit meeting at the White House the next day, November 18.

But when you need friends, it's too late to make them. Boehner hadn't been consulted about the summit, and with the incoming House Republicans deep in internal battles over realigning committee jurisdictions, he had no interest in hurrying down to the White House the next day. Along with Senate Minority Leader McConnell, Boehner slapped the offer away. They wanted it postponed until after Thanksgiving.

The tables had turned. They had the votes.

The delayed summit began in the Roosevelt Room of the White House the morning of Tuesday, November 30, 2010. The outgoing Congress had failed to pass a budget—only funding the government through December 3—and because it was illegal for the executive branch to spend money not appropriated by Congress, the country was three days away from possible government shutdown.

"It was a hard-fought election," the president began. "This is the first of regular meetings between us." It was a new world. They would meet, talk and listen. "We've gone through tough times." But they had a responsibility, jointly, to grow the economy. There are "going to continue to be serious political differences," he said, but "let everyone get something done."

The Democrats got "shellacked," he admitted, repeating what he had said in a press conference the day after the election. He focused on the party, not on himself. But it wasn't just Democrats. "People aren't happy with everything that is going on. We all read the polls," a not very subtle reference. Polls showed an approval rating of Congress at 17 percent and Republicans at 31 percent.

"I haven't reached out as effectively as I should have," Obama acknowledged. "Let's have honest cooperation, not just photo ops."

He had a list of what needed to get done in the lame-duck session—while the Democrats still controlled the House—and what could wait until the Republicans took over the House in January.

The first big question was what to do about the Bush tax cuts, due to expire at the end of the year. If the rates for all but the highest income brackets were extended for another 10 years, it would cost the U.S. Treasury $3.2 trillion.

They went around the room.

"Congratulations to John Boehner and Eric Cantor," Pelosi said graciously. "Two things we need to do: create jobs and control spending."

"I am a transparent guy," Boehner said. He called for more direct communication, saying they all "need to have more time together." Jobs and spending were his focus also.

"Thank you for the spirit in which you have welcomed us," said Cantor, whose connection to the Tea Party made him a new power center in the House. "Thank you for the pay freeze," he said, referring to Obama's recently announced two-year pay freeze on federal workers that would save $5 billion. He proceeded to list what he hoped would be "common ground"—deficit reduction, spending and bureaucracy cuts, and jobs.

On taxes, Cantor emphasized his belief that all the Bush tax cuts needed to be extended. He urged the others to "look through the prism of people that have to pay taxes." Getting on his favorite hobbyhorse, he said, small businesses are asking, "Where do we get the money?" They had to let those folks who would create jobs keep their money so they could invest in their own businesses and expand.

Cantor urged them to act on the Bush tax cuts during the lame-duck session, and not start in January when the Republicans would control the House. Otherwise, he more or less threatened, it would have to be done "retroactively."

"How do we get out of here?" Senator Reid half joked. How could this be done before the December holidays? "Try to be reasonable," he urged. No one has "a magic wand," he said, and reminded everyone that the Senate was different, meaning slow and burdened with many procedural hurdles.

McConnell, the Republican Senate leader, saw it somewhat differently. "American people prefer periods of divided government," he said. "Sometimes divided government can be productive." This was because any deal that passed would necessarily have both parties' fingerprints on it. The key questions, according to McConnell, were what to do about tax cuts, how to come to an agreement on the budget, and yes, how would they get out of town before the holidays? He said he hoped that something productive would come out of the Simpson-Bowles commission, and said he was prepared to do some business.

"The long term needs to be our goal," said Jon Kyl, the Senate minority whip.

Kyl, at 67, had been representing Arizona in Congress for 23 years, first as a member of the House, and since 1995 as a senator. One of the most conservative members of the Senate, Kyl also knew how to exert political pressure.

Without any attempt at subtlety, he said, the "sooner we get to agreement on taxes and spending, the more time we will have for START." Kyl was referring to a major strategic arms reduction treaty that the administration had painstakingly negotiated with Russia and which Obama had been pressing the Senate to ratify. It had support from both Republicans and Democrats, but Kyl was concerned that the treaty did not invest enough in weapons modernization.

The "this for that" suggestion was not lost on anyone.

"We have gotten some stuff done," Obama interjected. He was pleased they had agreed on setting aside $1.2 billion to compensate black farmers who had faced discrimination from the Department of Agriculture. And, he pointed out, they had toughened economic sanctions on Iran.

Geithner said the economy was growing annually in the 2 to 2.5 percent range, "but not very strong," noting there was "some risk of double dip recession." Next year "could be slightly stronger, 2.5 to 3 percent." The economic conditions in Europe were "very messy," and Europe was the main risk that could damage the U.S. economy.

Larry Summers added that the economic demand for goods and services was less than the capacity to produce. "Private spending is sluggish," he added. "Unemployment claims are dropping . . . not terrific, but better than we have seen."

Obama went to the nub, taxes, noting that Boehner and Cantor had raised the issue. "I would love it to not tax anyone," he added. "I'm not hung up on the notion that we have to 'sock it' to the rich." Simultaneously reducing the deficit, spurring economic growth, and adjusting tax policy was a complex blend of policies. They might not all work together, he warned. Under Keynesian economic theory, cutting government spending hurt economic growth.

So he had an idea that, not coincidentally, his 2012 campaign team would endorse: "Not doing anything too drastic in 2012, then medium-tough measures in 2013 in spending . . . then taking on long-term entitlement."

Turning to what would later become his campaign focus, he said, "Our view is the middle class have been impacted" by the recession and as a result those who make $250,000 a year or more should be taxed at the old Clinton-era top rate of 39.6 percent, while everyone below should be protected from any tax increase.

"This doesn't negate the need for spending cuts," he added, but "we can't cut our way out of this deficit.

"Why not decouple?" he asked. "Then have debate on higher incomes?" He wanted Republicans to consider extending the tax cuts for people earning less than $250,000 separately from the issue of what to do with upper-income rates. "That way we can achieve 98 percent of what we agree on.

"Unemployment insurance is very important," he added. It benefited small businesses.

He turned to Cantor. "Eric," he reminded him, "Walmart says pass the middle-class tax cuts . . . get unemployment insurance extended."

The president suggested that each of them assign someone at the staff level to meet with Geithner and Jack Lew, who had replaced Orszag as head of the Office of Management and Budget.

"We need to extend the estate tax," Kyl said, because the generous exemptions were expiring also.

Obama said they had to get to "what are our options . . . what are each other's bottom lines?" Then they could set up a process for implementing the agreed-on recommendations.

"We all need to step into the rowboat together," Biden said, using one of his favorite analogies, so it won't tip and no one will fall in the water.

"I don't see enough of the growth" coming from the Simpson-Bowles fiscal commission, Pelosi said, citing "green jobs" as an example. On taxes, she wondered if there should be a size limitation on small business, "so we aren't giving benefits to companies that don't need it." She added, "We can reward success, but this is about fairness."

Reid urged his colleagues not to "waste time" on other pending issues like the DREAM Act, which aimed to create a path to citizenship for certain illegal aliens brought to the country as minors, or the Zadroga Act, which expanded compensation for rescue workers disabled as a result of their actions in the aftermath of 9/11. They needed to focus on "just taxes and funding," he said.

Obama turned to Kyl about START. "This needs to get done. The U.N. Security Council would not have gone along with Iran sanctions if the Russians hadn't come along. Can we turn Russia more towards the West? This is worth doing on the merits. Absolutely vital to our national interest."

Missile defense, which used to be very controversial, had just sailed through. It was all part of a larger strategy with the Russians, he said.

"No politics involved," Kyl said. "The resolution or ratification needs to be amended . . . priorities have to be established." Then he reissued his threat. "If we agree on taxes and spending, we will have enough time to take up START."


Just before lunch that morning, one day before the fiscal commission was due to vote, Simpson and Bowles went into the House Ways and Means Committee's private library to see the fiscal commission's three Republican House members: Dave Camp, Jeb Hensarling and Paul Ryan.

Of the three, Ryan, a 40-year-old Wisconsinite, was the only one with a national public profile. Six weeks earlier he had published the book *Young Guns: A New Generation of Conservative Leaders*, with co-authors Minority Whip Eric Cantor and Deputy Whip Kevin McCarthy. Ryan was seen as a major new deficit reduction force in the Republican Party, a policy intellectual who would chair the House Budget Committee in the incoming Congress.

Camp and Hensarling, though, would also play important roles in the new Congress. Camp, from Michigan, would head the powerful tax-writing Ways and Means Committee, and Hensarling, a Texan, would be Republican conference chairman, placing him fourth in the ranks of House leadership.

All three had told Simpson and Bowles that they would not support the commission's final recommendation.

The plan the commission was about to release had changed only slightly from the chairmen's earlier proposal, and nothing had been held sacred. As Simpson later put it, everyone "had to agree to shoot one of their favorite cows." Democrats would still have to accept deep cuts to entitlement spending, and Republicans would have to sign off on increased tax revenue. Controversially, it proposed bridging the gap between current policy and full implementation of the plan by, in part, eliminating the Bush tax cuts for high earners.

"I hope and pray that you didn't vote against this because of pressure from Grover Norquist," Simpson told the Republicans. "Because if you did, I've lost all respect for all three of you."

Norquist is the leading conservative anti-tax activist who successfully elicits pledges from about 95 percent of the House and Senate Republicans not to vote to raise income tax rates.

This is not about Grover, Ryan said. You're broadening the base and lowering rates. That's the kind of reform we all agree with. The problem, Ryan said, was the impact of the commission's plan to eliminate the tax deduction for employer-sponsored health insurance plans.

If you remove the tax exclusion for health care, then you're going to dramatically accelerate employers' dumping their employees into Obamacare, Ryan said. You will eviscerate the employer-sponsored health care market. Everyone will be shoved into Obamacare and the cost will explode.

Ryan feared the government would find itself with an open-ended commitment to paying for the health care of more than 100 million people. On top of that, he added, the commission hadn't addressed the increasing costs of Medicare and Medicaid.

We're going to accelerate a debt crisis if we put this thing together, Ryan said.

Camp and Hensarling said they agreed with Ryan. Camp was also worried that the commission's proposal was a backdoor method of raising government revenue, which the plan envisioned capping at 21 percent of GDP—well above the historical average. He thought it should be in the range of 19 percent.

If you're going to do reform, you need to do reform, Camp said. If you're going to raise money, you need to raise money. And I think to try to pretend that it's reform when it's really raising revenue makes the reform harder to do.

"That's a good answer," Simpson told them at the end of the hour-long meeting. "I sure will accept that answer. That's honest."

Stalemated at 11–7, Simpson and Bowles never called for a formal vote on the plan, ensuring it would not be sent to Congress. The panel held a final meeting on December 3, two days past its official deadline.

"The Fiscal Commission has been a success," Ryan wrote in a statement appended to the final report. "Although I could not support the plan in its entirety, many of its elements surely are worthy of further pursuit."

The president was visiting troops in Afghanistan on the day of the commission's final meeting, and the White House released a statement in which Obama praised the commission's overall work.

"The commission's majority report includes a number of specific proposals that I—along with my economic team—will study closely in the coming weeks as we develop our budget and our priorities for the coming year."

But he cited no specifics, and did not endorse the commission's conclusions.

In an interview on July 11, 2012, the president recalled that when the fiscal commission's plan was released, "none of the House Republicans vote for it, including Paul Ryan, which also was a harbinger of things to come.

"A lot of people ask, well, why not immediately embrace Bowles-Simpson? The reason that we did not was that the revenue that they obtained involved eliminating the home mortgage deduction, health care deduction, charitable deduction, etc.," he said.

"If people knew exactly what that was, it could not pass Congress. It would be wildly unpopular. We could not get that done. And the Defense cuts were actually much steeper than, responsibly, I could sign on to when we were still winding down the Afghan war. So what I said to my team was, rather than just embrace, whole-hog, Bowles-Simpson, let's take the framework—which is the right one, a balance of spending cuts and revenue—and let's affirmatively present to the country what we think would be a path to bringing down our deficit and stabilizing our debt. And I said internally, let's not have any sacred cows. Let's look at some things even if Democrats are uncomfortable with it."

In his State of the Union address the next month, in which he focused on the nation's budget problems, the president barely mentioned the fiscal commission. His proposed budget, released in February, bore no resemblance to Simpson-Bowles.

The commission's plan seemed dead.

*8*

On Thursday, December 2, Nancy Pelosi, who had a month left as speaker, rammed a bill through the House extending the lower- and middle-class Bush tax cuts without the high-income tax cuts the Republicans considered essential. The bill passed on a largely party-line vote, 234–188.

The lame-duck force play agitated incoming speaker John Boehner. "I'm trying to catch my breath," he told reporters, "so I don't refer to this maneuver going on today as chicken crap, all right? But this is nonsense. All right? The election was one month ago. We're 23 months from the next election, and the political games have already started." Pelosi's move was contrary to the spirit of cooperation the president had just promised, he said.

Each side had the same problem. Far apart on tax policy, they had to agree on a way forward. Otherwise, the Bush tax cuts would expire and taxes would go up for everyone, which neither party wanted.

The Democrats still controlled the Senate. But Pelosi's tax bill would not pass there because Minority Leader McConnell could order a filibuster. And in the new Congress he would have 47 Republican senators, up from the current 42, giving him even more of a stranglehold on legislation.

Biden had seen this coming even before the House vote. If there was a window to get something done, it was now. Sometimes it came down to one man. He told Obama he wanted to make a back-channel call to McConnell.

Sure, Obama said. Why not? Try everything.

Biden was known in the White House as the "McConnell whisperer," the person who knew the right combination of sympathy and gentleness, never force, needed to work with the minority leader.

In an October 2010 interview with *National Journal*, McConnell had said that for Republicans, "The single most important thing we want to achieve is for President Obama to be a one-term president." The statement was widely reported in the press and was cited by Democrats as evidence that Republicans in Congress prized defeating Obama above the good of the country.

But the coverage largely ignored the rest of what McConnell had said.

Asked if his strategy involved constant confrontation, McConnell said, "If President Obama does a Clintonian backflip, if he's willing to meet us halfway on some of the biggest issues, it's not inappropriate for us to do business with him."

"I don't want the president to fail," he said later in that interview. "I want him to change."

Working with McConnell would be tricky, but he and Biden had served together in the Senate for 25 years, and both knew the foremost Senate club rule: You get some, I get some.

Biden enlisted his chief of staff, Ron Klain. Klain had been an editor of the *Harvard Law Review* three years before Obama became the *Review*'s first black president. Laurence Tribe, a Harvard Law professor, said Obama and Klain were two of the most brilliant students he had taught.

Klain, 49, saw the president's economic philosophy as technocratic. It seemed to him at times that Obama was seeking mathematical answers to questions that did not always have them. The president was a progressive but clearly had a Blue Dog streak. He saw the perils of unsustainable federal spending.

Losing the House, Klain thought, put them in uncharted territory.

At times like this, Klain would say, "Scary *Jaws* music was playing in the background."

McConnell and his top domestic policy aide were direct with Biden and Klain.

You've got a problem here, Joe, McConnell said. There are things you want, like the START treaty, and for that to pass, you're going to need some Republicans. You don't want a party-line vote, so the anti-START people need five, six, seven days of Senate floor debate. If you don't give them a fair hearing, I have to round up the Republicans to vote down START to validate their procedural rights. As their leader, my job is to protect their right to be heard on this. McConnell said he would order a filibuster if necessary.

Fine, Biden said. The START treaty would be held hostage until the Republicans got their debate.

And there was another problem, McConnell explained. We can't even do the START treaty until this tax thing gets done. Because for my guys, getting the tax thing done is the most important matter. If you guys drag out this tax thing, I can't get anybody to focus on anything else. "For us, taxes is the thing."

The "tax thing" meant the extension of the Bush tax cuts for everyone. McConnell said that the tax thing was so important that he would consider anything that Obama and Biden might want in exchange.

Okay, Biden said. A door had opened.

The vice president and Klain weighed the realities of late 2010. Larry Summers and Biden's own economic advisers said that raising income tax rates while the recovery was still shaky would hurt the economy, and failure to extend the tax cuts before the Christmas season could ruin it. Even prolonged uncertainty would have a negative impact. And Biden realized that the Republicans were more adamant in their position—no one's taxes should go up, especially in a down economy—than Democrats were about ending cuts to the upper-income brackets.

Although raising taxes on just the upper brackets remained White House doctrine—the president had reiterated the pledge before the

2010 congressional elections—Biden was sure the Democrats would cave. "Our guys will blink," he said. If they didn't get a tax deal in the 30-day lame duck, everyone's taxes would go up and the economy would likely take a hit. Republicans would quickly pass an extension of all Bush tax cuts. In the Senate, a lot of Democrats would fold quickly. So, as long as there was going to be a deal, Biden said, strike it now. Get that done and they could get the START treaty ratified.

The president didn't want to give up that easily. I still want to extend the tax cuts for everyone but the wealthy, he told Biden.

Biden told him it wouldn't sell to McConnell.

Let's try, Obama said.

Biden tried, and McConnell repeated that it was not going to happen. He wouldn't budge on the tax thing. His feet were in cement. But, tell me what else you want.

Biden wanted START. He wanted help for working people to send their kids to college, help for the working poor, the very poor, the unemployed. And he wanted to extend Making Work Pay, a program of $400-a-year income tax cuts from the president's original 2009 stimulus program. The cost would be about $60 billion a year.

No way can I sell that, McConnell said. Making Work Pay was refundable, which meant that it gave money to people who didn't pay any income taxes, either because they were poor or had a lot of deductions. A married couple could get a check from the federal government for as much as $800 even though they paid no income tax. Won't fly.

The deadline was running out on the tax thing, but McConnell's adviser Rohit Kumar proposed a solution.

A 37-year-old attorney, Kumar was a Boston native, educated at Duke and the University of Virginia. An expert in taxes and financial policy, he had served as an adviser to the two Senate Republican leaders who preceded McConnell.

Suppose we adopt Making Work Pay, but just for those who pay taxes? he suggested. No tax due, no check in the mail?

Klain took this idea to his old friend Gene Sperling. Sperling was a veteran of eight years in the Clinton White House, the last four as head of the National Economic Council—Clinton's economic czar. Now 51, he had played critical roles in the 1993 and 1997 budget deals and was one of the strongest advocates of progressive causes in the Democratic Party. Since he had supported Hillary Clinton in the 2008 presidential race, he had not been given a top economic post in the Obama administration. Uncomfortable on the sidelines, Sperling had accepted a position as Tim Geithner's counselor at the Treasury Department, handling much of the White House business on deficits, taxes and jobs. He had an office just down the hall from Geithner's, and was a fount of new ideas. He had hired a small army of young, hardworking number crunchers who worked in a section of the Treasury Department that other staffers referred to as the BoG, Bureau of Gene.

When Klain confided that they were considering dropping the poorest citizens from Making Work Pay, Sperling went nuts. "That would be immoral," he said. If you do that, we'd be run out of town. No way could Obama abandon those at the bottom.

All right, said Klain, but Republicans owe us. If the president gives in on the high-income-bracket extension, that's $60 billion a year. "So they should give us $60 billion. That's fair. McConnell knows that."

The task now was to find another way to get what was theirs. Sperling suggested payroll tax cuts.

He knew the tax code and federal budget inside and out. A famous workaholic, Sperling believed in preparation. He and his bureau had already gathered the research to show that many Republicans, including McConnell and Boehner, had been proponents of cutting the payroll tax that funds the Social Security Trust Fund. The payroll tax was currently set by law at 12.4 percent, with half paid by the employer and half by the employee. A cut in the tax would apply only to those who paid it, so nontaxpayers wouldn't benefit. Republicans loved tax cuts, and this one would apply to 160 million workers.

Sperling went back to the Bureau of Gene and put together Power-Point slides showing all the different Republicans who had been for a payroll tax cut. Biden and Klain presented the idea to McConnell in a conference call.

McConnell liked it, and he and his deputy, Jon Kyl, went to the soon-to-be leaders of the new House majority, Boehner and Cantor.

McConnell announced that they were going to get an extension of the high-income Bush tax cuts, holding the top rate down to 35 percent. This was a big victory for Republicans. As their share of the pie, Obama and Biden wanted a one-year payroll tax cut that would cost $60 billion.

Boehner was fine with the deal.

Wait, said Cantor. A payroll tax holiday was not great policy. Since Reagan, the Republican Party had been about low income tax rates to grow the economy. The $60 billion cut in the payroll tax would technically come from the Social Security Trust Fund, which Reagan and Tip O'Neill had saved in 1983. He looked down the road into the 2012 tax year. The White House would argue that the cut had to be extended for another year. Republicans would have no choice but to go along. They could hardly be for allowing taxes to go up, especially in an election year.

McConnell and Kyl insisted, so Boehner again said fine. But given Cantor's hesitation, McConnell told Biden that if they went along with the payroll tax cut, he needed something more to sweeten the deal. Kyl wanted to change estate tax rates, which were scheduled to rise to 55 percent with a $1 million exemption when the Bush tax cuts expired. The White House would have to accept a drop in the estate tax rate to 35 percent with a $5 million exemption for two years. This was a pet plan of Kyl's and of Arkansas Senator Blanche Lincoln, a Democrat.

"It's just terrible," Sperling said when he heard the proposal. Obama and Biden were outraged. This was classic special interest legislation that might apply to only 6,000 to 7,000 families and would cost the Treasury $25 billion.

Geithner told the president there was a principle involved. "The only way you can possibly do Kyl-Lincoln is if they give us everything."

Biden knew House Democrats were anxious about the White House cutting its own deal with the Republicans, so on Saturday night, December 4, Biden had the Democratic leaders, Pelosi and Hoyer, and Maryland Representative Chris Van Hollen, a top Democrat on the House Budget Committee, to dinner at the vice president's residence. There as backup were Geithner, Lew and Schiliro. Biden mentioned that all kinds of ideas were being explored with the Republicans. We're not really negotiating, he said. He did not mention extending the Bush tax cuts, the most explosive issue. You'll be in the loop, don't worry about it, there's no deal yet.

As usual, there were a great many players to be kept in the loop, and with the "tax thing" deadline coming closer each day, the loop was beginning to feel like a noose.

The next day, Biden and McConnell agreed to a basic two-year extension of all the Bush tax cuts ($544 billion), the payroll tax cut for a year (now $112 billion), the Kyl-Lincoln estate tax plan (at least $25 billion), and extension of unemployment insurance for 13 months ($56.5 billion). Other provisions favored by the Republicans allowed businesses of any size to entirely write off the cost of equipment or other capital investments for the next year. Businesses would save an estimated $150 billion in taxes. In addition, the highest rate on capital gains and dividends would remain at 15 percent for two years. Other details remained unfinished, but both men knew they were close to a deal.

On Monday, Biden called Pelosi and other key House Democrats to the White House Roosevelt Room to give them the good news.

"We got a good deal," Biden said. "I told your leaderships on Saturday night when they were at my house that we were working on this," and here it is. He attempted to summarize, mentioning now that the Bush tax cuts for all would be extended for two years.

Blindsided, the House Democrats erupted. There were raised voices, raw emotions, even shouts of anger.

"I thought we were going to be part of these negotiations," said Van Hollen. "I thought I was going to be at the table. We weren't at the table."

This is brutal, thought Sperling, who was backstopping the vice president. He knew it was a bitter pill, having to extend the Bush tax cuts for the top income brackets. In the White House they were grieving too, but they'd had time to come to terms with the idea.

"Speaker Pelosi," Sperling interjected, "remember what we did in '93? Remember when we passed the Earned Income Tax Credit? I went back and totaled up how much difference that made. It was like $150 billion to $200 billion." The EITC, a "refundable" credit, reduces the tax burden on poor and middle-class families, and if the amount of the credit exceeds taxes owed, the difference is "refunded" to the taxpayer. It will be extended under the new agreements, he said, and they should consider the power of that.

"In the Recovery Act [the stimulus of 2009] you fought to increase the child tax credit of $1,000, and to increase the refundability. The Republicans are saying they'll extend it for two years. If they extend it for two years, it could go on and on. This could be a great legacy for you."

Sperling rolled on. Under the deal, 2 million people would have their unemployment insurance extended for 13 months, and 8 million students and their families would see an extension of the American Opportunity Tax Credit, which provided college tuition assistance.

Pelosi replied that the vice president was going to have to personally present the deal to all the House Democrats. She wasn't going to sell it for him.

Ron Klain also sensed the grief in the room, and he knew it wasn't just the result of giving in on a fundamental tax issue. The sorrow was amplified by the recent election results. Pelosi—just two years earlier the first female speaker of the House—was suddenly going to be minority leader. They would all be moving to smaller offices, giving up committee chairmanships and the larger staffs and status that come with being "Mr. Chairman." And for the 63 Democrats who had either been voted out or were retiring, passing this deal would likely be their last act as members of Congress. The political setback was enormous.

When Obama entered the Roosevelt Room, having just returned from a speech in North Carolina, the mood was still angry.

"I'm drawing a line in the sand after this," Obama promised, trying to rally the group. This was his final compromise on taxes. "Let's protect the fragile economy. Come the next round when these things expire, I'm holding. Not happening again."

Biden had walked over to the Cabinet Room to break the news to the leading Senate Democrats. Most seemed resigned, but not Senator Chuck Schumer of New York. Schumer was a showman, and the joke among reporters on Capitol Hill was that the most dangerous place in Washington was between Chuck Schumer and a television camera. He had personally engaged the tax issue with a so-called Schumer amendment to continue the Bush tax breaks for everyone except those who made $1 million a year or more. That meant 315,000 Americans would pay at the pre-Bush top marginal rate of 39.6 percent. McConnell and the Republicans voted unanimously against opening debate, which Schumer said was proof that they loved and protected rich people.

"Joe," Schumer said to Biden, "you've got to let this go on." Schumer planned to make the Republicans vote again and again and again, to embarrass them.

"Chuck, you had your vote," Biden said. "You got your press release. You've got whatever political gain we're going to get out of this." Time to move on. "If we do this now, we can get the tax thing done. We can also get START done. We can also get Don't Ask, Don't Tell done." The nuclear weapons treaty and the elimination of the ban on gays serving openly in the military were two of the Democrats' major goals. There is too great a cost for waiting. Scoring political points two years before the next election? Biden asked. No one would remember.

Biden's most sensitive conversation was with Harry Reid, who had not been included in the negotiations.

Reid was frosty. "You guys went and did this deal," he told Biden. "You go sell it. Not my deal, not my problem. Not telling you I'm against it, not telling you I'm for it, not yelling at you, just saying you guys made this deal. Hope you can line up the Senate Democrats behind you because I'm not going to."

Later, the president wanted Reid to come to the White House to discuss the deal. Obama's life and his operating style had been built

around avoiding confrontation. Reid's had been about having con-
frontations. "I'm not going to come in after the fact," Reid said. "No,
Mr. President, you went and did this. You're going to have to live
with it."

At 6:30 that night Obama announced the deal from the White House.
The Republicans, he said, wanted to "make permanent the tax cuts for
the wealthiest 2 percent of Americans," and he had held the extension
to two years.

It was spin. The Republicans would have liked to make the cuts
permanent, but it was never a serious part of the negotiations.

"There are things in here that I don't like, namely the extension of
the tax cuts for the wealthiest Americans and the wealthiest estates,"
the president said. "It's not perfect."

However, he said, the result would keep taxes from going up by
"$3,000 for a typical American family."

"I'm not willing to let working families across this country become
collateral damage for political warfare here in Washington."

In the end, Biden and Klain realized, it had been an easy deal to make.
Everyone had gotten what they wanted. "We walked in with a big bowl
of candy and said, 'What do you want?' " Klain said. "Allocating goodies in negotiations is a little easier than allocating pain."

But not all Democrats were happy with the distribution of the
goodies. Many on the left viewed the president's compromise as tanta-
mount to betrayal. Ohio Senator Sherrod Brown accused the president
of "blowing a $700 billion hole" in the budget in order to give tax cuts
to the rich.

It was in this atmosphere that Obama appeared before reporters
on December 7, and held forth on the necessity of compromise. He
sounded as if he had been robbed at gunpoint.

"The middle-class tax cuts were being held hostage to the high-end
tax cuts. I think it's tempting not to negotiate with hostage takers, un-

less the hostage gets harmed," he said. "In this case the hostage was the American people and I was not willing to see them get harmed."

Looking back on the negotiation, the president later told me, "There's no doubt that the politics of it, as well as the substantive policy of extending the high-end tax cuts as well as the middle-class tax cuts, was very difficult and hard to swallow, partly because it was hard to justify that [top] 2 percent contributing significantly to economic growth. But we were in a political situation, having just gotten slaughtered in the House races, and the Republicans feeling ascendant, where we felt that what we did end up negotiating would give the best chance of continuing to grow the economy. Essentially, we were willing to swallow some stuff that was not as helpful to get all the stuff that was helpful."

On Wednesday, December 15, the Senate voted 81–19 to approve the tax deal, and the next day the House passed it 277–148. Most of the no votes came from 112 Democrats.

What was noted only in passing in most news accounts was that the cost was about $900 billion over two years, more than the controversial stimulus bill. It would be funded by increasing the deficit and the national debt by that amount.

In other words, it wouldn't be paid for.

Bruce Reed, who had been the staff director of the Simpson-Bowles commission and who would soon take over for Klain as Biden's new chief of staff, said, "The era of deficit denial is over. They're just having a big year-end close-out."

On December 15, Don't Ask, Don't Tell repeal passed the House, and three days later it was approved by the Senate and went to the president. On December 22, the START treaty was ratified by the Senate 71–26.

Privately, McConnell thought the Republicans got the better end of the deal. If they had not taken over the House and picked up five seats in the Senate, he reasoned, they never would have gotten the deal. The victors didn't roar into Washington and pillage like in the old days, but they had momentum on their side.

Biden felt that in the 45 days since the staggering political defeat of early November, Obama had stabilized his presidency. They were back in the game.

On February 11, Biden spoke at the University of Louisville's McConnell Center, which had been personally endowed by McConnell. A 1964 graduate, McConnell loved the university and was a self-described "rabid" fan of its sports teams. He had invited Biden to speak. The McConnell whisperer's theme was that the political system was not broken, that progress could be made, and that not only could Republicans and Democrats work together, but they often like each other. "They do," Biden said. "They really do."

At the White House, Biden's Senate style of doing business had, for the moment, supplanted the House approach, exemplified by Rahm Emanuel's "We have the votes. Fuck 'em."


The administration's success in getting several of the more controversial items on its agenda through the lame-duck session of Congress gave rise to criticism, from Democrats, that the White House ought to have pushed to settle the upcoming debt ceiling issue as well.

"We saw coming that this debt ceiling could end up being a problem because, historically, that's always an unpopular vote. Nobody, certainly on the other side of, or in the other party to, the White House, feels like this is a winner to them," Obama later recalled.

"A whole bunch of people would say, Why didn't you get a deal on the debt ceiling back in December? Because you should have anticipated this was coming. We knew it was coming," he said.

"Mitch McConnell, who knew he was gaining seats, and John Boehner, who knew they were gaining seats, were not going to go along with a situation in which we got a free pass on a debt ceiling, or were they going to put on a whole bunch of votes to let us off the hook on the debt ceiling," he said with a laugh. "They were very explicit about it. So it wasn't for lack of trying or lack of awareness. We just couldn't get it."

# 9

Summers resigned as head of the National Economic Council effective the last day of 2010. Later, one night at Harvard, he gave an associate his private conclusions about Obama and what was driving him. "I don't think anybody has a sense of his deep feelings about things. I don't think anybody has a sense of his deep feelings about people. I don't think people have a sense of his deep feelings around his public philosophy." He found Obama to be a judicious manager who did not have driving, long-formed and long-held convictions on the issues. He was not ideologically driven.

Once, in a conversation on the longtime liberal cause of disability insurance, the president said he realized that sending excessive payments to people who were not working would lead them to not return to work. There was what Summers told others was an "excessive pragmatism" in the president, causing him to have some difficulty in taking a line and sticking with it. It is not a political triumph to have the left outraged at you and the business community think you're a socialist, Summers said.

One day, he said, the president would decry the "fat-cat bankers," and then later call top bank CEOs like Jamie Dimon of JPMorgan Chase and Lloyd Blankfein of Goldman Sachs "savvy businessmen," adding that he didn't begrudge them their success or wealth. Summers said he thought Obama should have taken a consistent line more reassuring to business. Though he had been the chief business contact for the administration, Valerie Jarrett was the ambassador, and Summers said the president paid a price with the business community for keeping her in that role.

"And she sure talked like she was speaking for [the president]," Summers said, "and he didn't disabuse them of that, so I think they felt patronized and offended by Valerie."

Summers found the president defensive in some interactions with business leaders, which wasn't effective. The Jarrett solution was often, "We'll just set up three more lunches with the president and business leaders." She had the view that if you simply arranged more meetings, that would solve any problem. But the interactions had an emptiness that made the problem worse. Sometimes, it's not a good idea to have a meeting and discussion.

According to Summers, "excessive pragmatism" meant Obama's views and actions were not easily pigeonholed, leaving the chief advocates from both the left and right perpetually unsatisfied.

But the president was not satisfied either, Summers said. "Obama really doesn't have the joy of the game. Clinton basically loved negotiating with a bunch of other pols, about anything. If you told him, God, we've got a problem. We've got to allocate all the office space in the Senate. If you could come spend some time talking to the majority leader in figuring out how to allocate office space in the Senate, Clinton would think that was pretty interesting and kind of fun. Whereas, Obama, he really didn't like these guys."


Another problem for the president and his economic team was brewing in the House. The new Budget Committee chairman, Paul Ryan, seemed determined to challenge the president on basic federal budget issues, especially spending on Medicare and Medicaid.

When he had first come to Congress in 1999 at age 28, Ryan had been so youthful-looking he had problems getting into the House chamber. His slight frame and a mop of dark hair led the Capitol police officer guarding the door to assume he was staff.

Ryan believed his most important challenge was learning how to be an effective lawmaker, and he began charting a path right away. Having lost his father at the age of 16, he had always sought mentors, working as a speechwriter for former Republican Congressman Jack Kemp and former Reagan Education Secretary Bill Bennett. Now he reached out again, asking a number of the House's senior members to breakfast or lunch, seeking guidance.

He sat down at one point with Representative Barney Frank, the Massachusetts Democrat known for his biting wit and powerful intellect. Though they were ideological opposites, Frank gave him what Ryan considered the best advice he got about how to be an effective congressman. Be a specialist, Frank told him, not a generalist. Focus on one set of issues. Get on the committee that you care about, and then learn more about the topic than anybody else.

Ryan also sought out Bill Thomas, the Republican chairman of the powerful House Ways and Means Committee. Talk to all the experts you can find, Thomas told him, and read everything you can. Know these things inside and out.

Having majored in economics and political science as an undergraduate at Miami University of Ohio, Ryan didn't take long to decide that the Budget Committee was where he wanted to be.

Following the advice of Frank and Thomas, he threw himself into the world of economic policy wonks, consulting with experts and issuing detailed legislative proposals for balancing the budget and getting the federal debt under control.

Ryan had come into Congress thinking that health care was a Democratic issue, and not so much a financial one. But the more he pored over budget numbers, the more he came to believe that unless drastic changes were made to health care spending, the United States could never get its budget under control. This isn't a social issue, he concluded, this is an economic issue. On one level, it was not complex— the drivers of runaway spending were Medicare, Medicaid and Social

Security. Spending on these three entitlement programs would double in the next 10 years.

By 2007, the beginning of his fifth term, he had worked his way up to the highest position available to a Republican on the Democrat-controlled House Budget Committee: ranking member.

Some congressmen aim for such titles because they covet prestige or authority. Ryan coveted computing power.

As ranking member, he gained access to the actuaries and economists at the Congressional Budget Office. His research requests would be honored, and he could test his budget plans against the powerful computer models used by CBO staff to analyze federal spending.

In 2010, still in the minority, Ryan released his "A Roadmap for America's Future"—a plan he said would bring the federal budget into balance by the middle of the century, eventually eliminating both the debt and the deficit.

The centerpiece of the "Roadmap" was a plan to replace the existing Medicare system with vouchers that recipients could use to purchase health insurance on the private market. The plan drastically cut federal spending on Medicare in the coming decades. But the method raised howls of protest. The value of the vouchers would grow at a rate lower than the rate of health care inflation, meaning that unless growth in health care costs suddenly slowed, recipients would have to use more of their own money each year in order to maintain the same level of coverage.

In a hearing on February 2, 2010, Democratic Representative Allyson Schwartz of Pennsylvania said the Ryan plan would "end Medicare as we know it," a phrase that would become a standard talking point for Democrats.

But not all Democrats had trashed Ryan's ideas. The president had appeared at a House Republican retreat in Baltimore on January 29, 2010, where he praised parts of Ryan's proposal.

Ryan posted a clip from the event on YouTube. What mattered for

Ryan was Obama's tone. The president sounded like he wanted to avoid partisan trench warfare.

Obama called Ryan's Medicare plan "a serious proposal. I've read it. I can tell you what's in it. And there's some ideas in there that I would agree with but there's some ideas we should have a healthy debate about because I don't agree with them."

The president indicated that he and Ryan were on the same page when it came to understanding the federal spending problem. "The major driver of our long-term liabilities, everybody here knows, is Medicare and Medicaid and our health care spending. . . . Nothing comes close. That's going to be what our children have to worry about."

In the videotaped discussion, Ryan made it clear to Obama that under his plan those currently 55 or older would see no change in conventional Medicare, but those who were younger would pay more. "It has to be reformed for younger generations," Ryan said, "because it won't exist. It's going bankrupt."

"As I said before," Obama continued, "this is an entirely legitimate proposal. There is political vulnerability to doing anything that tinkers with Medicare. And that's probably the biggest savings that are obtained through Paul's plan. And I raise that not because we shouldn't have a serious discussion about it; I raise that because we're not going to be able to do anything about any of these entitlements if what we do is characterize whatever proposals are put out there as, 'Well, you know, that's the other party being irresponsible . . . the other party is trying to hurt our senior citizens.'

"That's why I say: If we're going to frame these debates in ways that allow us to solve them, then we can't start off by figuring out a) who is to blame and b) how can we make the American people afraid of the other side. And unfortunately that's how our politics works right now. Every time somebody speaks in Congress, the first thing they do, they stand up, have all the talking points, I see [pollster] Frank Luntz up here, he's already polled it. . . . I've done a focus group, the way we're going to box Obama in on this one, or make Pelosi look bad on that one. That's how we operate. It's all tactics. It's not solving problems. And so the question is: At what point can we have a serious conversation about Medicare and its long-term liability, or a serious conversation about Social Security or a serious conversation about budget and debt in which we aren't simply trying to position ourselves politically?

"That's what I'm committed to doing."

It was a remarkable on-the-record olive branch, and Ryan took the president at his word, hoping for a real dialogue and negotiation.

On April 5, 2011, Ryan, now chairman of the powerful Budget Committee, released an updated version of the "Roadmap" called "The Path to Prosperity." He highlighted stark differences between his plan and the annual budget request that Obama had sent to Congress earlier in the year.

The administration had claimed its plan would reduce the deficit by $1.1 trillion over the coming decade. The Ryan budget claimed to cut the deficit by $4.4 trillion.

The administration proposal would continue deficit spending indefinitely. The Ryan budget would create a budget surplus by 2040.

Ryan had provided the plan to the Congressional Budget Office in advance and simultaneously issued the results of the office's analysis.

The CBO largely confirmed Ryan's claims about cutting the deficit and bringing the budget into balance. But it warned that Ryan would accomplish that by pushing a large and growing share of health care costs off the federal government's balance sheet and onto individuals and states.

"Under the proposal," the CBO found, "most elderly people would pay more for their health care than they would pay under the current Medicare system." Ten years into the Ryan program, total spending on Medicare patients would be higher, because private plans do not hold costs down as effectively as Medicare. The government would save money only because its share of those increased costs would be much smaller. The CBO found that the percentage of total costs paid by seniors enrolled in Medicare would increase from 25 percent to 68 percent.

The Ryan proposal would also turn Medicaid into a block grant program, with the amount of money given to the states each year increasing at a rate slower than the expected increase in health care costs. The proposal gave states more choices about how to spend the money, the CBO found, but:

"Even with additional flexibility, however, the large projected reduction in payments would probably require states to decrease payments to Medicaid providers, reduce eligibility for Medicaid, provide less extensive coverage to beneficiaries, or pay more themselves than would be the case under current law."

In the end, the elderly and the poor would pay more for their health care, and the government less. Would this be manageable for seniors and the poor? Ryan hoped that it would be made so by an economic renewal that he expected to result from stabilizing the federal deficit and cutting taxes.

But many Democrats, like Chris Van Hollen, the ranking member on the House Budget Committee, thought it was fantasy.

The CBO had noted that when the plan was in full effect in 2022, the average Medicare recipient would be receiving $25,560 in annual Social Security payments. These would be retired seniors with few potential sources of additional income. Even if an economic boom were to occur, it was hardly going to change their circumstances. The Ryan plan would increase their health care costs by more than $7,000 a year.

Congressional Republicans had their hands on a political atomic bomb.

The legal limit on government debt, which was currently set at $14.7 trillion, would have to be increased in the spring or summer. If not, the United States would default on its obligations. Financial markets considered U.S. Treasury securities the world's safest investment. Investing and trading strategies around the globe were built on the assumption that they were essentially risk-free assets. If the U.S. stopped paying its bills, confidence in Treasuries would be shaken, and the economic turmoil that would result was almost unthinkable.

In a January 6 letter to Harry Reid, copied to all members of Congress, Treasury Secretary Geithner warned, "Default would effectively impose a significant and long-lasting tax on all Americans and all American businesses and could lead to the loss of millions of American jobs. Even a very short-term or limited default would have catastrophic economic consequences that would last for decades."

For most of the past decade, increasing the debt limit had been a routine matter. That had changed significantly in 2009, when Senator Conrad's group of Democrats held it hostage in order to force Obama to appoint the Simpson-Bowles fiscal commission.

Now Republicans led the House, and the takeover had been spearheaded by candidates affiliated with the Tea Party, whose opposition to deficit spending animated their campaigns. With the Treasury nearing the debt limit again, House Republicans were certain to up the ante and use the extension to extract spending and tax cuts. Boehner had for months made it clear that a debt limit increase would only pass if it were accompanied by real spending cuts and serious deficit reduction.

The White House had a more immediate problem: funding the government through the rest of the year. Without a budget, the country's day-to-day operations were funded under a series of short-term "continuing resolutions." Each time one neared expiration, Republicans warned of a looming government shutdown.

There was a new team at the White House. Emanuel had returned to Chicago to run for mayor. He was replaced by former Clinton Commerce Secretary William Daley, 62, an affable lawyer who had strong business contacts and sympathies. Born into the legendary Chicago political family—his father, Richard J. Daley, served 21 years as mayor, and his brother Richard M. Daley served 22—Daley's background was business. He had been president of SBC Communications and a member of the executive committee at JPMorgan Chase.

Jack Lew was now head of OMB, a job he had also held during the Clinton administration. A strong supporter of Hillary Clinton during the 2008 Democratic primary, Lew had followed Clinton to the State Department, where he served as deputy secretary for management and resources for two years. Lew, 55, was a Harvard graduate who wore round wire-rimmed glasses, and had a head of thick black hair streaked with gray. He was a committed progressive, unafraid of wading into political fights. A soft-spoken budget technician, he had been trained in the office of House Speaker Tip O'Neill, where he had been deeply involved in negotiating the 1983 deal between President Reagan and O'Neill to save Social Security. The deal included an acceleration of a planned increase in payroll taxes from 10.8 percent to 12.4 percent. Lew had taken away a key lesson. O'Neill publicly described it as a tax increase and Reagan as a benefits cut. As long as neither challenged the other's statements, the deal was accepted. Lew kept a picture of himself and O'Neill in his office. Next to it, under the frame, was a personal "Dear Jack" letter of thanks from Reagan, dated April 26, 1983.

After two years of struggling, Gene Sperling was elated when he finally made it to the White House inner circle. Obama picked him to replace Summers as head of the National Economic Council. After a decade in exile, he returned to the second-floor West Wing suite of offices where he had virtually lived during the Clinton administration.

Obama appointed Rob Nabors, 39, director of legislative affairs. A budget expert who had worked closely with Lew in OMB during Clinton's second term, and then as OMB's deputy director under Orszag, Nabors had been majority staff director on the House Appropriations Committee during the Bush administration. His father, a Vietnam draftee, stayed in the Army, eventually retiring as a major general. As a child, Nabors lived in places as diverse as South Korea, Italy, Arizona and Massachusetts. The family finally settled in Virginia, where Nabors finished high school before going to college at Notre Dame and graduate school at the University of North Carolina–Chapel Hill. His former boss, David Obey, the ranking Democrat on the House

Appropriations Committee, once said of Nabors, "He understands
the House, he understands the committee, he understands the town,
he understands the bureaucracy, and he doesn't take any crap from
anybody."

The White House now had four Clinton veterans at the top: Daley,
Sperling, Lew and Nabors.

# 10

For perhaps the most important role in the West Wing, the president turned to someone he had worked with intimately for years, David Plouffe, his 2008 campaign manager.

Plouffe, 44, replaced David Axelrod, the political adviser for the administration's first two years, taking over the most strategically placed office in the West Wing. Though the office was small, it was closer to the Oval Office than any other, including the chief of staff's.

Small-boned and almost frail-looking, Plouffe (pronounced Pluff) was a disciplined political tactician, brought in to align the White House's day-to-day policies with the long-term goal of making sure Obama won reelection in 2012.

Plouffe had dropped out of college in 1989, after his junior year, to work on his first political campaign. He completed his degree in 2010. Now, after more than two decades of total immersion in Democratic electoral politics, he knew the entire landscape—the Congress, grassroots organizing, fundraising, messaging, advertising and strategy.

Within the West Wing he had the most orderly desk. All papers, files and schedules were carefully arranged. He was in on every important presidential decision, quick to anticipate the second, third and if need be the fourth and fifth bounce of any move.

To any request that he deemed in Obama's interest, he would say,

"I'll facilitate that" or "I'll make sure that happens." And it then would. In many respects he was running the White House.

Careful but occasionally profane, Plouffe seemed almost egoless on the surface. But he was not modest about his accomplishments, skills and place in history. His 2009 campaign book, *The Audacity to Win*, began with an account of a conversation he had with David Axelrod, Obama's other top political aide. "We had just elected the president of the United States," Plouffe wrote. Not that they had managed it or that Obama had won it, or that the voters had selected Obama. He and Axelrod—the "we"—had won it. He also reported immodestly what Obama had said to him when he told him he wanted him to manage the campaign. "I've been impressed by your judgment, temperament, organization and strategic sense. . . . I can see you understand the rhythm and contours of a race like this."

Plouffe also wrote that when President-elect Obama spoke at the Lincoln Memorial the Saturday before his inaugural, he asked Obama if he was looking up at Lincoln. "Very observant, Plouffe," he quoted Obama as saying.

As Plouffe involved himself with war-room-like intensity with the economic decisions before the president, he returned to a theme that went back to the 2008 election about Obama. "He is, in his gut, a fiscal conservative," Plouffe said. "There is a Blue Dog streak in him." And that was likely to play against the president's political interests within the Democratic Party.

The current continuing resolution to fund the government was due to expire on March 4, so Daley reached out to Boehner to open negotiations. Daley's appointment had seemed like a good sign to Boehner, who knew and trusted the new chief of staff.

Hey, he told Daley, you ask for this much. I'll ask for this much. We'll end up somewhere in the middle.

You know what? Daley reported to the president, Lew and Sperling. Boehner is a partisan, but you can cut a deal with the guy.

The speaker wanted several billion dollars shaved off of federal spending, and the White House complied.

But a longer-term agreement was elusive. Boehner seemed willing to deal, but Lew and Nabors ran into problems as they tried to work out details on the Hill. Barry Jackson, Boehner's chief of staff, was not nearly as accommodating. First he would send them off to different congressional offices. Go deal with the members of the House Appropriations Committee, Jackson suggested. Then agreements would slide or get fuzzy. It was never-ending. Sperling joked that Jack Lew swore more times in a day than he had in all his eight years in the Clinton administration.

Late on the evening of April 8, Boehner and Obama met in the Oval Office and settled on the terms of a final deal. But up on the Hill, Republicans on the Appropriations Committee didn't get the message. Lew and Nabors found themselves in the Capitol until 4 a.m., being asked to make changes to a deal they thought was done.

We're not going to renegotiate what the president and the speaker signed off on at eleven in the Oval Office, Lew said. The president and the speaker are going to have to talk.

At eight the following morning, Obama called Boehner.

"John, you're the speaker of the House, the leader of the Republican Party," Obama said. "I'm the president of the United States, leader of the Democratic Party. The country depends on the two of us being able to do our business together. When I give you my word, it has to mean something. When you give me your word, it has to mean something. And it can't be that people go back and agreements that we make don't stick."

Then, the president later told senior staff, the most perplexing, troubling thing happened. Instead of denying that things weren't going as he'd promised, Boehner seemed to apologize. As if embarrassed, Boehner told the president that, at the time, at least, he had meant what he said. There were obviously things Boehner couldn't control, the president said.

Finally, on April 9, Congress passed its seventh and final continuing resolution, and agreed on a budget that would carry the government through the end of September.

The speaker thought the continuing resolution fight had given him a chance to seize the moral high ground and force spending cuts. He got the House to pass legislation that funded the Defense Department for nearly six months while cutting an additional $12 billion from other departments and only funding them for one week.

Finally, Boehner won $38.5 billion in cuts for the year. He was the toast of the town at Republican dinners and fundraisers and in his own conference, where more than two thirds of the Republican freshmen had voted with him. In an internally circulated six-page chronology, Boehner's staff hailed the continuing resolution fight as "the first big challenge of the new majority." Boehner touted the $38.5 billion in cuts and said, "The agreement enacted the largest non-Defense spending cut in dollar terms in American history."

But on Wednesday of the following week, members of the Republican conference got some unwelcome news. The Congressional Budget Office, which produces nonpartisan analysis of federal spending, had taken a hard look at the numbers. The true savings for the remainder of 2011 would be more like $352 million—less than one percent of what the speaker was claiming. The speaker's numbers hadn't included funding for overseas operations by the military and other agencies in Afghanistan and Pakistan. Add them to the mix, and discretionary spending would be $3.3 billion higher than in 2010.

Proponents of the deal, it turned out, had counted dubious sorts of "savings" in the plan, including money that, by all accounts, was never going to be spent in the first place. Once the gimmicks were swept aside, it became clear that Boehner was asking Republicans to approve what amounted to a spending increase.

The battle over the continuing resolution, Obama later recalled, had been "somewhat painful" and "a little bit annoying." In the end, he said, "We were able to avoid a shutdown. The only thing that happened there was I missed, I think, a long weekend with Michelle, so I got in trouble at home."

What stuck with the president was how differently the deal was perceived by Democrats and Republicans.

"Some of our friends on the left would howl and act as if we had dismantled the New Deal in this continuing resolution deal," Obama said, "when in fact, in retrospect, actually, we did a pretty darn good job of negotiating and protecting things that we cared deeply about. Ironically, while the left thought we'd been completely out-maneuvered by John Boehner, his caucus thought that he had been completely outmaneuvered. That sets the stage, then, for the later ne-gotiations."


Another skirmish in the battle over the continuing resolution grew into a well-fortified battle line. During the heated negotiations, Barry Jackson, Boehner's chief of staff, reported to David Krone, Reid's chief of staff, that Bill Daley, the White House chief of staff, said there was a breakthrough.

"I talked to Daley," Jackson said. "He told me that you guys could get to at least $70 billion in cuts." It was much more than the White House had been proposing.

Reid and Krone were surprised. Daley said his statement had been misinterpreted. But Krone and Jackson had developed a strong rela-tionship, and Krone believed the speaker's chief of staff over the White House chief of staff. So did Reid, who was outraged that Daley would insert himself in the negotiation.

"Mr. President," Reid said in a talk with Obama, "this has to be a relationship between you and me." Dealing with the new Republican House majority was going to be difficult, and Daley was talking to Boehner's chief of staff. "What's your chief of staff doing going around and having his own conversations without telling us?

"I'll tell you when I want your chief of staff coming up here. I'll let you know when I need him."

• • •

Media reports cast the coming debt limit debate as a major showdown. The business and financial communities issued dire warnings. Failure to raise the debt limit in a timely manner would be "a recovery-ending event," said Federal Reserve Board Chairman Ben Bernanke. It would be "catastrophic and unpredictable," said JPMorgan Chase CEO Jamie Dimon.

Republican House freshmen vowed not to increase the debt limit, or to do so only under the most stringent conditions. "The only way I would even consider to vote for raising the debt ceiling," said Representative Raul Labrador, a Tea Party–affiliated lawmaker from Idaho, "is if we have passed, in both the House and the Senate, a Constitutional balanced budget amendment."

A budget based on Representative Ryan's "Path to Prosperity" was expected to pass the House with the promise of cutting $4 trillion in spending over the next decade. The administration had not responded. The $1.1 trillion in cuts in its own budget request, sent to Congress earlier in the year, looked paltry.

In the White House, Obama and his staff knew they needed a basic framework to counter Ryan.

Lew and Sperling, reflecting their budget wonk roots, told the president that the only way out of partisan gridlock was to propose their own major budget, spending and tax deal with the Congress. The only times in recent history when big deals like this had actually worked were when the president brought together the key players—House and Senate, Republicans and Democrats. They cited Reagan and Speaker Tip O'Neill in 1983 on saving Social Security, George H. W. Bush and the Democrats in 1990 on raising taxes, and Clinton and Speaker Newt Gingrich on the budget in 1997.

"You bring everybody in the room," Sperling said, "you hold hands, and you jump together."

The senators in the so-called Gang of Six—an unofficial bipartisan group of three Democrats and three Republicans—had been promising to put out their deficit reduction and tax plan. Maybe the White

House could adopt theirs somehow. But despite frequent promises that the plan was imminent, the Gang didn't get it done.

"We're not waiting," the president said in exasperation. He wanted to rip into Ryan's plan. He was holding several meetings a week with his economic and speechwriting teams to figure out how best to do it and on the weekend of April 9 and 10, the president summoned them to the Oval Office. He wanted a credible alternative plan. Democrats didn't want him to cut Medicare. But to prove his seriousness about deficit reduction, he said, he wanted to propose hundreds of billions of dollars in Medicare cuts and additional cuts in other cherished programs. He would also propose some cuts in Medicaid, the health insurance program for the poor. But there was a line that couldn't be crossed, and Ryan's plan had crossed it. The Ryan plan was a model of excess.

Obama was jotting notes as he talked. A speechwriter and aides also took down what he said.

"I want to say this idea that we can't get our deficit down without brutalizing Medicaid, it's a dark view of America," he said. He wanted that idea in the speech.

The Ryan view is that "we can't afford to invest in our infrastructure." In mid-March Obama had visited Brazil, Chile and El Salvador. "Can you believe in South America, they're doing this stuff?" He had met with heads of state and they said, "The main thing in our country is to build up our infrastructure." And these were the conservative leaders, he said acidly.

Obama was getting fired up as he worked through what to say and how to say it. He wanted a $4 trillion deficit plan too, but the cuts were too severe. The progressive and liberal base would be deeply distressed.

Sperling suggested an old trick from the Clinton years: Stick with the $4 trillion—that was easy to understand—but instead of projecting it over the traditional 10 years, do it over 12. No one would really notice. Few would do the math. By stretching the plan out and loading most of the cuts into its final years, the early cuts were substantially smaller.

As the draft was being polished, Obama recognized that he had gone past an opening offer to his final one. He had negotiated with himself and was presenting a compromise. His Blue Dog had risen; under this framework, there would be pain for all. When he announced the plan, he realized, he couldn't describe it as a starting point for discussions. The framework was, simply, "where we have to be."

He had been absent from the public debate for some time. It was now time to let the world, and the Republicans, know where he stood. "I'm not splitting the difference on Medicaid," he said. He had gone as far as he was going to go. The speech was ready.

# 11

---

In the White House congressional relations office, preparations were under way for the president's speech, scheduled for April 13, at George Washington University. A junior staffer noticed that Alan Simpson and Erskine Bowles, the co-chairs of the president's fiscal commission, were invited, and suggested in an email that the other members of the fiscal commission should be too.

Including the seven who didn't vote for it?

Well, someone said, that would be the polite thing to do.

Done. Do the polite thing.

So Ryan, Camp and Hensarling—three Simpson-Bowles no votes—received invitations to Obama's speech.

Aha! Ryan reasoned, Obama is going to pull a Clinton-type compromise. He was going to "triangulate," meaning he'd take ideas from both sides and devise what he thought would be a higher order or "third way." Well, that was pretty much to the good, Ryan thought.

When he learned that Simpson and Bowles were invited, along with all the commission members, he thought, "Obama's going to endorse Simpson-Bowles!" Maybe some health care entitlement and Medicare reforms could be devised. "We can get an agreement," he thought.

So, on April 13, Ryan, Camp and Hensarling piled into Hensarling's Jeep Cherokee for the trip across town to George Washington University.


At 10:40 a.m., Obama gathered the eight top congressional leaders from both the House and Senate in the Cabinet Room of the White House to preview his speech.

"I will speak about long-term debt resolution today," Obama said, noting that the debate over the last few months on the continuing resolution had been just a "warm-up." Not being totally frank, he added, "I feel good about how the negotiations proceeded."

The president was going to urge repeal of the Bush tax cuts for the wealthy when they expired at the end of the next year, and he would not support Ryan's proposals for Medicare change. Revenue and Medicare were going to be areas of contention. When Congress returned from its upcoming recess, they would have "a very short runway."

Obama said he wanted the leaders to work toward a package that identified $4 trillion in savings—similar in size to the Bowles-Simpson plan. He wanted them to take a balanced approach, which would include increased tax revenue. "For us to do nothing on revenues is not a balanced approach.

"I'm calling on Joe Biden to lead a working group of House and Senate members from both parties. I'm asking everyone to work seriously to come to an agreement."

Geithner reminded them that the federal government would run out of money in just over a month. He placed the date at May 16, but repeated what he had said in congressional testimony the previous week: He had financial tools that could push the drop-dead date out a further six to eight weeks, possibly to July 8. So the length of the runway was not clear. "We can't get too close to the brink," he said. "It will be too hard to undo the damage."

It was a small window in which to act, Boehner agreed. "We need more revenue," he added, contradicting his party's line that excessive spending, not too little revenue, was the problem. Then he seemed to catch himself and steered back to orthodoxy—"but we can get them through economic growth."

Boehner's claim relied on so-called dynamic scoring of the federal budget. The idea was that if the economy grew, people would make more money and pay more taxes. It seemed logical. The problem, however, was that the Congressional Budget Office could not calculate hypothetical revenue and accordingly would not count it in the official budget score. Even Congress's own Joint Committee on Taxation gave limited credit for expected economic growth.

Harry Reid was exasperated. "We have all these theoretical plans," he said, "but we need to figure out how to get this done." They had a lot of work ahead. "I don't know how we get from here to there," he said with dreariness in his voice.

Biden turned to process, suggesting that each side appoint four people each from the House and Senate. He believed that each side would want someone from leadership as well as representatives of the Budget, Finance (Ways and Means in the House), and Appropriations committees. That would be a total of 16.

"Sixteen seems like too big of a group," McConnell said.

Pelosi, to no one's surprise, said she favored tax hikes for the wealthy, and recommended a budget developed by Chris Van Hollen, the senior Democrat on the House Budget Committee.

Obama said they could streamline or reduce the Biden group if necessary.

"Politics should stop on the debt limit," said Senator Dick Durbin, the No. 2 in the Democratic Senate majority. To the president he said, "I disagree with you on Defense." They should be able to find another $500 billion to cut over 10 years.

"I join the speaker," Cantor said. "We don't want to default on the debt." He projected a penetrating gaze from behind his glasses. They needed to decide what parts of the budget were open to negotiation. Referring to the Republicans in the House, he said, "I, we as a conference, won't raise taxes."

It was a direct challenge to a main tenet of Obama's proposal— that taxes should go up on the wealthy. But to Cantor, the consummate vote counter, it was also a simple statement of the facts. The new Republican majority had dozens of Tea Party adherents who not only would never vote to raise taxes, but were on the record saying they wouldn't raise the debt limit. Virtually all the House Republicans saw spending cuts as the path to long-term resolution of the deficit. Obama didn't have the votes to raise taxes.

At first, Obama avoided answering Cantor's comment and shifted to what he said was a "very good point" on the need to define exactly what would be on the negotiating table. Each side, he said, would "have to give a little bit" to show the markets they were serious. Then he returned to the revenue issue. "You have all said we can't deal with revenues." That was "a thing that we can't give on too."

The president stated what everyone knew: Revenues and Medicare would be "the central areas of disagreement." Maybe a down payment could be made, "with a little pain for everyone.

"Give Ryan credit. There is a choice; we can't have everything and not pay for it."

Steny Hoyer, now the House Democratic whip, suggested they should shoot for solving this in the next month—by June 8, not July 8. "The more we hold the debt limit hostage, the worse off we are."

"We can't play chicken with the debt limit," Obama agreed. But, he added, "We can't ask either side to swallow something that is fundamentally irreconcilable with their beliefs."

Biden laid out his theory of the case: "Find the sweet spot on what we can get done and leave something to be resolved in the next election." You get some, we get some.

Geithner expressed his concern. "We can't have a 'Countdown to Default' on every TV station."

The president made a final point. These talks would be serious. "Whoever is at the table has to be able to speak for you."


A few hours later, Obama headed half a mile down Pennsylvania Avenue to deliver his speech at George Washington University. Sperling was mingling with the crowd when someone waved at him. Who is that tall man who waved at me? he wondered as he put on his glasses.

It was Ryan. And his two Republican cronies. None of the three had voted for Simpson-Bowles. How had they been invited? And this was the day the president was taking off the gloves. Sperling hurried back to Daley with the warning, and Daley sprinted backstage to get to the president.

Too late.

Michigan Representative Dave Camp, a tall, spare Midwestern Republican, arrived sharing Ryan's assumption that Obama was about to endorse Simpson-Bowles. Camp, who had taken over the chairmanship of the House Ways and Means Committee in January, had been surprised when he received the invitation. But if the president was endorsing Simpson-Bowles, Camp figured, it was important for him to be there—to show that he wanted to be part of the process.

He took his reserved seat in the front row, on the end and next to Ryan.

Waiting for the president to be introduced, Camp looked off to the side of the auditorium and spotted Sperling peering toward him and his companions. People were milling around the room, greeting one another.

Why doesn't he come over and say hello? Camp wondered. He's looking at us.

When the president took the podium he was only about 25 feet away from the first row of the audience, but with the spotlights in his eyes, he didn't spot the three Republican House members. As Ryan took his seat, he glanced over to his left and saw a photographer with a long telephoto lens, on a unipod, aimed straight at him.

That's weird, Ryan thought. Why me? It was like a photographer at a football game zeroing in on the end zone.

Obama rolled gently into the subject, speaking of American unity. "We're all connected," he said, and then he jabbed.

The plan and vision, he said, "presented and championed by Republicans . . . would lead to a fundamentally different America than the one we've known, certainly in my lifetime. In fact, I think it would be fundamentally different than what we've known throughout our history.

"A 70 percent cut in clean energy, a 25 percent cut in education," he said. "These are the kinds of cuts that tell us we can't afford the America that I believe in and I think *you* believe in."

Ryan sat stiffly in his chair, refusing to give the man with the telephoto lens a hint of his chagrin. This wasn't an olive branch. This was not Bill Clinton, not triangulation, not Simpson-Bowles. This was what he called "game-on demagoguery."

Ryan's worst suspicions about the president were realized: Obama wasn't just phoning it in for Pelosi and Reid, he really believed this stuff.

In one of the speech's harshest sections, Obama attacked not only Ryan's plan but his entire vision. "It says that 10 years from now, if you're a 65-year-old who's eligible for Medicare, you should have to pay nearly $6,400 more than you would today. It says instead of guaranteed health care, you will get a voucher. And if that voucher isn't worth enough to buy the insurance that's available in the open marketplace, well, tough luck. You're on your own. Put simply, it ends Medicare as we know it."

He warned that "up to 50 million Americans" would lose Medicaid coverage—grandparents, the poor, the middle class, "children with autism or Down syndrome."

Over the top, Ryan was thinking.

Camp felt the same way. Ryan's initial plan had included vouchers. But the Ryan budget that was on the verge of passing the House did not. It offered premium support, which meant the amount of government support would rise in response to premium increases—very different from a flat voucher program, he thought.

Camp thought the president was deliberately mischaracterizing the

Republican position. It seemed the sort of attack that would have been more appropriate on the campaign trail.

All these cuts, Obama continued, are offered in exchange for a $1 trillion tax break for the wealthy. "They want to give people like me a $200,000 tax cut that's paid for by asking 33 seniors each to pay $6,000 more in health costs. That's not right. And it's not going to happen as long as I'm president."

The Republican plan, he said, was "less about reducing the deficit than it is about changing the basic social compact in America."

As soon as Obama concluded, Sperling dashed to intercept Ryan. But Ryan had gotten up quickly and headed out with Camp and Hensarling. This is going to be a long two years, Ryan was thinking, a hard slog. Obama had just doubled down on his ideology. The debt crisis was only going to get worse. He prayed they could hold the bond markets at bay "long enough to get somebody new to fix this problem."

Striding out of the auditorium, Ryan heard someone shouting, "Mr. Chairman! Mr. Chairman!" He thought it was a reporter. He was not going to stop and answer questions, so he ignored the voice.

Then he saw it was Sperling running after him. Catching up with him, Sperling practically grabbed Ryan's coat.

This wasn't planned, he said. This wasn't a setup. Sperling saw that Ryan was genuinely ripped.

"I can't believe you poisoned the well like that," Ryan said quickly, and kept walking. Sperling kept talking and following. Ryan kept walking and didn't listen.

Back in Hensarling's Jeep, the three congressmen vented. This was outside the normal boundaries of partisan discourse—right between the eyes from the president himself. Why did he invite us? Why did he invite the whole Simpson-Bowles commission? What was he up to?

Ryan took out his BlackBerry and began punching out a statement calling the Obama speech "excessively partisan, dramatically inaccurate and hopelessly inadequate to address our fiscal crisis."

Back at the Capitol, Ryan took a call from Alan Simpson.

"I'm going to go throw up in the tulips," Simpson said. The president's words and demeanor, he said, were way over the line.

Then Erskine Bowles called. "I was disgusted," the longtime Democrat said. "I couldn't believe that he did that. And I'm going to talk to the president about it." He said he was apologizing.

"It's not your fault," Ryan replied. "You don't need to apologize for anything."

Ryan's presence at the George Washington University speech fundamentally changed the public and media perception of what the White House had hoped would be a major budget moment. Instead of reshaping the debate, the speech widened the partisan divide. The contrast between the cool bipartisan talk at the White House in the morning and the attack on the Republicans was stark.

Ryan felt betrayed. He'd expected an olive branch. What he got was the finger.


At the White House, there was no witch hunt launched to uncover who in the congressional relations office had failed to tell senior staff and Obama that Ryan and company would be at the speech.

Sperling waited several days and then called Camp and Ryan.

That's our speech, Sperling said to Ryan. Proud of it. But it wasn't a setup. He tried to explain how and why the president didn't know the trio of Republicans was in the audience.

There are fights, Ryan said, and of course, we beat the hell out of the president. But we're just Congress. He's the president. Isn't he supposed to be kind of above it all?


"I was not aware when I gave that speech that Paul Ryan was going to be sitting right there," President Obama later acknowledged in an interview.

Had he known Ryan was in the audience, Obama said, "I might have modified some of it so that we would leave more negotiations open, because I do think that they felt like we were trying to embarrass him.

"We made a mistake," he said.

For Dave Camp, the 57-year-old chairman of the House Ways and Means Committee, the White House claim that the invitation to the George Washington University speech had been an honest mistake didn't sound right. No White House did anything that wasn't calculated. That they had been given reserved front row seats by accident was hard to believe.

Camp was puzzled. This administration's approach to Congress was different from what he was used to.

He had first come to Washington as a congressional staffer during the Reagan administration. Reagan had deployed administration liaisons all over Congress. White House aides were everywhere on Capitol Hill. Camp could remember Reagan getting on the phone with a lowly freshman congressman to discuss legislation. Not coincidentally, Reagan was often able to get things he wanted out of Congress, whether by cajoling or muscle.

Camp was a congressman himself by the time Bill Clinton, another president who often bent legislators to his will, took office in 1993. A self-described "nobody" on the Ways and Means Committee, he had gotten a call from Hillary Clinton about a bill he had introduced. As Reagan had, President Clinton deployed congressional liaison staff across Capitol Hill to develop relationships and create trust.

But from the Obama administration there was virtually no outreach or contact.

During Obama's first two years in office, Camp was the ranking Republican on the Democrat-controlled Ways and Means Committee. He was one of the more politically moderate House Republicans. Yet the administration's Hill staff didn't even seem to know who he was. He never saw them.

After Republicans won control of the House, the administration didn't seem to know how to connect with them on either personal or policy terms. They hadn't found their bearings. The Rahm Emanuel approach to congressional relations—"We have the votes. Fuck 'em."—wouldn't work anymore. They didn't have the votes. Obama's post-election promise of regular meetings and better communication had never materialized.

More than four months later, with Camp sitting in the Ways and Means chairman's seat, one of the most powerful and coveted positions on Capitol Hill, nothing had changed. Polite and approachable, he was the tax man in a time dominated by debates over taxes, and he still felt like a stranger to the White House and the president.

The result was a lack of trust that made even the most bipartisan legislative efforts impossible at worst, and a chore at best.

Not long after the April 13 speech, Camp spoke privately with Geithner about three free trade agreements the administration had negotiated, with South Korea, Colombia and Panama. They had broad support from both parties—Republicans could sell them as good for business, and Democrats could pitch them as creating good middle-class jobs.

Roll out these trade agreements right away, he told Geithner, and I can guarantee you, they will pass the House with a large bipartisan margin. It wasn't an idle promise. Camp was close to Boehner and knew the importance of free trade to the Republican leadership.

Geithner didn't have much of a response.

Camp raised the issue with Sperling. And with White House chief of staff Daley. But the agreements still didn't come to the Hill. It was clear to Camp that the White House wouldn't take him at his word. The administration seemed paralyzed by uncertainty. Where were the administration's legislative representatives? Where was the president?

Does Obama want to chair the Democratic National Committee, or be president of the United States? Camp wondered. Why isn't Obama doing what presidents are supposed to do?

The three free trade agreements didn't come before Congress until October of 2011, when they were introduced, passed and sent to the president in the space of six days. All three passed with large bipartisan majorities in the House on October 12. The vote on the South

Korea agreement was 278–151, on Panama 300–129, and on Colombia 262–167.

Two days later, on October 14, Obama traveled to Camp's home state of Michigan, where he touted the benefits of the agreement with South Korea, noting that it "won support of business and labor, from auto makers and auto workers, from Democrats and Republicans. That doesn't happen very often."

# 12

Not long after the president's speech at George Washington University, Joe Biden tracked down Gene Sperling and deputy National Economic Council director Jason Furman in the White House.

"Sperling, I know Furman's your principal deputy," the vice president began. "For the next few months, he is my principal briefer. He's mine; I'm taking him."

By way of explanation, Biden told a story about a confrontation he had with Senator Russell Long, the son of the flamboyant populist Louisiana Governor Huey Long, during Biden's early days in the Senate in the 1970s.

I was talking about a tax expenditure benefiting oil companies, Biden explained. "I had a great staffer, and he wrote these great talking points for me." And he had delivered them with all the confidence of a new senator.

A senator since 1948, Long was one of the old breed of larger-than-life Washington pols. He chaired the Finance Committee, and was the Senate's preeminent tax expert. Being from Louisiana, he knew a lot about drilling for oil.

"Son," Long told Biden, "I know you're from Delaware, so I'm sure that you know all the details about how you get this type of oil out of the ground."

Biden obviously did not, and Long began defending the tax break, going through the oil drilling process in excruciating detail.

"As I sat there humiliated," Biden told Sperling and Furman, "I thought to myself, I am never going to speak on something that I don't know about again."

The president had asked him to lead a group of lawmakers in an effort to deal with the mounting federal deficit, and the debt ceiling extension, Biden explained, and he was going to need preparation. A lot of it. He had once voluntarily given up his seat on the Senate Budget Committee because he disliked budget work so much.

"I am not a budget guy, but you're going to brief the hell out of me," he told Furman, a 40-year-old Harvard Ph.D. economist. Day after day, the two spent hours poring over the budget with other experts from the Office of Management and Budget and the National Economic Council.

On a sunny spring Thursday, May 5, 2011, at 10:35 a.m., Biden convened a meeting of some 25 top congressional Democrats, Republicans, senior Obama administration officials and staffers at Blair House across Pennsylvania Avenue from the White House. The question before them was whether they could forge a deal to prevent the United States from defaulting on its $14.3 trillion debt. The only way was to pass legislation to increase the debt ceiling.

The new reality was that the Republicans in the House had the leverage. Democrats were going to have to agree to large cuts in federal spending if the Republicans were going to support a debt increase. There was no way around that central truth. But a large number of the new Tea Party–affiliated House members had vowed not to raise the debt limit, so Democratic votes would be needed to pass anything.

Biden saw the group as a sort of search party being sent out into the jungle of federal spending. The key Republican at the table was Eric Cantor, and all eyes, including Biden's, were on him.

Biden began by clearing the room of everybody except the congressmen and senators, the standard way to ensure confidentiality.

Their topic was the federal budget, but with the exception of Representative Chris Van Hollen, the ranking Democrat on the House Budget Committee, the members of the group were not budget experts. Van Hollen, a 52-year-old attorney and a certified budget wonk, was a favorite of Pelosi's. He was a strong progressive voice in the Democratic caucus.

Biden saw the group's lack of budget expertise as an advantage. While preparing for the meeting, he had told his staff that after 40 years of dealing with politicians—and being one himself—he had come to the view that "most elected officials don't know squat about the details. Because they're doing so many things, they know the shorthand and they know the talking points and they have a general sense."

Politicians are always better when you push them off their talking points, Biden said. You can spend a whole career on Capitol Hill without ever having to defend the weaknesses of your positions. But when everyone is learning together what the facts are, then you can see where the real differences are and it's a lot easier to reach agreement.

He was trying to create that atmosphere. He believed that the best way to do it was to keep people in the same room for a long period of time, give them a stake in the outcome, and make sure there were no leaks.

When staff was called back into the room, Biden was soothing. "There are no ultimatums here. Our purpose is to find agreement. Our operating concept is that there's no deal till there's a deal." That meant that, even if they reached consensus on certain specifics, nothing was set in stone until a comprehensive package was completed. "And we want to keep it in the room," he continued, meaning no leaks to the media. "The objective today is to have no doubt where everyone starts out." We will have a set of marathon meetings over the next weeks, but now I want opening bids.

President Obama's and his: "We want $4 trillion in deficit reduction over 12 years. Everyone else is very close to that. Our proposal is three-to-one, cuts to revenue." That meant roughly $3 trillion in cuts with $1 trillion in new tax revenue.

Tamping down expectations, he said, "We won't settle the Bush tax cuts here." The across-the-board tax cuts were currently due to expire at the end of 2012.

"We want a debt cap with enforcement that's tied to spending and taxes." The debt cap would set a limit on government borrowing. Exceeding it would trigger an enforcement mechanism that would automatically cut spending and raise taxes in amounts equally painful to both Republicans and Democrats.

"There's mutual agreement that we need discretionary caps," he said. He was referring to a ceiling on spending by domestic departments and agencies, such as Education, Defense, Transportation and the Environmental Protection Agency, which then accounted for about 39 percent of the federal budget. "We'll support that."

Biden then took another popular idea off the table: generating savings through tax code reform.

"We agree the tax code is broken," he said. "And we want to produce fundamental reform next year, but it's really an issue for Ways and Means and Finance," he said, meaning the committees in the House and Senate that handle taxes.

Geithner took the floor to describe what lay in store if they failed to act.

"Our number-one objective is to avoid a catastrophic loss of confidence. The debt is a more serious problem today than it was in the '60s or the '90s. If we don't do something now, we're jeopardizing the future."

If international creditors began to doubt the safety of U.S. debt obligations, the country was in danger of losing its ability to continue borrowing. If that happened, the Treasury would be unable to fund the national debt.

They were facing "a test of our credibility," he said, and issued a challenge: "Weaker countries are doing tougher things, and we need to do tough things."

Geithner repeated his conclusion that annual deficits needed to be reduced to 3 percent of the Gross Domestic Product, a level that a wide range of economists had concluded was sustainable. It would demonstrate that the United States was at least moderately disciplined.

It was a wildly ambitious goal. The current annual deficit was running close to $1.3 trillion, or 10 percent of GDP.

Geithner laid out the administration's ultimate goal. "We want to get to primary surplus in 2015"—meaning a surplus excluding interest payments on existing debt. "And the good news is, everyone does."

The Simpson-Bowles commission and the House Republicans had similar goals.

The treasury secretary reiterated Biden's call for a strict enforcement mechanism. "We have to have a real trigger" backed by the force of law, which would force deficit reduction if we don't reach agreement, he said.

It was not possible to postpone action until the next election cycle. "Reforms have to be broad-based to be credible." The chief audience was the bond market, the global web of bond traders whose collective decisions about the stability of the country's fiscal situation dictated the interest rates the Treasury paid on new debt.

"We can't do it without more revenue," Geithner continued. "If you try, the world will laugh at us."

The Republicans present resented his challenge.

Geithner had earlier publicly mocked the Republican refusal to extend the debt ceiling, calling it "political theater," and effectively deriding them as showboaters and bluffers.

"We have to do something to reduce long-term health care costs," Geithner continued. "There's a way to start without resolving all this, but we can't rely solely on targets and triggers" to force cuts.

Jack Lew, the budget director, took over. He wanted to make sure everyone understood that this crisis was of a different magnitude than debt crises in the past. "Now I'm always meeting with the bond markets," he said. "That wasn't true in the '90s. They want to know, 'Are we serious?' "

They had to act decisively. There would be no partial credit from the bond market for "a Band-Aid" solution. It had to be comprehensive. Lew walked through the proposal the president had made at George Washington University three weeks earlier. This was the plan Biden had opened with: $4 trillion in deficit reduction over 12 years, rather than the usual 10 years. It included spending cuts, Medicare and Medicaid reforms, changes to the tax code, and limits on itemized deductions for the wealthiest taxpayers.

On the national security side, including Defense, the State Department, Homeland Security and Veterans Affairs, Lew said, "We are beginning a strategic review—a fast strategic review is being initiated. But it's possible to talk about the numbers without Defense being on the table."

"Veterans Affairs," Biden interrupted in some wonderment. The military was sacred, and it could be political suicide for Democrats to consider cuts for vets. "This is a dangerous area," he acknowledged, "but we should look at it."

"Medicare," Lew continued. "We should cover the Doc Fix." They should continue to stave off the dramatic cuts in Medicare reimbursements to doctors as Congress had been regularly doing.

"Again, we're going to treat Medicare and Medicaid separately," Lew said. The administration thought it would be possible to save $5 billion on reimbursement rates for doctor-prescribed durable medical equipment—in-home medical items such as wheelchairs, hospital beds or diabetes-testing equipment.

There were lots of potential savings in other mandatory entitlements, though Lew pointed out that the House had voted for significantly more in the Ryan budget—$700 to $900 billion in such cuts. The distance between the $5 billion for medical equipment and the $700 to $900 billion from the House was a long one—a Grand Canyon–sized gap.

But this meeting was about reaching agreement between the Democrats and Republicans in the room. "There's a lot of overlap between where you are and where we are, but this isn't going to be easy," Lew said. He cited agriculture subsidies and various education programs that both sides agreed could be cut.

Lew said he was concerned about low-income taxpayers and the impact cuts would have on the poor. Then he turned to tax reform, despite the fact that Biden had pretty much taken it off the table only a few minutes before. "We should have a tax expenditures discussion," he said, referring to deductions, such as mortgage interest, charitable contributions and health insurance costs. He suggested the next step should be laying out the White House and Republican plans side by side.

Biden then called on Sperling to talk about a proposed debt cap. This would set a specific dollar amount for the national debt which, if exceeded, would trigger automatic spending cuts and revenue increases. It was the alternative to default. Including both spending cuts and tax increases, he said, was intended to make the consequences of exceeding the cap unacceptable to both sides.

"The goal is for it not to take place," Sperling said. "The goal is for it to be equally offensive [to Democrats and Republicans] so that we are forced to act. Getting the debt under control is the ultimate target. It's not just me who says this." Jim Nussle, a former OMB director, and Doug Holtz-Eakin, a former CBO director, both Republicans, agree, he said.

Geithner offered a positive spin on the situation, saying the "projected deficit paths" that the administration and House Republicans were on "are not that far apart, though revenue is the big issue."

Eric Cantor was next.

"Our budget assumes a debt limit increase as well. So we're both kind of dealing with that. But we have a lot of savings. The Affordable Care Act—" He kind of stuttered as he made a deliberate point of not calling the 2010 health care reform legislation by its often disparaging name, "Obamacare."

"You're not going to go there," Cantor said. "So we're not going down the revenue path."

It was a categorical statement. If Democrats wanted tax increases, the only acceptable trade-off would be changes to Obamacare. He was taking both off the table.

"We disagree on how to get revenue," Cantor said. The Republicans wanted revenue by growing the economy, the Democrats by raising taxes.

"We deal with the safety net issues very differently. We block-grant Medicaid." Lump sums would be given to the states for medical care for the poor. This left the states responsible for covering additional costs, but also allowed them to set eligibility requirements. Medicaid would cease to be an open-ended entitlement that guaranteed care to all who qualify, regardless of cost. The Republicans, he said, also had a "vastly different" approach to Medicare in Ryan's premium support proposal.

"Ultimately," Cantor said, "this is going to be for the next election to decide, but we shouldn't take everything off the table. There may be areas in Medicare and Medicaid where we can come to agreement."

"Areas of commonality" definitely existed in the approach to cuts in military retirement programs and agricultural subsidies, he offered.

Responding to Sperling's debt cap suggestion, Cantor stated bluntly, "Our problem is we view your proposal as a tax trap." If the Republicans went along, the Democrats would have a strong incentive to hold out because, at the end of the stalemate, there would be not only spending cuts, but an automatic tax increase.

"That said, there's plenty of commonality on the spending side. The Government Accountability Office says the deficit won't go away unless we deal with the entitlement programs. Let's start where we can agree. We need real enforcement."

Cantor said he concurred with Geithner that the need for action was urgent. "I agree we need to get policies done and enacted by year end. We can't rely on out-year triggers."

"There's no deal without a debt cap," Geithner retorted. "No deal without specific savings. If we don't solve the revenue, Medicare, Medicaid problems, then we have to agree to debt targets . . . automatic enforcement."

Senator Kyl wanted them to explore other ways to curtail spending, such as legislation introduced by Senators Claire McCaskill, a Democrat, and Bob Corker, a Republican, that would mandate across-the-board cuts to federal spending, or a balanced budget amendment to the Constitution. "I'm deadly serious on Constitutional spending limits," he said.

"Without revenues, it will not pass," Biden said. "There's no constituency for that to pass in the Senate." Even if it did, Obama held the hammer: "And it will face a veto pen."

"Let's plan on the next three or four meetings. What can we do that might pass the smell test? Each of us needs to bite the bullet. Keep moving through each meeting and see what we can do."

Geithner aimed at the heart of the Republican argument that growing the economy would increase revenue. "One of the things we should do is take off the table growth assumptions that help us wish away the problems." Growing the economy would increase tax revenue, but nobody knew by how much. He was saying what they all knew. The Congressional Budget Office refused to use assumptions about future growth. Even Congress's Joint Committee on Taxation, while slightly more willing to consider the future impact of tax proposals, wouldn't base future revenue estimates on growth assumptions.

Senator Daniel Inouye, the Democrat from Hawaii who chaired the powerful Appropriations Committee, had a single remark. The 86-year-old World War II veteran, who had lost his right arm in combat, warned about cuts to the Department of Defense. "We're not assuming another 9/11," he said. "We can't assume that it won't occur again."

"You're right, Mr. Chairman," Geithner said.

Inouye, who was in his ninth six-year Senate term, lamented the George W. Bush years. "We responded to two wars with tax cuts and more spending. We can't do that."

Baucus interjected, "There's waste in DOD."

"Yes," Biden agreed. "Military health care is a huge contributor."

"We should do something there," Lew agreed. But if military cuts were going to be recommended, he said, "We've got to do it together" in a bipartisan effort.

Representative James Clyburn, the third-ranking Democrat in the House, said, "I agree we need to take a look at Defense." Clyburn, whose district in South Carolina is heavily dependent on military spending, added that cuts to the military would be "very tough for me."

Biden instructed the staffs to come up with an agenda for the next meeting. "We'll try to pull together one summary of what we all did."

After a few pleasantries, the meeting ended.

Cantor was surprised. When he had been put on the Biden group, Boehner had warned him it wouldn't be a serious effort and that he wanted him to just sit through each day, grin and bear it. Though the first meeting had revealed big differences, he thought the vice president was attempting to mediate. He told his top staff, "Maybe it's not just going to be a charade."

# *13*

---

Biden convened the next meeting on Tuesday, May 10. The goal that day was to identify $150 billion in proposed cuts over 10 years, and by the end of the meeting they had agreed on $123 billion in cuts, including $9 billion from federal employee retirement programs.

"We could improve upon this," said Jack Lew, "if we looked at national defense."

He got no immediate takers. With its annual budget near $700 billion, counting extra appropriations for the war in Afghanistan, that was where the money and savings could be found. But it would have to wait for another meeting.

"We've got to go to the big numbers if we're going to get this done," Cantor said.

Reactions were mixed. It was a start, there had been some progress, but they were not there. Yet Neil Bradley, Cantor's policy director, remarked, "Where else do you walk into a room and find $123 billion in savings?" And it had only taken a few hours.


At the third meeting, May 12, Biden gathered the group at Blair House.

Early on they came to the Supplemental Nutrition Assistance Program (SNAP), commonly known as food stamps. It covered some

44 million Americans and it was one of Cantor's favorite targets. Significant savings were available because of the number of "scams," he said.

One such scam was connected to the Low Income Home Energy Assistance Program (LIHEAP), which provided money for home heating. In many states, qualifying for LIHEAP granted automatic eligibility for food stamps. In some cases, the heat-and-eat policy meant that a $1 heating assistance check established categorical eligibility for food stamps. Investigators had found that some LIHEAP checks were going to people whose heating bills were included in their rent.

We believe states have too little incentive to prevent otherwise ineligible individuals from receiving food stamps, Cantor said. He had examples from New York and Vermont and, he whispered to Van Hollen, he also had some from Maryland.

In addition to tightening eligibility requirements, Cantor wanted to eliminate SNAP's nutrition education funding, increase work requirements, and eliminate duplicative job training programs. This could add up to huge savings.

As the group gathered in Room S219 on the Senate side of the Capitol on May 24, day four of their meetings, Jack Lew was seeking someone to do some political wet work. Before everyone was seated, he pulled Van Hollen aside.

Will you take on Baucus on farm subsidies? he asked. The White House wanted to cut them, and Baucus, a 32-year Senate veteran, was deeply committed to the special interests of farmers and ranchers in his home state of Montana. A sign in his office read "Montana Comes First." He had said he was going to revisit the issue, and the White House did not want to challenge the powerful Senate Finance chairman openly. Would Van Hollen take on the task?

The House Democrats had $20 billion in proposed agriculture cuts, and Van Hollen thought they should be higher. The House Republicans had $30 billion in their budget.

Van Hollen agreed to do the deed.

"We're not leaking!" Biden began in some wonderment as everyone sat down. Three days of meetings and no leaks to the media! They must be serious! It was a sign of their commitment. He was proud of them, almost gleeful.

But then he dampened the mood by turning to Medicare. After Social Security and Defense it was the government's most expensive program. It would cost $520 billion that year, and the price tag was expected to double to more than $1 trillion a year in the coming decade. An April 11, 2011, *Washington Post*/ABC News poll showed that 78 percent of the public "oppose cutting spending on Medicare as a way to chip away at the debt."

They talked about "reform"—avoiding the word "cut"—but no one had much to suggest.

Talking about Medicare cuts was dangerous territory for Democrats, and Biden moved them on to a topic at least as sensitive for Republicans.

"We're going to insist revenue's on the table," he said. "We know you don't agree to that," he added, looking at Cantor. "But the key from our perspective is that we be very unambiguous about the need to have a discussion about it." It had to have an airing. "From our perspective, it has to be part of a final agreement."

Cantor and Kyl jumped in hard.

You have to understand, said Cantor, we need to get to 218 votes in the House. "My guys don't even believe default is a problem," he said, referring to the Tea Partiers in the Republican conference.

The Democrats knew that Cantor wasn't kidding. The Republican presidential primary debates were in full swing and Tea Party–backed candidates such as Representatives Michele Bachmann of Minnesota and Ron Paul of Texas were calling loudly for Congress to refuse to raise the debt limit.

Biden stood firm: Revenues had to be part of the deal. You don't get to have a one-sided deal just because your side is more unreasonable than ours, he said. We can't take credit for our Luddites—neither can you.

Kyl, who often called tax revenues "the subject which shall have no name," said he and Cantor had already agreed to some aviation and pension fees.

"That won't do," Biden said. These collections were not counted as tax revenue by the Congressional Budget Office and other experts.

Kyl disagreed. Fees are revenue. It was money going into the federal coffers.

Biden asked Lew to go over some previously agreed-upon savings. Lew raised farm subsidy savings. They were between the Democrats' $20 billion and the Republicans' $30 billion.

They were taking too much from subsidies, Baucus exclaimed.

That was Van Hollen's cue. "Commodity prices are through the roof," he said. Farmers and ranchers were cashing big subsidy checks at the same time their crops and livestock were selling for more than ever.

I might be willing to agree to the proposed agriculture subsidy cuts, Baucus said, but only if other things took a big hit too. And, he noted, the high commodity prices on corn and other produce were sure to drop someday, so the overall issue should be put off.

It was finally agreed that Baucus would come up with a detailed plan for agricultural cuts. There was skepticism among the negotiators that he would provide a serious proposal, but they agreed to wait.

Lew raised the issue of drug reimbursements for those eligible for both Medicare and Medicaid, the elderly poor. Under Medicaid, pharmaceutical companies were required to sell drugs to the government at a price equal to the best price offered on the private market or about 15 percent below the average private market price, whichever was lower. If Medicaid paid more than that over a given period of time, pharmaceutical companies were required to pay a rebate to the government.

Lew asked if it were possible to get more rebates from the drug companies.

Many Republicans, including Cantor, saw the attempt to reduce payments to pharmaceutical firms as dangerous. We need higher prices, he said, surprising many. Higher prices incentivize innovation by the drug companies. If we make the drug companies pay more, we will kill innovation, new drug development, it could even kill the industry.

Wait, said Van Hollen. The Medicare prescription drug benefit program for seniors, so-called Part D, which had passed under the Bush administration with some Democratic support, had been a boon to the drug companies. More seniors could now afford drugs, a good thing, and the drug industry sold a staggering number of additional drugs. They should pay rebates.

"You're getting into a big issue," Baucus said. The pharmaceuticals industry had already sacrificed a lot under the Obamacare legislation, agreeing to take $100 billion less over 10 years from Medicare.

Senator Daniel Inouye showed his impatience. "Outside groups think we're not serious," he said. His tone indicated that he didn't necessarily disagree. "We need to make cuts and vote on them next time."

Yes, Biden agreed, they had to prove they were serious. But he deflected the idea of voting in the near term.

After the meeting, Biden pulled Van Hollen aside. They agreed that discussing Medicare reform had put them in the extreme danger zone.

"We started these talks in water up to our ankles," Van Hollen said, "and it is rising fast and is about up to our chests, but still not over our heads."

He wanted to make sure they didn't drown. Later, he spoke with Pelosi, urging her to tell Biden that the Democrats had to meet with the president. They needed to be sure they knew where they were going.

On May 26, Biden called the group together for its fifth meeting, a perfunctory session where little was accomplished.

By this point, the vice president was hoping to hit $2 trillion in deficit reduction and then fight out the big Medicare and taxation issues in the 2012 election.

With $1 trillion in agreed-upon cuts to general spending over 10 years, $250 billion from mandatory programs such as food stamps, farm subsidies and federal retirement, and another $250 billion in Medicare and Medicaid cuts, they could get to $1.5 trillion. Add in 20 percent interest savings over ten years—from not having to borrow that $1.5 trillion—and the deal would be up to $1.8 trillion.

If Biden could get the Republicans to kick in $200 billion in revenue, they'd be up to $2 trillion. It seemed possible.

Biden convened the sixth meeting in Senator Reid's ceremonial office, S219, on Thursday, June 9. Once again, he insisted that revenue was going to be necessary, and asked Baucus, as longtime head of the Finance Committee, if he wanted to make the case.

The short answer was no. Baucus wasn't used to having ideological arguments during a negotiation, and on taxation issues he often voted more like a Republican than a Democrat.

As Senate Finance Committee chairman in 2001, he was one of the 12 Democrats who voted for the Bush tax cuts (which passed the Senate 62–38). He was the only one of the six senators on the Simpson-Bowles commission to vote against that $4 trillion deficit reduction plan.

So Biden turned the floor over to Geithner, who spent little time on income tax rate increases, focusing instead on Obama's plan to limit deductions for people filing in the top brackets. It could raise $290 billion.

That should be considered part of overall tax reform, the Republicans responded.

Kyl teased Van Hollen, who had apparently missed a meal, for devouring an entire bowl of popcorn that was sitting on the table.

Baucus pushed for closing a fossil fuel tax loophole.

What about the loophole on mining activity, Max? Kyl inquired mischievously. He knew Baucus didn't want to close that. Mining was big in Montana.

They kept coming back to the question of revenue, and the Republicans' refusal to address it.

"This is our come-to-Jesus moment," Biden said.

"Yeah," said Cantor, who is Jewish, "but I'm not very good on that point."

Cantor's joke masked a serious point: Biden shouldn't expect any sudden conversions from the Republicans on taxes.


Biden was encouraged by the fact that he and Cantor seemed to be settling into a comfortable working relationship, based in part on mutual recognition that neither was running the show.

You know, if I were doing this, I'd do it totally different, Biden told Cantor during one of the private asides they frequently had after the meetings.

Well, if I were running the Republican conference, I'd do it totally different, Cantor replied.

They agreed that if they were in charge, they could come to a deal.

# 14

---

Biden called the Democrats in his group to his Senate office on June 14 before the seventh day of talks. They were not happy.

The White House was changing the numbers, Van Hollen complained. The president's proposal in April had contained cuts of $900 billion to general federal spending, including Defense, over 10 years. It was the largest number they had discussed. Now the administration was suddenly talking about $1.1 trillion— $200 billion more in cuts. What was going on? Were they measuring something different?

No, it was an additional cut, Lew said.

That's a very big number, Van Hollen said, and it would be difficult.

"I'm confident we can get to a minimum of roughly $1 trillion," Biden said.

Van Hollen was disheartened. It sounded to him as though the vice president was beginning to adopt the Cantor-Kyl position. The administration seemed to be retreating.

The sudden addition of $200 billion in cuts was a clear illustration of how squishy all the numbers were. How could this big number appear out of the blue at the same time as they were having niggling debates over a $10 billion or $20 billion cut?

. . .

At the full meeting later that day, Kyl joked that he wanted to make sure there was a full bowl of popcorn for Van Hollen.

The House budget, Cantor pointed out, had $1.7 trillion in cuts to general federal spending. That was $600 billion more than the $1.1 trillion the White House was now proposing. Whatever number they agreed to, they should have one number and no firewalls—partitions between Defense and all other spending that assured a certain percentage of cuts came from Defense. "Let the Senate and White House battle it out," he said. Since the Democrats controlled both, he was telling the Democrats to negotiate with themselves.

Van Hollen said firewalls had a precedent. Budget agreements in 1991, 1993 and 1997 all had them. He said the 193 Democrats would not go for deep general cuts without firewalls.

But the administration might be able to go without firewalls, Biden interjected, eager to get an agreement.

Not helpful at all, thought Van Hollen.

Biden later backtracked some, suggesting a 50–50 Defense/non-Defense firewall for just two of the 10 years.

Inouye repeated what he had told the Democrats in their pre-meeting: Defense could be cut. Domestic programs needed protection.

A growing feeling of incredulity came over Van Hollen. The administration didn't seem to have a strategy. It was unbelievable. There didn't seem to be any core principles.

First Kyl, then Cantor, said they needed deeper cuts or they would not be able to sell it to Republicans in either the House or Senate.

Some revenue, Baucus said, almost pleading.

"We really have members who don't get the need to raise the debt ceiling," Cantor repeated. "It's an existential question for them."

"So you're looking for Democrats to be more responsible than you?" said Biden. "You can't use the irresponsibility of your own members to get your way."

"I'm frustrated, because I think you don't get our perspective," Cantor said.

"Republicans want Democrats to sell their sisters!" the vice president said. They wanted Democrats to give up "everything we hold dear" without making any sacrifices themselves.

Cantor threw his hands in the air.

"Why don't you just say it's the crazy Republicans made you do it?" he asked.

After the meeting, Biden called a Democratic huddle. They agreed to say something positive to the media—that these are tough issues but everyone is still at the table. The whole enterprise was very tricky politically, Biden conceded, and he was not sure how to navigate.

There was little show of confidence in the administration at Pelosi's message meeting that day. Most were skeptical that the president would stand firm in the end, afraid instead he would cave to the Republicans as he had in extending the Bush tax cuts six months earlier.

The eighth meeting was in Reid's Senate conference room on June 15. Biden opened with the enforcement mechanism that would kick in if the budget cuts they identified weren't imposed. The trigger should include revenue, so everyone had skin in the game. The Republicans disagreed. They certainly would not go along with a trigger that would mean automatic tax increases.

A trigger requiring revenue would be more credible to the financial markets, Geithner said. He pointed out that the new Conservative government of the United Kingdom had included revenue in its deficit reduction plan.

Saying he was speaking only for himself, Biden said if they included sufficient revenue in a down payment, a chunk of money up front, maybe they would not need revenue in the trigger.

Van Hollen argued that they would have to have revenue in the trigger.

Kyl pressed for only spending cuts.

The retirement of the baby boomers would drive up all federal spending, Biden said, even if costs were frozen.

Kyl kept hammering. They had to try to get more Medicare savings, especially through increased co-payments from seniors or through a process called means testing, which would raise the costs of care for high-income seniors.

Some Democrats are opposed to means testing, Biden said. It could erode the near-universal support for the program.

Kyl again urged more Medicare savings.

Medicare, Biden said, was going to be one of the big issues in next year's elections. Whoa! he blurted out, letting off some steam. They all recognized that they were not going to resolve all this right here around the table. Somewhat wistfully, he went through the possibilities for the next year. Who might win the White House? The Senate? The House?

Each of them could dream of breaking the electoral bank and taking all the chips home—the big prize of one-party government. With all the chips, there would be no need for meetings and negotiations like this.


In a private discussion after the meeting, Biden and Van Hollen agreed that the talks were getting difficult. Van Hollen noted grimly that polarization had increased among the Democrats.

Ugh, Biden said, Pelosi had hit him hard on the issues the night before.

Later, Baucus met with Van Hollen and Clyburn.

We have to limit agriculture subsidy cuts to $20 billion, Baucus said.

Clyburn said he would agree to that, but Van Hollen held out for getting to $30 billion.

If it was not kept down to $20 billion, Baucus threatened, he would walk away from the negotiations.

• • •

On June 16, day nine, at about 11:20 a.m., Biden had the group's Democrats meet in his ceremonial Senate office. He laid out his slightly modified blueprint—$1 trillion in 10-year general federal spending cuts; $200 billion from other programs, including food stamps and unemployment insurance; and $300 billion from health programs. Add in the reduction in interest payments—about 20 percent of the total measured over 10 years—and it came to $1.8 trillion.

Van Hollen repeated the need for revenue. He said he could not support a deal without significant revenue, maybe as much as $600 billion. He knew a figure that high would be a stretch without any income tax rate changes.

Too much, not realistic, some countered. Van Hollen was worried that the administration was wobbling on revenue and too eager to cut a deal.


The full group was supposed to meet that morning, but a marathon series of votes had been scheduled in the House, which meant half the negotiators were unavailable.

With their bosses all busy voting, Biden called the group's key Democratic staff into his ceremonial office.

"Speak for your bosses," Biden said. "What revenue can you live with?"

The administration's idea for limiting tax deductions in the upper brackets might work, one staffer offered, but Republicans would never go along. As Biden went around the room, the staffers made it clear that their bosses would not support lots of revenue ideas.

Biden became increasingly annoyed.

"You keep asking us to ask for more revenue, but you have trouble finding even $400 billion worth of revenue that you would be willing to vote for," he said. "We can't ask for more than our side is willing to support."

•        •        •

At 4:15, the full group convened in Reid's conference room.

Baucus had been waiting to launch his counterattack on the proposed cuts to agriculture subsidies.

I will "walk away from any deal" with $30 billion in cuts, he announced. It was a 20 percent cut—huge compared to what federal employees were being asked to contribute, for example. This was the clearest threat anyone had issued so far.

Baucus pulled out a three-page alternative, proposing cuts in other programs that were technically part of the Agriculture budget but had nothing to do with agriculture subsidies paid to farmers and ranchers. His proposed 10-year savings included $3 billion from the ethanol tax credit, $4 billion from eliminating duplicative job training in the food stamp program, and nearly $7 billion from reducing the Strategic Petroleum Reserve from 727 million barrels of oil to 650 million.

Participants in the meeting said it was difficult to tell whether the Democrats or Republicans had a harder time containing their laughter.

Dodging the conflict, Biden said the chairmen and ranking members of the Agriculture committees should work this out, but his frustration boiled over. This was "Mission: Impossible," he said, and adjourned the meeting.


Biden called Van Hollen the next day, Friday, June 17.

Hope you and the president seal the deal on the links tomorrow, Van Hollen said. Obama, Biden, Boehner and Ohio Governor John Kasich were scheduled to play golf.

I'll call you from the golf course if we get a deal, Biden promised.

Use the House and Senate Democrats as the bad guys with Boehner, Van Hollen suggested. Tell him that the Democrats would not agree in principle to any Medicare cuts or changes without an agreement in principle on revenue. I'm afraid that if we leave revenue to the end, the

Republicans will say we had a deal on everything, but the Democrats wanted to raise your taxes. The Democrats had to position themselves so they could say the Republicans had demanded Medicare cuts but refused to get rid of special interest tax breaks.

"I won't screw you," Biden said. "We're all together on this."

# 15

On Saturday morning, June 18, Boehner and Obama teamed up to beat Biden and Ohio Governor Kasich in a round of golf at Andrews Air Force Base outside Washington. "The president and I whupped 'em pretty good," Boehner said. "But it was just golf." The president and speaker, who shot a very respectable 80, collected two dollars each in winnings, and the foursome was photographed enjoying cold drinks on an outdoor patio afterward.

Later, the president recalled the conversation, noting that he and Boehner had already agreed that they were both interested in pursuing a "big deal"—something with deficit reduction of as much as $4 trillion over 10 years.

"You know what, Mr. President? I meant what I said. I still believe we can do a big deal," Boehner said.

"John, I completely agree," said Obama.

Boehner said he didn't think trying to negotiate a deal with the entire congressional leadership would be productive. "Maybe our teams should start talking," he said.

"John, I'm all there with you," Obama replied.

•   •   •

Back at the White House, Obama took Nabors, the head of White House congressional relations, aside.

"Rob, I just wanted to let you know, this is what Boehner said to me." The speaker thought they should get together, just the two of them, to see if there was something they could get done here. "So he's going to come up to the White House."

Obama seemed energized. Boehner was a type he knew well, he said. "He reminds me of people I worked with in Springfield, Illinois," he told his inner circle, referring to his eight years in the state legislature. "John Boehner is like a Republican state senator. He's a golf-playing, cigarette-smoking, country-club Republican, who's there to make deals. He is very familiar to me."

Nabors and others in Obama's inner circle knew that the president believed that a large number of Boehner's rank and file—the extreme Tea Partiers—were dangerously irresponsible.

"John's just not going to be able to force these people," Obama said. "You know, I have some sympathy for him."

Several aides disagreed. Boehner might appear softer, but he was the political opposition. The speaker represented the problem, and they had to be careful.

"I have some sympathy for him," the president repeated. "You see how crazy these people are. I understand him." Boehner was not one of the crazies. "His motivation is pure." He wanted to do the right thing. "He just can't control the forces in his caucus now."

Plouffe thought Obama had developed a soft spot for Boehner.

"We'll see what comes of this," the president concluded.


Nabors had spent a lot of time analyzing the House Republican conference, and had concluded that Boehner was struggling to find balance among four distinct constituencies: the "Paul Ryan folks" who wanted structural entitlement reforms; the Tea Party, who wanted to shrink government and slash spending at almost any cost, but didn't really understand numbers and policy; the members who would face tough reelection races in 2012, and didn't want their fingerprints on legislation attacking popular entitlements; and the old guard, in safe seats.

In Nabors's view, Boehner would never be able to balance the concerns of the Tea Party with the concerns of Republicans in swing districts. No matter what he proposed, Nabors told Obama and the White House senior staff, the speaker "was going to have people who were complaining that the cuts weren't deep enough, or that they were misplaced, or that revenue was part of the equation." On any proposal, Boehner would always lose a significant portion of his now 240-member conference. It was hard to come up with precise numbers, but clearly there were blocks of dozens or more that could sink any proposal.

On Tuesday, June 21, day 10, Biden told the Democrats that he had met with the president and they had agreed that they needed to have increased tax revenue. There could be no deal without it. But I want to present it in a way, he said, that doesn't prompt a Republican walkout. It was sometimes "Kyl's style," he said, to just get up and leave, donning the cloak of shock and dismay. That kind of stunt could overshadow the important speech on the war in Afghanistan that the president would make the next day. "Make sure if there's a walkout, it's not before Thursday."

Later, the meeting with the entire group was tense. There would be no cuts to Medicare, Biden began, unless there was an agreement on revenue. Period. He noted that McConnell had said on *Face the Nation* over the weekend that if the group did not tackle entitlement reform, "then we'll probably end up with a very short-term" debt ceiling for only a few months. "And we'll be back having the same discussion again in the fall."

Biden wanted a debt ceiling extension that would take them through the 2012 election.

I agree with the vice president, Cantor said. McConnell might welcome another set of negotiations, but Cantor wouldn't. Everyone knew the House Republicans were going to hate voting to increase the debt limit, and some never would. The difficulty of rounding up his conference's votes made Cantor eager to ensure he would only have to do it once.

The vice president had mischaracterized McConnell's statement, Kyl said. It was not a wish, but a reflection of the state of their talks. I told McConnell that based on the pace and progress here, I didn't think we could get a comprehensive deal that would justify lifting the debt ceiling through the end of 2012, Kyl said.

I did not intentionally mischaracterize Mitch McConnell's position, Biden replied.

But Kyl's assessment was both depressing and realistic. So they went back to a new version of the old issue—Medicare cuts, with Democrats repeating that they would go along only if there was real revenue.

Kyl, wagging his head, groused about the linkage of Medicare cuts and revenue. As Van Hollen had warned, Kyl was saying that both sides had agreed on a bunch of cuts which were now being held hostage to revenue.

As they probed into rural health care cuts, Baucus, thinking of Montana, said, "We need proportionality between urban and rural cuts."

"Totally parochial," Van Hollen scribbled in his notes.


"REVENUE" was the dreaded word at the top of the two typed pages in Eric Cantor's hand when he connected by phone with the vice president the morning of Wednesday, June 22.

It was day 11 and the group was scheduled to meet later.

"What do you need?" Cantor asked. "I know you're going to need revenue. We're going to need revenue neutrality." Taxes raised in one area would have to be offset by tax reductions in another. "There are some things we all want to do that people want to get done." Both sides wanted the extension of payroll tax relief for the next year, a tax cut that could cost between $100 and $200 billion, depending on how much the rate was reduced.

Cantor had more than once told Biden privately that he understood revenues would have to be part of a final agreement. Now he was offering a deal, but only of sorts, because there would be no revenue increase to the U.S. Treasury. He mentioned a $20 billion "guesstimate" increase in revenue from limiting the home mortgage interest deduction for some of the wealthy; eliminating the mortgage interest deduction for second homes—another guesstimate revenue increase of $20 billion; and tightening the tax treatment of retirement accounts.

Cantor's proposed offsets for these increases were the $110 billion from payroll tax relief, and another $50 billion guesstimate from reducing employers' contribution to the Social Security payroll tax by one percentage point.

He also proposed some $50 billion in corporate tax raisers, including the $3 billion for deductions related to corporate jets, and $20 billion in oil and gas subsidies for large companies. That money would have to be offset by an equivalent amount of corporate tax reductions.

Cantor felt he was being creative, offering proposals that would be controversial with his House Republicans.

Biden was listening. It wasn't much, but getting the Republicans to say they would agree to revenue was progress. On the question of payroll tax cuts, the Democrats would be happy to accept revenue neutrality. It would pump money into the struggling economy in the short term, and could be recouped slowly over 10 years.

The vice president said the most the Republicans would get out of the administration would be increasing the age at which people became eligible for certain entitlement programs, limiting access to entitlement programs for higher-income beneficiaries, and a change in the way the Consumer Price Index was calculated. And to get those, he added, Republicans would have to give on the Bush tax cuts for the wealthy.

# 16

At 12:30 p.m., Pelosi met with Van Hollen, Hoyer and Clyburn to discuss a meeting they had scheduled with Obama for the following day.

We should focus on insisting that the president ask for $600 billion to $700 billion in revenue, Van Hollen said. He knew that would be a stretch. His goal was now between $400 billion and $500 billion but he needed to start the bidding higher because he was worried that the White House would go for much less, something in the $150 to $200 billion range, the convoluted "revenue neutral" number that Cantor had been floating. The question was: how to stiffen the administration's spine?

Pelosi's biggest concern was Medicare cuts—especially co-payments from beneficiaries. Half of Medicare recipients were receiving $22,000 or less in yearly Social Security benefits. How could they afford to pay more?

I agree, said Van Hollen, but if the Republicans give in any significant way on revenue, we will have to include some savings from Medicare, by both lowering payments to providers and requiring higher beneficiary co-payments, at least in limited areas.

Pelosi said House Democrats would not know the details of Biden's talks because of the confidentiality agreement, and they would be "swayed by perceptions and atmospherics." If the perception was that Democrats were caving on Medicare, it would be bad. She said she would hang tough if the deal was balanced with real revenue. But she needed to prepare her caucus.

That day's Biden meeting started a little late. After the vice president's usual statement of the need for balance and revenue, Cantor began with a proposal he called Option Two, to be implemented after the 2012 elections. It would increase Medicare premiums for the upper-income bracket by 10 percent, saving $38 billion over 10 years.

I'm not interested in talking about Option Two, Van Hollen said, unless Republicans engage on the revenue question. He turned to Cantor. "We will address these issues with the same degree of seriousness that you discuss revenue."

"Oh, you know," Cantor replied, "that's theology."

"You're talking your theology."

"Well," Cantor said, referring to Medicare, "that's your theology."

"We're not going to keep going down this road, Eric," Van Hollen said. "We will agree to these reforms, but we're not going to keep talking about them until you talk about revenue. Just tell us which of these items you hate the least? Corporate jets?"

Cantor ignored the question but thought, Whoa! What was this new aggressiveness on the part of the Democrats? Where had it come from?

Remaining on the offensive, the Democrats moved next to the drug companies. They wanted more money in rebates for drugs purchased under Medicare.

For God's sake, said Kyl, the current system for purchasing Medicare drugs is a model program that's coming in under budget. More rebates would screw up the program. Don't touch it.

Under budget because of low enrollment, Van Hollen said, and all drug prices had come down.

The Republicans swung back. What about the Medicaid provider tax?

It's a scam, Biden agreed. The states were gaming the system, tax-ing doctors and hospitals so they could get federal reimbursements and then returning the money to the providers. Let's call it like it is, and let's just do this. For a moment, Biden sounded like a Republican. It could save $40 billion. "If we can't do this—" the vice president said, "come on!"

Lew and Sperling said that it would force the states, which would get less money, to provide fewer services to the poor.

Yeah, Van Hollen said, it would encounter resistance from House Democrats.

We're going to do lots of hard things, Biden said, pushing Van Hollen's concerns aside. We might as well do this, he said. The adminis-tration would adopt the Republican view on this.

Cantor didn't need to say a thing. This was a huge deal. Biden had caved on the provider tax, agreeing they could save $40 billion.

After that peace offering, Biden and Sperling brought up the es-sence of the problem: revenue. Sperling suggested limiting itemized deductions to 35 percent for the upper-income taxpayers, potentially raising $130 billion over ten years.

Cantor realized it was innovative, but he said he did not want to discuss it at this point.

The other idea was on the corporate tax side—the possibility of increasing revenue by changing the rules about how corporations' in-ventories were treated for tax purposes.

None of these tax ideas are wild or over the top, Geithner said. They weren't trying to raise revenue for the fun of it, but to reduce the deficit.

The Republicans still refused to engage.

"We may as well call it quits!" Biden finally said, pushing back his chair and starting to get up.

We should keep talking, Cantor and Kyl said.

That is my preference, Biden said, but it is hard to see us getting anywhere with this impasse. All the serious bipartisan plans, such as Simpson-Bowles, had included revenue.

Yeah, Kyl replied, and since Simpson-Bowles had about $1 trillion in revenue and $3 trillion in cuts, they should just agree on the $3 trillion in cuts first. If there were four things being negotiated and they could agree on three, why not go ahead if the agreements on the three were serious? The fourth could be addressed later.

To his increasing annoyance, there were no takers. At one point, he turned to Sperling. "So you're saying to me that even though there are Medicare savings that you think are reasonable—that we could do—you won't do them unless we're going to raise taxes on somebody?"

Sperling looked around the room for a few seconds.

"Well, yeah," he replied. "We can't agree to all your stuff without any of our stuff."

Under the Kyl logic, Cantor said, he thought they were gaining ground.

No, Lew replied. "We are slipping today, clearly going backwards." Whatever the case, he said, they would need firewalls—the agreed-upon division between domestic and Defense cuts—especially if the number on general spending cuts was low.

Kyl, who hated Defense cuts, pushed back on firewalls.

Cantor said he also opposed firewalls and wanted a relatively low number on the general cuts because he felt the serious cuts should come from entitlements like Medicare and Medicaid.

While the House and Senate Democrats might disagree, Lew said, the administration might be willing to live without firewalls if the number on general cuts was on the higher end.

After the meeting, Biden gestured to Cantor to come out to the hallway.

"What is going on?" Cantor asked, perplexed by the way the Democrats had turned up the heat. "You think these talks are kind of hitting their end?"

"Look," Biden replied, "you're right. There's something going on." He had met with McConnell several times over the course of the spring, and was trying to work something through a back channel. The word was also getting out to rank-and-file Democrats that they were cutting health care entitlements, and Van Hollen had asked for a meeting of the concerned House Democrats and the president the next morning. But the group should keep meeting.

"Yeah," the vice president went on, "we've probably got one or two left. Oh, by the way, that's why Boehner and Obama are meeting now."

Cantor was stunned. He had no idea that the speaker and the president were planning to hold separate talks. He needed to get back to his office to think this over. There were two ways out of the hallway where they were speaking. One led directly to a throng of waiting reporters, the other down a back staircase. Cantor and his communications director, Brad Dayspring, took the back way.

Cantor explained what he had learned. He'd been blindsided.

"I get more information out of Joe Biden than I do my speaker," Cantor said.

He had spent five weeks in the Biden talks—on Boehner's direct instructions—and now the speaker was making an end run around him by negotiating secretly with the president.

Boehner had always been dismissive of the Biden group's efforts. "I'm sorry I'm making you go sit in a room for three hours and wasting your time," he told Cantor once. The speaker had repeated his conclusion that the talks were useless on multiple occasions. But Cantor had jumped into the process with a purpose, and he felt that he had forged a valuable connection with Biden and that the group had made real progress.

He had told Boehner all about it. They spoke every day, and Cantor had always kept him up to date. And Boehner hadn't even mentioned that he was planning to meet with the president?

Cantor felt he had been lied to.

That day at 5 p.m., Boehner and Obama met privately at the White House.

"I came in through the South Entrance. Very unusual," Boehner later recalled. "Went through the Diplomatic Receiving Room, waited for a few minutes, they took me upstairs to the residence, and we went outside on the Truman Balcony."

They agreed to keep their discussions—even the fact that they were taking place—confidential.

I want to look at significant structural reforms to all the major entitlement programs, Boehner told the president.

You would have to give on tax increases before we consider entitlement reform, Obama replied.

You can't have tax increases, Boehner said. But he did offer a path to increasing federal revenues: comprehensive tax reform.

"If we lower all the rates, clean out all the garbage in the tax code, you know, there could be some revenue," Boehner said.

The speaker believed they could get additional revenue from economic growth and better tax compliance. It had been done with the 1986 Reagan tax code overhaul—the gold standard of tax reform—which reduced the number of personal income tax brackets, cut the top rate from 50 percent to 28 percent, and eliminated a host of tax deductions.

Obama said he was in favor of reform. They would have to work together on it. If the Republicans insisted on reforms that made the system less progressive, he would walk away and end the Bush tax cuts for the two upper-income brackets.

"We're not going to change progressivity, all right?" Boehner said. "We've got a progressive tax code, people get it. You know, I see that as being neutral, the issue of progressivity."

As for the president's threat to let the Bush tax cuts for the wealthy expire, Boehner said, "We're not going there. We're just not going to go there. You're getting into an area where you're tying my hands. We're never going to get anywhere."

He got the impression that the president was focused on being the one who got rid of the Bush tax cuts for the rich. He was acting as if he had the leverage.

Boehner said he and Congress had the leverage because the president only had about five weeks to get the debt limit extended.

You're fighting on a playing field that cannot be resolved, all right? the speaker said. We can't work in this universe of the current tax code. It's too polarized. You caved in the 2010 lame-duck session by extending all the Bush tax cuts. We've got to start from the premise that the whole code is getting thrown out. Let's try to work out a way to get reform done. We've got to try to stay out of the mind-set of the battle over the Bush tax cuts.

"It was a good start," Boehner later recalled.

Asked about the conversation with Boehner, the president said in an interview that it proceeded as follows:

"I want entitlement reform," Boehner said.

"John, I cannot ask seniors to make a series of sacrifices if people like me are not making any to reduce our deficit. So I am willing to move on entitlement reform—even if my own party is resisting, and I will bring them along—as long as we have significant revenues so that people feel like there's a fairly shared burden when it comes to deficit reduction."

"I can't simply vote to raise taxes," said Boehner. "I can't get the votes. But there should be a way of raising revenue."

The speaker suggested using tax reform as a way to increase revenue without increasing tax rates.

"John, I'm all for tax reform," Obama said. "But I'm not going to have a situation in which we have a vague promise of tax reform later—because tax reform would take a year, year and a half to actually get done, rewriting the tax code—but all the entitlement cuts are locked in on the front end. I just can't move my folks. So there would have to be a mechanism in which we had a guaranteed amount of revenue that was raised, and that revenue would have to be coming from not the middle class, but would have to reflect the progressive principles that exist in current tax policy."

Asked if he felt that he and the speaker were on the road to a deal, the president said, "Let me preface this by saying generally that I like John Boehner. I genuinely think John wanted to get a deal done. And I don't think John actually is, in his bones, an ideological person. I think he's a pretty practical, old-school, country-club Republican.

"And I like him. I mean, by that time I'd quit smoking, but I was making sure he had an ashtray," he said with a laugh. "You know, he'd be having a sip of wine. We could have a good conversation. And I personally think he genuinely wanted to get something done. So I'm feeling fairly optimistic after the meeting on the Truman Balcony."

After the meeting, Obama briefed his staff.

Boehner seemed eager to do something, he said. And we're not getting anything done through the Biden talks or anything else. He and I agreed, at least, on the need to take some sort of action.

Boehner would consider accepting some additional revenue through tax reform, Obama said, mentioning that he had told the speaker that retaining progressivity was a condition of any tax reform deal.

"We need to stabilize the economy. We realize that this is a crucial moment in time," Obama said. "See if you can make this happen."

Afterward, Daley assembled Lew, Nabors, Sperling, Plouffe and Bruce Reed, Biden's chief of staff.

"Should we engage at all?" was the question.

It was all very well for Boehner to talk about ignoring the issue of the Bush tax cuts, but within the White House they viewed their looming expiration at the end of 2012 as the president's sword in the debt limit battle.

The thinking was that if they were allowed to expire, it would be an automatic decoupling. The popular lower- and middle-class cuts could be reinstated. That would be easy. But the high-income cuts would never get through the Senate. The government would collect $800 billion in new revenue, and the president would get credit for ending the Bush tax cuts for the wealthy.

Politically, this was a big deal. Many Democrats hated the Bush tax cuts and wanted them dead. This had been the single biggest fiscal issue separating the Republicans and Democrats since 2001.

Did they really want to get into negotiations about trading entitlement cuts for an unspecified amount of revenue that would come from unspecified tax reforms?

They would get hammered by their political base, many of whom thought Obama already had a clear path to $800 billion by vetoing any legislation that extended the Bush tax cuts.

"Well, we all know it ain't that easy," Sperling argued. "Vetoing means vetoing the whole thing."

Plouffe agreed. It was "pure insanity, politically and economically," to let the cuts expire with no guarantee that the tax cuts for the middle class would be brought back. "I'm not part of the Democratic Party that signed up to raise taxes on working people $3,000 a year," he said.

Plouffe wanted to negotiate with Boehner. His analysis of the politics was that while the individual components of a deficit deal all polled terribly, the whole was greater than the sum of its parts. People believed Washington was dysfunctional. If they saw their leaders coming together on a big deal to address a serious problem, there would be a huge political upside in addition to the economic benefits.

Sperling and Reed, who had been at the Biden meetings, knew this was their best shot at additional revenue. Cantor wasn't going to give much, if any, on the issue, and everyone in the room knew Cantor's position had the backing of a large element of the Republican conference.

Boehner's probably a little over his skis here, Plouffe said. But he's the speaker of the House, and historically, he's been a good vote counter. We have to engage, he advised. We can't be naive about it, but we have to engage.

The others agreed. Maybe they would get something bigger in scale with Boehner.

And in the worst scenario—Republicans demanding that the tax code be made more regressive—the president still had his sword. He could veto an extension of the Bush tax cuts and hope it got them $800 billion in revenue.


A few hours later, the president appeared in the East Room. In front of a nationwide television audience, he announced a drawdown of 33,000 U.S. troops from Afghanistan by the next summer.

"America," he said, "it is time to focus on nation building here at home."

Back at the Capitol, Cantor called his senior staff together. One staffer passed on what he believed was good intelligence about the Democrats. They were pissed that the talks had gone into Medicare, had demanded a meeting with Obama at the White House, and were planning to scuttle the talks and blame the Republicans, especially Cantor.

Gee whiz, Cantor thought, it's going to blow up. The Democrats are going to blow up the Biden discussions and finger me.

Maybe he should act first. He talked with Paul Ryan, Kevin McCarthy and Jeb Hensarling, his brain trust. It was late that evening when they finished, too late to call the speaker, who was often hard to reach after 9 p.m.

After the meeting, Van Hollen ran into Representative John Larson, a Connecticut Democrat, on the House floor. He neatly summarized the Biden meetings to the third-ranking leader in the Democratic minority: "We are all fucked."

Later that night Van Hollen called Senator Chuck Schumer to hear the Senate perspective on potential cuts on Medicare prescription drugs. Baucus was lining up with the Republicans.

"Not just Baucus," Schumer said. "If so, we could end-run him— but also Harry [Reid]." The deal had been that the drug companies would support Obamacare and not come after Senate Democrats—like Reid—who had been up for reelection in 2010. The deal had held and Reid, for one, had won reelection.

Baucus is using his perch as Finance Committee chairman to pursue his parochial interest in agricultural subsidies, Van Hollen complained.

The problem, he continued, is that Biden is discussing the merits of Medicare cuts while the Republicans refuse to engage in a serious discussion of revenue.

Schumer and Van Hollen pretty much agreed that the White House was talking about $2.4 trillion that would apparently include the $1 trillion saved from drawing down troops in Afghanistan and Iraq—the Overseas Contingency Operations fund to some, "funny money," to others.

Van Hollen said he would be surprised if the Republicans went for that. But if there was no revenue in the package, the use of funny money might be the only way to get to $2.4 trillion in deficit reduction.

# 17

Early on the morning of Thursday, June 23, Cantor gave an interview to *The Wall Street Journal*. "We've reached the point where the dynamic needs to change," he said. "It's up to the president to come in and talk to the speaker. We've reached the end of this phase."

He then sent one of his aides to the speaker's office to see Boehner's deputy chief of staff. The Democrats are going to the White House at 10 a.m. They are going to blow up the talks, which are no longer useful. They will blame us. Eric thinks we need to blow it up first and punt this thing to the speaker and the president.

The aide then went to Kyl's chief of staff and repeated the plan.

"Makes sense," she said.

Cantor went to see Boehner, and told the speaker exactly what had happened. "The meeting was vastly different yesterday. The mood was bad," he said. "I know that you're meeting with the president now."

Silence.

Biden had told him, Cantor said. If the president's chief deputy knew, why hadn't he, as the speaker's chief deputy?

Boehner said the president had insisted on absolute confidentiality, which had obviously been breached by the vice president. They had only met once, the day before.

The speaker apologized to Cantor. Boehner said he was sorry it had happened this way. They agreed they needed to salvage something, save face, move forward, and work together.

The Democrats are meeting at the White House right now, Cantor said. There was a rumor they were going to blow the whole thing up. We could use that as a reason to act first.

"We are going to do it on our own terms, so we don't get blamed for this thing," he told Boehner.

Shortly afterward, Cantor placed a call to Biden, but the vice president was in a meeting. Cantor wanted to give Biden the courtesy of telling him personally that the Republicans were pulling out, rather than letting him hear it from the media.

After several tries, he got through.

"We're not going back in," he said.

"Oh, my God," Biden said. "I get it. Let me call you back."

"It's your meeting," Obama said around 10 that morning, in the Oval Office. "I'm here to listen."

Hoyer, Van Hollen, Clyburn and Pelosi sat on chairs and sofas in the office. Biden, Geithner, Lew, Sperling and Daley represented the administration.

"This is an opportunity to do something big," Pelosi began, characterizing it as "a Nixon to China moment" in which they could do the totally unexpected. At minimum, they could extend the payroll tax holiday. If the Republicans agree to do bigger revenue, we'll agree to some significant reforms, she said. "And we need a jobs program," she added, reminding Obama of his call for investments in energy, education and infrastructure.

Hoyer, the fiscally conservative Democratic whip, said he supported the Simpson-Bowles approach and was actually against extending the payroll tax holiday.

Nancy! Steny! the president interrupted sharply, you are "contradicting" each other. "Practical politics" and the effort to boost the economy now required action. "Only a payroll tax holiday will fly," he said.

Van Hollen said that though he was not thrilled with the extension of the payroll tax holiday, "I agree it is the only politically viable option." However, a debt extension of only one year was a bad idea. "It puts us right back in the soup, that's for sure." They would be having this debate again in the middle of next year, right as the presidential election heated up. They needed the big deal with large spending cuts and significant revenue.

"We've got to get past the election," Obama agreed emphatically. Otherwise the Republicans could threaten to shut down the government or stall out the economy every six months. He had to have an extension of 18 months, at least.

He laid out his concerns. First was the soft economy, and the economies of Japan and Greece. Second were the Republicans, who were in "the political bunker with the Tea Party and taxes."

If they could get the big deal, with the Republicans giving in on "big revenue" and income tax rates "that would be accompanied by some Medicare structural reforms," the media could consider it a "game changer."

The congressional Democrats in the room wondered if the president realized the danger of talking about "Medicare structural reforms." That was Paul Ryan's language. But Obama insisted he would support a hard line with the Republicans on "big revenue."

Van Hollen had some specific revenue proposals: the previously discussed "cats and dogs" of corporate tax loophole closers—oil and gas subsidies and corporate jet depreciation. Second was an idea to phase out income tax deductions for those making over $500,000 a year, and giving a tax cut to those earning between $170,000 and $250,000. That was appealing because they would be able to argue that the overall effect was to give more people a tax cut than a tax increase.

The third idea was Sperling's proposal to limit personal income tax deductions for those in the highest brackets. It could raise $130 billion over 10 years.

As the Democrats left the White House they got word that something dramatic had just happened with Eric Cantor.

Cantor was having lunch at a Capitol Hill restaurant when Biden called.

"You've got to come back in," Biden said. "We've got to go back into that meeting just so we can say that we are agreeing to stop right now, but we're all on the same page."

"There is no way," Cantor said. They were not on the same page, not in the same book, or even the same library.

"What do we tell the press?" Biden asked.

Cantor said they should just say the talks were in "abeyance," not necessarily over.

"I get it, I get it," Biden said. Just one more try? "Any chance you could come back in the meeting and take a photo?"

"I can't," Cantor said, "given the statements I've already made to the press. I can't go back in there." There was some utility to the talks, he added. "But again, I gave you the background about we don't think you go and put good money after bad if you're not fixing the problem.

"The entitlement trajectory here is going to bankrupt the country."

Biden hung up the phone. His search party had been a failure. They'd discovered plenty of things they could agree on. But they had come home empty-handed.

The breakdown of the Biden talks was treated by the press as an act of willfulness by the House Republicans in general and by Eric Cantor in particular.

"Deficit Talks in Danger as Cantor Bails," read the headline on Politico.com that morning.

The next day, the *New York Times* editorial board, under a headline accusing the House Republicans of pitching a "temper tantrum," observed that "this bit of grandstanding has brought the nation closer to the financial crisis that Republicans have been threatening for weeks."

Boehner tried to portray Cantor's walkout as a necessary and unremarkable part of the process.

"I understand his frustration. I understand why he did what he did," Boehner said publicly, "but I think those talks could continue if they are willing to take tax hikes off the table."

The following morning, June 24, Boehner effectively replaced Cantor as the Republicans' chief negotiator on the debt ceiling. In a press conference, he laid out three criteria for a deal: It had to commit the government to spending cuts greater than the increase in the debt limit; restrain future spending growth; and contain no tax increase.

"A tax hike," the speaker said, "cannot pass the House of Representatives."

On June 29, 2011, President Obama appeared in the East Room of the White House at 11:40 a.m. for a press conference on the economy and the need to raise the debt limit. He went after Republicans for their unwillingness to raise any revenue through tax increases. "I spent the last two years cutting taxes for ordinary Americans, and I want to extend those middle-class tax cuts," he said.

Ridiculing Republican "sacred cows," he said, "The tax cuts I'm proposing we get rid of are tax cuts for millionaires and billionaires; tax breaks for oil companies and hedge fund managers and corporate jet owners."

In John Boehner's office on Capitol Hill, the president's appearance was met with anger and derision. The repeated references to corporate jets—six in all—were particularly annoying. Eliminating the tax break for corporate jets would have a trivial impact on the overall deficit, saving perhaps $3 billion over 10 years.

A statement released by the speaker's office said, "The President is sorely mistaken if he believes a bill to raise the debt ceiling and raise taxes would pass the House. The votes simply aren't there—and they aren't going to be there because the American people know tax hikes destroy jobs."

Later that day, Obama met with Senate Democrats, who wanted to introduce a short-term debt limit extension. Reid didn't believe that a large deal including spending cuts and revenue was possible, and he thought a series of temporary increases was inevitable. He knew McConnell felt the same way. Reid wanted to get started.

No, Obama said. The talks with Boehner are making progress. We're still going for the big deal.

That evening, Boehner left a message for Cantor, informing his second in command that the talks with the president about a big deal were ongoing. He had sent a proposal for a basic framework to the White House.

At the White House, Nabors, Lew and Sperling began putting a formal offer on paper to submit confidentially to Boehner. The speaker's framework wasn't specific. They knew any deal was going to be about two things—Medicare and revenue.

They went to work on Medicare. It was, in some respects, the prize. Paul Ryan's budget had gone after it. Sperling's sense was that the Republicans were looking for something iconic—a clear, understandable, structural entitlement change that they wanted, but didn't want to do without political cover from the Democrats. And not incidentally, Sperling noted, it was a change that would cause Democrats the maximum amount of political pain.

The starting point was raising the Medicare eligibility age from 65 to 67. It was a seemingly small change, but tampering with Medicare—Lyndon Johnson's Great Society contribution to the well-being of the elderly—was almost forbidden among Democrats. The AARP, which had spent more than $20 million on lobbyists in 2010 alone, would rise in protest. But the president said it was Boehner's requirement.

The Ryan budget had proposed increasing the age of eligibility by two months per year beginning in 2022, so that by 2034, a senior would have to be 67 to be eligible. "I don't care what they say," Sperling said. "We're not starting more aggressive than Paul Ryan is."

Sperling thought they should raise the age more slowly than Ryan. The White House team finally settled on raising the eligibility age by one month a year, meaning the full two-year increase wouldn't be complete until 2046. Even putting such a proposal on paper was dangerous for the White House, should it leak.

So, the total 10-year savings would be a mere $15 billion, with a few small changes in cost to wealthy Medicare beneficiaries.

In addition, they proposed $1.1 trillion in general spending cuts, spread over 10 years, plus another $490 billion in cuts to other programs including the federal employee retirement program, Medicaid, and other health-related cuts.

Sperling, Nabors and Lew decided to take a hard line on revenue and proposed what Boehner would consider a $1.4 trillion increase. But overall, the proposal cut the deficit by $2.7 trillion.

On July 1, the White House sent the offer to Boehner's staff.

In his remote windowless fourth-floor office in the Capitol, Brett Loper, Boehner's policy director, sat down to read the proposal. Loper, age 37, was one of those very important figures, little known outside Washington, who did the excruciating detail work. He headed a team of 10 policy experts.

With closely cropped hair, at 6-foot-2, Loper was the ultimate Republican efficiency man. Before coming to work for the speaker, he had worked in the White House Office of Management and Budget during the Bush administration and had been the Republican staff director on the House Ways and Means Committee. Prior to that, he served as deputy chief of staff and floor coordinator for Representative Tom DeLay, the former Republican majority whip and majority leader whose vigorous enforcement of party loyalty earned him the nickname "the Hammer."

In bold type on the first line of the White House offer were the words "Medicare structural reform." Loper's eyes flicked over to the right side of the page, where a column of numbers estimated the savings from each part of the proposal. The Democrats were estimating $15 billion in Medicare savings over 10 years.

Loper couldn't believe it. Just $15 billion in cuts over 10 years? Medicare was the single biggest driver of the country's long-term debt problem. The program would cost the government trillions of dollars over the next decade, and the best they could do was $15 billion in savings? This was almost too ridiculous to put down on paper.

Loper's eyes plunged down the page.

Under the White House plan, the Medicare eligibility age would be increased by two years, from 65 to 67, but not until 2046. That was 35 years away. Talk about kicking the can down the road.

Next on the list was "Medicaid and Other Health." The number there was $270 billion over 10 years. Okay, that was more like it.

But when Loper flipped to the third page, where the Medicaid cuts were specified, he realized that much of the savings weren't coming from Medicaid at all, but from Medicare prescription drugs. It was a confusing mishmash. Loper knew this would never fly with the speaker. It wouldn't even make it to the runway.

He turned to the section headlined "Revenues" and found yet another surprise. The Democrats were proposing the government collect what amounted to an additional $1.4 trillion in taxes over the next decade. It was an eye-popping number. Boehner had expressed willingness to increase revenue through tax reform, but there was no way to sell a number this big to the House Republican conference.

The revenue number was couched in a discussion of "fundamental tax reform" but included a wish list of changes to the tax code that the White House wanted up front that would increase taxes by $510 billion. Guaranteed to provoke Republican opposition, it targeted oil and gas companies, the estate tax, business inventory accounting rules and corporate jets.

If there were tax increases up front, where was their incentive to follow through on tax reform? This was basically bullshit, Loper concluded. He took the plan to Barry Jackson, Boehner's chief of staff.

Jackson, heavy and rumpled, with shaggy gray hair and glasses, was an Ohio native like the speaker. He had helped run Boehner's first congressional campaign in 1990, and served as the speaker's first chief of staff before taking over as the executive director of the House Republican Conference. He had left Capitol Hill in 2000 to work on the George W. Bush presidential campaign and spent eight years in the Bush White House, the majority of that time as deputy to senior adviser Karl Rove.

At 50, Jackson was the key figure in Boehner's inner circle, often serving as the speaker's proxy in negotiations with the Democrats in Congress. He knew a bad deal when he saw one.

He got on the phone with Boehner, who was back home in Ohio. This is a step back, not forward, Jackson said. The paper offer did not match the president's willingness, as you perceived it, to make some hard choices.

Boehner agreed and said he had to reject the offer.

He sent a simple message to the White House: Call when you're ready to get serious.


On Sunday, July 3, Boehner had a bunch of high school buddies and their wives visiting from Ohio. He was scheduled to go out to dinner with them that night, but the White House called. The president wanted to meet with him to see if they could get the negotiation back on track.

"All right. Six o'clock. I can do that and still make my dinner," Boehner said.

It was a brutally hot summer evening when the speaker arrived in the Oval Office, but Boehner wanted a cigarette and he knew there was no smoking allowed inside the White House.

"Hey, why don't we go outside on the patio?" he asked the president.

Boehner asked for a glass of Merlot and lit up a cigarette, sitting in the blazing heat across from the president, who had publicly admitted to his struggle to quit smoking. The discussion turned quickly to the administration's last proposal.

"Look, this isn't cutting it," the speaker said. "You're way too high on revenue. I can't do all these tax changes up front because, one, I'm opposed to them. But two, you will have no incentive to do tax reform." McConnell wouldn't go for it. The House Republicans wouldn't go for it. "This is no good. If you need the revenue, we've got to find a way to make tax reform work as part of this and not do this splitting out of these other things." And your entitlement reforms are inadequate. I can do revenue. But we need to have structural reforms of the entitlement programs.

I got it, I hear it, the president replied. Let's make another run at it.

Boehner said that among their options—a small deal with minimal reforms, a big deal with major reforms, or something in between—it was the big deal that stood the best chance of passage. "We could bring the votes together better if we are really accomplishing something. Just going in and nicking everybody is going to be that: a whole lot of nicks without a whole lot of success. The overall package wouldn't be big enough to really have accomplished much."

By the end of their discussion, Boehner thought he had convinced Obama that the big deal was the best option.

"The more I got into this, it became clear to me and frankly it became clear to the president that the only way to actually do this was to do the big deal," he said in an interview.

Boehner also remembered the meeting as a moment that crystallized his view of the difference between himself and Obama.

At one point in the meeting, he recalled, "I look at myself, I look at the president, and I just started chuckling to myself. Because all you need to know about the differences between the president and myself is that I'm sitting there smoking a cigarette, drinking Merlot, and

I look across the table and here is the president of the United States drinking iced tea and chomping on Nicorette."

"That's exactly right. And that's true," Obama said, smiling broadly and unwrapping another Nicorette during an interview in the Oval Office. "And then it started raining, and so we had to move back in. And it was very hot."

Asked to recall the meeting with Boehner, Obama said he told the speaker the same thing he had been telling members of Congress about the debt limit.

"I want to take this issue off the table," he said. "Because part of my view is that even though we were not largely responsible for these deficits and this debt, the public cared about it deeply. And we could not move an affirmative agenda forward as long as this debt and deficit was looming over the horizon.

"And I'm saying to them, look, there are three components to this. There's discretionary [general and Defense], there's mandatory [for instance, food stamps], and there's entitlements [such as Medicare and Medicaid]. I said, I'm game to do the discretionary, it's in our budget anyway. Biden and Cantor have done some good work on the mandatories, the nonentitlement mandatories. And we should be able to come up with something on that. And I said, the entitlement issues, from our perspective, are co-joined entirely with how far you guys are willing to go on revenue. So what I said was, you can—you have a menu of options here. You can go small, and we'll just do the discretionary. We can go medium, where we also do some of the mandatories. Or we can go large, with some of the entitlements. But if we do the large piece, then you've got to have significant revenues with us.

"I said, here's a menu of options. You guys can select whatever options you want, and I'll work with you to resolve this. We can go big. Maybe you guys can't deliver. Maybe we'll go small."

# 18

Inside the White House on the 4th of July, senior staff were irritated. Daley, Lew, Sperling and Nabors had been talking with Boehner's staff for several days without making much progress, and now here they were giving up family time for negotiations that still didn't feel serious.

Nabors found the whole situation aggravating. Why weren't they getting to some point of closure? Every time the White House took a step in one direction, the Republicans took a step in the opposite direction.

On Tuesday, July 5, the president made a short statement in the White House Briefing Room. Without offering any details, he said that talks on the debt limit had continued over the July 4th weekend, and that progress had been made.

There was still work to do, he cautioned, and solving the crisis would require a balanced approach that included both spending cuts and increased tax revenues. "This will require both parties to get out of our comfort zones, and both parties to agree on real compromise," he said.

He reiterated his opposition to a short-term debt limit extension and announced that he had asked the top eight congressional leaders to come to the White House for a meeting on July 7.

In a statement released later, Boehner said, "We're not dealing just with talking points about corporate jets or other 'loopholes.' The legislation the president has asked for—which would increase taxes on small businesses and destroy more American jobs—cannot pass the House, as I have stated repeatedly."

Regarding the requested meeting, he said, "I am happy to discuss these issues at the White House, but such discussions will be fruitless until the President recognizes economic and legislative reality."


Jack Lew and Rob Nabors went to Capitol Hill on Wednesday, July 6, to meet with Jackson and Loper in advance of another private Obama-Boehner meeting.

Loper handed them Boehner's counterproposal for a $2 trillion deficit reduction deal, which, they believed, offered $788 billion in new revenue. The proposal also insisted that yearly revenue not exceed 19.1 percent of GDP—a giant goal, given that government spending had increased to an annual average of 23.2 percent of GDP.

The plan had been bouncing around Boehner's office since the spring, Boehner later recalled.

"When you look at current tax policy it produces about $35.5 trillion plus over 10 years. If you look at current tax law, it produces $39-plus trillion. Out of tax reform the goal was to hit $36.2 or whatever, and so the idea was, and our proposal was that tax reform would produce up to—underline a hundred times 'up to'—$788 billion. And then roughly 19.1 percent of GDP. Which was a way for us to put revenue out there and unlock my box and their box."

Where the administration proposed saving $15 billion from Medicare over 10 years, the Boehner proposal sought $250 billion. He wanted to overhaul the system, combining Medicare's various parts that covered doctor's fees and hospital care separately into a single plan that looked and functioned more like a conventional insurance policy. The two-year increase in the retirement age would begin seven years earlier, in 2015, and be completed 19 years earlier than the White House proposed.

Combining the hospital care and regular medical care segments of Medicare might be the right policy, Lew said, but it's very complicated. You're going to create winners and losers. This can't be sold as part of a budget-saving policy. It's got to be done on a no-cost basis, just for good policy, because you're screwing some of the healthy and creating more of a safety net for the unhealthy. You have no idea what the political ramifications are going to be, he added. This is going to be bad politics for you.

This was the sort of thing Jackson couldn't stand—the White House telling House Republicans about their own politics.

"Jack, I know my politics," he said. "I don't pretend to know yours. Don't pretend to know mine."

Boehner's counteroffer applied the modified Consumer Price Index to Social Security and made other changes to the Democrats' treasured retirement program.

Lew said the administration would consider the CPI change, but any other changes to Social Security would need to be balanced with an increase in payroll taxes. He suggested creating a "donut hole" system for payroll taxes. Currently, everyone paid payroll taxes on their first $106,800 of income. Lew suggested keeping the cutoff at $106,800 and reinstating the tax on income over $250,000.

Loper found Lew obnoxious. The budget director was doing 75 percent of the talking, lecturing everyone not only about what Obama's policy was, but also why it was superior to the Republicans'.

Jackson found Lew's tone disrespectful and dismissive.

Lew was incredulous when he considered the Republican proposal as a whole. The changes they were considering sounded simple. But the speaker's office was laying down general principles and looking to apply them to extremely complex programs. The devil was always in the details. What mattered was what impact those general principles would have on people's lives if they were implemented.

When the speaker's office made a proposal, Lew would return with an analysis of what it would mean for the average Medicare retiree and people at different income levels. It complicated the negotiations, and in Lew's experience, the answer "things are complicated" was not highly appreciated by the speaker's office.

Lew felt that Loper understood the issues and, if he had been given the freedom to negotiate, would have been able to come to a deal. Jackson, on the other hand, was a political strategist. He had little interest in the substance of the debates—his eye was always on the Republican conference, making sure Boehner wasn't too out of step with what they would support.

To Lew, it seemed the speaker and his staff were constantly complaining about the problems they had with their caucus. It wasn't as if the White House would have an easy job selling the deal either. Democrats in Congress weren't exactly clamoring for cuts to Medicare and Social Security.

Lew tried to explain the magnitude of what Republicans were asking the White House to support. Their proposed changes to Social Security, Medicare and other social programs would overturn decades of Democratic orthodoxy. Even the Ryan budget, viewed as unacceptably radical by the Democrats, didn't change things so quickly. He said the Republicans had fundamentally misread the politics of the budget debate.

"You realize that all the Democrats think we've got you by the balls because of that Paul Ryan budget you voted for? And we're going to give it up in one fell swoop?"

Later, at the White House, Nabors and Sperling looked over Boehner's offer.

We can't do most of this Medicare stuff, Nabors said, and the Medicaid pieces are completely unworkable. The Republicans were pushing for funding levels that could only be reached by turning Medicaid into a block grant program—something Democrats would never accept.

The cuts to entitlements, in general, were higher than the Democrats would tolerate. The proposed $788 billion in new revenue was a fiction. It assumed a new and lower starting baseline.

"We can't do this," Nabors said. "And they have to know that we can't do this. This would be suicide." He thought the Republicans were pulling away from a deal.

"Oh, my God, why are we in this negotiation?" Sperling said. "It's a fraud."

Sperling had focused on the requirement that government revenue be tied to GDP. This was the killer line: "Projected revenue could be no higher than 19.1 percent in any year." It would be a potential revenue cut of $600 billion, not a revenue increase. The 19.1 percent was something the *Wall Street Journal* editorial board fantasized about, but the federal government's obligations to seniors through Medicare and Social Security were skyrocketing with the retirement of the baby boomers. There was no way to go back to the Reagan 1980s with some arbitrary 19.1 percent cap. They wanted to cap revenues at an already low percentage of GDP when the country was coming out of a recession?

"No fucking way," Sperling said.

We can't do this, Nabors told Jackson.

This is a fair deal. It's reasonable, Jackson replied, pointing out the offer of $788 billion in revenue.

As much as anyone in the White House, Nabors was eager to cut a deal. But this was just insulting.

"If you can't sell it to me," he told Jackson, "there's no way you're going to sell it."

During the course of the week, the approximately $1.1 trillion in discretionary cuts negotiated by the Biden group had become an assumption. They would be part of whatever deal could be worked out.

When Boehner went to meet with Obama on the evening of July 6, he remained convinced that the offer his staff had delivered the previous day held the key that would unlock the box each side was trapped in. It would allow the Democrats to say they were raising additional revenue while protecting the Republicans from having to support a tax increase.

"Listen, $788 billion was real simple," Boehner recalled. "Flatter, fairer code, you're going to get more economic growth. Secondly, you're going to have a more efficient tax system."

He said that Internal Revenue Service data shows that the current tax system produces about 85 to 86 percent of what it's supposed to. Boehner's staff had estimated that it could be increased to 93 percent with a flatter, fairer code.

"Thirdly, I'll call that opportunity savings, nobody knows what the tax rates are going to be. We got [the Alternative Minimum Tax] hanging out there, we got the Bush tax cuts all going to expire. There's some value into locking this down. Well, I was entirely comfortable—well, entirely, that's an overstatement—I was comfortable."

The demand that revenue be limited to 19.1 percent of GDP would have made it an easier sell to Republican hard-liners, but it "was not something I was going to fall on my sword over," Boehner later recalled. "But the up to $788 billion, I was comfortable enough to put it on the paper. I don't want to say I was that comfortable, because I knew I was going to have a battle here, but I was willing to do that if there were real reforms in the entitlement programs. You know I think at this point they were pretty excited about us putting revenue on the table and we were making progress."

But at the end of the meeting, despite their previous discussion about pressing staff to find an agreement, they remained far apart on the key issues of taxes and entitlement reform.


On the morning of Thursday, July 7, a *New York Times* story headlined "President Looks to Broader Deal in Deficit Talks" revealed that Boehner and Obama were engaged in secret negotiations. The report said the speaker had shown a "new willingness" to bargain over revenues, and mentioned that a figure of up to "$1 trillion or more" was in play.

David Krone, Reid's chief of staff, told Jackson that the White House had briefed Pelosi and Reid, and it looked like the leak had come from Senate Democrats.

On the $1 trillion figure, Boehner insisted to Cantor and others, "That's not accurate. I'm not doing that." He was proposing tax reform exclusively. It was the only way.

However, he added, "I want something big." It would be easier to sell than something small or at the medium level. "I want something big."

"I don't know that you can," Cantor replied. "Our members aren't there. Maybe we should go for the Biden thing." He was trying to convey skepticism, even animosity, without rocking the boat too much. Additional debate about a split between the speaker and majority leader would generate headlines reading "Ambitious Cantor Wants to Overthrow Speaker."

The internal House Republican dynamic, as viewed by their staffs and by the House press corps, was Cantor vs. Boehner. They were obviously in different places, and any disagreement by Cantor was gauged in terms of a leadership challenge. Cantor referred to it as "the soap opera," but it was real.

Boehner's staff worried that the president thought if he got Boehner in a room with the rest of the leaders and announced a deal, Boehner would fold in front of everybody. Loper tried to get the speaker to beg off even going to another meeting. It was ridiculous. The distance was too great, and Pelosi would never agree to support a deal with big Medicare cuts.

Boehner and Obama spoke on the phone in advance of the scheduled White House meeting.

I'm going to lay out three potential paths to an agreement, Obama said. The choices would be: a smaller deal with roughly $1 trillion in deficit reduction, a medium-sized $2.4 trillion plan, or a big deal that would require tough cuts but provide close to $4 trillion in deficit reduction.

"We aren't there" on any agreement of any size, Boehner reminded him. He was nervous. The deal was so unformed that he was afraid discussing it in a meeting would only confuse people. Even the other

Republican leaders "didn't have any clue" about what he'd been discussing with Obama.

"This ain't going to cut it," Boehner said. Why have the meeting at all?

"Well, we've already got it scheduled and I feel like I have to bring them down here," Obama insisted.

Boehner wondered if Obama was using the meeting as a means of managing Reid and Pelosi, who were increasingly upset about being cut out of the negotiations.

Boehner met with Cantor, McConnell and Kyl to discuss the White House meeting that day, and then called the entire Republican conference. Negotiations are ongoing on a number of options, he told them, including structural entitlement reforms, spending caps, and comprehensive tax reform. All of these things could be part of one significant framework, but there will be no tax increases.

In case there was any doubt, Boehner spoke to the press after the meeting. In the debt limit negotiations, he said, "Everything's on the table except raising taxes on the American people."


As promised, Obama laid out his three options when the top eight congressional leaders met at the White House that morning.

The big deal was impossible, Cantor and Kyl said immediately. The $4 trillion deal, which required $1 trillion in new revenue, would never pass the House, Cantor said.

The president cautioned them that he wouldn't sign anything that didn't get the country through the 2012 elections without another debt limit crisis.

Boehner remained convinced that the president's insistence on a single-step debt limit increase was purely political.

"Okay, so, he wants to get reelected," he recalled in an interview. "Doesn't want to have to deal with it more than once. Okay, so, he kept saying it. This had nothing to do with anything other than the convenience of his own reelection."

Did you say that to him?

"No, no, no. I didn't have to state the obvious."

They made little progress during the 90-minute meeting, but agreed to meet again on Sunday evening.

The president spoke to the media at about 1 p.m., calling it "very constructive," but admitting that "the parties are still far apart on a wide range of issues."

Afterward, Pelosi expressed concern that cuts to Medicare, Medicaid and Social Security were on the table. "We are not going to balance the budget on the backs of America's seniors, women or people with disabilities," she said.

Later, Boehner met with the rest of the House leadership: Cantor, McCarthy and Hensarling.

They discussed options for a Plan B, in case the White House negotiations didn't pan out. They neared a consensus to pursue a medium-sized package, based largely on the Biden group's work.

Boehner's decision to send the rest of the Republican leadership in search of a Plan B had two purposes. First, he had no confidence the negotiations with the president would produce a deal, and second, he had to cover his own back by keeping McConnell, Cantor, McCarthy and Hensarling busy doing something because they were really nervous about what the hell he was up to. And he realized that was an understatement.

Did they ask you? I asked the speaker.

"Oh, hell yeah!"

What did you say?

"Well, you know, I couldn't get into what we were actually talking about, because hell, you know, everything around here is like a sieve."

So what did you say to them?

"I'm working on this, working on this. They kept saying we're not going to do a big deal, can't do a big deal, can't do a big deal, and so I said why don't we work on a deal that we think we can do. So there was effort under way, one, in case this thing did fall apart, and two, to keep them engaged in something."

·          ·          ·

Late that day, Jack Lew went to the Hill to meet with an angry Nancy Pelosi. She had asked him to brief senior Democrats on the debt limit talks, but she also wanted to send a message to the White House.

House Democrats are being excluded from the talks, she said, and obviously, we are going to be necessary to pass any bill. The contingent of right-wing Republicans in the House will never vote for any debt ceiling increase, she said. Everyone knew this.

The president had to deal with the House Republican majority, Lew said, attempting to defend the secret talks as a strategy of necessity.

"Don't insult us," Pelosi retorted. "You guys don't know how to count."

There was often theater in these meetings, Lew knew, particularly when a leader like Pelosi was speaking in front of her extended leadership team. He was being chastised in order to send a message to the White House and to other House Democrats that she was asserting her rightful role.

The Democrats had 192 votes in the House. "Next time around," Pelosi added, "you better make sure that you—*we*—use the leverage. If you're going to ask for House Democrats to put the vote over the top, we want to make sure that our concerns are more fairly reflected."

# 19

At 8:30 a.m. on July 8, the Labor Department announced that job growth had slowed in the previous month and that the unemployment rate was stuck at 9.2 percent. Within an hour, the House Republican leadership was holding a news conference.

"After hearing this morning's jobs report," said Boehner, "I'm sure the American people are still asking the question, 'Where are the jobs?' " It was a theme he had been pushing since the 2009 stimulus package.

Asked about the prospects for a debt ceiling deal, he said, "There is no agreement, in public or private. . . . It's not like there is some imminent deal about to happen. There are serious disagreements about how to deal with this very serious problem."

What were the prospects for progress in the meeting scheduled for Sunday?

"I don't know," Boehner said. "There's a lot of conversations continuing, but I don't—in all honesty, I don't think things have narrowed. I don't think this problem has narrowed at all in the last several days."

Senator Kent Conrad sat down for a private meeting at the White House requested by Obama and Biden.

Though Conrad had been the impetus behind the Simpson-Bowles fiscal commission and had served on it and voted for the final product, he had urged Obama not to endorse or embrace it because it would mobilize Republican opposition and "House Republicans would automatically oppose it." A longtime veteran of the budget wars, Conrad was one of the six senators in the bipartisan group called the Gang of Six that had been trying to come up with its own deficit reduction plan that combined increased tax revenues and spending cuts.

How would the revenue piece for the Gang of Six, which had not officially released its plan, actually work? Obama asked.

"You've got two pieces," Conrad said. First, $800 billion in revenue over 10 years came from not extending the Bush tax cuts for the upper brackets; second, another $1.2 trillion, also over 10 years, came from tax reform.

"You've spent all this time negotiating with Republicans," Obama said. "In all those hours of negotiation, what have you found works?" He had to crack the code. How do you get revenue out of these guys?

"There is only one thing that works," Conrad said. "And that is fundamental tax reform that actually lowers marginal rates." Reagan had dramatically reduced income tax rates in 1982 and 1986, and it had been a Republican obsession ever since. Most of them had signed a pledge originated by anti-tax lobbyist Grover Norquist vowing never to raise taxes. It was holy writ. The extremist Tea Party wing of the party was smaller and consisted of 40 to 60 "crazies," or "barbarians at the gate," according to Nabors. Their power, however, was not within the House Republican conference. Rather, it was the threat of a primary challenge, which they could engineer and help finance.

Tax reform was a possible way around Norquist—eliminating loopholes raised revenue, which in turn could be used to both lower tax rates and reduce the deficit.

The reform would include elimination of tax deductions, including those for mortgage interest and employer-provided health care insurance. Technically these deductions were called "tax expenditures," as the president and Biden knew, because they cost the Treasury money—more than $1.1 trillion, each year. It was an astonishing number: The government lost more through the tax code than it spent through the annual appropriations process.

The key to generating revenue through tax reform, Conrad said, was not to raise the income or corporate tax rates, but to lower them while eliminating deductions.

"Combined with entitlement reform and with going after wasteful spending," Conrad said, it was possible to get there.

One lesson, he said, was to look at Defense spending. Lift the veil over there at the Pentagon, he said. Savings could be found that would not compromise the military's real capacity an iota. While serving on the Simpson-Bowles commission, Conrad said, he heard a witness testify that 51 percent of all federal employees, including uniformed military, were at the Department of Defense. That did not count the Defense contractors, so Conrad had asked how many there were. The answer had an astounding range—1 million to 9 million. He had been unable to get more precise numbers, though the Pentagon had acknowledged they had a contractor problem.

"They've got a huge contractor problem," Conrad said.


In his first meeting with the president-elect during the transition in 2008, Nabors, then an OMB expert, had spent 10 minutes discussing tax reform.

"It's a necessary part of our reform agenda," Obama had said. "It has to be, because it's so screwed up."

Since then, senior staff had spent many hours with Obama discussing tax reform. Nabors considered them surreal conversations. "Let's just give them two to three months to come up with tax reform," the president said at one point. It only seemed reasonable, Nabors realized, until they got into the details. He found himself walking the line between his old role as a technician and his new one, as a political guy.

They called in the tax experts from the Treasury Department—Nabors called them "the trolls"—who said even six months would be fast. Realistically, it would be 12 to 18 months.

Later that day, Lew and Nabors went back to the Capitol to meet with Loper and Jackson. They hadn't brought any new paper with them, but they were ready to talk about some of the details in the Republicans' latest offer.

The White House was willing to compromise on some of the changes the Republicans wanted to make to Medicare, such as transforming the confusing Medicare Part A and Medicare Part B systems into a single entity. They would agree to that if the change could be pushed off to 2021 or 2022, and if there were guarantees that the policies would be affordable for low-income seniors. The net change in costs had to be zero. Republicans could change Medicare, but they couldn't generate any savings from doing it.

The White House was willing to compromise on the Medicare eligibility age. They still wanted to raise it at the slower rate of one month per year, but would agree to start the process four or five years earlier. The Republicans were asking too much. "We can't do this," Nabors said. "You know we can't do this. This would be suicide if we did this."

"Medicare is going to be tough on us as well," Jackson replied, noting that they had already voted, in the Ryan budget, for more radical cuts. "I'm not stupid. Come on, guys."


Despite their frustration with some of Boehner's positions, White House senior staff hoped there might be some substance to the negotiations. They had to be hopeful to work this hard. They were exchanging documents with Boehner's staff, red-lining each other's proposals, and returning them for further discussion. Sperling said he took it as a sign of seriousness that built confidence on both sides. "We both know there's shit on this paper that would kill either of us."

On Friday, July 8, Nabors came to Sperling. "They sent their tax principles and we've got to send a reply. Oh, and I need to do it by tonight."

He handed Sperling one sheet of paper containing Boehner's goals for tax reform.

"Go consult with Geithner," Nabors said. "Consult with Reed. Get back."

Sperling went down Boehner's list.

"Maintain an income-based system without adding any new tax structures," he read. They could agree on that and on trying to reduce the number of personal income tax brackets to three.

In Sperling's view, some of Boehner's principles were standard right-wing dogma. The speaker wanted to reduce taxes on investment income, make the cuts to the estate tax implemented the previous December permanent, and "exempt from federal income tax all or substantially all dividends received from foreign subsidiaries."

Sperling drafted a set of principles for the administration. It accepted some of the Republicans' proposals verbatim and ignored others. On the question of the estate tax, the administration would propose reverting to a system similar to what was in place before the Kyl giveaway from the previous year.

Sperling knew the president was determined to keep the tax code progressive. Had the White House made a terrible negotiating mistake by leaving the definition of "progressivity" vague?

He decided to leave no doubt. Tax reform, he wrote, should "maintain or increase the progressivity of the tax code, compared to the Fiscal Commission baseline in 2013. Progressivity will be measured by the percentage change in after-tax income for each quintile as well as the top 2%."

In an interview, the president recalled that he had been concerned by the Republicans' tax principles because they didn't appear consistent with Boehner's promise to retain the current level of progressivity.

"So we've got to do an evaluation: Can you maintain progressivity of the sort that we have right now with only three rates?" he said. "And the answer is no. So that all would have had to have been rewritten."

•      •      •

Nabors sent the White House's response to Boehner's office that night. Loper looked at it in disbelief. The White House had eviscerated the Republicans' tax principles. The section on progressivity stood out in particular. The Democrats' proposal would push progressivity to record levels.

Loper knew this wouldn't work. Republicans believed the burden of paying for the government was already too concentrated on middle- and upper-income earners, so changes that made the system more progressive could be seen as not enough reform. Loper took the administration's principles to Jackson. The gap between us is too large, they agreed. We're not going to be able to close it. They began drafting a pessimistic memo for Boehner.

On July 3, 2011, President Obama and Speaker John Boehner met on the White House patio outside the Oval Office to discuss raising the federal debt ceiling.

"All you need to know about the differences between the president and myself," Boehner said, "is that I'm sitting there smoking a cigarette, drinking Merlot, and I look across the table and here is the president of the United States drinking iced tea and chomping on Nicorette." The drinks had apparently been removed for the photo, because the president confirmed what Boehner said. "That's true. And then it started to rain, and so we had to move back in."

**2**

During his first year in office, President Obama said that addressing the country's growing budget deficit was of the utmost importance to him. He told fiscal hawks in Congress, "I believe so strongly in what you're saying, I'd be willing to be a one-term president over this."

**3**

"This debt issue bothered me before I got here 22 years ago," said Speaker Boehner. When the Ohio Republican became speaker in 2011, he said, "I'm sure as hell going to do something about it."

**4**

Treasury Secretary Tim Geithner warned that a debt default could trigger a depression worse than the Great Depression of the 1930s. "Everything comes crashing down and you cannot rebuild it," he told the president. "It's something that will be lasting for generations."

**5**

As the Obama administration prepared its first full-year budget in late 2009, National Economic Council Director Larry Summers, left, urged the rest of the economic team, including Treasury Secretary Geithner, center, and Office of Management and Budget Director Peter Orszag, right, to "just gimmick it up," because any long-range spending cuts passed into law could be changed by a future Congress.

**6**

"Our internal process is a fucking debating society," complained White House chief of staff Rahm Emanuel—the man in charge of that process—in a February 8, 2010, email. President Obama's fellow Chicagoan left the House leadership to help guide the relatively inexperienced president through the intricacies of Washington politics, and his aggressive approach to dealing with congressional Republicans in the early years of Obama's first term was: "We have the votes. Fuck 'em."

Senator Kent Conrad, Democrat from North Dakota who chairs the Budget Committee, created a precedent for the debt limit crisis of 2011 when he told President Obama that he would block a vote on the increase of the federal debt limit unless the White House backed a fiscal commission with extraordinary power to cut spending.

Vice President Biden, pictured here on May 24, 2011, was called on to negotiate through back channels with Senate Minority Leader Mitch McConnell on sensitive budget and tax issues. In the West Wing, he was called "the McConnell whisperer" because he knew the right combination of sympathy and gentleness, never force, needed to work with the minority leader.

Erskine Bowles, left, former White House chief of staff to President Bill Clinton, and retired Senator Alan Simpson, center, a Wyoming Republican, were tapped to chair a bipartisan fiscal commission that would seek ways to reduce the federal deficit. In announcing their appointment, President Obama said the two were "taking on the impossible."

President Obama calls future speaker John Boehner on election night, November 3, 2010, after the Republicans won 63 seats in the House, giving them the majority. White House staff at first couldn't find a phone number for Boehner, but Obama eventually reached him and said he was "looking forward to working with him and the Republicans to find common ground, move the country forward, and get things done for the American people."

"I haven't reached out as effectively as I should have," President Obama told House Republicans in a meeting November 30, 2010, after the election. "Let's have honest cooperation, not just photo ops." From left, Speaker Nancy Pelosi, just outside the door; Virginia Republican Eric Cantor, the incoming House majority leader; Obama; Senate Minority Leader Mitch McConnell of Kentucky; Senate Minority Whip Jon Kyl of Arizona; and Senate Majority Leader Harry Reid of Nevada.

**12**

"The single most important thing we want to achieve is for President Obama to be a one-term president," Senate Minority Leader Mitch McConnell said. Often forgotten is what he said later in that interview: "If President Obama does a Clintonian backflip, if he's willing to meet us halfway on some of the biggest issues, it's not inappropriate for us to do business with him....I don't want the president to fail; I want him to change."

"My guys don't even believe default is a problem," House Majority Leader Eric Cantor explained to Democrats. Cantor, closely connected to the more extreme conservative Tea Party wing of the House Republicans, was skeptical of a $3–$4 trillion grand bargain to reduce the deficit with entitlement reform and a tax increase.

**13**

**14**

Wisconsin Republican Paul Ryan, left, took over as chairman of the House Budget Committee in 2011. His April 2011 budget proposal, "The Path to Prosperity," was designed to slash the federal deficit, but drastically reduce benefits for people on Medicare and Medicaid. After President Obama publicly criticized what he called Ryan's "dark view of America" in a speech when Ryan was in the audience, Ryan told White House staff, "I can't believe you poisoned the well like that."

House Majority Leader Eric Cantor, left, and Vice President Biden on May 5, 2011, the opening day of initial talks to address the federal deficit and raise the debt ceiling. The two forged a close working relationship but Cantor opposed any tax increases and Biden said they had been sent on "Mission: Impossible."

**15**

**16**

Representative Chris Van Hollen, a Maryland Democrat, was frustrated during the Biden committee meetings by Republicans' refusal to consider increasing federal revenue or taxes as a way of reducing the deficit. "We're not going to keep going down this road," he told Republicans.

Senator Jon Kyl, one of the two Republicans on the Biden committee, couldn't understand why Democrats wouldn't just accept spending cuts without revenues. "So you're saying to me that even though there are Medicare savings that you think are reasonable—that we could do—you won't do them unless we're going to raise taxes on somebody?" he asked.

Democratic Senator Max Baucus, the chairman of the Finance Committee, aggravated members of both parties during the Biden talks, saying, "I will walk away from any deal" that would make large cuts to the agriculture subsidies important to farmers and ranchers in his state of Montana.

David Plouffe, Obama's 2008 campaign manager, took over as senior adviser to the president in January 2011. When President Obama promised to veto a debt limit extension that didn't last past the 2012 election, Plouffe realized he had drawn a line in the sand. "If he caves," Plouffe said, "it will have long-lasting political repercussions that we may never get out of."

President Obama with Rob Nabors, the White House director of legislative affairs. Discussing the Democratic vote count for a grand bargain deficit reduction deal, Obama asked Nabors, "How many people do you think are going to vote for it?" Nabors replied, "How many people are you going to tell to vote for it?"

Director of the Office of Management and Budget Jack Lew with President Obama. Lew was the administration's point man during staff-level negotiations on the debt limit. Obama joked that Republicans hated negotiating with Lew because he "knew the budget better than anybody." But Republicans said their real problem with Lew was that he didn't know how to "get to yes." Lew became White House chief of staff on January 27, 2012.

**22**

President Obama with Bill Daley, the White House chief of staff in 2011. Senate Majority Leader Harry Reid did not like Daley's involvement in congressional budget negotiations. "I'll tell you when I want your chief of staff coming up here," Reid told the president.

**23**

Barry Jackson, chief of staff to Speaker of the House John Boehner, looks on as Boehner speaks to the president by phone. "The White House is brilliant at getting out early and defining things their way," he warned, so it would be essential for Boehner to give his version publicly.

**24**

Senate Majority Leader Harry Reid leaves the White House with his chief of staff, David Krone. "It is really disheartening that you, that this White House, did not have a Plan B," Krone told the president after the debt talks with Boehner fell through.

**25**

Brett Loper, Boehner's policy director, couldn't believe the impact the Gang of Six proposal had on negotiations with the White House. Who cared what six senators said? he asked.

**26**

Steven Stombres, Cantor's chief of staff, was not shy about challenging senior Republican leaders. "You are crazy," the former Army intelligence officer told Speaker Boehner, who said he could get 170 Republican votes for a large revenue package.

**27**

Neil Bradley, Cantor's deputy chief of staff and policy director, thought the Biden committee showed promise at the start. "Where else do you walk into a room and find $123 billion in savings?" he asked after one of the first meetings.

**28**

President Obama with Nancy Pelosi, the House Democratic leader. "Nancy has always been there for us," Obama said. Rob Nabors, the White House director of legislative affairs, said of Pelosi, "She is absolutely nails."

Majority Leader Harry Reid negotiated with the Republicans and almost joined them in making a deficit reduction deal, but President Obama pulled him back. Reid complained, "Republicans can't deliver the big deal. They're jeopardizing the future of the country."

**29**

When Boehner suggested that he and the president begin face-to-face discussions on the debt limit, the question among White House staff was: Should we engage at all? From left, President Obama, chief of staff Bill Daley, director of legislative affairs Rob Nabors, National Economic Council Director Gene Sperling, deputy NEC director Jason Furman, Office of Management and Budget Director Jack Lew, senior adviser David Plouffe, and Treasury Secretary Tim Geithner.

Speaker John Boehner, Vice President Joe Biden, President Obama and House Majority Leader Eric Cantor meet in the Oval Office on July 20 when they seemed to be getting close to a budget deal. On revenue, Boehner told the president, "Our necks are out as far as they can go."

President Obama at a press conference after Speaker Boehner pulled out of their talks for a second time. "I've been left at the altar now a couple of times," he said, adding that Republicans would have to take "responsibility" for the failed talks. The president's press conference took place right after he hung up with Boehner. "He was spewing coals," Boehner said of their conversation. "I was pretty angry," Obama later recalled. "And look, the reason is, here we've got a national crisis that needs to get resolved. The entire world is watching."

Senate Majority Leader Harry Reid and Speaker Boehner in the White House Cabinet Room on July 23, 2011. "Mr. President," said Boehner, "as I read the Constitution, the Congress writes the laws. You get to decide if you want to sign them." Reid then asked the President to leave the room so congressional leaders could speak privately. "You know, the truth of the matter is, at that point, all I'm concerned about is getting this thing done," the president recalled. "And so I'm not concerned about protocol."

Rohit Kumar, far right, McConnell's chief domestic policy adviser, conducted key negotiations for the minority leader. When he showed up at home at 8 p.m. on July 29, his wife, Hilary, was stunned that he wasn't still at work. "The fact that I'm here at eight o'clock," he told her, "tells you how screwed we are. We're nowhere. We have no deal."

By July 31, just two days before the Treasury would run out of money, White House staffers were exhausted from a month of intense negotiations. Bruce Reed, the vice president's chief of staff, said it was comparable to an economic "modern-day Cuban Missile Crisis." From left, President Obama, National Economic Council Director Gene Sperling, chief of staff Bill Daley, Reed, director of legislative affairs Rob Nabors, Office of Management and Budget Director Jack Lew, Vice President Joe Biden, and White House senior adviser Valerie Jarrett.

**36**

President Obama in the Oval Office on July 11. He told his senior staff he would not sign a short-term extension of the debt limit. "Under any scenario we risk a default," he said. "That's not my control. The Republicans are forcing the risk of a default on us. I can't stop them from doing that. We can have the fight now, or we can have the fight later on, but the fight is coming to us."

**37**

President Obama, chief of staff Bill Daley, National Economic Council Director Gene Sperling, and Treasury Secretary Tim Geithner. "This is insanity," said Geithner, as the final debt ceiling negotiations threatened to come undone over cuts to Defense spending.

**38**

Representative Jeb Hensarling of Texas, left, number four in the House Republican leadership, and Senator Patty Murray, of Washington, number four in the Senate Democratic leadership, were the co-chairmen of the supercommittee. It was supposed to find $1.2 trillion in additional deficit reductions, but failed in November 2011.

"There's no process for making a decision in this White House. There's nobody in charge," Speaker Boehner, left, said about the failure of the debt limit negotiation to cut spending. "John was in a tough spot. He couldn't get it done," said President Obama. "I think that him trying to spin it is understandable."

# 20

On Saturday morning, July 9, the president was still determined to "go big." He would agree to sharp cuts in Medicare and Medicaid, adopt the modified CPI measure, and get some revenue. He realized the Democrats, especially in the House, were up in arms as details were getting out. Yet he felt he was chipping away at the barriers to a deal. He believed Boehner had agreed, for example, to big cuts of $50 billion or more on prescription drug rebates, previously a Republican no.

Obama also believed he was gathering some important intelligence from his talks with Boehner. First, the speaker acknowledged that Cantor was working against the deal.

The president and Boehner joked about the tension between the speaker and the majority leader.

You know Cantor's trying to get your job, the president told Boehner. He's trying to screw you. He's stirring up stuff inside your caucus, and he walked away from the negotiations with Biden in part because he doesn't want the failure to be around his neck. He wanted you to take the blame if this thing falls apart.

In addition, Boehner had confided that he believed another reason Cantor had walked out of the Biden talks was because he learned of the secret Obama-Boehner meeting. Eric, Boehner had said, considered that an "end run."

If they didn't get a big deal, Obama realized they would have to go back to some of the core ideas that came from the Biden meetings—not a hopeful sign, given that the Biden work was tentative and had broken down over the revenue question.

So where were they?

"You know what?" the president told Daley. "We've got a 50–50 shot at getting something done." But in phone calls that morning he had told some Democrats it was only a 25 percent chance.


Most of Obama's economic team gathered early that Saturday morning in the West Wing. Nabors reported that he was somewhat optimistic. Though there were big differences, the distance between Obama's offer of $2.7 trillion and Boehner's $2 trillion ought to be something they could bridge in a normal negotiation. "They're looking at it," he said. The speaker, of course, wouldn't take Obama's first offer any more than they would take the speaker's. And they had exchanged drafts of tax principles.

An immediate answer seemed unlikely. It was a hot summer Saturday, and Nabors said he thought the speaker might be playing golf. It wasn't unusual, in complex negotiations, to unwind with a little time on the fairways. After all, this—at least the current phase of *this*—had all begun three weeks earlier at the Golf Summit.

Golf, a game of recovery, was a good metaphor for what they were doing. A bad or unlucky shot wasn't fatal. Follow it up with a good second or third shot, and you could still find yourself on the green with a chance at par, or even better. Negotiations were similar. If your first offer is a bust, you can always follow with a second one.

Everybody should take time off, they decided. People fled to play golf or tennis or spend time with family.

•          •          •

That same morning, Cantor read *The Wall Street Journal*, especially focusing on an editorial headlined "Boehner's Obama Gamble." The *Journal*'s editorial page, with its hard anti-tax line, was a kind of *Daily Racing Form* for Cantor and the new Republican, Tea Party–inspired majority in the House.

"A tax increase now for the promise of tax reform later won't fly," Cantor read. The *Journal* was issuing an explicit thumbs-down on the talks aimed at a big $4 trillion deal. "Especially risky is his [Boehner's] willingness to 'decouple' the Bush tax rates," Cantor read. "Taken by itself this would be a tax increase pure and simple and violate the GOP's campaign pledge." Talk of forcing tax reform over the next several months with a "trigger" was an insufficient guarantee. "We'll see a unicorn first," the *Journal* warned. "Republicans who embrace this logic deserve the Tea Party's disdain." The worry was that Obama would "bull-rush Mr. Boehner into a bad deal. . . . Mr. Boehner shouldn't bet his majority on Mr. Obama's promises."

This was more than a small fire alarm. The *Journal* had a lot of influence with House Republicans. When it said their speaker was about to agree to a tax hike they shouldn't support, the members would react.

Boehner had told Cantor that if he got significant entitlement reforms, specifically on Medicare, he would be able to sell what the White House would call a tax increase as tax reform that would generate revenue through economic growth.

Cantor begged to differ. A big number would be considered a tax hike. To sell that to their members would require large entitlement cuts that addressed the deficit problem—something transformational. And he knew from the Biden talks that the Obama administration wasn't even close.

"I want something big," Boehner kept repeating. "I want something big." He and Jackson talked about the Boehner legacy, and how fine it would be to do something on the order of the dramatic 1983 Social Security deal between President Reagan and House Speaker Tip O'Neill or the tax reform deal of 1986.

"I didn't run and become speaker to do small things," Boehner told Jackson. "I did it to do big things."

Cantor spoke with some of the members. The *Journal* editorial reflected their sentiments. Some of the members called the speaker's staff and the speaker himself. The message: What are you doing? Don't get too far ahead. Ease up. They would never agree.

Michael Steel, Boehner's press secretary, thought the editorial was incoherent, failing to make the critical distinction between pure tax hikes and additional revenue through comprehensive tax reform, which Boehner had made a precondition of any deal. But it was too late. Inside information on the negotiations was unavailable. By stepping into the vacuum, the *Journal* had defined the issues.


Paul Ryan spoke with Van Hollen. The *New York Times* story on $1 trillion in revenue has blown any chance of a grand bargain, he said.

Van Hollen appealed to Ryan for a big package.

"The window is already shut," Ryan replied. "It just isn't going to fly." They needed to go back to the Biden framework.


Boehner was not playing golf that Saturday morning. The speaker was at his home in West Chester, Ohio, for the weekend, where he spent part of the day riding his bike. Then he tended to his lawn mower.

This was a ritual the speaker enjoyed—often telling staff how much he looked forward to it. He would tip the push mower over on its side, remove the blade and sharpen it with a hand file, then, like any suburbanite, mow the lawn.

That morning, Boehner looked over the three-page tax reform memo that Loper and Jackson had sent the night before, and called them. The memo was titled "Tax Reform Principles: Key Areas of Disagreement," and it highlighted several of them.

The first was the overall level of taxation. Republicans wanted to cap tax revenue at a percentage of GDP, which could require revenues to fall in a slow economy. The Democrats wanted revenue targets set at a dollar figure, which would preserve revenues at a specific level regardless of economic conditions.

The White House memo was "cryptic," its business tax proposals "vague."

The two sides also disagreed about what sort of enforcement mechanism, or trigger, would be in place to assure that tax reform was enacted, and whether the system should be made more progressive.

We're too far apart to get to a big deal, Loper said.

Boehner said he was concerned that at the White House meeting the next day, the president would announce that he and the speaker were close to a deal. He didn't want to be railroaded or to have to contradict the president in front of the other congressional leaders, so he directed staff to draft a statement taking the big deal off the table.

But his reluctance to embarrass the president wasn't Boehner's only problem. Both the *New York Times* article and the *Wall Street Journal* editorial had focused on tax increases instead of tax reform.

Boehner knew that the predominant school of thought in the conservative movement held that you shouldn't ever negotiate with Obama. You shouldn't do any sort of big deals, because Republicans believed they were going to take the White House and the Senate back in 2012, and then they wouldn't have to negotiate with Democrats at all.

Boehner and Jackson viewed this as a high-risk strategy. The deficit was too big a problem and with the country nearing the debt limit, they had leverage.

They discussed how to reframe the negotiation.

No matter how much time you spend on the phone explaining what the talks were really about, Jackson said, you're losing that fight. The story has broken out and gone viral. You can't talk to everybody.

Boehner needed time to focus the debate for the House Republicans—to get them to understand that the talks were taking place in the context of his demand for real, measurable spending cuts and tax reforms.

It was time to make a tactical retreat to advance his strategic interests, Boehner and Jackson agreed, to get out from under the "tax" definition forced on the debate by the rush of media coverage.

Boehner called the president.

The big deal isn't going to come together, the speaker said. I don't want you to walk into that meeting tomorrow thinking that it is. I'll be at the meeting, he added, but I think we're going to have to find some other way to get this done. The gap between us is too great.

Boehner said House Republicans needed to start looking for a Plan B, and would start a second set of negotiations in Congress.

Disappointed, the president tried to talk Boehner out of it. "I still want to make this pitch. I still think we can get there." He was going to present the big deal as a possibility anyway.

In an interview, the president recalled that he had been feeling "fairly optimistic" about reaching a deal. He had gone to Camp David for part of the weekend, which was where Boehner reached him.

"He calls me and says, you know what? I'm going to have to walk away from this right now. And to his credit, he said, I'm not closing the door to ever doing anything on this, but right now, I've just got to pull away from the negotiations. And I spent probably half an hour to 45 minutes trying to persuade him not to leave the negotiations.

"I said, you know what? The country is anxious and it is scared. And we'd just gone through the worst financial crisis since the Great Depression. And if you and I announced a deal, I think that the public would overwhelmingly support it. And despite resistance from both your caucus as well as the Democrats on Capitol Hill, we would win over the American people. Because it would be stark evidence that government can still solve big problems. So my basic pitch was—and I continue to believe this—that if he and I walked out together and said, we have arrived at a deal that is going to reduce our deficit, reduce our debt in a balanced, fair way, that overwhelmingly we could have won the support of the American people."

Speaking to others in the White House, Obama had wondered if the pullout was just another symptom of Boehner's inability to control the Republican conference. Boehner had realized that doing a deal with Obama would put his speakership in jeopardy, and didn't want to take the risk.

Nabors, wearing shorts and sneakers, was out enjoying the beautiful summer day when his phone rang.

"We're going to go public," Barry Jackson said. "We can't accept the offer. We're pulling out."

"What?" Nabors said. "But I sent you a piece of paper. And we haven't heard back from you on the piece of paper."

They had just exchanged one set of overall offers and another set of tax principles.

It was the decision, Jackson said. "Necessity."

Nabors called the White House and gave Daley the news. Daley ordered the senior staff called back in.

Gene Sperling's BlackBerry was ringing, but the NEC chairman, playing tennis, couldn't hear it.

Eventually, he looked over at the phone and saw there was a message from the White House. Everyone come back, it said. The tone suggested big news—almost an Osama-bin-Laden-is-dead kind of urgency. Get to the chief of staff's office at once.

Whoa, thought Sperling, immediately starting to rush back. He phoned the White House at once. "What's this about?"

Boehner's threatening to pull out.

Oh man, Sperling thought, this thing is accelerating! A threat was a good, even necessary, sign. They were going to cut a deal. It was going to happen. A veteran of the budget, tax and deficit negotiations during the Clinton years, Sperling knew a threat to walk generally preceded serious negotiations. It meant: Time to put your real cards on the table. He was excited as he raced back to the White House.

By the time Sperling arrived in Daley's office, Nabors was handing out a single sheet of paper with Boehner's statement:

"Despite good-faith efforts to find common ground, the White House will not pursue a bigger debt reduction agreement without tax hikes. I believe the best approach may be to focus on producing a smaller measure, based on the cuts identified in the Biden-led negotiations, that still meets our call for spending reforms and cuts greater than the amount of any debt limit increase."

What's this? Sperling asked. Is this what they say they're going to put out? The threat? Clever making it sound so final.

They've put this out, Nabors said.

"What do you mean they put it out?" Sperling demanded. "It's already to the press?"

Yes and yes. The wire services had picked it up a little after 4:30 p.m.

Sperling was stunned. It's just over? An exchange of paper and no call, no contact, not even a word or a hint about how to get to a deal?

Was it possible that *The Wall Street Journal* had such influence? Was the Boehner-Cantor tension so great that the speaker could not construct a graceful, face-saving exit? Was it so tense that Boehner could not even be seen as negotiating? Or was it that they didn't have Grover Norquist on board? What was clear was that Boehner had just got blown up. If someone doesn't come back to the table, they don't want a yes in any form.

Sperling was baffled. Hundreds of years of the history of negotiations suggested, strongly, that this is not the way you do it. There is discussion, an offer, then a counteroffer, and so forth, round after round. How could you ever get to closing with these people if they wouldn't even talk? If Boehner wasn't willing to come back to the table, it meant he didn't want to hear. God, Sperling said, I sure wouldn't want to date these people.

Or maybe Boehner knew it was going to blow up in his face, Sperling thought, and he was going back to build support. Where? How? Was it because Boehner seemed to be willing to play with this idea of decoupling the Bush tax cuts, letting them all expire and then only voting for a continuation for the lower brackets? Or had they misread that? Obama still clung to the idea that Boehner and the Republicans could then technically say they hadn't raised taxes. They could say they had not done anything but cut taxes again for the middle- and lower-income taxpayers.

What the fuck? Sperling said.

The president's estimated 25 percent chance of a deal with Boehner now appeared to be zero.

Lew saw it differently. The Boehner offer of $788 or $800 billion was their limit. It was the most they could do and still go back and say "We're not raising a dollar of new taxes," he told a White House colleague. "And they had to be able to say that."

The Boehner announcement of a pullout was a bit abrupt, Lew conceded. However, he said, "I viewed it through the lens of, what does this tell you about where the House Republicans are? And not necessarily where the policy is."

Later Sperling questioned Jackson. "Barry, someday when this is over, you're going to have to explain to me how a negotiation is: Someone gives their first offer, the other side gives their first offer, and you end it with no discussion?"

"It's not over yet!" Jackson said loudly, wagging his finger.

Jackson knew Boehner's view was simple: They had no choice but to succeed. "We will not default," Boehner had said time and time again, both publicly and privately. But they would falter if the debate was about tax increases. The speaker had to shift the debate to the more abstract issue of tax reform. But how, in the cauldron of the moment?

Boehner's announcement had caused a separate but related set of headaches for Nabors. The speaker had publicly announced the end of talks that the White House had never publicly acknowledged in the first place.

It wasn't long after Boehner's press release that Nabors's Black-Berry began lighting up with calls from angry Democrats in Congress.

"What talks?" they wanted to know.

In an interview later, Boehner described his decision to withdraw from discussion of the big deal as a sort of strategic deception.

"I was trying to push the president," he said. "I always believed that the big deal was the only way to get there and I still wanted the big deal. But I was trying to make him understand, hey, this isn't working, and try to rattle him a little bit into getting serious."

Boehner said he was concerned that they were running out of time to act.

"It's July. I know how long it takes to move a bill and to write a bill," he said. "This stuff doesn't happen overnight. But they don't have a clue. He doesn't have a clue and his staff doesn't have a clue."

Boehner said the upshot of his conversation with Obama was that "he understood he'd better get serious. I think I'd succeeded in what I was trying to accomplish."

Asked about Boehner's explanation for pulling out, Obama said in an interview, "At this stage, I know what my bottom lines are. So I'm not rattled, and I'm never overly optimistic. I just want to solve the problem. So what I say to him is, John, we'll keep on talking. And let's see if we can still get something done. Either way, we're going to have to resolve this debt ceiling situation."

After speaking with Boehner, he said, "I'm disappointed, because my feeling is we've missed an opportunity to resolve this in a way that would have as much upside in the markets and for the economy and world confidence as we ended up having on the downside when it didn't, when things almost came to the brink."

# 21

Obama was being subjected, dramatically, to the long, torturous ways of budget negotiations and Washington deal making. There is nothing quite like it. But he also saw his particular responsibilities as president constraining his ability to bargain.

"We have to acknowledge we're governing," he told his inner circle. "It's like King Solomon. We just have to accept we're the mom who's not willing to split the baby in half. And we're not going to have as much leverage."

To Jack Lew, the president's analogy was crucial to understanding Obama's position in the debt limit battle. Obama was saying that, as president, he had to be able to go out into the world and explain what he was doing with the U.S. economy. Unlike some in Congress, he couldn't pretend that default was an option.

Obama was admitting that he was constrained. He would have to take a worse deal than he would normally accept. The Republicans knew it, and they knew he knew that they knew it. This gave them extraordinary power. So they were pushing their agenda to its outer limits.

The question remained, just how bad a deal was the president willing to consider? And how much could he allow Republicans to push before defections from the Democratic side scuttled any chance of a deal?

And there was a broader problem, the president had warned them. It was quite possible that some would be willing, consciously or unconsciously, to drive the car off the cliff. There were Democrats who would rather have the political fight than get a deal.

Too many were focusing on who was winning the political exchange of the moment. Yes, Obama said, he would get support for the deal from the business community, the media and the opinion pages. But was that enough? Even at great political cost, he was going to have to be responsible, be the adult.

There was the chance that the economy would go under. If that happened, it would be on his head. The Republicans would bear some responsibility, but the headlines and the history books would record unambiguously that the economy sank during the Obama presidency.

Plouffe had been sitting in on the pre-briefs. There was no more important business. He agreed with the president's constant assertion, "We can't default."

"By stipulating to that," Plouffe said, "you've lost an enormous amount of leverage." He was worried that the economy was beginning to deteriorate significantly. It couldn't take much more of a beating. If there was a default, it could take not weeks or months, but years to recover from it. And it would sink Obama's reelection.

If I get criticized by Democrats, Obama said, for taking a deal I can defend on policy and substance, I'll have to take it.

Senior staff were painfully aware that the Democrats in Congress had caught the scent of some kind of political victory. Nabors would often hear it: Just let the thing default, and we blame the Republicans.

"We're actually running this country," Nabors argued back. "We're not going to run it into the ground. We have a Constitutional responsibility to solve this problem."

•    •    •

In an interview, Obama later recalled using the King Solomon analogy.

"That's true. There's no doubt that the challenge we had here was ultimately I and Tim Geithner were responsible for averting another financial meltdown, two years after we'd just had a financial meltdown. And so my interest in not playing chicken, or seeing any miscalculation here that leads to a default, was profound.

"And there's one other context to all that, though. By the time you read this quote—by the time I said those words—what's already becoming apparent is that this new House is not feeling a similar sense of urgency. And you have very prominent members of the House Republicans who are not only prepared to see default, but in some cases are welcoming the prospects of default. Think it would be a good thing, that it would be a tonic to shock the system. So I'm already at this point getting concerned that Boehner may miscalculate and not be able to deliver on his caucus even if we end up striking a deal. And as a consequence, throughout these discussions, I am very concerned about not making Boehner look weak. And I'm understanding of the fact that he, every time he goes into his caucus, has to throw them a bone. And they can't see this as a victory for me.

"Which raises one other problem, and that is that there were very prominent Republicans in the caucus who told me—to my face—that the view in the caucus was that getting a deal with me would ensure my reelection.

"Very reliable and prominent Republicans say to me, the view among many in our caucus is if we give you a deal, you have taken a major issue away from us. You are seen as the bipartisan leader, and you are a lock for reelection."

So inside the White House it was generally understood that you were negotiating with Republicans from a position of weakness?

"True," Obama said. "Now, keep in mind, I never said this to them."


In a near-crisis atmosphere, Obama summoned congressional leaders to the White House at 6:10 p.m., Sunday, July 10, 2011.

The feeling in the White House was that Cantor was perhaps the single biggest stumbling block between them and a deal.

"Cantor needs to be in the room," the president told his senior staff. "I want to look everyone in the eye."

But if Cantor was in the room, then Hoyer, the minority whip, needed to be there, too. And if Hoyer and Cantor had to be in the room, then so did the Senate whips, Durbin and Kyl.

So it was an unwieldy eight who gathered in the Cabinet Room with three weeks to raise the debt ceiling or face the unthinkable prospect of a debt default.

"We talked about options," the president began soberly. "We need to talk about what we should do. We need to talk about if there are other alternatives. I asked you if there were other alternatives." They were practically starting from scratch. He seemed to be groping for a solution, even something unconventional or against the grain. They had a lot to do. "I want to talk about the process for the week and how we're going to get through this."

He said he still hoped for the "big deal" of some $4 trillion in deficit reduction. All the leaders in the room had said they were for the "big deal," except Cantor and Kyl.

On the agenda, Obama said, were "changes in Medicare, Medicaid, potentially Social Security. We would keep the structure of these programs, but bend the cost curve."

The House Republicans wanted an overhaul: to change the structure and concept of these entitlement programs. It was a profound difference.

The president continued, "A commitment to work for middle-class tax cut extension, tax reform by a date certain that would capture the revenue necessary to meet whatever target we set as part of the tax reform exercise. Discretionary cuts of a significant amount, such as those that the vice president's been talking about in his discussions. This would achieve a sustainable deficit and debt, even with CBO's numbers."

He maintained that this would leave them with an annual deficit of only 3 percent of the Gross Domestic Product in the out-years, compared to the current 10 percent.

"If the goal is to solve the problem," Obama said, "I don't understand why we don't seize the opportunity. It would not violate either party's positions. Revenues wouldn't come from a vote. I understand this pledge that all these Republicans have taken."

The Republicans thought he really didn't understand at all. The scheme to decouple the middle- and lower-income tax brackets from the higher brackets was a transparent gimmick.

Obama said he had Speaker Boehner's statement. "I understand Eric and John anticipate this couldn't be done. But I told John, 'If not now, when?' Then let's admit that we're more into playing politics. And maybe I overstated what the traffic will bear. We need to get this through this year. It's unacceptable to do this every three months. We are not going to do this again."

Biden jumped in. They all knew that the big deal was the way to go, he said. "We're not going to become a banana republic. So what is it going to be? Or are we going to live or die on the election?"

"Everyone is being well meaning," Boehner said. "We've been in sincere discussions for weeks, but as I said, the cuts have to exceed the debt limit increase. There is more than one challenge to the big deal. My only concern isn't just the revenue increase. This could be impossible to draft, as far as my people understand, in terms of the time line of getting this done. And since this has to pass, given the time frame we have, simpler could be better. There might not be enough time for a big deal at this point." The Biden group's framework is our most viable option, he concluded.

Reid proposed they consider a procedure similar to that used to deal with the complex and politically charged problem of closing military bases around the country. In the Base Realignment and Closure (BRAC) process, Congress had to vote to close all or none of the bases selected by a panel of outside experts; the legislation could not be amended. The process was more or less working, though he noted some key Republicans had voted against some closures.

Warming to the topic of what he considered Republican intransigence, Reid said, "We had Bowles-Simpson. The Republicans walked out."

They hadn't walked out. Three of the Republican lawmakers on the panel had voted against it, but so had three of the Democrats. And the president had never embraced or adopted it.

"Then we had the Biden commission," Reid said. "We had another walkout," referring to Cantor and Kyl's exit from the talks the previous month.

Biden knew it was not a walkout. Given the circumstances of the speaker's end run, Cantor had handled the matter straightforwardly, and been a gentleman, Biden thought, but he didn't say anything.

"Then there were talks between Boehner and the president, and there was another walkout. Republicans can't deliver the big deal," Reid said caustically. "They're jeopardizing the future of the country. If Republicans send something at the last minute, a three-month deal, we're not going to do it."

"Thursday," Pelosi said, "the speaker said a bargain was possible. Now he says we don't have time. Democrats won't vote for anything that the president won't sign."

She turned to Boehner. "Do you have the votes to do it on your own?" Wouldn't he need some Democrats?

Boehner didn't answer. Votes were a touchy subject for the speaker, and everyone knew it.

McConnell wanted to work something out. "Let's see if we can build a deal on what the Biden group did that passes the smell test." He mentioned a cap on general spending for fiscal years 2012 and 2013. But then he added unhappily, "There's just no time to put together the big deal."

"All of us want to get to 218," Cantor said, ever the vote counter. The Republicans had a majority of 240 seats. He praised the spirit of the Biden group and how collegially they had worked together. He said he agreed with McConnell that, "We have the blueprint that we can build upon. We can exceed the amount that we raised the debt limit. We wouldn't have to raise taxes, and then frankly we could focus on jobs." He disagreed with the Senate leaders on timing. "And we could do it in the next couple weeks."

Cantor also said he could not accept the president's notion of letting the tax cuts expire and then reinstating them for the lower brackets. "You're asking us to fundamentally breach our position on the tax issues. That's where the difference is. For us, a vote to decouple with no guarantee is breaching our position." The big issues, such as taxes, might have to be left for the 2012 election.

Durbin, the affable Illinois Democrat who was second to Reid in the party leadership, threw some cold water. There was "no indication that the Biden plan could pass the Senate," he said. "Any indication otherwise is misguided. With no revenue, it can't pass."

"Eric," said Steny Hoyer, "I disagree with you. The oxygen will be taken out of it if we don't lead." To Boehner, he added, "John, I want to thank you for your leadership you've shown, and you've taken some flak for it."

Kyl tried to focus on the big numbers. "We're not talking about short-term solutions," he said. "Mitch McConnell's talking about entitlement reform. That's not a short-term solution. The vice president is saying entitlement requires tax changes now, but let's be clear: Social Security, which people are now discussing, was never discussed in the Biden group. The biggest change we talked about in the Biden group was means testing for those who are already means tested." That meant only seniors who were well off would see reduced payments.

"So here's the big question," Kyl said. "Are you saying even with Biden you have to have revenue?"

Biden responded, We're going to have to agree not to agree on estate tax or rates. We've had these discussions, but we didn't agree. We can get to $200 billion in revenue.

He seemed to be accepting Cantor's insistence on revenue neutrality.

Cantor reinforced Biden. "I said yes we can do something on loopholes, but it has to be revenue neutral. If you need to do something on billionaires and corporate jets, etc., for $3 billion, then fine. Let's just find an offset, use it for some further tax relief."

So the discussion had gone from Boehner's $1 trillion, through tax reform, to Cantor's $3 billion. To anyone paying attention, there was no progress, and the rift between the speaker and his majority leader was plain to see.

"Listen," the president said, "we're going to go back at it tomorrow, day after day, until we get it done. I'm not persuaded by the argument of time. The work has got to be done by someone, somewhere. Let's come up with a term sheet tomorrow. Eric, you've quoted back to me about the next election. I'm appreciative of that. But keep in mind the debt limit was not my choosing."

The Republicans were leveraging him. Addressing Boehner, he continued, "You said the biggest problem is spending and the deficit. So I am taking you at your word."

Then, looking squarely at Cantor, Obama said, "You refuse to talk about revenues. If the notion is that you're going to pocket the stuff you negotiated in Biden and set aside the stuff you have heartburn over, then that's probably not going to work. I'm not going to be under illusions that the Biden package, that everyone agrees to it. Because that only seems to have the stuff you like in it."

"I want to make clear," Kyl interjected, "to us, we look at that and we think there is revenue from these fees and other things of about $150 billion. And 60 percent of the health care savings comes from providers, not from beneficiaries. We believe that's a real compromise." The Republicans wanted health care savings to be replaced by increased co-payments from the beneficiaries, not cuts to providers, so business would not take the hit.

Addressing Kyl, Obama said, "Jon, hold on. The point I'm making is you guys got 70 percent of where we need to go, but nothing was agreed to till everything was agreed to." Referring to the Biden group, he said, "You did not have a full package. It can start unraveling. The work has not been completed on balancing it out. If we have to do dollar for dollar, then without revenue, entitlements or OCO [Overseas Contingency Operations—funding for the wars in Afghanistan and Iraq], then that will be hard. Something has got to give. Eric, you said people want to talk jobs. But you said the fiscal situation is the most important thing to do. We weren't asking you to vote on a tax hike. We would've voted on maintaining the tax rates for 95 percent. You wouldn't have had to take a vote. There has to be some give from you guys."

The president was still pushing for decoupling. Boehner, Cantor and the other Republicans couldn't believe it. Even the White House staffers realized that the president still saw it as his sword.

Cantor rebutted at length. "Our meetings in the Biden group were productive," Cantor said sharply, defending himself, Biden and the others. "We could get to $2 to $2.3 trillion," he said, referring to the $1.1 trillion in general spending cuts, $500 billion to $600 billion in entitlement and other cuts, plus $300 billion in interest and perhaps even some revenue. "We still have to work on caps and the control-type mechanisms. This is a viable option. What other choice do we have? You believe in more taxes. The vice president did say consistently that nothing was agreed to till everything was agreed to. We can talk all day long about who was right and who was wrong, but the bottom line is we have a blueprint in place we could use to build off of to get a deal."

The White House team saw clearly that Cantor did not want to be responsible for scuttling a deal.

Biden turned to Boehner. "John, I believe you wanted a big deal, but you don't have the votes. Absent revenues from Medicare and Medicaid, you can't get something for dollar for dollar that can pass." In addition to the $1.1 trillion in general spending caps, he said, here's where we are: If we can get over $200 billion in revenues, then we'll do $200 billion and Medicare and Medicaid. If $300 billion, then $300 billion. At the very end, though, if we can't do that, we refrain from leading here."

"The big deal doesn't look so good now," said Reid, undermining the president. He was upset that they were not counting the $1 trillion that the independent Congressional Budget Office counted for OCO. "Here's what I resent: OCO is now apparently a piece of shit."

"We always said we would do revenue neutrality," said Cantor. "So don't say we wouldn't do revenues; we always said we'd do revenue neutrality."

"Can we just go through the numbers?" Pelosi asked impatiently.

Cantor said $260 billion to $350 billion was available in health care savings.

"There's no agreement on that," Lew said.

"The whole package, revenue and offsets, then," Biden replied, reaching very high, underscoring the necessity of revenue, "slightly over $2 trillion."

"I want paper tomorrow," Obama said. He wanted it spelled out in writing. What was real?

Lew joined Biden in pushing on revenue. "I can't get to more than $2 trillion if you're insisting on revenue neutrality," he said. "We have to have the revenues to get to $2 trillion. And that's even at the outer limit. $2 trillion is aggressive."

"Okay," Obama said, "well, $2 trillion. What happens after that in the second 10 years?"

He knew the answer. He had seen the charts with the trend lines. But Lew answered, "That's $2 trillion for 10 years. Then what happens is the deficit path trends back up."

There was a sickening silence. This was the elephant in the room. They were not addressing the long-term problem.

"I believe the larger deal still is achievable and preferable and is the right thing to do," the president said. "In the meantime, I will listen to the ideas about a smaller deal. $2 trillion, it's a lot of pain, it's tough votes, and we have not solved the problem. We're going to reconvene for an hour or two tomorrow. We'll walk through what we are talking about. We should all be explicit. The speaker has always said it's easier to do a big deal. In the meantime, I don't want anyone trying to move legislation to make points."

Reid said he wanted to bring a couple of other members of Congress to the meetings.

"If we do . . ." Obama replied, his voice trailing off. "No," he added politely, "we're not going to expand. Then everyone else is going to bring their people." They would then have to move to a bigger room, he added.

"If we have to offset the revenue," Biden summed up, "then we can't get above $2 trillion."

With $2 trillion in cuts, they could add an equivalent amount to the debt ceiling. "How long would $2 trillion get us?" Obama asked.

Geithner said, "$2.4 trillion would get us to February of 2013. $2.1 trillion debt limit increase would get us to December of 2012." That would be a month after the election.

If they didn't get to that $2 trillion, they could be bumping up against the debt ceiling before the election, requiring another night-mare negotiation at the worst possible political moment.

Afterward, Reid approached Cantor. "I don't know you that well," the Senate majority leader said to the House majority leader. "I appreciate your honesty."

They didn't agree but, perhaps meaning other than himself, Reid said, "You were the one person in the room who said what you actually thought."


In Boehner's office, his staff couldn't believe the president's demand that congressional leaders meet daily at the White House until an agreement was forged.

Boehner had already concluded that the whole thing was a point-less dog-and-pony show. Was the president really naive enough to think that he could get all those members in a room and come to an agreement on a deal? That never happened.

Just the fact that Obama thought this might be productive was a sign to Boehner's people that the president simply didn't understand how Congress worked and didn't know how to negotiate. Boehner said he hated going down to the White House to listen to what amounted to presidential lectures.

In McConnell's office, the feeling was the same. Rohit Kumar, the minority leader's top policy adviser, thought the White House meet-ings showed that the White House didn't understand how legislative deals were made.

These agreements aren't struck by the president and congressional leaders meeting face-to-face, Kumar said. They were done by people like him. You have guidance from the leaders. You have principles you have to adhere to. You're given a set of red lines you can't cross.

Watching his staff prepare for a series of White House meetings frustrated Kumar. It was a waste of a dwindling resource: time.

# 22

During the eight years he spent working in the Bush White House, Barry Jackson believed he had developed understanding and respect for the office of the presidency.

"You do not be disrespectful of the office of the president," he told the staff in Boehner's office. "You just don't. It's the worst job in the world. They don't need people kicking them in the shins for the heck of it."

But in the speaker's office, respect for the office didn't extend to the man who occupied it.

Jackson believed that Obama lacked courage, was a poor negotiator, and was completely out of his element in dealing with Congress.

When Boehner returned from some of his first private meetings with Obama, he and Jackson discussed what they saw as the president's psychological motivations.

In one discussion of entitlement reforms, Boehner reported that Obama said, "John, I make $2 million. You can't expect me to ask somebody to take a cut in their benefits if I'm not willing to take a cut."

It's almost like he's ashamed that he's been blessed and he's made money, they concluded. It's as if he's guilty of his success.

"Oh, my God," they imagined the president saying, "I'm so embarrassed that I've done well, and I need to make sure that I do my self-flagellation."

On top of that, Boehner felt that the White House underestimated him. He had negotiated No Child Left Behind with Ted Kennedy in 2001. He negotiated the Pension Protection Act of 2006. He was a guy who knew how to do big deals and how to work with Democrats.

The White House didn't respect him. They dismissed him.

At 11:15 a.m. on July 11, the president appeared in the White House Briefing Room for a long press conference to explain what was going on with the negotiations. It was classic Obama. You had to listen very carefully and read the transcript several times to spot the inconsistencies.

"The things I will not consider are a 30-day or a 60-day or a 90-day or a 180-day temporary stopgap resolution of the problem," he said. He would not bend. But later he said the problem was the inflexibility of the Republicans. "I do not see a path to a deal if they don't budge, period. I mean, if the basic proposition is, 'It's my way or the highway,' then we're probably not going to get something done."

Later, the president issued his equivalent of a "my way or the highway" declaration. "I will not accept a deal in which I am asked to do nothing. In fact, I'm able to keep hundreds of thousands of dollars in additional income that I don't need, while a parent out there who is struggling to send their kid to college suddenly finds that they've got a couple thousand dollars less in grants or student loans."

At the end he temporized, "So this is not a right or left, conservative/liberal situation."

But everyone knew that was precisely what it was, try as the president might to smooth the edges of the partisan divide.

Later that morning at the Capitol, Boehner held a press conference in response, saying, "The American people will not accept—and the House cannot pass—a bill that raises taxes on job creators." He reiterated his requirement that any agreement include spending cuts larger than the increase in the debt limit.

"This is the message we will take, again, to the White House today, and hope that we can work our way through this."


"We're going to start by hearing from the Republicans on a possible trimmed-down version, kind of the medium-sized deal," Obama began that day's meeting in the Cabinet Room. "I'm in listen mode."

Cantor handed out copies of a six-page PowerPoint presentation.

The Republican majority leader claimed there was agreement on some $233 billion in cuts to various programs such as federal civilian retirement plans ($36 billion), military retirement plans ($11 billion), postal reform ($11 to $26 billion). Attacking waste and fraud could save up to $40 billion and reducing agricultural subsidies could net $31 billion. Various other cuts or savings, such as requiring increased co-payments for the retired military personnel covered by the TRICARE health care plan, would save $17 billion.

There was at least another $30 billion in higher education and food stamp cuts. They were highlighted in yellow on his PowerPoint because the Democrats had not agreed, he said.

"Well," Obama said, "my ranges are a bit different. When we look at civilian retirement and military, you have bigger ranges. Some say that should be more like $10 billion, not $36 billion. Let's set aside higher education and food stamps. If we do that, then the range is more like $200 to $280 or $290." It looked like a good start, but not bold. "So I look at this and say we could pocket around $200 billion without much controversy."

Lew mentioned undergraduate student loans, higher education and undergraduate food stamps.

"Maybe there's something in there we could do," Obama said.

On the food stamp program, Cantor said, "High error rates have been associated with the program. Since the feds fund the program but the states administer it, there's not a lot of incentive to control for errors." So policies and reforms could be put in place to yield some significant savings.

Durbin thought Cantor was being hypocritical. The only fraud Cantor saw involved poor people. But when he spoke, Durbin tempered his language, simply reminding Cantor that plenty of fraud existed in other programs too. He specifically noted "gross abuse" in federal payments to for-profit schools.

On food stamps, Obama said if there was error, "then let's go after it. If it makes it more complicated to get into the system, then I'm opposed to it.

"So on military and civilian retirement," he continued, "it looks like there's a wide separation. We would propose some additional savings out of aviation [fees] and program integrity that's higher than what you said."

Lew noted that the administration anticipated getting no more than $2 billion out of food stamp error rates. The Republicans saw 10 times that, up to $20 billion, but that included some $4 billion from duplicative job training programs.

On job training, Lew said, "I'm a proponent of consolidation . . . so I'm happy to have that conversation."


In Cantor's health care slides, the depth of the division was evident. There was roughly $17 billion in agreement on a dozen small-scale Medicare and Medicaid cuts, plus supposed agreement on $50 billion in savings from home health care and skilled nursing facilities payments. He identified another $38 billion in savings, but according to his deal, these would not happen until after 2019—eight years hence. The two sides disagreed on more than $208 billion in health care cuts.

Cantor had taken about 10 minutes. To experienced hands, it sounded increasingly like a congressional subcommittee debate.

"It's a reasonably fair presentation," the president said in response. "There are some ranges in dispute, particularly home health. We're more like 30 and you have 50. On [Medicare] bad debt, there's no philosophical objection here, but we have a difference in ranges. On beneficiaries, we have a difference."

Biden said the savings on Medicaid might only be $50 billion instead of the $100 billion on Cantor's chart. Some of the other numbers were also too high. "So we look at this as that we're closer to $200 billion" than to Cantor's $334 billion.

"Listen," Cantor said, "this is a package that can get 218 votes."

"Well," Hoyer declared, "you're not going to get any votes on our side without revenue."

Pelosi echoed Hoyer. "This is really hard to sell without revenue."

"Time is of the essence," Reid said. "I feel like we're talking past each other. Let's face it, the Republicans won't agree to the grand deal. The Democrats in the Senate won't do this middle-of-the-road with Medicare and Medicaid, so the middle deal is gone. Then the only option is some small package."

It was an accurate, if bleak, summation of where they were.

"Hold on!" Obama insisted, putting the brakes on Reid. "Let's just complete this exercise."

Reid was unrepentant. "We can do something for two years," he replied. "We'll create a commission. Equal Republicans and Democrats. Only members of Congress." The committee would present a deficit reduction package and both the House and Senate would give the unamended package an up or down vote.

Cantor noted that the House-passed budget saved $1.7 trillion in general spending and the administration had proposed saving $813 billion on domestic and Defense. Splitting the difference would be a total savings over 10 years of $1.2 trillion. "We had talked about $1.1 in the Biden. We can clearly get to $1.2, $1.3."

"Partially correct," Durbin said, "but we have to have equal cuts to security and nonsecurity." This was the firewall.

"We never agreed to firewalls," said Cantor. Republicans did not want equal cuts to come from Defense spending.

"In the absence of firewalls," Obama said, "we wouldn't even agree to $1 trillion."

"The Appropriations Committee is the place for these discussions to choose between Defense and non-Defense," Cantor said, "security and nonsecurity."

"If we did that," the president said, "we'd have a shutdown on every bill. We'd end up playing three-dimensional chess. Discretionary [general spending] is the least of our problems. We can have that debate later."

Boehner seemed to agree. Simply put, the White House and the Democrats were going to be able to sell a deal to their rank and file because of Defense cuts. Republicans would sell the same deal on non-Defense cuts. "Any kind of firewall creates problems on both sides," Boehner said. "Why are we creating problems for ourselves today?" In other words, they could fight it out later.

McConnell urged them to "lock down numbers" for the next two fiscal years.

Lew said they had to address the short-funding of the Pell college grants, a Democratic and Obama favorite aimed at assisting college students, because the annual cost was now more than $20 billion.

"Eric," Obama chided, "it looks like there's a page missing: revenue."

"If you feel you need revenue," Cantor replied, "then just offset it somewhere else."

"How about the payroll tax cut as an offset?" Obama said enticingly. "You don't have to answer that now." In his secret offer five days earlier, Boehner had proposed extending it another year. The payroll tax cut was popular with both Republicans and Democrats. It reduced taxes for all workers. The only problem was that it added to the deficit.

"Let me do some rough math here," the president said. "If you take health care mandatories that don't fall on the beneficiary, with the possible exception of means testing—which Pelosi and Reid have said they will oppose—plus other mandatory, plus discretionary, you're at $1.4 to $1.5 trillion. I warned you about this. But maybe I wasn't explicitly clear. You came in on the high end and presupposed the high end on all your numbers. So I'm going to take the lower end. I want you to listen to me."

Obama totaled up to "a little under a trillion," and saw how they could get to $1.7 trillion with interest savings and the $1 trillion general spending cap. In budgeting, CBO allowed them to count interest that would be saved by not having the debt. Interest savings generally were calculated to be 20 percent of the debt savings. "If no revenue, then you can't get to" $2.4 trillion. "I don't know how you're going to do it without going to revenue. That's the reason why the big deal is better."

Obama went on. They might need $2.7 trillion in the debt ceiling to take them beyond the next year, the election year. Since the speaker insisted on at least equivalent cuts, dollar for dollar, they were not going to get there. "Either we're going to do less than $2.4, $2.5 trillion in cuts, so we're not doing dollar for dollar, or we're going to go back to the big deal. But this isn't just about politics. Imagine doing this in the middle of a presidential race?" He added, "So I want you all to go back to your caucuses and figure this out. We can probably get to $1.7 or $1.8 when you include interest, but that's as high as we're going to get."

Obama, the precise technocrat, returned to his talking point. "Why aren't we asking more of the people who are making the most?"

"We ought to be clear that spending is the big problem," Boehner said. "Even if we wanted to, we couldn't take it all from the rich. No one here is jumping to cut Medicare."

"You already did," Obama replied, referring to the House Ryan budget.

"Excuse us for leading!" the speaker snapped.

"I didn't intend to get us started on a debate on taxes," said Obama, who had opened the subject. "What I'm saying is we're at $1.7, maybe $1.8. We still have to resolve the firewall, the Doc Fix and Pell. We agreed to a trillion [on discretionary] but that's about all the traffic will bear."

Looking ahead to the next day's meeting, he said, "We need to go back and figure this out. Everyone needs to give me specific ideas on how to move forward."

"We're nowhere near agreement here," Reid said. "I think we need to do a commission with an expedited approval process."

Addressing the Republicans, Biden said, "You keep saying it's possible to do revenue if neutral." How was Pelosi, he asked, supposed to do that with her Democrats?

Ignoring the question, Cantor replied, "We've got to get through this and start talking about jobs."

"If we're cutting spending," Obama said, "that doesn't have anything to do with jobs. We lost half a million jobs in the public sector, and if we hadn't put the [stimulus] money in, unemployment would be higher." Instead of being 9.2 percent we'd be half a percent higher, he maintained. "We can have the macroeconomic debate at some other point," he said, postponing discussion over whether the stimulus money had worked to boost the economy.*

"What is fair?" Biden asked. They could get at least $100 billion from the wealthy with tax increases. "No economist will say that will impact jobs. So what you guys have here is a political problem. Harry's saying he can't get this deal done."

"Give me something," Reid pleaded. "Give me $250 billion in revenue."

Oh, no, the speaker said, "We've seen that before. The tax increases are immediate and the cuts never happen."

Pelosi said, "You've made a real commitment here to be the president, Mr. President," to lead and do the negotiations yourself. In the Bush administration, during the financial crisis and bailout at the end of 2008, Bush had been much less involved. "The White House wouldn't even let me call the president," Pelosi said. "I mean, I love President Bush," she said. "I actually sent him flowers for his birthday, and I called him and I thanked him" after Osama bin Laden was killed. To Obama, she said, "But you, Mr. President, you listen to all sides."

"I only get to $803 billion," said Hoyer, after making some calculations.

"Listen," Obama said, "we haven't agreed to anything."

---

* In February 2012 the University of Chicago surveyed a range of 40 prominent economists and 80 percent agreed with Obama that the stimulus had helped the economy, while only 4 percent disagreed.

"Well," Hoyer said, "I certainly haven't agreed on $1.7."

"I was only speaking for myself," the president replied.

"We're no closer to an agreement," McConnell summarized.

That evening by 8:30, *Politico* had an article on its website headlined "Cantor Ascends as GOP Voice."

The debt limit talks with Obama had placed Cantor in the spotlight, center stage, as he made the Republican presentation, the article said. "Cantor has gracefully positioned himself as a guardian of the conservative line while Boehner worked to find the kind of shared-sacrifice deal Obama wants."

# 23

The next morning, July 12, Boehner spoke with reporters. Wearing a gray suit and an eye-catching lime green tie, he publicly stuck his finger in Obama's eye.

"Republicans have a plan," he said. "We passed our budget back in the spring, outlined our priorities. Where's the president's plan? When's he going to lay his cards on the table? *The debt limit increase is his problem.*" He reiterated his position—spending cuts larger than the increase in the debt ceiling, no tax increases, and real control on future spending.

Noting that he had been in conversations and meetings with the president, Boehner said, "The president talks a good game, but when it comes time to actually putting these issues on the table, making decisions, he can't quite pull the trigger."

McConnell pulled no punches on the Senate floor that afternoon, declaring the president guilty of "deliberate deception" by taking what should be a deficit and spending debate and now insisting on more taxes.

Sounding as though he was suggesting a coup, McConnell praised Biden as "a man I've come to respect as a straight-shooting negotiator." But, he said, as long as Obama remained president, "a real solution is unattainable."

• • •

That afternoon, CBS News released excerpts of an interview with Obama that would be aired on the evening news.

In response to a question about what would happen to Social Security benefits if Republicans and Democrats could not come to a deal on the debt limit increase, the president said, "I cannot guarantee that those checks go out on August 3rd if we haven't resolved this issue, because there may simply not be the money in the coffers to do it."

Asked about his relationship with the speaker, the president said he liked Boehner personally. "I think John would like to do the right thing."

Did he trust Boehner?

"I do trust that when John tells me something, he means it. I think that his challenge right now is inside his caucus."

The president criticized Congress for delaying action on the debt limit and other matters until conditions reached a crisis.

He was asked for his reaction to McConnell's statement that no deal was possible while he remained in the White House.

"Well, then he's going to have to explain to me how it is that we're going to avoid default, because I'm going to be president for at least another year and a half. And I don't think the American people would expect that the leader of the Republican Party in the Senate would simply say that we're not going to do business with the president of the United States."

At 3:55 that afternoon, the president convened the closed-door meeting at the White House with the congressional leaders. "John," Obama began, "you said this is my problem. I would be happy for it to be my problem if I didn't need votes in the House and Senate. As this concerns all of us, we all have a problem. I continue to believe that we ought to be able to do, we ought to take the approach of doing something big. Raising dollar for dollar to deficit reduction is a constraint.

This is also a constraint on Nancy and Harry if we can't do revenue. We're at $1.6 to $1.7 to $1.8. What is it people think they can do?"

Geithner had some words of warning. In Europe, he began, "there's been a big escalation in panic. It's spreading through Greece, Ireland, Portugal. Italy's seen a big increase in the price of default insurance on their debt. Bank stocks are down 25 percent. They're nowhere close in Europe to a viable strategy." In the United States, he said, "Rating agencies are looking at, one, the risk that Congress fails to raise the debt limit, and, two, the shape and contour of the fiscal restraints. If there's no clear path maybe this week, then we're going to be put on negative outlook or watch, downgrade if we don't act by August 2." They would be kept "negative" if they didn't deal with the fiscal problems.

"Europe's a bigger problem with many fronts," Obama said. The financial markets need some solid underpinnings, and symbolic votes in a show of party solidarity were dangerous.

"Default is not an option," McConnell said. "We should be reassuring the markets of that."

Neither he nor Obama addressed McConnell's assertion earlier that day on the Senate floor that the president was guilty of "deliberate deception."

McConnell then introduced a proposal to put the entire burden of raising the debt ceiling on the president. His complicated idea was that Obama should first raise the debt limit on his own authority, and then Congress would pass legislation disapproving of the increase. The president would then veto that legislation, but the Democrats would have enough votes to sustain the veto so the debt ceiling would be increased.

It was confusing and complex—but similar structures had been used in the past to provide legislators with political cover for difficult votes.

Some in the White House saw McConnell's proposal as a realistic approach to a thorny political problem. After the meeting Jason Furman, Sperling's chief deputy, sent an email to Rohit Kumar, who had helped devise McConnell's scheme. He jokingly thanked Kumar, on his wife's behalf, for his positive contribution to the discussion. His wife's birthday was coming up, Furman said, and he was worried he would miss the celebration if the debt limit battle dragged on too long.

For his part, McConnell was direct about the thinking behind the proposal to make the president the sole person responsible for raising the debt ceiling.

"I decided to make him own it," McConnell said in an interview. "We thought he ought to own it. It's part of my job to protect my members, if I can, against having to vote for it."

Boehner returned to the issue of whose problem it was. "I feel like I need to defend myself," he said. "Tim [Geithner] sent me a letter two days after I was sworn in as speaker talking about the need to raise the debt limit. No one wants to vote to raise the debt limit. You requested it. We said cuts, not taxes, and controls on spending. What is your plan that you want us to pass?"

"John," Obama replied, "as we've discussed . . ." Lew and the White House congressional liaison have been "sitting with your guys. I want the biggest plan possible. Revenue, entitlements, discretionary. We've been talking about revenue changes or revenue neutral, payroll tax cuts, $120 billion. That's $1,000 per family."

"How far are you willing to go on structural entitlement changes?" Boehner asked.

"We would not be prepared to do some hard things on entitlements if we don't get net positive on revenue," Obama said.

Suggesting he had read something in the newspapers, he added, "Mitch has been clear on the revenue issue about not raising taxes. So the conclusion I accept is you do not accept net positive revenue."

"Is that correct?" Biden asked.

"Yes," Cantor replied. He had been saying it—and meaning it—forever.

Boehner had a qualifier. "If the deal was big enough, we could talk about entitlements, corporate tax reform and individual tax reform," he said.

When Boehner said he was open to a big deal, Plouffe glanced at Cantor. The majority leader was staring angrily at the speaker.

The disconnect between Boehner and Cantor was a topic of conversation among White House staff. The tension was so obvious, Nabors joked, that he felt awkward being in the same room with the two of them.

To Sperling and the rest of the White House team it couldn't have been clearer. Cantor was a firm "No," Boehner a qualified "Yes."

On tax reform, Obama said, "I was willing to put my full weight behind it." But an enforcement mechanism would have to be put in place in case tax reform didn't get done.

"Fundamental reform would equal more growth and more revenue," Boehner said, offering the conventional Republican wisdom. "That's why we all have an incentive to do it."

Obama said that whatever the assumptions about more revenue from tax reform, "it wouldn't be coming immediately. But if there's an appetite for that, we can return to that discussion. I would love to."

"We need to spend more time on real enforcement mechanisms," Boehner said. "My members want a balanced budget amendment. It's the ultimate enforcement mechanism."

Obama said he did not consider a balanced budget amendment serious enforcement.

Some of Cantor's presentation on health care from the day before had shown up in *Politico*. "Witness what happened last time we came in and brought paper, Mr. President," Cantor said. "Witness what's going on. Totally inappropriate. It shouldn't have happened. Our members keep asking for what is going on. We bring it here and it ends up in the press. So we keep asking you what's going on. We'd like to see the specifics of your plan. Let's go through the same exercise that I went through yesterday, line-by-line specifics on your plan. And that's what our members want. I came in here, I did it, it got leaked. Shouldn't have happened."

"Completely agree," the president said. "Shouldn't have happened. I will take responsibility for it. And if it happens again, we'll have to kick out the staff.

"What I propose doesn't violate anything Grover Norquist says," Obama maintained. "These high-end tax rates are scheduled to lapse.

I proposed tax reform. We'd use that to make up the revenue from the higher-end tax rates going away."

"Where's the paper on this?" Cantor asked tartly.

"Your speaker has the paper," Obama disclosed. "My assumption is you've been working with him. Nancy and Harry don't have paper."

"Let's have the paper," Cantor snapped.

"I'll describe it," Obama said. "It's a big chunk of the Biden group. Health care and non–health care. Minimum of decoupling [Bush tax cuts] with tax reform of an equivalent amount. Raise the age on Medicare."

"What are the tax rates?" Cantor asked sharply.

"Maybe I was naive," Obama replied. "You took a pledge. I'm offering you the opportunity to lower everyone's rates" with tax reform. "What happens if tax reform breaks down?" Obama asked. "Which you all think would be great for my politics." Tax reform would be good policy, but they needed a fallback. "What happens if tax reform doesn't happen? What's the default? I'm saying revenues consistent with what we were promised from decoupling. And you're saying that's not acceptable. So here's my question: If people want to discuss that, we are game. If not, the clock is ticking."

"Mr. President," Cantor began more politely, "what you're talking about would actually be $1 trillion in additional revenue the way we look at it." Letting the upper tax brackets rise to 39.6 percent would raise at least $800 billion. "So we're going to end up with a higher tax increase than what you're saying." Tax reform is about lowering rates. "What is the top rate you're willing to agree to on tax reform?" This was the guts of the matter.

"If we're making a deal on the deficit," Obama said, "then the cuts have to be scoreable, so you can't count on economic growth. So I can't say growth and I have to have a default. If things played out and we didn't need the extra money, then fine."

It was almost a joke to think they might have extra money.

"I only had this discussion because it was the only way to do tax reform," Boehner said, justifying his private conversations with the president. "We'd need pain on both sides. We're having problems with the principles for tax reform. I want to lower, I want to go to three rates, broaden the base. And we're far apart on one principle—progressivity."

"That's accurate," Obama replied. "We have to maintain some level of progressivity. That doesn't preclude going to lower rates. And we never came to agreement."

"If we're talking about a top rate of 25, 28 percent, that would be one thing," Cantor said. "But if there's no agreement and you automatically get $1 trillion in tax revenue, where is your incentive to act?" The Democrats would stall on tax reform and then the trigger would go off, giving them a bonanza—$1 trillion in new tax revenue.

"We've been working with the speaker in good faith," Obama said. Bypassing Cantor, the president turned to the speaker. "John, if you think your conference is open to the larger package, then let's go back to it. If so, we can pass the debt ceiling deal . . . or at least the stuff we agreed to, along with some kind of deficit cap and the pathway towards tax reform. This would not involve your guys raising taxes. But we'd have an identifiable revenue source."

"One concern I have on a small or big package," Boehner said, is the lack of consensus on payroll taxes, Pell education grants and food stamps. "If we push the spending cuts off, then the markets will say, there they go again. We need to spend less now."

"You all want to go back to 1890 levels of spending," Obama joked. "But pulling that spending back has an economic impact just the same as you claim raising taxes would."

Biden chimed in, "If we don't have time for entitlements and tax reform, let's pass the $1.7 in cuts now and begin the discussion on entitlements and taxes."

This, of course, was what the Republicans wanted—a cuts-only agreement.

Reid addressed the president. "You are patient. I am not. There's no revenue. The Republicans won't help." He shook his head in disgust. "And lower rates sure have helped the economy," he added, in a snide reference to the Bush tax cuts. "We need to now spend some time on the McConnell approach."

They turned to Sperling for details about a compulsory trigger if they didn't cut spending or raise taxes in an amount at least equivalent to the debt ceiling increase.

"A trigger would lock in our commitment," Sperling explained. "Even though we disagree on the composition of how to get to the cuts, it would lock us in. The form of the automatic sequester would punish both sides. We'd have to September to avert any sequester"—a legal obligation to make spending cuts.

"Then we could use a medium or big deal to force tax reform," Obama said optimistically.

"If this is a trigger for tax reform," Boehner said, "this could be worth discussing. But as a budget tool, it's too complicated. I'm very nervous about this."

"This would be an enforcement mechanism," Obama said.

"Are health care savings included?" Kyl asked.

"Could include some health care," the president answered tentatively.

"If you subtract from the package," Kyl said, "meaning you start dropping things out of here, we're going to subtract rural hospitals and medical education."

"I just said $1.7 as a number," Obama said. "The staffs need to get together and go through each one. That's a rough estimate. Eric was at $2.2 trillion. I already discounted that."

"We're not touching Medicare and Medicaid without revenue," Reid declared.

"We don't have paper on your plan," Cantor said again.

"I've been dealing with your speaker," Obama said. "You all need to talk to the Republican caucus. Eric, if you want to go to the big deal, then we've got to talk about decoupling. Absent decoupling, no big deal. Harry and Nancy may have different views."

On the current annual spending level, Obama said, "Our proposal is 1048," meaning $1.048 trillion for general spending for fiscal year 2012.

On enforcement, Kyl said, "There's a huge gulf in there. We can't agree to a mechanism to reduce spending if it leads to tax increases."

"There's been no growth in the last 10 years in nonsecurity spending," said Senator Durbin. "Eighty-four percent of the growth has been in Defense." He pointed out that the pending transportation bill had cuts of 30 percent. "That's the first time in 56 years. Doing all these cuts in the discretionary part of the budget is unfair."

If they were limited to what his working group had done, Biden said, addressing the speaker, "There's no way we're above $2.2." So they couldn't stretch to the debt limit of $2.7 trillion or whatever it was and get dollar for dollar.

"Unless it's coupled with an idea like Mitch's," Obama said, meaning the complicated scheme of legislation and vetoes that would put it all on the president.

"What the president described as the work we have to do is right on target," Boehner agreed.

"We don't need to go out and get our bases ginned up," Obama said.

"No mandatory health care cuts without revenue," Pelosi said, speaking for her base. "And it's got to be net positive revenue."

As if it weren't already clear, Biden turned to Kyl. "Are you saying anything beyond revenue neutral is off the table?"

"It's off the table," Kyl said.

Cantor added, "$1.7 without revenue is all you say you can do. If you're talking about getting to above dollar for dollar, revenue neutrality comes in. We can credit the revenue toward a corporate rate reduction, for example."

"That is ridiculous," Pelosi said.

"Let's try to end on a constructive note here," the president intervened. "One, let's go find the areas of overlap. Two, let's work on firewalls. Three, let's work on trigger enforcement. I'll think about net neutral revenue."

Cantor said he would like to add health care mandatories and food stamps to the things to do.

Obama said they could do those things if they got revenue. "Allows us to do it, if revenue." Could be done, the president repeated, "if revenue."

• • •

When Cantor got back to the Capitol, he spoke to reporters about the progress of the talks.

"We both agree on entitlements," he said, "and in fact we would both agree on what the president's prescription for entitlement reform is, and we know what that is. So why don't we do that?"

Asked about other plans, the majority leader said they were stalemated. "Nothing can get through the House right now. Nothing."

In an interview later, Boehner said he did not understand why the president insisted on having the daily meetings. "It was all the small ball little stuff," he said. "All we were going to do was nick everybody and irritate everybody and not accomplish anything. I just labored my way through this, because it was a sideshow. It wasn't the real deal."

# 24

Before the meeting on Wednesday, July 13, the president gathered his budget and economic team in the Oval Office for a pre-briefing. He was fretting. There was an unusual edge in his voice.

The economy was shaky once again. They could feel tremors. The stock market had been down for three straight days and with most public companies preparing to report third quarter earnings, predictions were for the lowest profit growth in two years.

Plouffe felt that confidence in the economy was beginning to unravel.

"I've decided that I am not going to take a short-term debt extension under any circumstances," Obama said. He looked around at Daley, Lew, Geithner, Sperling, Reed, Nabors and Plouffe. What was occurring was fundamentally altering the founders' vision of the presidency. The United States had always honored its debts—it was a tradition that stretched back to the Revolutionary War—and for somebody to be able to hold that tradition hostage was truly unfathomable and unacceptable. He was not going to go through this again.

"I want you to understand, I am not going to do it. This is altering the presidency. I am not going to take a short-term extension, no matter what. I want everyone to understand it, and I want it to be in all your body language when you talk. Because you need to understand: I have made a decision. I am not going to do this."

People, Republicans, anyone can criticize us, he said, they can fight, they can shut down the government. He would not permit the Republicans or anyone else to hold the creditworthiness of the United States hostage, to threaten to put the country into default as a budget or political tactic. "I am not going to do it. This hurts the presidency." If they did a short-term deal, they would be going through this spectacle again in a few months—they'd have no time for anything else.

"This wasn't why I came to Washington," Obama said. "This wasn't why I was elected, to be forced into these situations. This is bigger than me. This is about the presidency, and it's about the nation. This is not the way this situation is going to be resolved. I can't let that happen."

Plouffe, for one, could see his boss was out on a limb. No one, including the president, was sure they could bring this in for a safe landing. But Plouffe said they had to realize what a huge cave-in it would be for Boehner and Cantor to agree to extend the debt ceiling beyond the election. That was their leverage, and they would cling to it. If possible, Plouffe said, it would be great if they could push the debt ceiling even further into the fall of 2013.

Lew was astonished that raising the debt limit had acquired such extraordinary power. A short-term debt limit would be terrible for the economy, and allow the Republicans to run the same play again next year, taking the whole economy to the edge of the cliff. "That's not a way to run a great country," he said.

"It's hijacking the presidency," Obama repeated, "putting a gun to the head of the economy."

He seemed to be fortifying himself.


In an interview, the president said, "The one thing I'm not going to do is a short-term deal.

"The reason that's so important is because, given how spooked the markets already are about this whole process—which is unprec-

edented in modern American history—for us to repeat this in incre-
ments every quarter would be disastrous for our economy. And we will
not do that.

"Now, they painted this as, well, he just wants to get past the election. And I kept on trying to remind them," he said laughing, "I said,
look, everybody in the world is paying attention. This is not just a U.S.
issue. This is a global financial issue. We can't do business by threatening to default every three months."

"I'm comfortable that we're up to about $1.7 trillion," the president
said at that afternoon's meeting with the congressional leaders. "We
need to talk about if there's anything we can do to plus it up. Additional mandatory, if there was net additional new revenue. By Friday, we need to make decisions. Are we going big, small or Mitch's
proposal?"

"Moody's has just put America on negative watch," Geithner said.
The credit rating agency said the U.S. government's sterling Aaa bond
rating was in jeopardy because of failure to reach a debt ceiling agreement. The Moody's report stated, "There is a small but rising risk of a
short-lived default."

"What is meaningful to them?" asked Boehner.

A "comprehensive" deal, said Geithner. If it was only a down payment, the agencies would look for "something substantive that is com-
plemented with enforcement."

Boehner again said their focus should be to cut more than the increase in the debt limit. "This is basically a turd sandwich with fries,"
he said. "So let's just do the right thing."

"Default would be a cataclysmic event," Cantor said. "I want to go
back to Thursday. When we were discussing the Biden proposal, it was
roughly $2 trillion. On Sunday, questions were raised about the Biden
proposal. On Monday, Mr. President, you said it was $1.7 trillion."

He wanted to know what amount of deficit reduction the president
really believed was possible.

"We've never cut it this close before," Obama said. "Some folks in your caucus don't want to vote for it at all. I imagined the situation back in February. I said the first time that you presented that we're short of the full package. Maybe the number's smaller than what I said. Maybe it's $1.4 rather than $1.7. I find $1.7 achievable." Answering Cantor, he added, "No one is walking back on anything."

"Well," Cantor replied, "then the problem must be other folks on your side."

"The $1.7 doesn't include anything you don't like," Obama insisted again.

Reid had a different number. From the Senate Appropriations Committee, he said, "I'm hearing, well, we can get $1.1 trillion" but $300 billion would be cuts in security spending.

"Can we just walk through the numbers?" Obama said in exasperation.

Cantor said there was "$1.1 to $1.2 trillion in discretionary" general spending cuts.

Jack Lew said that "stuff was not nailed down." He thought they were at about the number from the Biden meetings but reminded them that "the last meeting never happened" when Cantor and Kyl had refused to meet again. But he threw the Republicans a bone: "We are open to a higher number on civilian retirement." Simpson-Bowles had recommended $161 billion in savings over 10 years, more than five times the administration's $29 billion.

Hoyer, whose district was home to tens of thousands of federal workers, balked, saying there had to be compatibility between federal civilian workers and the military.

"We want to do more on military retirement," Lew said without giving a number, and dove even deeper into the weeds. "Nutrition assistance is below what Eric says. It's $2 to $5 billion, and I think we have it at $20 billion."

Obama noted the Republicans had not included unemployment insurance, "which is something we don't agree on. If I look at this sheet, Eric and John, if you take out the nutrition and take out the education, which is two areas of disagreement, you're at 282 and we're at 279 on ours. So there's a minimum area of agreement."

Kyl objected that some of it had not been agreed upon, including agriculture subsidies and how they would get there.

Did they all agree on unemployment insurance? Biden asked.

"I thought the idea was to cut spending," Boehner lamented. When you consider where we started from our end, it's going to be difficult to accept starting at $1.048 trillion, referring to that year's annual spending. "We're in a different era now in the House. This is about cutting spending."

"Yeah," Obama replied, "in the abstract everyone wants to cut, but not when they get to these particulars." He said that tax cuts were effectively spending because they increased the deficit.

"Tax cuts aren't spending," said Boehner. He believed they spurred the economy that would then yield more tax revenue.

"I'm not proposing any tax cut," said Kyl.

"This is Bizarro World," said the president.

"Let's take Doc Fix and unemployment insurance off the table, since those are spending," Boehner said.

"What matters to the market is the long-term trend," Geithner interjected, noting that the financial markets wanted a demonstration of serious engagement over the long haul.

"We need to deliver credibility to the American people," Boehner said. "We won't be able to do this in later years."

"Okay," Obama said, "maybe we need additional negotiations. At a minimum, we're at $1 trillion or so in discretionary, $230 to $240 [billion] in other mandatories."

"Let's talk about $1.5 trillion," Boehner said. "Does anyone believe that is possible?"

"Can we add to it?" Obama asked. "Where can we plus it up? Those are questions for tomorrow." Getting to 1.5 would be hard, he said, "without some health mandatory and some revenue and some targets for enforcement."

"Nancy made a good point," Boehner said. "We're nicking everybody and we don't have much to show for it."

Kyl mentioned the firewall.

"The firewall shouldn't be controversial," Obama said. "Defense spending went up 84 percent in the last decade. Defense without fire-walls would not be subject to constraints."

"There have been four straight years of cuts to Defense," Kyl said.

Lew said any Defense cuts over the next two years would only be at the margins, and any freeze would not impact real strategic capabilities.

"The Pentagon is happy to spend," the president said.

Hoyer said it would be easier to get money from Defense.

Kyl started talking about caps on spending again.

The president rubbed his eyes and looked at his watch.

"Having a firewall makes it difficult for both of us," said Boehner, noting that with no firewall, the Democrats could say the cuts were coming from Defense, and they, the Republicans, could emphasize the cuts from elsewhere. They could then work out the details later.

Obama knew the Senate and House better than that. "Well, then the appropriators just add the money back later," he said. The powerful congressional appropriations committees had the final say on how spending bills were handled in both houses of Congress, giving them tremendous power within their areas of authority.

"We didn't pay for the wars," Durbin noted. The regular appropriations process had been circumvented with giant supplemental funding bills for Afghanistan and Iraq.

"You've got to constrain the appropriators," Obama repeated.

"If we don't have a firewall," Biden said, "and Congress wants to go over on Defense, then they wipe out agencies," like the Energy Department.

Durbin raised the issue of all the contractors who worked for the Defense Department, and the president raised the issue of enforcement. Without enforcement, Congress would just spend.

"I just met with a person today who's just out of college," said Pelosi for no clear reason. "They were optimistic and hopeful and we need to get this deal."

The president put his chin in his hand and started playing with his name card.

Pelosi went on with a long anecdote, finally lamenting their apparent failure at negotiations. "I don't know who is going to tell the children," she said.

Cantor and Hoyer, who were sitting next to each other, began a private conversation while Pelosi told her story.

"We listened to Cantor day in and day out," Pelosi said, "but he's not listening right now."

The president burst out laughing.

"The problem with the automatic enforcements," Kyl said, "is there's no exceptions except for military pay."

Sperling noted that such an exception had been introduced by Republicans. "So that's you all who did that."

"Okay," said Obama, clearly near the end of his patience. "We're going to have to layer this cake," he attempted to explain. "I said we're going to get to $1.7 and then add additional layers. Add a sequestration mechanism, health mandatory and net neutral revenue. Mitch's proposal is the safety card for Friday if we can't reach agreement on how to get to $2 trillion. The spirit that we have right now is why we can't do this thing." They did not have the right attitude. "We need to make a decision."

"Mr. President," Cantor mildly taunted, "we are still a long way from $2.4 trillion, which is where you need us to be" to reach equivalency with a new debt extension. "Mr. President, we are moving in opposite directions. Why don't we take the wins where we can?" He proposed doing agreed-upon cuts with just a short-term debt extension.

"I will explain and defend," the president said, adding, "I am not trying to cast blame," as he cast blame. "I will take it to the American people. You want cuts well above what is needed."

Everyone knew what he meant: The gap should be closed with more revenue.

"If you send me something that doesn't go all the way through the election," he said, "I am not going to sign a short-term debt limit increase." The White House staff had rarely seen him so combative in front of the Republicans. This was, to some, the Obama of the 2008 presidential campaign.

"I will veto it. At least Mitch, to his credit, gets rid of default. He says, 'I'm going to make Obama wear this jacket.' "

The president wasn't finished. "But that's something almost just as bad, because the people don't trust that we can do anything. I'm not proposing tax increases on every single American. I'll take this on tour. I want to be clear, Eric," he continued, looking at his real adversary for the moment. "My responsibility is to the American people. I've shown myself as willing to compromise. Do you think Ronald Reagan sat here like this? There comes a point where I say enough is enough. That point has been reached.

"Get on board the dollar for dollar or the big deal," he concluded. "I promise you, Eric, don't call my bluff on this. It may bring my presidency down, but I will not yield on this."

The president then stood up, pushed his chair back, and strode from his Cabinet Room.


On the way back to the Capitol, Cantor called his communications director, Brad Dayspring, a two-year veteran of the White House press office under George W. Bush.

"Fyi," Cantor said, "there was a little bit of a blowup in the meeting. Obama really got stern with me at the end, so if you start getting calls, I wanted you to know, okay?"

In a matter of seconds, Dayspring's phone began ringing from reporters who covered the White House.

"I heard Cantor pissed off Obama," one said. "What did Cantor do?"

By the time Cantor was back at the Capitol, Dayspring had fielded half a dozen calls, and more were coming in. He recommended that the majority leader give his side to the press. Cantor agreed and a press conference was quickly called in the Speaker's Lobby.

Cantor described Obama as "abruptly walking out."

"He got very agitated, seemingly, and said that he had sat here long enough and that no other president—Ronald Reagan wouldn't sit here like this, and he's reached the point where something's got to give," Cantor said.

"I was somewhat taken aback, because, look, I was compromising. We are very far apart right now. The progress we made seems to have been erased now."

In the speaker's office, Barry Jackson, who had attended the White House meeting, was thinking, "Huh, this certainly doesn't bode well." The president had overdone it by losing his cool. He'd let the Republicans see they were getting to him. Politics meant sitting across the table from people you might not like or who were annoying. Keeping cool was essential. In his eight years in the Bush White House and during a decade on the Hill, he said, "I'd never seen anything like it. Never heard of anything like it."

But Boehner let Cantor twist alone. He said nothing to him immediately afterward.

The president later recalled the confrontation with Cantor as a clarifying moment.

"What was clear to me was they kept on thinking that somehow sooner or later we were going to cave on this. And I think it was maybe the third or fourth time when Cantor comes back to, why don't we just do a short-term deal, Mr. President? Essentially what he wanted to do was pocket the discretionary cuts that we had already agreed to.

"And that would then buy us three or four months," Obama said with a laugh, "and then we'd go back at this thing again. So after the fourth or fifth time that he's repeated this, I say, Eric, I'm serious. Don't call my bluff on this. I've told you I'm not signing something like that. We're not going to put the country through an ordeal like this every three or four months. That's not how the greatest country on earth operates. And we should be embarrassed if it gets to the point where our government is running on three- or four-month patchwork agreements."

And then you walked out?

"I think people say I pushed my way off the desk, or something. It wasn't that dramatic. I just said, you know what? So when we get serious, and when you guys understand that that's the case, we're going to have another conversation. But you probably need to talk about this among yourselves. And I walk out of the room."

Was there a lot of theater in this? I asked.

"I wanted to emphasize to them that it was time to stop playing games and posturing. And there was just this constant sense of gamesmanship involved that the country simply could not afford, given the magnitude of what was at stake and what the country had already gone through. I mean, part of what I would say to some, including my own staff, was this wasn't the equivalent of the government shutdown in '95. When the economy's growing at 5 percent, and you can afford to have these Washington theatrics, but essentially the engine's going full-gear. This is a situation where we'd just come out of this tremendously difficult time, and people are still hurting really badly. And in those moments, you can't play games. And a default on the debt is not a government shutdown. This is not the same thing. And I think that some over on Capitol Hill seemed to think that the consequences of this would be similar. And you know, you close up the national monuments and folks are on furlough for a couple of days, and then it all gets resolved."

He said he feared what he called a "global cascade." The prospect of default would begin to have serious effects on investors' confidence in U.S. debt. The Treasury needed to hold regular auctions of its securities in the financial markets.

"If we have one failed auction, you don't know if you can put that genie back in the bottle again," he said.

"Things might then spiral in ways that could have plunged us back into a Lehman-type situation, or worse," he added, referring to the investment bank, Lehman Brothers Holdings, which collapsed in 2008 after investors lost confidence in its ability to pay its debts.

## 25

———————

Obama's exchange with Cantor at the previous day's meeting sent an angry Harry Reid to the Senate floor on the morning of Thursday, July 14.

"With so much at stake, even Speaker Boehner and Minority Leader McConnell seem to understand the seriousness of this situation. They are willing to negotiate in good faith, which I appreciate and the country appreciates.

"Meanwhile, House Majority Leader Eric Cantor has shown that he shouldn't even be at the table, and Republicans agree that he shouldn't be at the table."

He went on to call Cantor's departure from the Biden talks the previous month "childish."

Boehner was sick of the White House meetings. It was still mostly the president lecturing, he reported to his senior staff. The other annoying factor was Jack Lew, who tried to explain why the Democrats' view of the world was right and the Republicans' wrong.

"Always trying to protect the sacred cows of the left," Barry Jackson said of Lew, going through Medicare and Medicaid almost line by line while Boehner was just trying to reach some top-line agreement.

•        •        •

Boehner wasn't quite sure, but it didn't seem like Cantor was on his side.

The confrontation with Obama and Reid's criticism of the majority leader on the Senate floor focused a lot of negative media attention on Cantor, and that gave Boehner an opening.

At a news conference in the Capitol, reporters were hitting Cantor hard on his position on the debt limit talks. They were pounding the hell out of him, Boehner later recalled. "I just went up and put my arm around Eric and made it clear, listen, we're on the same team."

Boehner then said to the reporters, "Let me just say, we have been in this fight together, and any suggestion that the role that Eric has played in this meeting has been anything less than helpful is just wrong."

Afterward, when Boehner and Cantor were waiting together to get on an elevator, Cantor indicated he had needed that vote of confidence. "Thank you very much," he said.


That day's White House meeting was scheduled for late afternoon in the Cabinet Room. Before it got under way, Pelosi and Hoyer spoke briefly with Boehner.

"Look," Hoyer, a fiscal conservative, said quietly, "if you can get this nailed down, we're going to be there." He didn't promise any votes but Boehner assumed it meant he wanted a deal.

Even Pelosi indicated to the speaker that they were counting on him to pull this off.

Boehner interpreted this to mean that the House Democratic leaders were not confident in the president's ability to negotiate a deal and avoid default.


"Last meeting for this week," Obama said. "We could potentially get to $2 trillion or more if we did not do revenue neutral." He was sticking it to Cantor, pointing out that it was the House majority leader's insistence on revenue neutrality that was standing in the way of a deal securing $2 trillion in deficit reduction. "Standard & Poor's is putting us on negative watch," Obama added.

"It's not public yet," Geithner said. "It will come out in the next few hours. S&P is going to issue a statement regarding deficit risks," saying there was a 50 percent chance that the U.S. debt rating could be lowered in the coming three months. The problem was the long-term deficits.

"Nobody wants to be in default," Boehner said. "The second point Tim makes is valid." The long-term deficit was the Republicans' main concern.

The speaker was wound up. "We're one hiccup away from September '08 or worse," he said dramatically, referring to the onset of the financial crisis. "We've got to get this done right. I'm upset by what happened yesterday." The press had reported on the confrontation with Cantor. "But we're all going to be polite. I'm not referring to you, President Obama, relax." It was awkward. He seemed to be trying to break the ice and not get back into a pitched confrontation.

"I am relaxed," Obama said.

"We are going backwards if there's no new revenue," said Reid, getting back into it.

"Health and revenue are tied together," said Lew, reminding everyone that if the Republicans were not going to do anything on revenue, the Democrats would not do much on Medicare and Medicaid.

"Medicaid," said Durbin. "This hits the states hard back home." In his state, one in three children were covered by Medicaid. He said the provider tax might be a contrivance, but it was a contrivance that allowed Illinois to keep Medicaid afloat. Taking it away would damage the system. Unlike some other states, Illinois was reimbursed only 50 percent of Medicaid costs.

"Here's the upshot," Obama said. "There's some additional health-care-related savings that aren't structural. We could save about $200 billion, and we could use the revenue to offset extension [of the] payroll tax holiday. An approach like this wouldn't add to the gross savings but it would benefit the economy" because workers would have slightly more money from the payroll tax reduction.

"A down payment," Geithner said, "if we could get somewhere close to $2 trillion [total] savings, would be seen as credible if we combined it with a trigger."

"We could include next steps for tax reform," Obama said. Everyone was talking tax reform, the genie in the bottle that might be lured out to fix all their problems—a project that surely would take six months to a year or more and step on all the special interests.

Sperling then made another presentation on global caps and targets.

"This is mutually assured destruction," Boehner noted unhappily. They all knew it was designed to force decisions.

"Reagan, when he did cuts, weren't they 50–50 domestic and Defense?" Pelosi asked.

Lew and Geithner next walked through a presentation based on paper they had presented to the group.

Kyl didn't like it one bit. "He who controls the paper controls the negotiation," he said. "This paper excludes stuff we talked about, other savings that are not on this list, that we ought to talk about. We wouldn't pay for the tax changes you talk about, payroll holiday, etc. If you want to do those things for free, fine, but we're not going to raise other taxes to pay for it." He wouldn't even accept Cantor's revenue neutrality.

The president wanted to get back to the overall. "Let's assume $1.7 with nonhealth, discretionary and interest," he said. "We've discussed some revenue raisers that don't cause much heartburn." He had proposed capping itemized deductions—Sperling's brainchild from the Biden talks. "The 35 percent revenue may never materialize because you guys," the Republicans, "may be successful in replacing me, or we would get tax reform done. That's about as modest as it gets in terms of revenue raisers and net neutral. If it gets us to about $2 trillion, it'd be worth it."

"There's a better way to get to $2 trillion," said Kyl. "The stuff we put on the table that you took off. Discretionary caps. We could get agreement among staff. Enforcement. If you think that ours will agree that if Congress doesn't do its job then taxes go up, that's not something we're agreed to."

"We thought about this," Geithner said. They needed enforcement of some kind.

"That's not true," said Kyl. "You don't need enforcement to raise revenues." Don't make it automatic. "Congress can raise taxes anytime we want."

"You also have the right to cut spending anytime you want too," noted Obama.

"We have less revenue now because of the recession," Kyl said, "not necessarily the Bush tax cuts."

"We all have our own economic theories about what happened and why we don't have this revenue," Obama said.

It was, however, an economic fact that the recession, with less economic activity and income, resulted in less tax revenue. It was also an economic fact that the Bush tax cuts had meant the Treasury collected $1.5 trillion less in revenue in the last decade.

"Actually 50 percent of people don't pay taxes," Kyl said.

Hoyer protested, noting accurately that 50 percent of workers do not pay income tax, but all workers pay the payroll tax.

Reid noted the proposal was to get about $75 billion from the high-profit drug industry. "Let's face it," he said, "there's no chance in hell that Republicans agree to Part D rebates, so already we're $75 billion off of this."

He went on, saying that he had read the press accounts of the previous day's meeting and clearly some of the issues were carrying over. "Unless the deal has some revenue to it, I don't know how we do it."

"Are there any other comments?" Obama inquired. There were no more. "If not, here's where we are. I'm prepared to do the largest deal possible. Discretionary, health, mandatory revenue. Solve problems for the foreseeable political future." On the revenue question, he told the Republicans, "I don't expect a bedside conversion on your part. The American people want a balanced approach. Two out of three Republican voters want a balanced approach," Obama added, providing Republicans some raw polling data on what their voters wanted.

It drove Boehner crazy when the president told him what his party's voters wanted, but he didn't say anything.

"So option one, big deal," the president continued. "Option two, fallback, $2 trillion. The fallback, we can get a little over $2 trillion in savings with" what he carefully called *"some gestures on revenue."*

Boehner, Cantor and most of the others wondered what that meant. Gestures? They were still $200 billion to $300 billion short of the $2 trillion target.

"If we coupled that with a trigger," Obama continued, "it would buy us some credibility.

"Option three, some mechanism like Mitch and Harry. I'm happy to take responsibility, as Mitch proposed, but that is suboptimal. We've tried every angle. Hard to bridge the differences. The leaders all need to go take 24 to 36 hours, come back and tell me what you can accomplish. I prefer the big deal, but we're running out of time." He added that they might need to meet next week.

"Last point," the president said. "A short-term solution is not something I will sign." Just in case anyone had missed his message to Cantor the previous day, he repeated that he would only go along with a debt extension that took them past the 2012 election. A short-term extension, he said, "makes it harder, not easier. Not for me, but for you."

Boehner again cringed, but remained silent. The president was telling them again what was good for Republicans. It would be good for Republicans to relinquish their leverage? Unbelievable.

The president's assertion was highly debatable. He had acknowledged that it rested on him. He was president. He was going to wear that jacket.

Pelosi said, "I'm an optimist. I think we can tell you all right now where we are. So why do we need to wait 24, 36 hours?"

"Mitch and I have a plan," Reid disclosed, tantalizing everyone. "So let's just do that."

"This is a complicated dynamic," Obama said, understating the problem. "Both between the parties, the leaders and the chambers."

"Our caucus fully supports you, Mr. President," Pelosi said, "your bigger deal." That evening, there was the congressional baseball game, Democrats vs. Republicans, so she joked, "How about whoever wins the baseball game tonight decides?"*

Cantor had not said a word.

Durbin, a Chicago poker player, was watching him carefully, looking for a "tell," some cue that would betray what he was thinking. He decided the silence itself was the tell. It was a sign that Cantor knew he had been chastised. To Durbin, it looked like Cantor wanted to hide under the table, become a mouse and disappear. He was sure Cantor realized that, in holding the press conference, he had gone too far.

The consensus among Republican participants was that the White House meetings had run their course and that despite the fact that they had come to no solution there wouldn't be any more. But Boehner thought he saw an opening. Maybe they were closer than it seemed.

The president is scared, he told Cantor. He sees no way out.

The speaker asked Cantor if he would support one last effort to secure a grand bargain with the president based on serious tax reform.

Cantor had his own worries. Default would be disastrous for the country, but it would also be a political catastrophe for him. Media coverage of the White House meetings had painted him as the obstructionist standing in the way of a deal. Right now, if the country went into default, he could wind up taking a disproportionate share of the blame.

It would be easier to get to 218 votes with a larger package, Cantor conceded. "Yes, let's give it a try and see what happens."

The media was focusing on the possibility that the McConnell plan to allow the president to unilaterally raise the debt limit was becom-

---

*The Democrats won the game 8–2.

ing the most likely option. Reid had, that day, expressed support and Boehner had told reporters Thursday that the McConnell plan, while "less than optimal," might look increasingly attractive as the country neared default.

Reid thought the group was getting nowhere. His idea was that they push it off to a new special bicameral, bipartisan group, a kind of supercommittee. It would be made up of members of Congress and given the job of hashing out the details the high-level leaders were failing to agree on. The supercommittee's proposal would then be submitted to the Senate and House. The recommendations would have to be taken or rejected in their entirety. It would be an up or down vote on an expedited basis.

Boehner's old friend and golfing buddy, Ohio Governor John Kasich, phoned him to offer help on the impasse. Kasich had been House Budget chairman in the 1990s when Gene Sperling was Clinton's NEC director.

"Hey," Kasich said, "I know Sperling real well." They had worked on the 1997 budget deal together. "Can I help?"

Yes, Boehner said. Obama had to get serious. "I'm putting revenue up there, but they've got to have real entitlement reform and we have things on paper and it's kind of like everybody understood and then we get another piece of paper back." The paper did not reflect the rhetoric.

So Kasich called Sperling at the White House, suggesting that he meet with Boehner. Lew, he said, did not know how to get to yes.

Sperling realized it was not a compliment that they wanted him. It essentially meant, "Lew's being too tough. Can we get Sperling?" He reported the Kasich call to Daley and Geithner. Both said that the Republicans did not get to decide who they would negotiate with, and a private meeting between Sperling and Boehner did not happen.

# 26

_____

In the speaker's suite on the second floor of the Capitol, they felt the pressure of the clock.

"We don't want to go through another three weeks of Jack Lew nickel-and-diming," Barry Jackson said, banging his fist on the table, "and moving shit around when we've got to draft legislation."

We've got to get this back on the track of regular order, Boehner said. There was Senate process, House process. This had to be reduced to precise legislative language.

Would the White House bite? What was the path?

On the morning of Friday, July 15, Boehner called the president to follow through on Jackson's promise that it was not over.

Mr. President, I want to reopen talks on the grand bargain. He had a new offer, some big specifics. He was willing to do $800 billion in revenue over 10 years if there was comprehensive tax reform. "I'm willing to go this far on revenue. But I've got to make sure that the entitlement side is big enough to justify it. We need to get real entitlement stuff locked in, [so] nobody can touch it. That's what makes me comfortable." Would the president send Geithner and Daley up to the Capitol?

And Mr. President, the speaker added, please don't send Jack Lew. The budget director talked too much, was uncompromising, and Boehner's staff did not believe he could get to yes.

In an interview a year later, Boehner still had strong feelings about Lew. "Jack Lew said no 999,000 times out of a million," Boehner said, chuckling. Then he corrected himself, "999,999. It was unbelievable. At one point I told the president, keep him out of here. I don't need somebody who just knows how to say no."

For his part, Lew felt he could rest on his record of getting to yes in every other negotiation over 30 years. He believed Boehner was impatient with details, irritated when he asked hard questions and insisted everything be fleshed out. "He wanted to be a speaker who accomplished something great and important," Lew explained to a White House colleague, "but he wasn't willing to go back to his caucus and push on taxes."

The president was not comfortable with Boehner picking his negotiators for him.

"Look," Boehner said, "we're serious. We can do this." They just needed to sit down and hammer it out.

Okay, the president said.

Obama sent Geithner and Daley that evening, and with Cantor by his side, the speaker presented an offer. The tone was very much, "We've tried everything else. Let's try to get this done." None of them had taken a day off in a month, and everyone was exhausted.

Boehner handed Daley and Geithner a two-page offer.

The proposal extended the debt limit past the 2012 election, but it did so in two steps: an immediate $1 trillion increase in the debt limit backed up by $1.2 trillion in savings achieved by capping general spending over the next decade. The second step required cuts over 10 years to be negotiated in various programs: $250 billion in federal retirement, agricultural subsidies, higher education and various other programs; $200 billion in non-Medicare health programs; $250 billion in Medicare spending and altering the eligibility age; and additional cuts to Social Security by changing the eligibility age and reducing future cost-of-living increases.

Though couched in budgetary alchemy, the Republicans offered what amounted to $800 billion in new revenue over the next 10 years, to be achieved through major tax reform.

The $800 billion number had been floated before, but here it was in writing. It was a breakthrough. Geithner said the administration would accept it. Daley and he said they were less receptive to the two-step debt ceiling increase. As Boehner knew, the president was adamant on this and had vowed not to agree to a short-term extension. Just ask Eric.

"Go back and take it to the president," Boehner said. "Think about it, whatever you've got to do, and give me your reaction."

Geithner and Daley replied that clearly it was a serious offer, and agreed to take it to the White House.

Nabors read the two-page offer. The two-step process was unacceptable. The health care cuts were too deep, and why were they throwing Social Security into the mix? It really had nothing to do with the deficit. Doing so was just gratuitous piling on. It was a step backward. So he sat down at his computer to red-line the draft.


Later that evening, Pelosi and Hoyer, at their request, met with Boehner in his conference room. Pelosi had found out that Boehner and Obama were negotiating again.

If this is going to get through the House, it's going to need both Republican and Democratic votes, Pelosi said. You're going to lose some of your guys. Tell us what you need, and we'll tell you how involved we need to be in the process.

Tell me what you're willing to do, Boehner said. Would she and the Democrats agree to changes in Medicare that actually impacted beneficiaries?

Pelosi declined to answer. She fished for more details, but Boehner was not forthcoming.

"Why don't we let staff have a conversation about this?" he suggested, a tactic he often used to extricate himself from unproductive discussions.

•        •        •

It had been a tough week for the speaker. "There was one point before this," he later recalled, "in the week before this, the middle of July, when my senior staff came in. And one by one described to me how I was risking my speakership continuing this conversation" with the president. "I looked at them. I just listened to all what they had to say, leaned back, and said, 'So be it.'

"I'm sure most of my staff was scared to death of what the hell I was up to. Fine.

"I'm trying to use the debt limit to leverage the political process to produce more change than it will if left to its own devices. It's not rocket science. This debt issue bothered me before I got here 22 years ago. And I'm sure as hell going to do something about it. Because I need this job like I need a hole in the head. And I don't think what the president understood or some others understood is that I didn't really care." If he lost the speakership, he said, he would be comfortable.

# 27

Sunday morning, July 17, Boehner, Cantor and their senior staff entered a Secret Service building, and walked through a tunnel to the White House for a 10 a.m. meeting in Daley's office. The White House had two offerings. The first was fresh pastries from the nearby Corner Bakery. The second was a four-page counteroffer. Nabors had finished his changes to the proposal presented in Boehner's office on Friday night.

We appreciate the offer you made on Friday, Daley began. The White House viewed it as serious and constructive. He then turned the discussion over to Geithner.

The two-step debt limit approval process was not something the White House could live with, Geithner said. The debt limit negotiations were already having a negative effect on the financial markets. Why would they want to set it up so that the country would have to go through this again? "The president is just not bending on this issue," he said.

"We have to get this passed and out of politics," Daley said.

Barry Jackson chuckled to himself. This was about the president's reelection. It seemed to be Obama's only marker: How can I do this to my political benefit?

They went through the White House's counteroffer, beginning

with caps on general spending. This time, Jack Lew was in the room. Boehner and he immediately started haggling.

The Republicans hadn't been specific about a total budget number for 2012. Lew wanted $1.047 trillion. Boehner came back with an offer of $1.040 trillion.

The White House agreed to the $1.2 trillion in spending cuts over 10 years, but added a firewall that required that they be split evenly between Defense and other general spending. Republicans resisted. The congressional appropriations committees ought to be allowed to make those spending choices.

Geithner said that the savings from winding down the wars in Iraq and Afghanistan—the Overseas Contingency Operations fund—should be counted in the grand total. He conceded that this wasn't real savings, but it was a peace dividend and it made the overall total look bigger. "We need to have this because the ratings agencies and markets believe in this stuff."

Fine, Boehner said. He was past arguing about OCO.

The White House plan offered a level of cuts to other general spending that was comparable to what Boehner had proposed. But the administration plan envisioned plowing a portion of that savings into an extension of unemployment benefits. Boehner agreed to it.

The discussion moved to the debt limit. The White House wanted an immediate increase of $1.6 trillion and a guarantee that an additional $900 billion would be available to the president, subject to McConnell's plan that would allow Congress to express disapproval without actually preventing the increase.

The increase would be offset by additional spending cuts that would have to be negotiated by Congress, and the White House proposed a trigger mechanism that would automatically cut spending and raise taxes if Congress did not come to an agreement. The trigger was to be designed so that its impact was equally offensive to both parties.

Why is the White House so insistent on a trigger? Boehner asked. Wasn't the looming federal default trigger enough? If that's the hammer hanging over us, we'll find a way to get this done, he said.

The issue of a trigger unresolved, they moved on to additional spending cuts. The White House wanted to halve Boehner's $220 billion in proposed cuts to other health programs to $110 billion. The White House was willing to apply the modified Consumer Price Index to Social Security and other programs.

Boehner found the new White House offer on revenue of $800 billion as a minimum, or floor, unacceptable. He had previously made it a ceiling, meaning they could do less.

"We need some wiggle room to be able to sell this to our guys," the speaker said. "We need some flexibility to produce tax reform. We really need this to be a ceiling."

"I think we can do that," Geithner said.

Boehner said he wanted to maintain the lower rates on capital gains and dividends.

"That just hits too many of our people right between the eyes," Geithner said.

When the discussion turned to corporate tax reform, Boehner and Cantor thought they were onto something positive. The administration had tentatively—everything was tentative, it seemed—stated that corporations would only be taxed on domestic income and not from overseas income. This was a giant issue for companies like Apple, Microsoft and Google, any that operated abroad. Called a territorial corporate tax system, the business community would be overjoyed if it was adopted in an overhaul of corporate taxes. Not having to pay the U.S. corporate rate of 35 percent on overseas income would be a bonanza for corporate America.

"The goal is territorial," Geithner said, starting to pull back. "I'm not sure we can commit to completely territorial." Maybe 95 or 96 percent. He added pointedly, "We are prepared to move off decades of Democratic orthodoxies."

Treasury had been working on a corporate tax reform plan for some time. Decisions had been expected earlier in the year.

Where are you? they asked.

"Well," Geithner said, "we're still working. But complete territorial we may not be able to get. But we're going to get close, and we can work with you on that."

Nabors said that the president would just not do $200 billion on Medicaid. As they had said before, that would gut the program. It was achieving a policy outcome through radical cuts in funding. "We're not doing that," he said. He also had a table of $243 billion in cuts on 14 programs ranging from civilian and military retirement to agriculture subsidies. If they were going to sell a deal to Democrats, he said, these needed to be part of the package. They reflected the agreements reached in the Biden meetings. They couldn't have 14 negotiations, Nabors said. "We're not negotiating on the cuts, just agree to these cuts."

Then, unexpectedly, in walked the president. "How are you guys doing in here?" he asked. "You making progress? I was just at church."

Obama, in a suit and tie, struck a sharp contrast to the others, who had shown up for the Sunday session in khakis and blazers. Daley gave a status report that was slightly more positive than negative.

"Let me talk to John and Eric alone," Obama said.

The others wondered if they should leave. It was an awkward moment.

"We'll go down to my office," the president said, leading the two leaders to the Oval Office.

The president would later recall that he was pleased to see Cantor there.

It was "a good move by John" he said, "to bring Cantor in so that he could feel some ownership, but also because he was probably closer to a certain wing of his caucus. And so I was glad to have him participate."

Stombres and Bradley, Cantor's top aides, had earlier expressed their concern to their boss that the president was bringing him into the discussions only to get him invested in the process. Beware of some kind of pre-sealed deal Obama might slap down on the table and urge you to sign. Don't make any deals. Step out. Say you have to make a phone call. Don't get railroaded.

Now, in the Oval Office, Cantor told the president and Boehner that while he wanted to see if something could be done on a big scale, he had doubts, grave doubts, that he and the speaker had the capacity to sell something that would be perceived as a tax increase by their members. Cantor thought the president was saying in effect, you are the impediment here. I know I could get a deal with the speaker.

Boehner pushed. He wanted a deal. With $800 billion as the revenue figure, he said, even if our guys hate it, we can get it passed and cure all sins with robust tax reform.

Cantor thought the speaker had symptoms of deal fever.

Faced with both Obama and Boehner, Cantor said it would be a hard sell to their members, so it had to be made as easy as possible. In other words, "the best worst big deal possible."

Boehner later recalled, "We have an outline of a deal. It's done."

Meanwhile, in Daley's office, the House Republican senior staffers sat with their Democratic counterparts, eating muffins and watching the British Open golf championship on television.

After about 20 minutes, Boehner and Cantor returned. The speaker had just opened a door that led to a small outdoor patio, apparently intending to have a cigarette, when the president unexpectedly returned. Boehner stayed outside the door and lit up while the president spoke.

"I just talked to John and Eric and I think we're in a really good place here," he said. "We need to start thinking about how we put this thing together." How long will it take to get this drafted? He was looking at Geithner, but before Geithner could answer, he asked, "How much time do we have before we reach the limit?"

As of August 2, Geithner said, the Treasury would no longer be able to borrow money.

"Now," the president said, "this is going to be very tricky for us because you know the press will be climbing all over us. We may be speaking one language to our people." The Republicans would be speaking their language to their people. "And as stuff gets out it's going to make things very difficult for us. So we've got to keep this real quiet. My guys are under instructions not to say a word about any of this. We need to get this done, locked down and rolled out."

"I got 'em," said Boehner, on the ride back to the Capitol in his official car, running red lights and speeding through the empty streets of Washington. "I think if we give on the debt limit and go to a trigger—a policy trigger instead of a debt limit trigger—we'll get them on everything else," he told his aides. He was willing to do that. Get Cantor to my office as soon as possible.

In an interview later, Boehner said, "We're there. Now we've still got to figure out what the trigger is, so that if tax reform doesn't happen, you've got to have a big enough trigger behind it."

Boehner emphasized the importance of the trigger. "It had to be ugly enough where nobody would go there, so we'd get tax reform done. I knew we couldn't have decoupling or other crazy things in there."

Cantor left the White House with Stombres and Bradley.

It was crunch time, he told them, and it showed. He looked as though the weight of the world was on his shoulders. If they—meaning mostly he—screwed this up, it could be a disaster. If he or the speaker blew it up again, they risked being seen as unreasonable, going to the brink of a deal and then walking, yet again. He could see the headlines: There would be a big deal with tax reform if not for these crazy Republicans led by Eric Cantor. On the other hand, agreeing to a bad deal or one that the Republican members would choke on could be worse. "Can this work?" he asked. "Can this really work?"

One reality was his relationship with the speaker. In the House hierarchy, Cantor was the subordinate. But he was also the one plugged into the members, and that was why Obama and Boehner tolerated his presence, barely.

The deal was hanging by the thinnest thread. And so was he.

•     •     •

In an interview, the president recalled that after the Oval Office meeting with Boehner and Cantor, "What we have is a framework, not an agreement," he said.

"I have to say that Boehner could not have thought at that point that we had a deal. And the reason is—and I'll just give you one example—the principles of tax reform were completely unsettled. And I was always suspicious of the notion that tax reform, without an actual identification of where the revenues were going to come from, would be real enough for me to be able to extract what are very real changes to entitlement programs. And so I can't sell that.

"If Cantor's reading is we didn't have a deal yet, it's more accurate than John's. And frankly, we did not indicate to him that we had a deal. We were optimistic, though, at that point that we could get a deal done. I mean, I think that the last—when he leaves our office, I think the basic view is, you know what? This can get done. Here's a framework that can work. We've got to work out all these details and get an agreement.

"At this point, I'm probably feeling better than 50–50 that we'd get this done. And I feel sufficiently good about the prospect of getting it done that I start saying to my team, we've got to do some additional consultations with the House and Senate Democratic leadership. Because it is important that they don't start feeling blindsided."

Back at the Capitol, Cantor told his staff he had to make a sincere effort with the members. How the hell are we going to sell this? How can we get our members to support this? He couldn't get too far ahead of them.

"Where is Paul Ryan going to be on this?" Cantor asked his aides as they rode back to the Capitol. "What's he going to say?"

Ryan would understand the numbers, Stombres said, and the $800 billion looked conveniently, suspiciously, like the revenue from the expiration of the top Bush rates. Ryan's first question would be: "What have you committed us to? Have we committed to really bad policy that we can't support?" His second would be: "What have you locked us into going forward? Have you put us in an impossible position where we're damned if we do, damned if we don't?"

Ryan would worry that all this short-term deal making would retard the real cause: addressing the "real problem," as they called it, of runaway, unsustainable entitlement spending.

They all knew tax reform would take six months to a year or more to work out and negotiate. A complete or even partial transformation of the tax code, larded with decades of special interest provisions, was a monumental task. If a deal was reached and announced on the basis of tax reform, what would be the enforcement mechanism or trigger that would go off if tax reform did not work?

All the talk, Stombres said, would ultimately come back to that. The trigger would be make or break.

Yeah, Cantor agreed, returning to his own personal problem. He was living in a political no-man's-land among the largest political forces in the country—Obama, Boehner and the House Republican majority. He felt like one of those stretchable rubber dolls. Obama and Boehner had one arm and his 240-member conference had the other. "I want to find the exact spot where both arms don't get ripped off," he said.


In the early afternoon, Cantor, Stombres and Bradley went to the speaker's office.

Boehner was positive, optimistic as always about what they were working out. We are going to describe the deal this way, he said. Income tax brackets would be collapsed into three rates, no more. The White House had agreed. No rate would be higher than the current 35 percent. The White House had agreed. Efficiencies in the tax code and economic growth would lead to lower tax rates. The corporate rate was going lower.

"They can't say that Boehner is raising taxes by $800 billion," Jackson said.

Don't worry if it is received poorly at first by the members, Boehner said, we'll fix it with tax reform.

Well, let's see exactly what "it" was, Cantor said. After all the talk with the White House, they would see "it" differently. Let's get precise details. The speaker agreed. Also, they agreed that if there was going to be revenue in a trigger, the White House would have to agree to an Obamacare trigger. Brett Loper, Boehner's policy chief, and Neil Bradley were directed to capture the details on paper, make sure they were all comfortable with them, and then send them to the White House.

"Let's see what they come back with," Cantor said. One thing was for sure, the White House would have a different take and spin on the conversations.

So, Loper and Bradley drafted a proposal that stuck close to many of Boehner's original positions, but added a clause allowing for an unspecified trigger made up of spending cuts and revenue increases. Obama would get his full debt limit increase, up to $1.2 trillion right away with an additional $1.3 trillion available through McConnell's convoluted approval/disapproval process.

Cantor went upstairs to his office with Stombres and Bradley. Tax reform cures all sins? It was daunting to say the least, they agreed.

At 7 p.m., Loper sent a three-page offer to the White House. It gave a $2.5 trillion debt extension under McConnell's scheme. The trigger was "specific spending reductions and revenue increases." But, it noted, "further discussions necessary to finalize."

The White House said they could expect a detailed reply waiting in their email inboxes on Monday morning.


Boehner and Jackson discussed where they thought they really were. Obviously there were some worries about where they would get the votes for a deal. But Boehner believed that if he and the president agreed on something, they would get the votes. Joining together, going out, standing together, declaring publicly they had a deal, he said, would generate momentum.

"The president," Jackson said, "is supremely confident in his ability to deliver. You can't be president of the United States without having that sense of yourself." Once a deal was announced, Obama would have no choice but to rally whatever Democratic votes would be needed. Obama couldn't sign on and let it fail. He would be forced to use the power of his office to get the votes.

Boehner knew he was in the same position. He too would have to use the power of his office to rally the House Republicans as he had never before.

"How many people do you think are going to vote for it?" the president asked Nabors.

"How many people are you going to tell to vote for it?" Nabors replied. There were no natural votes. "No one wants to vote for this. If you throw it on the floor, it's going to get zero votes. Because there's something in here for everybody to hate." He believed he had an accurate whip operation with the Democrats and could get a vote count. "I have it name-by-name, this is who we're going to get, this is how we going to get them." The Democrats are cranky about this, he said, as he produced preliminary lists of House Democrats for the president. He said that he, Pelosi and Hoyer would be able to take care of 60, 70 or 80 House Democrats. Some would come aboard out of loyalty to Obama, some would have to be leaned on.

Obama seemed to agree.

"These are the members that you're personally going to have to call," Nabors said. "If we are putting the full power of the White House behind it, what can I get?" He had a list of about 50 House Democrats—a big number, a healthy number—that Obama would have on his list.

Nabors would long remember exactly what the president said to him. "At the end of the day," Obama said, "this is more important than health care, in terms of the fiscal condition of the country." He would have the meetings, make the phone calls. "I'll get it done."

So that would take them to about 120 or 130 Democrats, Nabors said, well on the way toward the necessary 218. There were, however, two questions.

Was the president going to put his political capital on the line, put everything on the line? Frankly, Nabors said, they did not have a lot of capital left, post–health care, post–loss of the House, and after the recent battle over the appropriations bills.

But, he added, it was an odd dynamic. In a face-off such as this with the Republicans and a willingness to double down with political capital, the 120 to 130 votes was reachable. "It's not a lot of votes to get."

The other question was Boehner's strength. "A speaker should be able to stand up and say, 'Vote for it because I'm the speaker. Don't even read it. I'm the speaker, vote for it,' " Nabors said.

The question, they agreed, was could Boehner deliver the additional 100 votes or more from the Republican side? Was that possible? Did he have enough clout?

Boehner was a mixture of confidence and uncertainty. In an interview he recalled a discussion with the president when they were alone. "At some point that week I said to the president, I said, 'Mr. President, don't underestimate the difficulty in getting this thing passed,' He must have been sitting next to me because he reached down, touched my forearm, and said, 'John, I've got great confidence in my ability to sway the American people.' It almost took my breath away. It was just one of those moments you never forget. And he was very serious."

Asked about this, the president said, "I don't recall that precise conversation."

Boehner told him he could persuade enough House Republicans.

It was really about votes? I asked.

"It's about votes," Boehner said.

Did you ever talk to the president about votes and ask how many votes are you going to get?

"Well, no, no, no. We never got into that. Never got into it."

I said I understood that the president thought he could get 120 to 130 votes from House Democrats.

"We always assumed that they'd have to get half the votes and we'd have to get half the votes," Boehner said, adding that he was confident he could deliver. "And I always assumed I could get half the votes."

## 28

By Monday morning, the White House had sent nothing.

It's coming, Daley and Nabors promised Jackson.

Boehner and Cantor kept their staffs at the office well into the evening, ready to get to work when the White House offer arrived. They had legislative language to draft. They had the responsibility of coming up with the precise definition of the trigger. Jackson in particular was focused on how they were going to sell this to the conference. Congress was out of session so not too many people were around. There had been no leaks that they were on the verge of a deal.

As a precaution, Jackson had begun discussions with staff from Reid's and McConnell's offices on a fallback plan in case they weren't able to reach agreement with Obama.

Sometime between eight and nine o'clock, Nabors called Jackson. The offer isn't coming tonight. We'll have it to you first thing in the morning.

At nearly every White House senior staff meeting for months, Sperling had said, "The Gang of Six might come out with something today."

The Gang was made up of six senators—three Democrats and three conservative Republicans—who had been working on a big, supposedly dramatic, deficit reduction plan. The bipartisan makeup of the Gang suggested it might have clout in the ongoing budget wars. The group had been formed in the wake of Simpson-Bowles and included Senator Conrad, the fiscal hawk and Budget Committee chairman, and Senator Saxby Chambliss, a Georgia Republican who was one of Boehner's closest friends.

Sperling's invocation of the Gang of Six had become a daily joke.

"You've said that every day for the last three months," Nabors told Sperling one morning. "Stop saying that."

But suddenly, on the morning of Tuesday, July 19, it was no longer a joke. Sperling reported that the Gang was going to have a meeting that morning to announce its framework.

Nabors called Jackson.

"This may end up being a potential problem for both of us in terms of votes," he said. The Gang undoubtedly was going to be more aggressive on spending cuts, thus appealing to the anti-government hardliners among the House Republicans. And it was also surely going to be more aggressive on revenue, appealing to the progressive Democrats who wanted more tax increases.

That's weird, Jackson thought. Given Boehner's closeness to Chambliss and McConnell, he would have expected a heads-up.

They're supposed to have a roll-out in the Senate in a little while, Nabors told him.


The Gang—Democrats Durbin, Conrad and Virginia Senator Mark Warner, plus Republicans Chambliss, Idaho Senator Mike Crapo and Oklahoma Senator Tom Coburn—had been crashing around in the forest since the previous December. But in a meeting with fellow senators that morning, they announced a plan calling for $3.7 trillion in deficit reduction, including new revenue of at least $1.2 trillion.

Because it was bipartisan, it drew a great deal of media attention.

Plouffe went to the president with the other senior staff. This is a very important moment, he said. Perhaps a watershed, because it was the first time Republicans were coming forward publicly and embracing the concept of more revenue. Three Republican senators, including Boehner's close friend Chambliss, were out there with a big revenue number. If Chambliss was coming out for more revenue, Plouffe said, while the president was having these negotiations with Boehner, it was probably not unrelated.

"Now, let me get this straight," Obama said. "So Saxby is saying he's willing to vote for $1.2 in revenue? And they can bring the Republicans along? Because if that's true, we definitely have a deal."

"We need to shape this for two reasons," Plouffe said. "One, let's build momentum around Republicans wanting to do revenue." It would help Boehner, giving him room to maneuver in the Republican world. Second, the Gang of Six was giving explicit support to the president's main argument that they should take a balanced approach to deficit reduction—spending cuts and a big chunk of additional revenue.

Daley, Lew and Sperling were fine with the idea. Nabors agreed strongly because they would look, he said, like "the weakest presidency in the history of mankind" if Obama was proposing less revenue than six senators including three Republicans. There was no further debate.

In the modern media age, it was important to act, get out there, be part of the daily conversation, shape the perception. No one tried harder at it than Obama. It was part of the permanent campaign, and at the moment the message seemed more important than the sensitive negotiation with Boehner. In the rapid-fire move and countermove of a presidential campaign, no one tipped the other side to the next move. One of the principles of campaign warfare was surprise. So, no one thought to give a heads-up to the speaker or his staff. The instincts of the former campaign manager carried the day.

At 1:32 p.m. Obama made a surprise appearance in the White House Briefing Room.

"Some progress was made in some of the discussions, some narrowing of the issues," he said carefully, hedging about the meetings with Boehner and the congressional leadership. "The good news is that today a group of senators, the Gang of Six, put forward a proposal that is broadly consistent with the approach I've urged." He went further, "I want to congratulate the Gang of Six." He also said that the plan McConnell and Reid were working on was "necessary" to ensure that the debt ceiling was raised if a larger deficit reduction deal could not be reached. "We have to have that fail-safe that Senator McConnell and Senator Reid are working on."

Jackson's head was almost spinning. "Why did the president come out and do a press conference to wrap his arms around the Gang of Six when they were in the middle of secret negotiations with us? We were so close to a deal. Why would he come out and say that he wants something, he applauds something that is so different than what we were so close on? We were just trying to nail down a few last pieces."

The Gang was the kind of high-profile, vocal and self-appointed group that could dwell in the world of fiscal and budget abstraction, relying on the high principle of less spending and more taxing. They did not have to live in the real world of the present crisis, in which the administration and Congress had about two weeks to avoid a calamity. That freedom also gave the Gang plenty of time to stir the pot and cause trouble.

Asked about his reaction to the Gang of Six, Obama later recalled that he had tried to walk a delicate line in discussing the revenue number.

"I did not endorse that number, precisely to protect that number," he said. "I praised the concept of Republicans being willing to actually do revenue in exchange for some serious cuts. Now, to be honest, part of the reason we didn't endorse it was because we knew that whatever they were coming up with in terms of revenue, over on this Gang of Six side, was fuzzy. They hadn't identified it, they hadn't specified where it'd come from. The cuts that they were looking for I think were substantially greater in exchange for the revenues.

"And so the notion here was not to try to embarrass Boehner or to force his hand. The notion was simply to lift up a principle, which was, if Republicans are willing to move on revenue, I'm willing to move on entitlements, and we can get a deal done."

• • •

Cantor invited Paul Ryan to his ceremonial corner office to dissect the Gang of Six plan with their staffs. With almost computer-like precision, Ryan and the others clicked through the proposals. It was a mix of the good, as they saw it, such as lowering the top marginal income tax rate to 29 percent, and the bad, including a failure to address what they believed were the budget-busting consequences of Obamacare.

The Gang of Six appeared to raise revenue of $1.2 to $2 trillion, through tax reform. A tall order, Ryan said.

But in their proposed deal with Obama, Boehner and Cantor were to raise "up to" $800 billion. They could not completely crap on the idea of tax reform because they might be driving down a similar road.

"We might be making the same argument in a day or two," Cantor's policy director, Bradley, said.

It also appeared that the Gang paid for cutting the top income tax rate to 29 percent with a massive tax increase on capital gains and dividends—Republican heresy.

So Cantor put out a statement praising the Gang's "constructive ideas" but voicing his concern about the revenue target and lack of detail.

Through a spokesman, Boehner said the plan "shared similarities" with the grand bargain he had been negotiating with the president.

Boehner and Jackson reviewed the situation. Boehner couldn't see why the Gang of Six plan should have any real impact on his discussions with the president. It was just a handful of senators getting together and making a point. It had no bearing on discussions between the White House and the House of Representatives.

"Senators being senators," Jackson said derisively. "We will come rescue the day because nothing's getting done and we're all in a panic."

Senator Tom Coburn, a member of the Simpson-Bowles commission and one of the Six, thought Obama had made a mistake. Coburn was one of the few in his party who regularly said that higher taxes were necessary to balance the budget. He thought that Obama did not realize how toxic he was to Republicans, who would see his embrace of the Gang of Six as a prelude to a tax hike. He said it showed how inexperienced a negotiator Obama was. He later told *The Washington Post* that the president's statement "absolutely killed anything we were doing with the Republicans."

Daley assembled the senior team in his corner West Wing office. The president was at $800 billion in revenue, substantially less than the Gang of Six's $1.2 trillion.

That $800 billion itself could be a "killer," Sperling said, because it was dependent on the elusive white whale of tax reform. They could chase tax reform all over the oceans and come back with nothing, as many Democrats were warning. "We'll say $800 billion," he said, "they'll say zero." So $800 billion might be too light, not enough.

Nabors agreed. "It's either zero or $800 billion, depending on who you are." The Gang of Six had changed the playing field. The $800 billion, he said, "looks really low in a world in which you've got Republicans who are willing to sign off on a higher revenue number. The Norquist pledge sort of has a hole in it all of a sudden. And so in a world in which President Obama needs to get 120 votes potentially, this is going to be tough. How do we explain this to Democrats?" Many in the party thought the White House cut bad deals, for example, the extension of the Bush tax cuts the previous year. "Just this day Republicans signed off on more revenue." Or, at least, three Republican senators had.

How about an extra $400 billion? That would take it to $1.2 trillion. If three Republicans—Chambliss, Crapo and Coburn—could go as high as $1.2 trillion, surely the president could not be much lower.

Would Boehner freak out?

"Look," Nabors said, "let's just talk to them. Let's just say, 'Look, we don't have the votes here, can we talk about this?' "

It would be a feeler. Several of them mentioned that the $800 billion number had been hard-won. They should not overplay their hand.

"You know what?" Nabors finally said. "I'm just going to float it as my idea." The son of an Army general, he knew about probing the enemy lines for weakness. He would, of course, run it by the president to make sure he approved, but by floating it as his own, Nabors would give the president some distance. He would ask for $1.2 trillion as the revenue number.

Daley gave the go-ahead, and Nabors explained his plan to the president. He would present the $1.2 trillion in his voice as a former deputy budget director and former House Appropriations Committee staff director. His plan was to say, "I'm just trying to get a deal. Is this something that can work? This isn't big macro politics."

Give it a shot, Obama said.

Nabors called Barry Jackson. He would prepare a formal offer under his name suggesting an increase to $1.2 trillion in revenue.

"We have to see how this shakes out," Jackson said, noncommittally. "We don't have any read of what's going on yet."

There had been no explosion from Jackson, Nabors told Daley. They were considering it. "You know what?" They seemed okay. "They understand."

There was this weird dance with the offers going back and forth, Nabors thought. They would want more entitlement cuts, and the White House would want more revenue. Every time one would go up, the other would go up. Enough crap, Nabors figured. Time to rip the Band-Aid off. When he was done he had a three-page offer and sent it at 6:27 p.m., clearly labeling it "Nabors draft."

"Barry," he said, "this is it. It's just me." He did not mention that the president had approved it.


When Jackson and Loper read it, they saw that Nabors left the debt limit increase blank. "$X Billion," it said. On revenue, he proposed the $800 billion plus what amounted to about $400 billion more, for a grand revenue total of $1.2 trillion.

"Whoa, whoa, whoa, whoa!" Jackson said. There it was in writing. He was dumbfounded.

"We can't do this," Loper said.

"It's a walk-back," Jackson told Boehner. Here they were in the middle of what were essentially secret negotiations with the White House, and the president comes out and throws his arms around the Gang of Six? Yes, it was the same framework—but these were very different numbers. The Nabors offer would trigger a whole additional round of offers and counteroffers.

Maybe the White House was trying to drag this out for some reason? But that made no sense. Geithner had read them all the riot act. They had a hard deadline.

Boehner was frustrated. He was willing to talk, and negotiate, about revenues. But in his mind, it was really about getting the economic engine of the country going again. It was about growth. And the things hampering growth were out-of-control spending and entitlements. He didn't, of course, want to quantify the revenue number. It was too explosive for his conference: Revenue meant taxes. But tax reform and economic growth were the remedies. The administration's demand that they get specific on the revenue debate confounded him. Numbers were poison. In the next 10 years the federal government was by all projections going to collect at least $38 trillion in revenue. And the debate had been about $800 billion—about 2 percent of that total. "It's minuscule," he said. But now the White House was talking about $1.2 trillion.

"Look," Boehner said, "we're not going to have time. I don't know why the president's walking back on this, but I'm done. We had an agreement. He's broken the agreement."

Those were Boehner's words, but he and Cantor decided that the best short-term course of action was to wait it out. Obama had invited them to the White House the next day.

In the meantime, Boehner had to make sure they did not default. The president was not a productive player now, so the speaker told Jackson that the focus would have to be on what could be worked out with the Senate—Reid and McConnell. So Jackson kept working with David Krone in Reid's office, and Loper with McConnell's key staff person, Rohit Kumar, trying to line up a Plan B.

•        •        •

The conservative intelligentsia, as they are called in Cantor's office, did not react favorably to the Gang of Six deal, especially the revenue number. It was panned by the American Enterprise Institute, the Club for Growth, *National Review* and *The Wall Street Journal*. Saxby Chambliss acknowledged it was a big number, but said they would make it up through tax reform and growth.

Not possible, said the propeller-heads of the conservative movement. That's a tax hike.

# 29

On Wednesday evening, July 20, Boehner and Cantor came to the Oval Office to review the bidding. The Republican leaders brought their senior staff—Jackson, Loper, Stombres and Bradley. Biden, Geithner, Lew and Nabors sat in for the administration.

They were close on a draft plan, Obama said, as he rattled off various cuts and savings. They were close on the cuts to the non-Defense, nonsecurity and nonentitlement spending. They hadn't settled on the final discretionary number, on language for entitlement reform, or the all-important trigger. And the Gang of Six, Obama said, has made this more complicated on the revenue front. Your buddy Saxby, he said to Boehner, has put me in a hard position.

"Revenue," Boehner said. "Mr. President, our necks are out as far as they can go." The "up to" $800 billion was it, the upper limit.

Nabors worried that they were again talking past each other. Boehner kept calling it $800 billion but the Republicans were going to say it was all through tax reform and so it would effectively be zero. How was the president going to sell what House Republicans would call zero revenue to Democrats when conservative Senate Republicans like Chambliss, Coburn and Crapo said they needed at least to get $1.2 trillion in revenue? But Nabors did not say anything, and his $1.2 trillion proposal did not come up explicitly.

"Social Security," Boehner continued. "I think there's a way to stay out of the problem." He mentioned a 75-year solvency test. The concept was they would avoid getting into particulars by just establishing a test on solvency. If the Social Security system was solvent in 75 years, then they would consider the problem solved.

"Let's say it's resolved," the president said, jumping on an agreement quickly. One issue settled, pushed off to a distant future.

On the trigger, the way to enforce an agreement, Boehner said, the "ultimate trigger is the debt ceiling" but he had conceded that—a big concession.

"We can't do that," Obama reaffirmed.

"Decoupling sends people over the edge," Boehner said, meaning not continuing the Bush tax cuts for the upper two brackets. Then the speaker played his best card. "If you're going to have decoupling, we would need Obamacare."

Awkward moment. Everyone tried to avoid the use of the pejorative, but there it was.

Ooh, okay, Cantor thought.

The trigger would have to contain two key parts of the president's health care reform, Boehner said. If the trigger went off, these two elements would be repealed. First, the controversial Independent Payment Advisory Board (IPAB), which was supposed to find savings in Medicare and curb costs. Second would be the individual mandate that required all Americans to buy health insurance.

"Creative thought, John," the president said. In other words, gut health care reform. No.

"Our members see a disincentive to act in the Senate," Cantor said. If letting the Bush tax cuts expire is in the trigger, the Democratic Senate majority could let the trigger go off and they would have killed the lower rates for the wealthy, a big accomplishment. That might be worth everything to them. "That is a nonstarter for us."

Why don't you just put in there that if it doesn't happen, then I'm impeached or removed from office? the president joked. Let me try to clear out the underbrush, he said. Medicaid and other health cuts need to be at $150 billion.

Cantor had been pushing for higher cuts, thinking they could do more. But the president seemed to be holding at $150 billion.

On the revenue side, Obama continued, you guys said you can't do more. "The only thing I'm thinking about is, can we do some cats and dogs? Corporate stuff, close loopholes."

Everyone knew these were small—$5 to $10 billion—and would have no impact except as symbolic political scalps. The president, apparently, wanted some.

"How do you explain that revenue plug?" Cantor asked. This was the $800 billion. The CBO score won't help. CBO is going to score that as a tax increase. It's not going to help us sell it when we're seeing CBO go, that's just a tax increase, and our guys are reacting negatively, obviously, on the Gang of Six.

We have to figure out, universally, Boehner said, how we're going to talk about it. They had to know how each side was going to define and market this "so we're not totally undermining each other's arguments." Though he had told Jackson he was finished with Obama, Boehner was talking as if they were still on track. He had invested so much, and so much was at stake.

"It has to be a jump ball for both of us," the president said. He said he wouldn't try to claim victory. "I won't spike the ball," he pledged, acknowledging the importance of perception. "I won't dance in the end zone. I guarantee you that I will get more shit from my base. I'm going to get ripped for caving $1 trillion below where the Gang of Six was."

Back to the trigger, he said, "You are right that health care spending is as sacred to us as decoupling is to you. But Medicare is the ultimate to us. Let's talk crass politics: You will have Democrats that agree to Medicare cuts. That helps you."

Boehner and Cantor acknowledged his point. It was McConnell's constant theme. Republicans were being attacked for the drastic Medicare cuts proposed in the Ryan budget. If Democrats agreed to cuts in Medicare, that political argument was gone, or at least much less effective. Because, look, both parties voted to reform Medicare.

A cut of hundreds of billions to Medicare beneficiaries is significant, Jack Lew said.

Our guys don't want to do it either, Boehner said. The pain isn't shared equally. If it's decoupling and you're just playing around the edge of Medicare, this is not viewed as equal by our guys. "The trigger would have to raise more than the debt ceiling." Boehner had consistently said that total deficit reduction would have to be greater than the hike in the debt limit.

Obama began listing what he would be giving up. "We're immediately engaging in discretionary cuts" such as education and transportation. Plus more cuts in the nonhealth mandatory, such as federal civilian employment pensions. "Lots on the front end. Tax reform happens later."

The president summed up, "The balance is, we are putting a big down payment with cuts but we don't get the revenues until later."

Boehner seemed to be nodding in agreement.

The cuts in education or transportation had to be set up front, Cantor said. "We don't believe that the caps"—the plan to put 10-year limits on that spending in the law—"our guys don't believe that they're real after the first two years, after the next Congress. So we've got two years of caps at max."

It was a point Larry Summers and others had always made to the president. Future Congresses could change the laws on spending to reflect their will. Instead of arguing with this fact, Obama tried to turn the tables. "We say the revenues are not real," he repeated. Tax reform would be far downrange.

"We all want a broader base and lower rates. I'm concerned that there are progressive and regressive cuts to reform the tax code. The trigger ensures a regressive policy if hit." From Obama's perspective, the poor and underprivileged on Medicaid and Medicare would be hurt the most. So the trigger would be very bad for him if it went off. "I'm not trying to get a scalp. I'm trying to ensure that the fallback doesn't hurt those who can least afford it."

"Our guys want something real," Cantor said. They wanted an ironclad enforcement mechanism. "How do we ensure that it happens?"

No one had an answer.

"Decoupling is a huge issue for our guys," Cantor continued. The trigger was unbalanced because Obama wanted decoupling in the trigger. If everyone has what is most important to them in this trigger, then everyone is motivated to get this done, he said.

"Tax hikes are bad politics for us," Obama said.

The Republicans did not believe this, especially Cantor. If so, why were the tax hikes on the wealthy the very centerpiece of Obama's political attack? For Cantor and Boehner, the claim was phony.

"The debt limit is the ultimate solution," Boehner repeated.

"No," the president said sharply. "Can't do that."

"I would bet anything," Biden said, "if there were secret polls of Democrats, they would say you Republicans would trade decoupling for the repeal of health care reform." Getting rid of health care reform would be too big an incentive for you guys. In other words, you're asking for too much. During his meetings with Cantor in the spring, they had taken those issues off the negotiating table.

"I think this is constructive," the president said. "The trigger needs to be decoupling." If it went off, the Bush tax cuts for the rich would expire—anathema to the Republicans. "Medicare is not enough for you."

Boehner said, hey look, cuts in Medicare aren't exactly great for us.

"You have asked us to come up with something you think is painful for us," the president continued.

"The logic behind the trigger was equal pain," Lew said.

"The trigger right now looks like you've been set on fire and stabbed," Obama said.

Laughter.

The Democrats had it better, he conceded. "We have just been set on fire."

More laughter.

"I think there's a way to do that creatively." So they needed to find something to add to the trigger that would stab the Democrats also. "Is there a way to work on the trigger?" A scalp for a scalp? He suggested that their staffs work on it.

"Both of you have been very solid in these negotiations," Obama continued, complimenting Boehner and Cantor. "And I know it's been hard. Some of your guys are unreasonable." He said nothing about his own guys. "We're running tight on time. John, how are you going to roll out?" The president was talking optimistically, as if it was all or mostly done. How would they publicly describe the deal and some of its components?

He had one request. "Help us say that the economy is not going to be in danger."

It was an unusual moment. On one hand, it was an appeal to the high purpose of his office and theirs to serve the larger national interest by helping him build and hold confidence. They would collectively reassure the markets, investors, businesses, and not least, the credit rating agencies, Moody's and S&P. It sounded high-minded. But it was also personal, because everyone in the Oval Office realized precisely what Obama needed to win reelection: public confidence that the economy was strong and wasn't on the verge of collapse.

Boehner turned to the next year's discretionary cuts to education, transportation and domestic spending, hoping to cut additional billions more.

"We want 1.040," he said, meaning $1 trillion 40 billion.

Obama jumped into the auction, wanting 1.048—$8 billion more. "I can't go to 1.040. Let's not nickel-and-dime each other, John."

Boehner said that $1.048 would not work.

"How about 1.045?" Lew suggested, adding another nickel.

Agreement was not reached.

It was almost funny. With the economy nearing disaster, the president, the speaker and the House majority leader needed to reach agreement on a deal involving trillions of dollars. But they couldn't reach token accord when positions differed by only $8 billion.

"All right guys," Obama said, "let's work on the trigger. See how creative we can get." Cantor interpreted this to mean, I'm keeping decoupling in there. Let's see what else you need to get there, but it's not going to be Obamacare.

The president continued, Work on the $150 billion cut in non-

Medicare health programs. Let's work on the overall discretionary number, the Medicare doctor fix, unemployment insurance, and the payroll tax cut, which will expire at the end of the year.

And the all-important revenue number. Go work on it, guys.

Driving away from the White House, Boehner and Jackson had two questions. What was the president trying to do here? Are we being gamed or not? Neither had answers. Boehner indicated he was trying to balance the interests and keep working the two tracks: one with Obama and the other with the Senate leaders.

After the meeting, Biden pulled Cantor aside and hustled him down to his office. He thought of Cantor as his contact, even his guy, in the House Republican camp, much like McConnell in the Senate. They could talk candidly.

"I trust you, Eric," Biden said. "You trust me. We've developed this relationship." I think we're close on a deal. Let's keep the line of communication open, let's not screw this up now.

Cantor could see a path to agreement. If he could get Obamacare into the trigger—and he was very skeptical—it was possible that he could deliver the Republican conference, or enough of it.

Would the administration really buy into an Obamacare trigger? Cantor later asked Stombres and Bradley.

Probably not, Stombres said. It was a fantasy. By discussing it, even seemingly putting the Bush tax decoupling and Obamacare on the table, they had identified the red lines for both sides. Didn't that really mean, let's talk about something else, find some other trigger that would not go over a red line? By defining where they couldn't go, they might figure out where they could, he added hopefully.

Cantor said it was clear the president was not open to doing Obamacare—his signature achievement. But he seemed to comprehend the political need of the Republicans. As a practical matter, Cantor could sell repeal of Obamacare or of its major parts to his members, but nothing else. But Obamacare in the trigger was just not going to happen.

The stakes were high for Cantor. Now that he had been brought back into the direct talks with the president, the tom-toms would start beating. Was he challenging Boehner? He concluded that if Obama and Boehner were committed to this big deal—and they seemed to be, even overly so—he would have to do everything possible to fall in line and help them get it. He could not be seen as the spoiler. So, he asked, how could he make the most of it, help get a deal that would upset the fewest of his members while still getting the necessary votes? All without violating the core anti-tax principle?

Though he was now majority leader, Cantor had never abandoned the habit, developed during his two years as Republican whip, of constantly staying in touch with the rank and file of the Republican conference. He had every member's contact information stored in his BlackBerry, and he emailed them constantly. Communication flowed both ways. Members came to understand that they were free to contact Cantor by email on almost anything, and that they could often expect a response within a few minutes.

His initial conclusion was that this $1.2 trillion would not fly. At the Capitol that night, he went to Kevin McCarthy's whip office, where a big buffet of Chinese food was laid out for Republican members. The buffet was a routine for nights like this one, when the House had late votes. Cantor took McCarthy, Ryan and Hensarling aside. This trio was the key. As whip, McCarthy knew the members better than anyone. Ryan was the bellwether for policy in the conference. And Hensarling, the No. 4 in leadership, had been chairman of the Republican Study Committee, an influential group of more than 170 conservative House Republicans.

Cantor told them that the speaker was getting too far out in front. The White House was floating a revenue number of $1.2 trillion. It seemed impossible to him, he said, but he didn't want to be the lone objector. "Tell me I'm not crazy."

All three said they agreed. He was not crazy. The number was too big to camouflage with tax reform.

So here was the bind, Cantor said. What if the speaker went for it? What would they do? Boehner talked tough in private but down at the White House he was acting as if they were on track. The speaker was like a runaway horse, he said. How best to pull back on the reins?

No one had an answer, and soon staffers from the speaker's office began asking about the meeting that Cantor was having in the whip's office.


The president called some Senate Democrats after the meeting to bring them up to date. They were getting anxious, not being part of the direct negotiations.

With $800 billion in revenue, the president said they would have to accept moderate entitlement cuts. But if the revenue could be increased to $1.2 trillion, they would wind up with significant entitlement cuts.

# 30

Nabors gathered key White House and Republican staff around the table in his large West Wing office the next morning, Thursday, July 21. Lew, Sperling and Bruce Reed, Biden's chief of staff, represented the president. Jackson, Brett Loper, Steve Stombres and Neil Bradley, Cantor's main policy staffer, spoke for Republicans.

We don't think we can get any more votes, Nabors said. We're going to need more revenue in order to convince more Democrats, and you're going to need more entitlement cuts to convince more Republicans. The $800 billion was not enough to get the Democratic votes they would need in the House. They needed $400 billion more in revenue, for a total of $1.2 trillion.

No one said yes, no one said no, but it sounded positive to the White House people. Jackson and the other Republican staffers said the revenue issue was way above their pay grades. It would be decided by Obama and Boehner.

They cleared away some underbrush, such as Pell Grant reforms. Left on the table was the trigger, though Cantor's staff said that if Obama wanted decoupling to be part of it, their boss would require that some major portion of Obamacare be included. That was the only plausible way to sell it to his members.

They turned to the Medicare age increase. It would be raised eventually over time to 67.

Yes, okay, everyone seemed to agree.

When would it start? In 2022 as Obama wanted? Or 2017 as Boehner proposed?

Well, they would have to work that out.

When would they eventually reach age 67? In 2046 as Obama wanted? Or 2029 as Boehner did?

That would have to be worked out also.

It seemed a century away to Jackson, and there was no agreement. He thought they were bypassing all the important decisions.

Nabors said the prospective deal was about four matters—Medicare, Social Security, Medicaid and revenue. As they went through them they were a little skittish.

"This is above all of our pay grades," Nabors said. "Let's just put that off on the side and keep working through the details." All four major issues would be left to Obama and Boehner. So they tackled some small things and seemed to reach agreement and took some steps on writing actual legislation. They discussed timing. Under House rules, legislation had to be publicly available for three days, so they looked at a calendar to calculate how much time was available.

"If we do this deal," Jackson said almost conspiratorially, "you guys have to wait till after the vote before you start describing it as raising $800 billion." If they did that, it was a deal breaker.

At one point Jackson accused Nabors and the White House of engineering the Gang of Six's decision to come out with their vague plan two days before.

"I don't know how you can say we engineered it," Nabors replied. "The speaker's best friend"—Chambliss—"is on the Gang of Six." Republicans must have known or been involved somehow.

We were surprised, Jackson insisted.

Lew and Nabors were scheduled to speak to the Democratic Senate policy lunch that afternoon. The weekly meeting of the Senate

Democratic caucus was an important communications forum for the White House.

"I'm only leaving now because I have to be up on the Hill," Lew said as he got up to leave. He was being served up as the administration's "sacrificial lamb," he added grimly.

Jackson turned to Lew. "We all agree we're going to get to yes, right?"

Yes, Lew said.

The meeting ended after two hours. A good meeting, thought the Democrats. It seemed like they had accomplished a lot, and Jackson's insistence they get to yes seemed to be a tip-off.

But there was no feeling of accomplishment on the Republican side. Cantor's staffers, Stombres and Bradley, and Boehner's, Jackson and Loper, felt the meeting was unproductive and that they were still not close to a deal.

Loper, in particular, was extremely pessimistic. They had been near a deal on Sunday. Then on Tuesday, the Gang of Six came out. Who cared what six senators were saying? Not Loper. Their math didn't even add up. The power was with the president, the speaker and the Senate. The Gang of Six was not a reason to step away from the deal. Maybe it was an excuse? he wondered.

Jackson, who was the most bullish on a deal because Boehner wanted one desperately, left thinking, perhaps for the first time, that they would not get there. He gave his assessment to Boehner.

The speaker wanted to talk about options for avoiding default. How quickly could they pivot to the plan they were working on with Reid and McConnell?

There was a confidence level with them, Jackson said. And Pelosi and Hoyer would deliver enough Democrats, he was sure. "The president would, in the end, have to accept this," Jackson said, "because when the congressional leaders say, Mr. President, this is what we can do, and the clock is ticking . . ." Well, it would be obvious. The president would have to give.

What about the trigger? Boehner asked. They had to come up with a better trigger and figure out how it would work. In the end, that would be about trust, he said. Neither he nor Jackson was sure they trusted the president.

Keep working with the congressional leaders, Boehner told Jackson.

*New York Times* reporter Jackie Calmes called Dan Pfeiffer, the White House communications director, to say she and her colleague Carl Hulse were about to post a piece on the *Times* website reporting that Obama and Boehner were near a $3 trillion deficit deal. The story was not precisely right, because it did not have the $800 billion potential revenue figure, and their reporting seemed to suggest there was not much revenue in the deal. Pfeiffer took the information to Bill Daley and the others.

"They can't report that," Daley said. "We've got to try to stop that."

Pfeiffer said it was impossible to stop; the horse was out of the barn.

On Capitol Hill, Lew and Nabors didn't have a chance to eat much of their lunch. They were accompanied by Plouffe because Harry Reid had wanted Obama's top political adviser to see firsthand the building wrath among the senators.

The majority leader stood to introduce them.

"The White House is here to explain the deal that they cut with Boehner," Reid said. "I don't know anything about it."

Nabors and Lew looked at each other in wonder. They had briefed Reid three days earlier. Reid had just thrown them to the wolves. As budget director, it was Lew they attacked most.

A band of angry Democratic senators, including former and likely future presidential candidates, cross-examined them on what kind of deal the president was trying to cut. Where was the revenue guarantee? Democrats had a winning hand, the public was with them on higher taxes on the rich. Why do we have to cut any Medicare? Don't cut anything. You are playing on Republican turf. Talk of big spending cuts was weak and played into Republican hands. This whole debate should be about revenue. Stare them down. Why were Senate Democrats cut out of the process? Force the Republicans to raise taxes on millionaires.

"You could raise all the taxes you want on millionaires," Nabors made the mistake of saying, and it would never raise enough.

It was about symbolism, and the political bounce, several senators retorted. Clearly, the White House did not comprehend the dynamic.

"This needs to run through regular order," Massachusetts Senator John Kerry, the onetime Democratic presidential nominee, said. "Let the committees do their business. Let the senators cut a deal. We can get there."

During the meeting, the *New York Times* story popped up on the Internet. Headlined "Push Intensifies for Larger Deal on Debt Impasse," the story said "new cracks were appearing among House Republicans." Boehner, it added, "has shown continued interest in a deal if it can be done in a way that emphasizes lower tax rates."

Lew and Plouffe told the senators it was premature and not really true, but Plouffe was alarmed. The story would push Boehner further into a corner.

Lew was less than forthcoming about the actual deal because of the sensitivity of the negotiations—the situation could not have been more delicate—and he knew that the senators would speak to the media afterward.

When Lew was done, Senator Barbara Mikulski, the outspoken Maryland Democrat, said to the others, "I haven't seen a meeting like this in my 35 years in Congress."

Reid was so angry that he talked to reporters off the Senate floor after the lunch, pleading for a deal with balance, fairness and necessary revenue. All the Senate Democrats agreed with that, he said. In a mildly threatening tone, he added, "Hope the president sticks with that, and I'm confident he will."

Lew, Nabors and Plouffe returned to the White House and briefed Obama. It had been a rough meeting, as anticipated.

"It was just one of the more awful experiences of my life," Nabors said.

"I'm glad it was you guys, not me," Obama said.


In the wake of the *New York Times* story, Plouffe was trying to count votes in the House. He thought Nabors's original estimate of 120 to 130 Democrats was too high. They would only get 70 Democrats now, he figured, so Boehner would have to come up with about 150 Republicans. That meant losing maybe 90—a big number for any leader. Whatever the count, they were dancing on a razor blade.

Nabors checked in with John Lawrence, Pelosi's chief of staff. Lawrence, who had a Ph.D. in history and been with Pelosi since 2005, had known Nabors for years. They could cut to the chase.

"The only way this is going to work is if we—not jam it through—but we have to move quickly," Nabors said. "Because if this thing sits out there, we're just going to get picked apart a thousand different ways. We need to cut the deal, we need to break the arms we need to break. We need to get this thing passed and signed before people lock into positions that will tear the package apart."

Democratic House members were responding to rumors, Lawrence said, because they didn't have much information.

"Please don't confirm or deny," Nabors said, "please don't let people lock into positions quite yet."

As Nabors talked to a few members, his theme was simple. "Holy crap," he said to one, "this is going to be really, really hard . . . 20 years of incredibly hard policy coming together in one package." On the table were Clinton tax increases of 1994, Bush tax cuts of 2001 and 2003, and big potential changes in Medicare and Medicaid entitlements. Possible Postal Service reform, and the biggest change in federal employee retirement in decades. The pay of millions of federal workers had been frozen and now they were thinking of increasing their retirement contributions. It was a big deal.

One Democrat told Nabors, "Let me get this straight. We are giving up specific cuts to entitlements for the promise of getting revenue in

the future? If there's going to be a process for revenue"—tax reform—
"we want a process for entitlements."

As Nabors traveled through the White House, especially the West
Wing, the common question was, "Does this actually have a chance of
happening?"

"The best indication that it has a chance of happening is that people are starting to panic," Nabors answered.


Nabors and Sperling went to see the president again with good news
about the earlier meeting with Boehner's and Cantor's staffs.

"Had you been in that meeting," Sperling said, "you would've bet
your house there was going to be a deal." He had been doing these negotiations for 20 years. Both sides had been told by their principals to
get a deal. "You can smell when people are trying to work it out. The
bullshit goes away. It was just totally honest."

The president, Nabors said, would have to reach agreement with
Boehner on the big-ticket items—Medicare, Social Security, Medicaid
and revenue. "Everything else is locked down. We could have this in
the can in an hour." It feels like a deal, he added. "So if Boehner calls,
cut the deal because we're ready to go on everything else."

Yeah, the president said. Fine. They were in good shape.


For about a year the president had had discussions with Geithner
about the overall fiscal picture.

"Geithner has two concerns," the president later recalled. "He has
an immediate concern about the catastrophe of a default on our debt.
He also has a longer-term concern about the markets and their assessment of our debt. And those are—one is a very technical, immediate
concern. And we're having meetings every week about, okay, what's
worst-case scenarios? How do we manage this? He's running fire drills
inside of Treasury to figure out how long can they extend it."

He and Geithner had come to agree strongly that they had to try
to "break" the Republicans on revenue. Without more tax revenue

the administration would not be able to do much on infrastructure, education and other spending the president deemed essential for the economy and the country. While it was important for the president to demonstrate that he recognized the country had to live within its means and cut some spending, it was crucial to get that revenue.

Lew was all for increased revenue. There was no way to dance around the need for new, real revenue—not just through tax reform, but through tax increases. The unambiguous message from the Hill Democrats was that new, real revenue had to be in the deal.

So rather than wait, the president picked up the phone and called Boehner. It was time for a vote count discussion. In the end, that was all that mattered. Did they have the votes or not?

According to one senior White House aide who was in the room when the call was made and then heard the president's description of Boehner's end of the conversation, this is what happened:

"John," Obama said, "this is going to be really tough." How many votes do you need?

I don't know, Boehner replied, it depends.

"If you need a decent number of Democratic votes," the president said, "we may need more revenue, in the $400 billion range." I'd like you to consider it.

Nabors had floated it but now the president was asking the speaker. "I really think that could help us get the number of votes that we need."

If they needed a lot of Democrats, Obama said, "I can't have the Gang of Six"—with their proposal for at least $1.2 trillion in revenue— "to the left of me."

Boehner agreed that would be hard for the president. But as he had said the night before, his neck was out about as far as it could go.

"If you can't," Obama said, "I understand. Come back to me. We'll figure out another way. Maybe there's another way we can lighten the Democrats' load to get some more votes." If the additional $400 billion was not possible, Obama said, "then we are going to have to look at the entire package." That meant, he said, "We're just going to have to look at the entitlements and we'll obviously keep most of what's in there." He was committed to the major entitlement cuts. "But we might have to dial some of that back a little bit."

The president said he was confident that the Democratic leaders, Reid and Pelosi, would go along. "I can get Nancy and Harry to be for this."

Boehner was skeptical. Reid was definitely in a different place. Keeping his options open, the speaker gave a vague response, along the lines of we should keep in touch.

"So think about it," the president said, "come back. And if it doesn't work for you, let's talk again. Get back to me."

Obama had just had one of the most important conversations of his presidency—one that he and Boehner later remembered very differently.

In an interview, Boehner, who was consulting notes of his discussion with Obama, vehemently disputed the White House version, saying that the president absolutely insisted on $400 billion more in revenue.

The Boehner version: "Then Obama finally calls me on Thursday and wants $400 billion more. I said, 'Mr. President, we've had this conversation now for a month. You know there's not a dime more on the table.' "

The president's response, "I have to have $400 billion more. I have to have $400 billion more."

"I said, 'Mr. President, it just isn't going to happen. No.' "

The president, according to Boehner, said three times, "I want you to think about it."

"So, I said okay."

According to Boehner, "We had a deal. That was the real shocker." He said he reminded Obama that they had met at the White House four days earlier. 'Mr. President, remember Sunday? We have a deal.' " Boehner said the president kept pushing and saying, "I've got to have more revenue. Got to have more revenue. I need $400 billion more."

Boehner added, "I pushed back a couple of times, because he knew there was not an extra dime on the table. But he was also, I'm sure, getting a hell of a lot of heat from Reid and Pelosi. And so, I understood the pressure he was under. But hell, I knew the damn pressure I was under."

I reminded him that the president later said he only asked that the $400 billion be considered and had not demanded it.

"No, no, no," Boehner said. "Hold on. No, no, no. No. No. I *need* $400 billion more revenue. I *need*. And I pushed back a couple of times. And he said, 'No, no, I need $400 billion more. You need to think about this.' I said, 'Okay, I will think about it.' And the president said, 'Call me back.' It was pretty clear to me then that he was blowing this thing up, and we'd better figure out what Plan B is.

"I immediately picked up the phone and called McConnell," Boehner said. He said he told the Senate minority leader, "We better be thinking about Plan B here."

Boehner summarized his view, "If you're going to drop your dance partner, you'd better make sure you've got another one. But understand, I did not want to get to August 2nd without an agreement." He added, "Eric and I believed we get past August 2nd, our leverage decreases, not increases."


Obama later told me that he presented the speaker with choices rather than a demand.

"At this point, Boehner and I, we've been talking a lot. We've been having a good discussion. And we think we're coming close to a deal. But now the question of votes is starting to come up. The Gang of Six has made its announcement. It's gotten a lot of attention.

"I say to John, here's the situation. You are going to need some Democratic votes to get this passed, no matter what. And at $800 billion, it is going to be hard to get the kind of Democratic votes that you may need to pass this through the House. And so if you are prepared to go up to $1.2 trillion, which matches more or less what the Gang of Six has talked about, we can probably get more Democratic votes. If not, you'll probably get fewer Democratic votes. So you need to give me a sense of, how many votes do you think you need for a deal? How many votes do you need to get this through? And based on that, we'll have to calibrate what we can do on my side. So get back to me, and let me know.

"We have two paths here. We can do the $800 billion and you'll get fewer Democratic votes. And I don't know exactly how many we'll get. Or we could go up an extra $400 billion, in which case you're going to get a lot more Democratic votes. And it will have a much easier time clearing the Senate if we can hang on to enough Republicans."

Told that some of his senior staff in the room during the call believed the two paths were $400 billion in more revenue or smaller entitlement cuts, the president initially said he didn't believe that was accurate but, "It may be that that is in the context of the fact that we still don't have a deal yet. So keep in mind, for example, Boehner's still asking for $125 billion or something in Medicaid cuts. So I may have said to him—which I would have been saying anyway—we can't go up to $125 billion. I might, if we have [revenue at] $1.2 trillion, might be able to do a little bit more and still hang on to Democratic votes. You see what I mean? So you've got a fluid situation in which we have not yet determined what kind of entitlement cuts are on the table. And we're in a situation in which the revenue has not yet been settled.

"You have at this point a set of variables. Variable number one is, how much revenue? Variable number two is, how significant are the entitlement changes? And variable number three is, how many votes can Boehner provide? And we're trying to see how this Rubik's cube gets put together. So that's the context of the conversation that I had with Boehner. I want to be very emphatic here: At no point did I say, John, take it or leave it. At no point did I say, John, I've got to have $400 billion more or we don't have a deal. What I said to him was, you have to tell me how many votes do you plan to put on this thing? Because I've got to then go back to Nancy and Harry and find out from them what it is that they think they can do. Because there's no point in us going out there if it turns out that we don't have the votes."

Jack Lew, who was among those in the room during the call, heard the president's end of the conversation and gave this account to a White

House colleague: "I remember Thursday extremely well, actually. The president called the speaker and said, 'We can go one of two ways. We could have a bigger package with more revenue or we could have a smaller package with less revenue. What we can't do is we can't be in the place we're at—the high end of our tolerance on entitlement cuts and at the low end of what is acceptable on revenue."

Lew summed up: "After the Gang of Six came out, our ability to get Democratic votes was just going to be different based on that. We still could get Democratic votes. We go higher on revenue, we'll be able to do more on long-term entitlement reform. If not, we'll still do changes. We'll still do things that are hard. But it's not going to have as much. And they were kind of path A and path B. I can go with either one."

Plouffe's version was still different. The president's political adviser believed the conversation focused on votes, with the president telling Boehner, "If you need a decent number of Democratic votes, we may need, for revenue, in the $400 billion range."

And the president, in Plouffe's version, was emphatic. He told Boehner: "If you can't do that, then we're just going to have to look at the entitlements and we'll have to obviously keep most of what's in there, but we might have to dial some of that back a little bit. . . . The president was very clear: If you can't do more revenue, then we're just going to have to look at the entire package."

Plouffe realized that no matter how the president had phrased it, he had offered "a door Boehner could walk through to shut this thing down. There's no doubt it was a lifeline for Boehner to say, ah, this is my reason to break this thing off—more revenue." Maybe it was a risk that had to be taken.

The Gang of Six was the stated reason, but it was also an excuse to try to get terms more favorable to the Democrats. The president had started the negotiations with one sword, the decoupling of the high-end Bush tax cuts, but had just handed another one to the speaker.


The president then met with Nabors.

"Rob," he asked, "what do you think our votes look like?"

In the House, Nabors said, instead of the 120 to 130 votes he had previously hoped they could get, it was probably down to 75 to 90. But if the president said he needed 120 votes, Pelosi would go into full operations mode. She would get the bodies; she would figure out a way to get to 120.

Nabors thought she was shrewder and tougher than anybody really knew. She would kick ass. She was an old-school leader. Pelosi wanted lots of hands—bloody ones if necessary—on the knife. "She is absolutely nails," he had concluded.

The president was in operations mode himself, acting like the chief whip. What about the potential Republican votes?

Because Boehner was apparently not doing a vote count, that was a bit of a mystery, Nabors replied.

How about the Senate? the president inquired.

"I think the Senate is going to be hard," Nabors said. "Absent any muscle, we'd be in the low 20s probably. But with some muscle, we're probably in the mid to high 30s to low 40s. As a result," Nabors went on, "we're going to need 15, 20 Republicans to show up to get us to 60. I don't think we should put what we think we can get on the table. We need to be prepared to go to McConnell and say—and overachieve— 'Mitch, are you prepared to put up 30 people? Because we can put up 30 people.' " Then if we got 40 to 45 Democrats, that would be fantastic. Added value, he explained.

Afterward, Obama said to Sperling and Nabors that he thought he had a deal. Get Reid and Pelosi in here.


Asked in an interview whether the Gang of Six releasing their plan had made it more difficult for Democrats to line up votes, Obama recalled, "I think that's kind of the buzz around Washington. And look, there's no doubt that there's a school of thought among some progressives that we shouldn't be even having this negotiation at all. And at this point . . . the whole legend that somehow we got outmaneuvered in the continuing resolution has taken root in the blogosphere among some folks."

Was it correct that Nabors felt, prior to the Gang of Six, that you could get 120 House Democrats?

The president disagreed. "The view was that if Boehner was willing to settle for 120, 130 votes, that we would work to make up the difference. I'm not sure we got up to 120. I didn't think that he would ever go for something where the Democratic minority in the House was supplying most of the votes for this thing. I didn't think that his caucus would abide by that. But I did think that we could get to a point where, if the deal had enough revenue, you could picture Boehner getting 120 or 130 votes, us supplying 90, or maybe even up to 100, and we could get something done." The magic number, of course, would be 218 total.

# 31

---

Pelosi was facing a rebellion among House Democrats. As just one example, Representative Corrine Brown from Jacksonville had said plainly and openly that Obama could kiss Florida good-bye if he messed with Social Security and Medicare.

Pelosi and Reid arrived at the White House and met with the president, Lew and Nabors in the Oval Office.

"I've got to do this," the president said. As part of a 10-year package he was offering Boehner over $1 trillion in domestic and Defense cuts plus another $650 billion in entitlement cuts—Medicare, Medicaid and Social Security. The minimal goal was $800 billion in revenue through tax reform. He also explained that he was trying to get $400 billion more on the revenue side, which would take it up to $1.2 trillion through tax reform. "I don't know if I'll be able to get it. If I can't, I'll try to make it more acceptable to us a bit."

"You guys went off and negotiated a deal without me," Pelosi said, echoing what Reid had said earlier in the day, "and you expect me to bring people along?" She rattled off a list of House Democrats, from the liberal Sandy Levin to Steny Hoyer, the whip, who would "hate" the deal.

"Why, Mr. President," she said, "would you give these guys anything for $800 billion in revenue? You're going to get that anyway."

She was referring to the prospect of ending the high-end tax cuts for the rich, which the president had insisted to her and to others that he would not extend. Time and time again he had told her, "Never again." He would not allow an extension of those Bush tax cuts as he had in 2010.

Putting Social Security cost-of-living adjustments on the table would take away an issue that had defined the difference between the two parties, she said.

"If we do anything on Social Security," the president said, "we're not using any of that money for deficit reduction. We're putting the money back into the system." This seemed contrary to the offer Nabors had sent to Boehner two days earlier, which had included "benefit changes."

Considering Medicare beneficiary cuts, she said, would allow the Republicans to get well on the Ryan budget. They would claim that the Democrats also wanted to cut health insurance for the elderly, again removing the distinction between the parties.

We think we can get all the Medicare savings from the doctor and hospital providers, Obama said, and not from the elderly beneficiaries.

The idea of raising the eligibility age for Medicare was a surprise, she said.

It would not change the standard of living for the elderly in a meaningful way, the president argued, and the change could give them 10 years to deal with Medicare's skyrocketing costs. He acknowledged that none of this was designed to fire up the party base.

What about Medicaid? she inquired.

It was under other health care savings, Obama replied, and the savings would be a very small component. "We think we can get it from sort of reducing improper payments.

"You need to understand how close we are to being downgraded," the president said, "and what the downgrade would mean, not just to us but in the context of the world economy."

"You have to understand how hard this is," Pelosi said.

"Most of this is in the range of conversations that we've all been talking about all along," the president said. "And at the end of the day, this gets us where we need to go. We all believe that we need to put the budget back on track."

Reid sat there stone-faced and hardly said a word.

"I totally disagree with this," Pelosi said. "I don't think you should do this." They were giving up way, way too much. But on the other hand, she said, "You are our president, and we are in a time of crisis." If he decided he had to do it, she would make sure he had every opportunity to present his case.

The president said he was expecting to hear back from Boehner. "When I get John on the phone," he asked, "can I tell John we can produce Democratic votes?"

"I'll see," Pelosi replied.

Reid would not commit and was grumpy. "You guys went off and talked to Boehner again," he said, shaking his head in disbelief. The administration had been screwed many times before. What did they think would happen this time? Reid was also not going to go along with a full 18-month extension of the debt limit, as the president was insisting. He wanted the Senate to retain some leverage.

After Reid and Pelosi left, Nabors turned to the president.

"I'm nervous," he said. In an understatement, he added, "I don't know where this is going."

Lew concurred.

"Nancy has always been there for us," the president said, and he was confident she would be again.

Though her words fell far short of a personal commitment, Nabors said he agreed. Her "I'll see" meant she was just trying to figure out how to get the votes. She would be all-in.

But they agreed they still had a Harry Reid problem.


The president later recalled the meeting with Reid and Pelosi this way:

"Well, I lay out for them what we're talking about. And then I say to them, with great specificity, I say to them, I don't know yet what Boehner is going to do. He is going to come back to me and tell me what his preferred path is. I need to get a sense from you, if he does not go along with additional revenue, are you guys still prepared to put up votes and work with me to go ahead and do a deal with $800 billion as opposed to 1.2 trillion? And I asked Nancy, I asked Harry, and I asked each of these folks. And I say to them, look, we're at white-knuckle time here, so you guys have to be straight with me. If you don't think you can do it, you let me know."

He agreed that Pelosi worried that cuts to Medicare beneficiaries could remove an important distinction between Democrats and Republicans.

"Well, I think generally speaking, all the Democrats felt that for Democrats to join with Republicans in anything that could be painted as a Medicare cut when there was a huge difference between Democratic and Republican positions on Medicare generally was bad politics. And I think Nancy felt that. And in fairness, I think substantively, they also felt—legitimately so—that these are very vulnerable populations.

"Now, what I told them is I had talked to my Medicare and Medicaid experts. And I was not willing to do anything that I thought was going to actually affect the care of vulnerable populations, and I felt confident that the package we had come up with would preserve and protect Medicare and Medicaid as the social safety net that we all care so deeply about. But I also told them it's an untenable position to say, we're not going to do anything on Medicare and Medicaid when that's one of the biggest drivers of our budget deficit.

"She was always open—all the Democrats were open to Medicare changes that affected providers," such as doctors and hospitals, he said, laughing.

Reminded of Pelosi's concern about changing the cost-of-living calculation for Social Security, Obama replied, "Well, Social Security was not on the table. There was discussion about Social Security, conceptually. But by the end of this thing—we've always been very clear. Look, Social Security is not the driver of our deficits. If you want to have a separate negotiation about Social Security, we're happy to. We're happy to listen to what your concepts are. But we're not going to collapse Social Security into this overall framework."

This, however, was not the case. In the offers White House staff exchanged with Boehner's staff, changes to Social Security benefits had been explicitly mentioned.*

Obama also recalled that during the meeting, "Nancy was fairly emphatic throughout this process: I need to know what Boehner can do. Because Nancy at this point has had the experience and witnessed Boehner not being able to deliver his caucus. And so she says, 'He's not having a conversation with me, but he's going to expect votes from me. He needs to know what it is that I can do.' "

The president said he was also concerned about Boehner's ability to produce votes.

"I think that even doing the $800 billion was a stretch," he said. "I'm not clear actually that he could have ended up delivering the votes that were needed for the $800 billion. That's part of the reason why the conversation about how many votes was he going to need from Nancy was so important.

"Now, keep in mind that that evening in the conversation, Nancy's not happy, Harry's not happy, I'm not happy, nobody's happy. But what I say to them is, ultimately the worst thing that can happen is a default. Then nobody will be happy, and the American people will be badly damaged. So if that's all they can do, are you willing to take that deal? And at that point, both Nancy and Harry say, well, we're not happy about it. We don't know how many votes it will take. But, Mr. President, if you decide that that's the best deal that we can do, we are willing to work with you to try to get something done."

Reminded that others in the White House reported Reid leaving the meeting unpersuaded, Obama was insistent: "Let me say this. That was Nancy's position. And that was Harry's position. Was he happy about it? No. Do we know how many votes ultimately could have been gotten by Harry or Nancy? We'll never know, because it wasn't tested."

---

*The draft proposal Nabors sent to Boehner's office on July 19 offered to apply the modified Consumer Price Index "to Social Security, mandatory programs, and the tax code beginning in 2015" and to "Reduce the 75-year estimated shortfall of the Social Security Program . . . with a balanced package of tax and benefit changes."

•     •     •

After Sperling was briefed on the meeting, he told some House Democrats that "Reid sold them out on the 18-month extension."

Boehner continued to put together his backup plan with Reid and
McConnell. Both seemed to be in agreement.

He called Cantor down to his office. The situation was serious.
The president had called him and said, "I got to have more revenue."
Obama was no longer hiding behind Nabors; he had now personally
floated the idea of $400 billon more, taking the revenue number up to
$1.2 trillion. Boehner quoted the president saying, "We can make this
deal work. I've got to have just a little bit more revenue. I can't sell it
to the senators, but I think we're real close. Let's make this final deal."

As Cantor knew, Boehner had told the president their necks were
out about as far as they could go. That was his position. But the president wanted more.

How many Republican votes do you think you can get for that $1.2
trillion? asked Stombres, Cantor's chief of staff.

In the range of "170," Boehner said.

"You are crazy," Stombres said. It wasn't polite. It was out of line,
almost unheard of, for a staffer to talk this way.

"John, can't do it," Cantor said, backing his chief of staff. The
House Republicans voted in blocks. The first block of about 50 was a
group they could get because of strong personal relationships with one
of the leaders, Boehner or Cantor. The leaders could call in the chits.
These 50 or so probably wouldn't have let even a $1.2 trillion revenue
deal supported by Boehner and Cantor go down with zero votes in the
House.

Another 100 House Republicans could be won with better conservative policy, taking them to 150 or 170. With strong conservative
policy—great policy from their perspective, policy with a heavy Tea
Party flavor—they could reach 230 or the 235 that passed the Ryan
budget earlier in the year.

So, Cantor said, a deal with $1.2 trillion revenue might get 50 votes. That was his count.

"Okay," said Boehner, ending the conversation. "We'll be in touch."

Leaving Boehner's office, Cantor felt they were done. The speaker seemed to buy that they could not sell the $1.2 trillion. Cantor and his staff had been counting votes for eight years, and experience had shown they were pretty good at it. They couldn't push this anywhere but over a cliff, particularly in light of the Gang of Six proposal. Cantor's Republicans were already trashing that. It was odd. The Gang, whose stated goal was a grand bipartisan coming together, could not have picked a worse time to release its plan. But Cantor felt that a smaller deal was still within their grasp. You don't wind up in the Oval Office unless you're close, he reasoned. So they had been close. How close was a matter of debate. But the president, who had to get a debt limit extension, was surely out on a limb. They all were, weren't they? Maybe by defining where they couldn't go, they had left some obvious areas where they could.

Once you get close, Cantor realized, deal fever overtakes everyone. Where was the middle ground? Where was the safe harbor? As Stombres put it, they had to ratchet back. Cantor's chief of staff looked for an analogy. "Maybe you're not ready to buy the Cadillac, maybe you don't want the Cadillac today, but can I put you in this nice sedan?"

Boehner was wrestling hard with himself. First, Brett Loper reminded him that the $800 billion in revenue had been coming from tax reform. Loper didn't think they could get to $1.2 trillion through tax reform. It would require the speaker to do what he had consistently said he would never do: increase tax rates.

We're not going to do that, Boehner said again. "Period, done, end of story." Obama was asking him to give up his principles for the president's political interest.

On votes, yes, he had told Cantor he thought he could get in the range of 170. It was not a whip count by any means. But on something major like this, they would get the votes. "If the president and I come

out and we have this agreement," he said, "we will get it over the line."
It was momentum.

It was a matter of votes as far as Jackson was concerned, and they
didn't have an answer.


Sperling concluded that if the speaker could not go along with the
$1.2 trillion, the $800 billion was nonetheless a salable deal. As was
his wont, he hypothesized that Boehner could make a potent political
argument. To his mind, Boehner could have gone to his Republicans
and said something like: "Guys, I'm giving $800 billion, but it's a win
for us. That's what I'm agreeing to. Let me tell you what I'm getting you
for that. Not extending the high-income Bush tax cuts is dead for the
2012 election. Big Medicare cuts are dead for the 2012 election. You
agree to this, we are in great shape. We have taken away their two best
arguments. So I know you don't like what I'm doing. You trust me, you
follow me, we will stay in the majority. And if not—I hate to tell this to
you guys—but whether we like it or not, if they can run saying we are
for deep Medicare cuts and tax cuts for the high-income earners, we're
going to have trouble in 2012. I am solving our problem."

But as Sperling's mind ranged across all the possible outcomes, he
realized that under any scenario, it might be that Boehner just did not
have, and could never get, the votes.


Obama called Boehner at 10:30 that night, leaving a message asking
that the speaker call him back.

Later still, the president remarked to Plouffe, "I still haven't heard
from Boehner. But it's fine. I guess I'll talk to him in the morning."

On his way home at about 11:30, Rob Nabors stopped to grab his
usual two-cheeseburger meal at the McDonald's on 17th Street, a
block up from the White House. His cell phone rang.

"So what are you hearing?" the president asked.

At the sound of the president's voice, Nabors instinctively stood up. McDonald's, at that time of night, was filled with two groups of patrons: the homeless and Secret Service agents. Looking around, Nabors decided it would be best to step outside.

"Where do you think we are?" the president pressed.

"Mr. President," he replied, "given that I just left you two hours ago . . ."

"What is the mood of the caucus?" Obama asked, referring to the lunch with the Senate Democrats. He wanted more detail.

"They feel they were cut out of the process," he said. Obviously the Senate and House leaders wanted more involvement.

What do you think about that?

"I've got to be honest, sir. We weren't going to get to savings by doing a pass the hat. If we subjected this to everybody's 'I'm okay with this/I'm not okay with this,' the whole thing would've fallen apart." He said he thought the concerns about process were exaggerated. "It's part of the game. They always believe that the process would be better if they would've negotiated this rather than you." Nabors said he didn't agree. "Sometimes you just need the president to get this done."

What was the vote count? Obama asked. Where are the bodies? "Who do you think I'm going to need to call?"

One was Steny Hoyer, the Maryland Democrat who was Pelosi's second-in-command.

"Is he going to be okay with where we are on federal retirement?" Obama inquired.

"I think so," Nabors replied. "It's going to be very hard for him." Hoyer represented thousands of federal retirees.

"Where are the progressives going to be?" the president asked.

"This is going to be a really hard sell to them because they're going to see Medicare cuts," Nabors said. The cuts could total as much as $250 billion over 10 years. It was going to be a shock, and Pelosi was on the record declaring she would not accept any Medicare cuts.

"Pharma is going to react negatively," Nabors added, using the shorthand for the pharmaceutical industry. "Pharma is going to think we walked away from a deal." In the health care negotiations, the drug companies had agreed to a $100 billion cut on drug benefits for Medicare, and now the administration was coming back with more cuts.

Both Obama and Nabors knew that Pharma had hooks into lots of people in Washington.

"We just need to be prepared to talk to Pharma," Nabors said, "talk about Pharma issues ahead of time, and wrap our arms around the members that we think we're going to lose." With an aggressive effort, Nabors said, he was optimistic these members could be won over.

Nabors was used to giving a two-minute report to the president on legislation, but this night, standing on 17th Street, he realized Obama wanted a full lay-down.

Okay, Defense cuts were going to be a giant problem, he said, especially with pro-Defense Democrats such as Ben Nelson of Nebraska. They would also hear from Senator Kay Hagan, the first-term junior senator from North Carolina and centrist member of the Armed Services Committee.

Defense was key in states such as Florida and Virginia. They reviewed the names.

Obviously Defense procurement was on the chopping block, Nabors noted. "That means the Boeings of the world," he added, "the Northrop Grummans of the world, the Lockheeds of the world. They're going to be quite upset." The senators and members from those states or districts were going to call and ask if they were being protected.

To win over a majority they were going to have to play this very hard, the president said, adding, "No sweetheart deals for anybody."

It had been a wandering, uneasy 20-minute conversation that showed how all the major elements—from revenue, to Medicare cuts, to the votes—remained up in the air.

# 32

"**B**oehner never called back."

The words rippled through the West Wing the morning of Friday, July 22. It was discussed at the morning senior staff meeting. Had anyone ever heard of someone not calling back a president for more than 18 hours? No one could come up with an example. At 10 a.m., the president called Boehner again. The speaker did not take the call, and the White House left a message: Please phone the president. The second failed call triggered a discussion of negotiating tactics within the West Wing. Some thought the second call was a mistake, making it too clear that the president was needy. No, others argued, Boehner already knew that. What was the best approach to show a needy Obama but not a desperate Obama? They were already in for two phone calls.

But why had Boehner not called back? The senior staff worried and, as was their habit, theorized. Maybe Boehner was trying to come up with his own plan? So they had to be patient. However, patience was not their strong suit. So the core group of six or seven worried some more.

Plouffe, however, figured that Boehner was caucusing with the Republicans. This was a big deal and it would obviously take time. He didn't feel very exercised.

But Jack Lew did. He was stunned. From his experience in Speaker Tip O'Neill's office during the Reagan years, O'Neill always got back in touch with the president immediately. They had deep policy differences, but it would have been unthinkable for O'Neill not to call Reagan back. To Lew, Boehner's radio silence was clearly bad news.

Boehner had concluded that there would be no deal with Obama. It was over. But he believed he could not show his hand publicly. He had three worries. First, the financial markets were now fixated on Washington, and it wasn't clear how they would react. Even the smallest signal, accurate or not, could cause them to explode.

Second, he knew how Obama operated.

"The White House is brilliant at getting out early and defining things their way," Jackson said. Boehner had to make sure he had an opportunity to tell his side of the story when it broke in public, before the White House smothered it.

Third, and most importantly, Boehner had to have the congressional plan in place, an agreement on how to proceed independent of the president—a Plan B.

He spent the morning struggling to move forward. He met with Cantor twice, with McCarthy, with McConnell, and then planned an all-important joint meeting with both McConnell and Reid.

This was the crucial move.

"Reid's an honorable man," Boehner said. "And when he says something I believe him." One of the most important communications back channels in Congress was between Boehner's chief of staff, Barry Jackson, and David Krone, Reid's chief of staff.

So Reid and McConnell went over to Boehner's office at 2:30 p.m.

"I'm out," Boehner told them. "I'm done. I'm calling the president this afternoon. I am done. There's no deal." Instead, he said he would do the deal that Reid and McConnell had been working. Even though he didn't like it, he said he was willing.

The debt limit was a "Rubik's cube" problem, as Brett Loper, his policy director, put it. But they could solve it. The solution was obvious and, in some respects, had been staring them in the face. It would include four elements, all of which they had been discussing.

First, the $1.2 trillion cut to general spending for 10 years that everyone, even the president, had agreed on for months.

Second, the supercommittee that Harry Reid had proposed more than a week ago. It would be responsible for coming up with another $1.2 trillion in deficit reduction through additional spending cuts and revenue through tax reform.

Third, McConnell's complicated mechanism to increase the debt limit so the Congress would not have to take an explicit vote to raise it.

Fourth, this would all be done in two steps. The first step would be an increase of only about $1.2 trillion, so they would hit the debt limit again in March. But the supercommittee deficit reduction proposal would then be ready so they could approve the second $1.2 trillion. Though this was exactly what the president had emphatically said was unacceptable, it was the only way for Congress to maintain its leverage.

I agree with this, McConnell said. "John, we know you did your best. You negotiated. Sometimes it just doesn't work. So let's go."

Reid said he too would agree.

Boehner told me later, "Harry and I understand each other, like each other. We don't agree on a lot of things. But we trust each other. And so when Harry says we got a deal, we've got a deal." The deal with Reid, Boehner said, was "absolutely" ironclad. "I reminded Harry that afternoon, one last time. Harry, I'm only going to agree to the supercommittee under one condition. And that's if you and Mitch tell me you're going to work with me to make it work. That's the only way I would go there. And they agreed."

Reid was irritated and disappointed with the White House. This could do the job, and he could see that the two-step plan was critical if Congress was to maintain its institutional role and leverage. He had fought all his 24 years in the Senate to protect the chamber's role and prerogatives, even when the White House didn't like it.

•      •      •

At 3:15 p.m., Boehner directed Jackson and his staff to prepare an announcement that the speaker was breaking off talks with the White House and would instead pursue negotiations with House and Senate leaders.

Obama made a third call to Boehner and was told that the speaker would phone back shortly.

"What happened to common courtesy?" Daley emailed to Jackson at 3:49 p.m. "Or do you figure you guys can stiff us? If so, good luck."

Six minutes later, at 3:55, Jackson answered Daley: "So, schedulers are working on a time for our bosses to talk."

At 4:06, Daley emailed: "It has been 24 hours since the President of the United States called the speaker, and he is unavailable. You guys are acting like amateurs."

Jackson did not respond.

At 4:10, Daley tried again: "Barry, your friends are saying you are walking away from trying to solve the deficit and trying to do a deal with the Senate to kick the can."

Jackson sent word through the schedulers that Boehner would call the president at 5:30 p.m.

Boehner and Jackson had decided on a media strategy that would let them tell their side of the story "before the White House went out and accused us of raping and pillaging," Jackson said.

Boehner's press office called a single reporter from each of the news organizations that regularly covered the speaker and delivered the message: Come here. Big story. We can't tell you why we are asking you here.

By about 5 p.m., some 20 reporters had crowded into the speaker's secondary conference room in the Capitol.


Reid sent word to Rob Nabors that Boehner was pulling out. At the White House the team gathered in the Oval Office.

"Reid just called," Nabors reported, "and said there's no deal, that things are sideways." It was bad if Boehner was talking to Reid but not to them. They were still in the dark. Maybe it was just because no deal had been finalized? But more news slowly started leaking out. Reporters called the White House: We hear Boehner's pulling out.

Oh, no. Not possible. Not again.

"Fuck," said Nabors.

But it was true. Now word was flooding in. Boehner had a conference call with his Republicans to inform them. He said he had delayed a formal announcement until the financial markets closed.

"That's bullshit," Nabors said, when he heard the speaker's reason for not calling back. If Boehner was genuine about this he would not be so willing to drive the entire economy off the cliff over what should have been a relatively routine debt ceiling vote. No, not calling, Nabors thought, was not just deeply insulting. It was the ultimate sign of weakness. Why wouldn't the speaker just call and say, "We can't get there. Sorry. Let's figure out something smaller to do."

Not long before that promised 5:30 call, Boehner went to his restroom, passing the secondary conference room where the reporters were gathered. He was smoking a cigarette and stopped. He wouldn't answer the reporters' questions. One reporter joked about his famous tan. Was he having a bad day? another asked.

"Have you ever seen me have a bad day?" he replied in his confident baritone. But then he recalled three years earlier when Congress had been forced to bail out the banks with the infamous Troubled Asset Relief Program (TARP), and the Dow plummeted 800 points.

"TARP was a bad day."

Boehner returned to his office and braced himself for the call to Obama at 5:30 p.m. He picked up the phone and was connected with the president.

"We can't go forward with this," the speaker said. "I'm sorry. I think we've run out of time, so we're going to proceed up here with a plan to make sure we don't default."

In the Oval Office, Lew, Nabors and the others watched and listened. The president was gripping the phone hard in his hand as he listened.

"I've taken my hits and the arrows from my guys," the speaker continued. "I bent over backwards. But you wanted more revenue—$400 billion more—and then less on the spending side."

"That's not a reason to cut off the conversation," Obama replied angrily. "I asked you to consider it. And you never got back to me. I've been trying to get in touch with you!"

Nabors would remember the look on the president's face for a long time. In years of dealing with Obama, it was the only time he had actually seen him visibly upset. Normally, when the president showed anger, he looked more like an average person who was merely perturbed—grimacing, agitated. Not this time. He was mad. There was a flash of pure fury. The president was looking up, holding the handset tighter and tighter. So tight that Nabors thought he might break the phone.

"We can put this back together," the president said. "How do we put this back together again?"

"That's the $64,000 question," Boehner replied. He was proceeding with the Senate leaders.

Wasn't Boehner comfortable with the terms they had been trying to agree on, the exchange of offers, the meetings? the president asked.

"I felt comfortable, or I wouldn't have continued these conversations," Boehner said.

Getting angrier, the president demanded to know why Boehner hadn't returned his call.

"I was trying to figure out what the right thing to do is, what can pass," Boehner said. "I just couldn't do any more revenue." So he had his plan with Reid and McConnell.

What about me? Obama asked. He was not exactly on the sidelines here.

"I understand your problem," said Boehner.

But Obama wasn't finished. Boehner sat there, enduring what he thought bordered on a presidential tirade.

"He was spewing coals," Boehner later told me. "He was pissed. I said, 'Listen, we've been round and round and round and round. And it's always the same thing. I told you I'd put revenue on there if we had real changes in entitlement programs. Every time we get there, you and I agree; all of a sudden you guys keep backing up, backing up, backing up. And now you call me and you want more revenue. It ain't going to happen. I'm done with it." Finally, at 5:42, they ended the call.

"Ooh," Boehner said, turning to two staffers in the room, one taking notes of Boehner's end of the conversation. "He was hot."

They asked for details.

"Wow," Boehner said. "He's really upset." The speaker lit up another cigarette. The president, Boehner said, had demanded that the combined congressional leadership come down to the White House at 11 the next morning.

Boehner later recalled, "He wasn't going to get a damn dime more out of me. He knew how far out on a limb I was. But he was hot. It was clear to me that coming to an agreement with him was not going to happen, and that I had to go to Plan B. And thank God, we'd been working on Plan B."

He recalled saying, "Trying to put Humpty Dumpty back together again would be almost impossible."


"I was pretty angry," Obama told me. "And look, the reason is, here we've got a national crisis that needs to get resolved. The entire world is watching. I've called him probably four times that day.

"And the speaker of the House is avoiding my phone calls. And then comes back to me, not saying, here's the best I can do, but rather just saying, I can't do anything, so I'm just going to try to see if we can work something out over in the House."

He said you were "spewing coals" like a furnace.

"Well, I . . . I was . . . Well, look, there's no doubt I thought it was profoundly irresponsible, at that stage, not to call me back immediately and let me know what was going on. Because this is the president of the United States calling to try to resolve a national crisis, and he's trying to reach the speaker of the House. And if he had called me and said, look, I don't know yet, or, I'm still trying to work it out, or, here are the problems that I have—any of those responses would have been acceptable to me. Because I was sympathetic to how difficult it was for him to manage his caucus. To leave us waiting . . . And it wasn't simply that he calls me back to announce that he can't do it. It's actually, we don't get the call until there's a readout in the press that these negotiations have gone down. Before I get the call."

What did you say to him?

"I don't remember my exact words. I think it's fair to say that . . . I think I was very insistent and very clear that I had not presented him with an ultimatum. Because at this point, you're already starting to hear spin. And he was trying to spin me. And I said, John, that's not the conversation we had. And I said to him at that point, if $800 billion is the best you can do, then you need to let me know, and I will be able to tell you how many votes I think I can get out of the Democrats. But to suggest somehow that I made a take it or leave it offer is not accurate, it's not the conversation that we had. And more to the point, I'm prepared right now to have a discussion with you about the $800 billion. So if you actually still think you can do that, you need to tell me that.

"At which point he just said, 'You know what, Mr. President? We tried. It got too close.' "


Plouffe saw Boehner's pullout as an immediate political problem. The president, he said, had to go out publicly and explain what he was trying to do, remind everybody why the debt ceiling was important, and why the deal fell apart. But politics aside, Plouffe had a larger worry. Like Boehner, he used the nursery rhyme comparison: "How on earth are we going to put Humpty Dumpty back together here?"

Within 45 minutes, Obama appeared in the White House Briefing Room to open his veins and bleed a little in public over his disappointment in the speaker. One White House aide said he seemed to want to sound a bit like Michael Douglas in the movie *The American President:* Damn the politics and full speed ahead on principle.

"I just got a call about a half hour ago from Speaker Boehner," the president began, "who indicated that he was going to be walking away from the negotiations." Obama said his offer had been generous. "What we said was give us $1.2 trillion in additional revenues." He was lumping the $800 billion from Boehner's offer in with his $400 billion request. This could all be done, he claimed, without raising tax rates and was "compatible with the 'no tax' pledge" of Grover Norquist.

"I couldn't get a phone call returned," he said. "I've been left at the altar now a couple of times." The bottom line, he insisted, was no partial extension of the debt limit. He would only sign onto a deal that extended the limit past next year's election.

He fired a broadside at the House Republicans. They had to take "responsibility" for any problems that might arise. Then, after making it clear that he blamed Republicans, he said, "Let me repeat, I'm not interested in finger-pointing and I'm not interested in blame. I just want the facts to speak for themselves."

He insisted that the congressional leaders be at the White House the next morning. "I want them here at 11 a.m tomorrow. We have run out of time."

Obama finished at 6:36.

"I'd sat here and watched his performance," Boehner later recalled, "which I thought was un-presidential. Angry."

Boehner and his staff thought the president had made a serious mistake appearing so emotional in public—it was the wrong approach, and could wind up scaring the country and the financial markets.

The message war was on, Jackson said, and he urged the speaker to make his own statement on television.

Boehner was not eager to jump into a public shouting match with the president.

"You're going to go out," Jackson insisted. "We're going to get you out. You've got to respond to this." There was, he said, a theme here for Boehner to adopt: "This isn't Republican/Democrat, this is the Congress versus the White House. We're equal branches of government, and you know, we're big boys and girls too up here."

So, 40 minutes after the president's press conference, Boehner appeared at the House Radio-TV Gallery. He wanted to appear calm and cool.

"There was an agreement with the White House at $800 billion in revenue," he acknowledged, but only through tax reform. The breakdown was because, at the last minute, the president "demanded $400 billion more."

"The White House moved the goalposts," he said. "Dealing with the White House is like dealing with a bowl of Jell-O.

"It's the president who walked away from his agreement and demanded more money at the last minute. That is—and the only way to get that extra revenue was to raise taxes."

"Do you trust the president?" a reporter asked.

"I do trust him as a negotiator," Boehner said carefully.

Later Boehner told me that he realized the importance of the question. "That's a dangerous question," he said, "considering the political climate we were in. I was more worried about how it would sound to the Tea Party. So I was trying to answer the question without getting myself in a whole lot of trouble."

He told me that the Tea Party had no objection to his phrasing. "I think it worked out pretty well. They were pretty happy about it."

The speaker felt he had maintained his cool.

Friday night, he sent a letter to the House Republicans saying, "A deal was never reached, and was never really close."


At the White House, Plouffe, Sperling and the others were outraged. It was a "lie," Sperling said. The president had not "demanded" $400 billion more, but merely asked Boehner to consider it.

"Obviously a cover story for why it fell apart," Plouffe said. "It wasn't true. It wasn't true."

They brought Jack Lew and others to the Roosevelt Room to tell reporters they hadn't moved the goalposts, but had only suggested moving them.

In the briefing, recorded by the White House, Lew said, "There was a great deal of zones of agreement and by the end we were really just focused on a few areas where we had to close. And if Speaker Boehner had called back and said yes, the American people would have a deal." Lew enumerated the issues that remained unresolved. First was the trigger if the supercommitee did not find another $1.2 trillion in cuts, second was the depth of Medicaid cuts, and third was revenue.

But Plouffe understood that this was just a battle within the broader war. Boehner had taken the lifeline. He had walked through the door the president had opened for him. Plouffe didn't think the White House could regret doing that—it seemed the only way to get more Democratic votes—but the playing field had suddenly shifted.

Plouffe and Nabors talked. "They were going to find a door," Nabors said. "Because at the end of the day, the political difficulty of passing this was not improved or diminished by the inclusion of more revenue. It was still an abstraction" buried in some future tax reform. "Like $400 billion of revenue isn't all that much—$40 billion a year over 10 years."

But the president was in one of the biggest political and economic jams of all time, and had no alternative way out.

# 33

Boehner scheduled a conference call with Reid, McConnell and Pelosi for the morning of Saturday, July 23, to discuss moving forward without the president.

Daley called Pelosi. You just can't do this to us, he said. You'll be leaving us hanging out there. Don't join the conference call. She agreed.

Leader Pelosi will not be able to join the call, John Lawrence, her chief of staff, emailed Barry Jackson.

David Krone called Jackson. Reid would be dropping out of the conference call too.

Jackson understood. "Poor Reid was left hanging," he reported. "It's becoming a political thing, and now Reid's got to go be a Democrat rather than a congressional leader, which I appreciate. It happens."

But that did not prevent Boehner from talking directly to Reid, so he did.

Reid said he was still on board with the congressional plan—$1.2 trillion in 10-year spending caps, his special supercommittee idea to identify the next $1.2 trillion in cuts, and McConnell's convoluted plan allowing Congress to duck a vote to increase the debt ceiling.

How do I get 60 votes? Reid asked. What can McConnell do? How many Republican votes would there be? He was in execution mode now. There was no time for philosophical debates. They weren't his style anyway.

Reid and McConnell talked, and the Rubik's cube package was on track. It was a deal.

Boehner spoke with McConnell, who said Reid was in.

As the president had requested, at 11 a.m. the four leaders—Reid, McConnell, Boehner and Pelosi—arrived at the White House.

In the West Wing lobby, Boehner pulled Pelosi aside. "We are not negotiating here," he said. The four leaders would work this out among themselves.

Fine, I agree, Pelosi said.

The four leaders went to the Cabinet Room. "We all came stumbling in there," Boehner later told me. "Nobody wanted to be there. The president's still pissed."

The president had met with Biden, Geithner and some of the others beforehand. It was agreed that Geithner would lay it on thick, reminding the leaders how short of time they were and how damaging default could be to the financial markets.

No congressional staff were admitted. Key White House players like Nabors and Sperling were left waiting in the White House lobby.

In the Cabinet Room, Geithner issued another warning to the congressional leaders, declaring there was a new deadline. This was not a Monday morning problem. Instead, if they didn't have a plan or a deal by late Sunday afternoon when the Asian financial markets opened, everything could begin to crack. Given the global importance of U.S. Treasuries and the U.S. dollar, he reminded them, if the debt limit was not extended and the country went into default, it could trigger a worldwide meltdown. Things were that serious.

You need to move off the idea that the cuts be greater than the debt limit increase, Biden told Boehner. As a starting point, to give them more flexibility, you've got to ease off on that.

Boehner refused. That had been his bottom line from the beginning: cuts equal to or greater than the debt limit increase. He was not budging.

Pelosi, who had not played a significant role in the discussions among the congressional leaders on their own plan, spoke up several times to insist that entitlements be protected.

You're not being constructive, Nancy, the president said, interrupting her. We need to get something figured out in the next couple of days. I have to have something that extends the debt limit past the election, he said. I won't take any kind of two-step process.

Boehner said that he believed he and the other three leaders had a plan. We think we can work this out. Give us a little more time. We'll come back to you. We are not going to negotiate this with you.

Obama objected, saying that he couldn't be left out of the process and wanted the negotiation to continue. "I've got to sign this bill!" he reminded them.

"Mr. President," Boehner challenged, "as I read the Constitution, the Congress writes the laws. You get to decide if you want to sign them."

Boehner later recalled, "Oh, God, if you could've seen the look on his face. I'm surprised he didn't storm out of the room."

Boehner's approach was now clearly at odds with the deal-making style he had employed for the past seven months. He had always negotiated with the president and the administration. But his new message was clear: We're going to take care of this. Time is out. We'll figure out what can pass. And he said it with a certain amount of relish.

Then Harry Reid spoke up. The four congressional leaders want to speak privately, he said. Give us some time.

This was it. Congress was taking over. The leaders were asking the president to leave a meeting he had called in his own house.

Fine, talk, the president said, knock yourselves out if you can get a deal. There is no pride of authorship here, just do it—if you can.

The president, vice president, treasury secretary and budget director all left the room.

"I think he was pretty happy to get up and leave," Boehner later recalled.

Boehner felt it was as if the president was saying, "You guys are children. You fix this." Well, Boehner believed, they were going to fix it, and they were well on their way to doing so.

When Nabors heard what had transpired in the Cabinet Room, he thought it sounded overwrought. No way could the president be cut out. They would need him to help get votes. On the Democratic side, if Reid and Pelosi cut a deal, there would be no way to sell any entitlement cuts to their Democrats without the president saying plainly that he was also on board.

Plouffe saw how disappointed the president was. It was clear the grand bargain was gone. So maybe it was best to let the congressional leaders meet. "Let's see what these guys can work out to get us out of the jam," Plouffe said. "Great opportunity missed. How do we salvage this?"

How did the president feel, being voted off the island in his own house?

"You know, the truth of the matter is, at that point, all I'm concerned about is getting this thing done," the president told me. "And so I'm not concerned about protocol. Essentially what I think McConnell and Boehner had decided was, maybe we can go ahead and work out something with Reid. And we can do an end run around the White House.

"They didn't like negotiating with Jack," he said laughing, "who knew the budget better than anybody. They didn't like negotiating with Rob. And they felt like they might be able to just get a better deal, for a short-term deal, with Harry Reid."

In the Cabinet Room, the four leaders didn't have to do much. They already had the three-part framework worked out. It had been the subject of discussions among staff from Boehner, Reid and McConnell for most of the week. They agreed to ask staff to continue working all this into a two-step plan to raise the debt limit.

The framework remained generally the same: It would have discretionary caps of $1.2 trillion over 10 years with a short-term debt limit extension. The debt limit increase would include McConnell's "disapproval" process. A supercommittee would be created to find additional savings by year end, and if it were successful, another increase in the debt limit would be authorized. One new addition required the House and Senate to vote on a balanced budget amendment to the Constitution, a perennial Republican favorite.

It was a deal in which Boehner, McConnell and Reid got what they wanted. Boehner got cuts greater than the increase in the debt limit. McConnell shielded his senators from ever having to cast a vote on raising the debt limit. And Reid got his joint committee on deficit reduction. Pelosi's insistence that entitlements be spared was not honored.

The other person who didn't get what he wanted was no longer in the room. The deal, if it passed, would guarantee that the president would have to revisit the debt limit during an election year.

Boehner arranged an afternoon conference call with his House Republicans.

"The administration says they need all of the increase up front so [the president] doesn't have to deal with this until after the election," Boehner told his conference. "He started the year asking for an increase with no cuts. He's trying to set this up so he gets a $2.4 trillion blank check—or to end in default so he can blame us. We know how bad both of those scenarios are.

"We have the opportunity to cut trillions instead," he said. "To stop him, we need a vehicle that can pass in both houses." He was no longer negotiating with the president.

The question was "What can we pass to protect the country from what the president is trying to do?"

He went on, "The White House tried to create buzz by saying there is some kind of grand bargain to be had. Let me be clear—that kind of grand deal cannot be had with this president."

He hadn't meant to inflame anyone by mentioning, during a recent public appearance, that there had been a deal on the table, he told them. "An agreement with the president was not possible and is not possible."

"There are no secret negotiations going on. So don't worry," he added.

"No one wants to default. If we stick together, we can win this for the American people. It will require some of you to make sacrifices. If we stand together, our leverage is maximized and they will have to deal with us."

He described the state of the discussions with the White House.

"The president wants a $2.4 trillion increase with no spending cuts. We won't let that happen," he said, despite the fact that the negotiations had explicitly included large cuts.

"They think they can win because they can divide us. They can't. We must stand together and take action," he said.

"When you get to town tomorrow, we'll have more detail for you," he promised. "We're doing the right thing. You all know the right thing isn't always the easiest thing to do."

Then Cantor stepped in. "Thanks to the speaker for his patience in working with the administration," he said.

But then he quickly undercut the speaker's claim that Obama had demanded there be no cuts.

"We are where we are because the president and his party do not want to cut anywhere close to what we do without raising taxes on people and small businesses," he said. "That has been the problem at each turn. The president's position of forcing us to give him a debt limit increase through the election is purely political and indefensible."

He echoed Boehner's call for a show of unity.

"Let me tell you, though, he has the microphone," Cantor said, reminding them that the president had some advantages. "The only way to overcome him is to remain united and insist that every dollar the debt limit is increased, we have equal or more dollars in spending cuts without any tax increases. Thank you all for your patience. This is a fluid situation. Let's stay united. We can do this."

Finally, Majority Whip Kevin McCarthy spoke.

"You see the battle the speaker is in," the California Republican said. "The president is throwing a fit because he's worried about the election. He doesn't want cuts, he wants increases. He lost his cool the other night because he knows he won't get what he wants if we remain united."

The speaker gathered Reid, McConnell and Pelosi in his office. No staff. Even Jackson and Krone were excluded, so they went down to Jackson's office and watched the Cincinnati Reds baseball game on television.

The leaders had essentially reached an agreement, but there was still a crucial question that had not been answered. What happened if the supercommittee couldn't agree on the second $1.2 trillion in deficit reduction? What would be the trigger or enforcement mechanism to make sure $1.2 trillion was cut from spending?

We would use the $1 trillion in imaginary savings from the Overseas Contingency Operations, Boehner and McConnell said. The wars were ending anyway.

Reid was particularly surprised; he had pushed dozens of times to use this OCO money.

"We can never put that in writing," Boehner said, "but you have our word." It can never even be talked about, McConnell and Boehner said, never be repeated outside the room.

Reid and Pelosi agreed. Pelosi was happy to use the imaginary money. It was better than more entitlement cuts.

The deal was done.

They began drafting a joint public statement that would report progress on their talks, and optimism that they were moving toward a solution.

At 5:21 p.m. Michael Steel, Boehner's press secretary, emailed a draft of a joint statement to Reid's and McConnell's communications directors, Adam Jentleson and Don Stewart. It read, "The leaders in both parties and both Houses of Congress are working together and making progress."

Krone told Barry Jackson that Reid and he had okayed it.

At 6:05 p.m., Steel emailed Jentleson, "I'm told that Mr. Krone signed off on this."

"That's a fact," Jentleson emailed back at 6:20.


Boehner met with the rest of the House Republican leadership, Cantor, McCarthy and Hensarling, to discuss the next steps.

There was a growing sense of urgency. Reid was under about as much pressure from the White House as he could take. What congressional leader could withstand a direct appeal from the president of his own party? Maybe not even the independent-minded Harry Reid.

The Republican leaders agreed that if the president forced Reid to step away from the deal, they would try to press forward anyway to pass the congressional leaders' three-part plan with 218 Republican votes in the House. That would put pressure on the Senate, where the bill should be acceptable, which would, in turn, put pressure on Obama to sign it.

At 8:11 p.m. Jentleson sent Boehner's staff an email: "Senator Reid will no longer be joining this statement. He will be releasing his own statement tonight."

"I will not support any short-term agreement, and neither will President Obama nor Leader Pelosi," Reid said in his statement.

Though Reid said this publicly, he was still riding both horses. His staff had continued working with the Republican leaders.


Around 10 p.m., Obama called Boehner, who was at dinner with friends.

I am not going to sign a bill that requires me to deal with this a second time before the end of 2012, Obama said. He was furious.

"Listen," Boehner recalled telling the president, "I understand it. All right? But you're not going to have a choice. We've got an agreement."

Obama said if the trigger could ensure a full debt limit extension, taking the country through 2012, he might support it.

That's not the agreement the congressional leaders have, Boehner said, despite what Reid might be saying publicly. The speaker wasn't interested in discussing it with the president.

Boehner recalled, "He was moaning and groaning and whining and demanding . . . threatening. . . . He was pretty desperate." Obama again said he would veto such a bill. Boehner said if the leaders could get the bill on Obama's desk, "I knew there wasn't a damn chance he was going to veto the bill."

The president repeated his offer. He would back off on the request for an additional $400 billion in revenue if the Republicans would give elsewhere.

We're too close to default to reopen the talks, Boehner said. Congress is going to move forward on its own.

Boehner believed that he had found a recipe that would work, especially for Harry Reid. If he could get it through the House in the form that Reid had agreed to, the president would be forced to accept it.

In a statement to the press, Boehner's spokesman, Michael Steel, said, "The Democrats who run Washington have refused to offer a plan. Now, as a result, a two-step process is inevitable."


Asked about Boehner's description of his late-night call, Obama said, "Listen, anybody who knows me knows, I don't moan, I don't groan, I don't whine." He laughed. "I'm not desperate. I was very angry about how he had behaved, and more concerning was the fact that we were now only a few days from there literally being $5 billion left in the Treasury for the United States government."

This was how precarious the fiscal situation had become. Just $5 billion was about half a day's worth of the federal government's expenditures. It had come down to the wire.


At the White House, the president told his senior staff that the call with Boehner had led nowhere. Boehner had said he had chosen his course, and insisted the congressional leaders were going to get this worked out. "I don't think he's going to bite," on the old $800 billion revenue plan, the president said. "So we've got to figure out Plan B. Which is, how do we get out of this thing?"

The problem was that they did not have a Plan B.


It was increasingly clear that no one was running Washington. That was trouble for everyone, but especially for Obama. Though running things was a joint venture between the president and Congress, Nabors thought a president had to dominate Congress—or at least be seen as dominating Congress. If the president succumbed it could be fatal. Reagan and Clinton were seen as presidents who had gained and largely held the upper hand with Congress. The last president to fold was George H. W. Bush, who gave in to Democrats' demands that income taxes be raised in a 1990 budget deal. And Bush had been a one-term president.

# 34

On Sunday morning, July 24, Boehner appeared on *Fox News Sunday* with Chris Wallace and said that if congressional leaders could not come up with a bipartisan plan, the House Republicans would move forward on their own.

He accused the White House of failing to offer a plan to deal with the debt limit.

"The conversations I was having with the president . . . there was never any plan from the White House," he said.

Senior staff members at the White House knew this was not true. The voluminous paper exchanges and meetings were proof.

"The whole plan came from us," Boehner continued.

Not true either, the White House knew.

"We laid out the framework," Boehner said. "And at some point they have got to lay their cards on the table."

Obama had laid out exactly what he would do, the White House believed, but so many numbers were fuzzy.

Boehner had been preceded on the show by Geithner, who had alluded to the possibility of reviving the grand bargain.

Chris Wallace asked, Would Boehner consider going back to his original offer of $800 billion in additional revenue?

"I have never taken my last offer off the table and they never agreed to my last offer," Boehner said.

"So your last offer, $800 billion in new revenue and entitlement cuts, spending cuts, that's still on the table?"

"It is still on the table," Boehner affirmed.

In an interview nearly a year later, Boehner said the purpose of his statement was not to reopen negotiations with Obama over an $800 billion revenue deal. "There were a lot of people panicking," the speaker said. "The goal of the appearance was to reassure people that—I know the president's having a meltdown—but Congress is getting this done."

At 11:30 a.m., Obama called Boehner to ask, How are we going to resolve this?

The congressional leaders are working on it, Boehner insisted. That was the answer, that was the solution, that was the path they were on.

Their talk lasted less than two minutes.

Did someone hang up on the other? I asked Boehner.

"No, no, no," the speaker answered, "No, no, no." He added, "It was clear to me they had no Plan B. Clear to me, frankly, for weeks they had no Plan B."

Later in the day, Boehner held another call with the Republican conference. He was holding them close. Though he had nothing to announce, he promised he would have something for them at the conference meeting scheduled for Monday at the Capitol Hill Club.

Boehner hoped that he could still keep Harry Reid on board with the congressional plan because the majority leader had kept his staff working with the Republicans.

Throughout the day, negotiations on finalizing the congressional plan continued, with a focus on language outlining the general spending cap and the firewall between Defense and other general spending.

•     •     •

David Krone called Nabors to explain the deal. It was now simple: the $1.2 trillion in general cuts over 10 years; the supercommittee backed up by a trigger of $1 trillion from the Overseas Contingency Operations; $400 billion in interest savings; and $100 billion in other mandatory savings, such as military retirement and health care, and also civilian retirement. The total came to $2.7 trillion. It was still in two steps.

"I don't know if the president's going to go for that," Nabors replied.

"I don't know what else I've got, Rob. I just don't know." Senator Reid, Krone noted, was hell-bent on OCO.

Nabors then briefed the president, Daley and Lew.

"The one thing I said I actually needed," the president noted, "they didn't get. I needed this to go past the election, and they didn't get it for me. This can't work."

Obama sent word to Reid and Pelosi that he wanted them at the White House at 6 p.m. No purpose was given.

Reid arrived with Krone. All were dressed informally, Krone in khakis, a button-down shirt and a pair of loafers without socks. To the president's personal assistant, Anita Decker Breckenridge, Krone looked tired, pasty and emaciated. Your boyfriend needs to eat a sandwich, she wrote in an email to Alyssa Mastromonaco, Obama's deputy chief of staff and Krone's girlfriend.

Pelosi and her chief of staff, John Lawrence, also arrived and went to the Oval Office. Obama, Biden and Geithner were there. Krone sat between Lew and Nabors.

"Harry," the president began, "I hear you have kind of an outline, a framework of something."

Reid began to lay out the two-step $2.7 trillion debt limit extension, then stopped. He was not a details guy. "Well, let David just tell you what it is," he said.

So the 44-year-old chief of staff began. It was highly unusual for someone to pass the ball so completely to a staffer. In all his years in Washington, Nabors had never seen a staff person from the Hill so on the hook.

Krone had always been nervous about the White House's ability to get a deal on the debt ceiling. He didn't think the Republicans wanted a deal in the first place, and warned everyone to be prepared for failure.

"Okay," Obama said.

Krone started reading.

"Do you have copies?" Obama asked.

Krone handed them out. The plan included the $1 trillion from OCO as the trigger for the second step. Boehner and McConnell had secretly pledged to honor it, Krone said.

"I don't trust these guys," the president said dismissively. "How can I trust their word that they'll agree to use OCO? I don't like it."

Sitting there on the Oval Office couch, Krone either would not or could not conceal his anger.

"Wait a second," the president said, interrupting someone else who was about to speak. "David has something else. I can tell David has something else to say." It wasn't hard to reach this conclusion. Krone was tightly wound.

"Mr. President, I am sorry—with all due respect—that we are in this situation that we're in, but we got handed this football on Friday night. And I didn't create this situation. The first thing that baffles me is, from my private sector experience, the first rule that I've always been taught is to have a Plan B. And it is really disheartening that you, that this White House did not have a Plan B."

Several jaws dropped as the Hill staffer blasted the president to his face.

"So I don't have a lot of options, in the past 36, 48 hours, to put together," Krone continued. All the leaders agreed on this plan. "So I'm going by what they said. You may not like it. But we are now finding ourselves in a situation where we're supposed to be the good guys. We're supposed to be the ones that fend off an economic catastrophe. And what we find ourselves is now, with no deal, we're going to have to root for the worst possible things to happen in order to prove to the Republicans that you cannot be so callous and let the debt limit expire.

"That is a horrible position that we're in," Krone continued. "And so this may not be the perfect deal, but it's the only deal that we have on the table right now in the situation that we find ourselves."

Nabors was watching Krone, whom he knew well, during his discussion with the president. Krone was extremely protective of Reid and of the Senate. But Krone's closeness to Boehner's chief of staff, Barry Jackson, meant that Krone was speaking through a big megaphone, essentially for the leaders of both the Senate and the House. What Nabors read on Krone's face seemed genuine. It said, I can't do any better. This is it. This is the best that we can get out of these guys.

"I understand what you think you're doing," the president said. "I'm not going along with that. I'm not doing that. The one thing that we need to bring stability to this economy is not throwing the debt limit increase back into the political arena. I'm not doing that under any circumstances. So if that means that I'm not signing this bill, I'm not signing the bill."

Krone wasn't finished. "If we're not going to come to an agreement on this two-step plan," he said, "then we're going to find ourselves saying, gee, hope really bad things happen." This would prove how immature the Republicans are, and the Democrats would be able to say look at what the Tea Party Republicans have done.

"David," the president said, "I get what you're trying to accomplish here. I can't trust these guys."

Reid believed he could trust them, although he didn't say so. He could trust them, he believed, because Boehner and McConnell were more scared of Harry Reid than they were of Barack Obama. And Republicans' reluctance to expose their secret agreement on OCO would only be another reason for them to make sure the trigger for the supercommittee never went off.

John Lawrence, Pelosi's chief of staff and a 40-year veteran of the Hill, realized that Krone's monologue, besides being extraordinary, revealed the extent to which Reid could not be controlled by Obama. Reid was a loose cannon. Though he would probably come around and succumb to party and White House discipline, at the moment he was flying on his own and jeopardizing a deal at the most delicate time.

Jack Lew agreed with Reid that the administration should take the counting of OCO more seriously. The Republicans had counted it as savings in the Ryan budget, after all. In this case, however, with verbal promises rather than something in writing, it was not acceptable. "Mr. Leader," he said to Reid, "we have to know what we are agreeing to. It can't be 'subject to.' It has to be something that we agree to now. It can't be 'trust me, we'll do it later.' If people aren't willing to say now what they're willing to do, there's reason to doubt that they'll be able to do it later."

As presented, the two-step debt limit increase relied on some absurd kind of double-secret promise that OCO would be okay later, but not now. It almost guaranteed another showdown.

Nabors agreed with Lew and told Krone, "If they could do OCO in the future, they can do OCO now."

Plouffe had an idea. If Boehner was introducing his bill, then Reid should introduce one also. That way the news stories the next day would say both Boehner and Reid were in the game with competing bills.

After the meeting, Obama made a beeline for Krone. The others, not knowing what might happen, stepped back so the president and Krone could talk, but they still overheard Obama's words.

"I'm sorry," Obama said, putting an arm around Krone's shoulder. "You didn't deserve that. I know how hard you're working, and I know we wouldn't even have a chance without you."

Obama later suggested to several staff members that he ought to call Krone and apologize.

"David doesn't get upset," Nabors said. "Don't worry about it."

•        •        •

Reid and Pelosi left the White House and said nothing to the crowd of reporters who, as *The New York Times* reported, "had been encamped there for the third consecutive weekend, awaiting an agreement."

Reid gave Krone a ride back to the Capitol. The majority leader was almost like a father to him.

It was a tough situation, Reid said, and Krone had handled himself well. There was no other path, no other option. "You stood up to him," Reid said. "He needed to hear it, and nobody was telling him."

Asked about the meeting with Reid and Krone, Obama said, "What I said to them is essentially, any short-term deal is not going to be acceptable. We can go back to the drawing board, but we're running out of time. They need to understand we're not going to do a short-term deal."

Obama also remembered having a conversation with Reid about a short-term deal, apparently later.

"Harry told me that he had never arrived at an actual deal that would involve a short-term debt ceiling increase. He did say that that was offered to him. I think he was sounding out whether I thought that was the only way to break the impasse. And I told him, 'You know what? It's not worth breaking the impasse to do that.'

"There were just practical elements to this. We would have already used up all the discretionary cuts that I thought, in good conscience, we could do. We're now in a situation where those have been pocketed, and now we're having a whole new negotiation about arriving at a whole other $1 trillion."

After more pressure from Obama, Reid changed course.

Late that night, the majority leader released a $2.7 trillion deficit reduction plan. At least publicly, it looked like he had given in. It differed from the plan put together by the congressional leaders in two key respects. There was a single-step debt limit increase that would last through 2012 because the OCO savings of $1 trillion was counted immediately. No second debt ceiling vote would be needed.

The plan, Reid said publicly, met the two key Republican criteria. "It will include enough spending cuts to meet or exceed the amount of a debt ceiling raise through the end of 2012 and it will not include revenues." These appeared to be big concessions because there was no new revenue or tax increases. But it also contained no Medicare cuts. And OCO was no longer going to be treated as a piece of shit.

Using OCO, Boehner later told me, "Just did not pass the straight-face test. I told Harry and Mitch and Jon Kyl and God knows how many others who looked at this, I said, guys, we aren't going to do any gimmicks here. No gimmicks. I told Harry, we're not doing gimmicks. Harry must've asked me a hundred times whether he could use that money. No. Oh, I know he believes in it. Oh, I know he does. It's an easy out. It's the same old Washington kick the can down the road. But he thought when it got down to the end, maybe I'd buy it. But I never did buy it. Reid's liberals were all over him."

This was not quite the full story. Boehner had made a secret deal with McConnell, Reid and Pelosi to use the OCO money.

## 35

On Monday, July 25, at a meeting of the House Republican conference, Boehner floated the congressional proposal, christened the Budget Control Act. It called for the $1.2 trillion in 10-year cuts, and established a supercommittee to come up with what he initially set at another $1.8 trillion in deficit reduction. The plan would increase the debt limit by about $1 trillion right away—the short-term extension Obama loathed—and would allow a second extension of $1.2 trillion only if the committee was successful in identifying the additional $1.8 trillion in cuts.

Boehner asked for support even as he admitted the deal was "not perfect."

The announcement set the House Republicans on a collision course with Reid's $2.7 trillion plan, which had been released the night before.

The White House publicly endorsed Reid's plan.

"Senator Reid's plan is a reasonable approach that should receive the support of both parties," said White House spokesman Jay Carney. Urging House Republicans to adopt the Reid plan, he added, "The ball is in their court."

On the Senate floor, McConnell said that Reid had gone back on his word. He said the majority leader had given his approval of the congressional plan over the weekend, and had only turned against it after Obama forced him, an accusation Reid vehemently denied.

In an interview later, McConnell said that he didn't think the president wanted a deal. "The president chose not to get a deal done," he claimed. "And the irony of it is, I remember saying this to the president himself, 'This would actually help you. Because people think you hide under your desk all the time and never do anything tough. And everybody who's knowledgeable in the country knows that a long-term solution to the entitlement problem is the key to the future of our country. I would remind you, Mr. President, that Ronald Reagan carried 49 out of 50 states the year after he raised the age for Social Security. I'm not asking you to commit political suicide here.' "

What did the president say? I asked.

"He just smiled," McConnell said, adding that he didn't think that the president could count on Pelosi and Reid. "It would have taken some political courage on his part. But I do know the way this town works, and when a president decides to make a big deal, his party falls in line." But it was "a failure of presidential leadership. He was not Reagan. He was not Clinton. At a critical moment, when we had a process in place to get solved the single biggest long-term threat to this country . . . It was very disappointing."

On Monday afternoon, Brendan Buck, part of Boehner's communications team, got an email from a White House correspondent for one of the major television networks.

The president is asking the networks for broadcast time tonight, it said. You guys need to do the same.

Boehner's staff quickly got on the phone to the television networks. If the president gets to make his case, we should get to make ours, they argued. The networks agreed.

Boehner was not pleased. Major public speeches were not his preferred forum, but he realized he had to do it.

Kevin Smith, Boehner's communications director, was worried. Even with time to prepare, delivering a response to a presidential speech was fraught with peril. On the day after the State of the Union address, nobody talks about the person who delivered the rebuttal unless they didn't do a good job. Boehner had only hours.

In dueling speeches, Obama and Boehner appealed for public support. Default and credit agency downgrading would have a direct impact on all Americans, Obama said. "Interest rates would skyrocket on credit cards, on mortgages and on car loans, which amounts to a huge tax hike on the American people. We would risk sparking a deep economic crisis—this one caused almost entirely by Washington."

Boehner called for real spending cuts and decried the Reid proposal as "filled with phony accounting and Washington gimmicks." There was no stalemate, and the House had a plan that he expected to pass and send to the Senate and the president.

Reid insisted his plan was the only option that the president might approve. "This isn't a game of chicken," he told reporters that night. "This is a game of reality. We're about to go over the cliff."

"The debt limit vote sucks," Eric Cantor admitted.

He was addressing a closed meeting of the Republican conference at the Capitol Hill Club on Tuesday, July 26. Cantor told the members that, while they might not like the Boehner plan to raise the debt limit, the alternatives—the plan being pushed by Reid or outright default— were far worse.

So, he said, members needed to "stop grumbling and whining and to come together as conservatives" in support of the speaker.

"This is a different fight now," Kevin McCarthy, the whip, said. "This is a much bigger fight. This defines who wins or loses. The whole nation is watching. The president is afraid of this bill. That's because in the end, this will *be* the bill."

McCarthy, a movie fan, had the lights dimmed. A short clip from the 2010 Boston crime drama and box office hit *The Town* appeared:

Ben Affleck: "I need your help. I can't tell you what it is. You can never ask me about it later. And we're going to hurt some people."

Jeremy Renner: Pauses and then, "Whose car are we gonna take?"

The Republicans roared their approval. But the speaker did not have their votes. Not even half of the 218, McCarthy reported.

Boehner's Budget Control Act, with a vote on the House floor scheduled for that day, faced significant resistance from the far right wing of the Republican conference. Many members elected with Tea Party support were saying they would not vote for a debt extension.

Later that day, the White House issued a warning that fell just short of a veto threat: "The president's senior advisers would recommend that he veto this bill."

Pelosi and Hoyer made public statements of support for the Reid proposal, and took all 193 House Democrats with them, which left Boehner scrambling to find 218 votes from the 240-member Republican conference. His job became more difficult that afternoon when the Congressional Budget Office reported the Budget Control Act would save not the $1 trillion Boehner had promised, but only $850 billion.

The combination of lack of Democratic support, resistance from Tea Party Republicans, and the CBO report forced Boehner to pull the bill off the floor rather than face a losing vote.


"Get your ass in line," Boehner told the House Republican conference in a closed-door meeting the next morning, Wednesday July 27. "I didn't put my neck on the line and go toe-to-toe with Obama to not have an army behind me."

Pulling the Budget Control Act from the floor the day before had been an embarrassment the speaker did not intend to repeat. Boehner and the rest of the Republican leadership spent the day furiously whipping votes, but were unable to get to 218, and Boehner pulled it again.

•   •   •

"The president," Biden told Pelosi, "is becoming increasingly fixated on this idea that Congress can hold him hostage anytime they want." Yes, they needed to compromise. "But instead of making it look like we are being held hostage we just have to change public opinion about what's happening here." They needed to identify the problem. "We have to get people to turn against the Republicans."

At 2:30 p.m. Lew and Nabors went to the Senate to meet with Reid and his chief of staff, David Krone.

"We have an idea for the trigger," Lew said.

"What's the idea?" Reid asked skeptically.

"Sequestration."

Reid bent down and put his head between his knees, almost as if he were going to throw up or was having a heart attack. He sat back up and looked at the ceiling. "A couple of weeks ago," he said, "my staff said to me that there is one more possibile" enforcement mechanism: sequestration. He said he told them, "Get the hell out of here. That's insane. The White House surely will come up with a plan that will save the day. And you come to me with sequestration?"

Well, it could work, Lew and Nabors explained.

What would the impact be?

They would design it so that half the threatened cuts would be from the Defense Department.

"I like that," Reid said. "That's good. It doesn't touch Medicaid or Medicare, does it?"

It actually does touch Medicare, they replied.

"How does it touch Medicare?"

It depends, they said. There's versions with 2 percent cuts, and there's versions with 4 percent cuts.

"I can't do that."

Once they started pulling things out of the sequester, they would never be able to stop. The idea was to make all the threatened cuts so unthinkable and onerous that the supercommittee would do its work and come up with its own deficit reduction plan.

Lew and Nabors went through a laundry list of programs that would face cuts.

"This is ridiculous," Reid said.

That's the beauty of a sequester, they said, it's so ridiculous that no one ever wants it to happen. It was the bomb that no one wanted to drop. It actually would be an action-forcing event.

"I get it," Reid said finally.

At 5 p.m. Thursday, July 28, Geithner appeared in the Oval Office with two senior aides. They had come to lay out the latest update on how they would handle a default and what it might mean.

A team at Treasury had been working steadily to try to understand the implications of a U.S. default. Some called their work "The Armageddon Project."

Geithner did not look so young anymore. He sounded like a general warning that the battle was coming and they were going to take heavy casualties. A U.S. default would be a first. A perfect credit rating, like virginity, couldn't be restored once it was lost. Going forward, American creditworthiness would bear the scar of default as long as the United States existed.

Cass Sunstein, the Harvard Law professor and Constitutional scholar who headed Obama's regulatory office in the White House, had been invited to offer his views on whether the 14th Amendment offered a way out of the crisis. The amendment reads, "The validity of the public debt of the United States, authorized by law . . . shall not be questioned." The issue was the phrase "authorized by law." Could the Treasury issue bonds that pushed the United States past its debt limit? It was not clear but everyone—including the other Constitutional law professor in the room—agreed it would not work. There would be lawsuits. The new bonds would be immediately downgraded. It would be a mess.

Mr. President, Geithner said, there are no more options left. The details were sickening. The federal accounts will be dry next week. He could sell assets, property, buildings, you name it, but it would look like a fire sale. He could delay some payments, juggle and shuffle. But all this would look like semi-default, which might be as bad. Even the perception of a U.S. default would change things permanently.

The economy was already weakening. What would happen in the markets? What would it do to job creation? Unemployment? Consumer confidence? Overall confidence? The moral authority of the government? The moral authority of the president? "Catastrophic," Geithner said.

The treasury secretary said he had a bottom line: A default could trigger not just a recession but a depression, one worse than the Great Depression of the 1930s.

One participant arched back in his seat, threw his head up and stared at the ceiling.

Plouffe found the projections harrowing. If that was his reaction, he wondered, how acutely was the president feeling it? As best Plouffe could tell, it was as if Obama had been seared.

A number of those in the Oval Office that day felt their stomachs turn to knots.

In an interview, Obama later said he had recognized that the stakes were high, which was why he and his advisers rejected ideas such as the 14th Amendment option.

"I am not prepared to put the country in a position in which a miscalculation results in default. And I think that one of the major arguments that would be lodged against us later was this notion that we gave leverage away. That we should have been prepared to say, we'll do this in the 14th Amendment route, and so forth," he said.

"And what I would have to explain to my folks is that the world financial markets, having already gone through trauma two years earlier, cannot afford to have uncertainty about what the world's reserve currency and its Treasury notes are worth in this environment."

•      •      •

Boehner brought his plan to the House floor again that afternoon. After nearly two hours of debate, which was supposed to culminate in a vote, House leadership abruptly shifted gears. At about 6 p.m., the House unexpectedly took up a series of bills to rename post offices.

Behind the scenes, Boehner had determined that he was still short of votes. It was down to 10 or 15 members who were resisting. The speaker pulled some of the most conservative members of the House into his second-floor offices for a late-night meeting. But only minutes after walking in, several of the members walked out.

We're going to the chapel to pray for our leaders, two of them told waiting reporters.

Shortly before 11 p.m., without voting on Boehner's bill, the House went into recess.

# 36

---

By Friday, July 29, Boehner was desperate. He was three votes short. He met with about a dozen House freshmen who were voting no. In exchange for their yes votes, they wanted a provision that made the second step of the debt limit increase contingent on both the House and Senate not just voting on, but passing a Constitutional amendment requiring a balanced budget. Okay, the speaker agreed, and brought the bill to the floor. It finally passed 218–210.

A clearly frustrated Boehner said after the vote, "I would say we tried our level best. We've done everything we can to find a common-sense solution that could pass both houses of Congress and end this crisis. . . . But some people continue to say no."

Where was the White House? he asked. Where was the Senate? He demanded they "put something on the table! Tell us where you are!"

Two hours later, the House bill was brought up in the Senate, where it was promptly tabled—meaning its chances of reaching the floor for a vote were slim.

What's next? Obama asked in a call to Boehner. I think we should meet.

Boehner wasn't interested. He said he would have Barry Jackson contact Nabors.

Jackson found that every time they went to the White House the result was unproductive. He took comfort from the fact that David Krone agreed with him. It was a pattern. Obama always wanted the principals to get in a room. It was another sign of the president's inexperience, Jackson believed. Putting the president and the speaker in a room together just increased the pressure. It was now down to detail. If Obama wanted to negotiate, he should send something in writing.

So Jackson called Nabors.

A meeting would not be productive, Jackson said, unless you send over a proposal.

We will, Nabors replied.


Rohit Kumar, McConnell's most senior policy adviser, went home about 8 p.m. Friday night, July 29.

"What are you doing here?" his wife, Hilary, asked. It was almost as if she was asking, Who are you? Are we still married? She had barely seen him during his past month of late nights and weekends. He'd often been rising before anyone, and arriving home after everyone was in bed.

"The fact that I'm here at eight o'clock," he said, "tells you how screwed we are. We're nowhere. We have no deal. I don't see how we get one." There was no path to a deal, he told her. Everyone was dug in. No one was moving; no one was blinking.


At the White House two hours later, 10 p.m., Daley, Lew, Nabors, Plouffe, Geithner and Dan Pfeiffer, the communications director, had not gone home. Daley called them to his corner office. The president was up in the residence.

Everyone was exhausted, wrung out, sleepless. It was so bad that at one point during the endless weeks of negotiations Lew had stayed at the office working until 6 a.m., gone home to shower and change, and been back at his desk by 7:30 a.m.

The situation was grim. The House Republicans had finally—after a week-long debacle—passed their bill. The group in Daley's office thought the final product was so ridiculous that it had no chance of passing the Senate.

But Nabors knew that there was a chance the Senate Democrats would fold, because the fastest solution would be to pass the House bill and get out of town. The House bill had the second debt ceiling vote, which was the president's final red line, and Reid had been wobbly on that issue. The subject for discussion: Would the president really veto a two-step process as he had promised? Was there an alternative?

"You can't veto," Geithner said. "You cannot be responsible for default." That would be a calamity, as they all knew. Anything had to be done to prevent it. Anything to preserve the global economy. They could not foreclose such an option, awful as it might be, if that was all that was left. Remember where they were: Europe burning, world economy very weak, young U.S. recovery.

"If he caves," Plouffe said, "it will have long-lasting political repercussions that we may never get out of. If we draw a line in the sand on something this important"—as the president had done unsparingly—"and cross it, we may never be able to come back." They all knew that Obama was under tremendous fire from Democrats. The view widely held by Democrats on the Hill was that the president caved to the Republicans. The evidence was his agreement to extend the Bush tax cuts the previous year. Those in the room might think it was an unfair description of what had happened, but Plouffe reminded them that they were not in a particularly good place politically.

So, accepting a two-step deal would not work, the senior White House political adviser said. "It'll be potentially devastating. We will not get credit for doing anything. We'll look like we got bullied by a bunch of very unpopular and irresponsible people."

Nabors said he basically agreed. "We are paying a heavy price now," he said, both politically and economically. "We will pay an even heavier price later" if the president signed the House bill. They would be buying a little short-term stability for a lot more long-term instability.

Lew reminded them that in the battles at the beginning of the year for the routine funding of the government through stopgap continuing resolutions, the Republicans had demanded more spending cuts every two or three months.

Nabors called it "paying at the pump," meaning the Republicans would insist on more and more cuts. Lew and Nabors had negotiated continuing resolutions for months. The president had held four Oval Office meetings with Boehner on them. The situation had been hell. "You can't send us back into that room," Nabors half joked. "I don't know how we get out of that room alive."

Pfeiffer saw the dilemma. On one hand the president could not cave, and on the other he could not knowingly trigger an economic disaster. "Here's what we have to do," Pfeiffer said. "We have to do everything we possibly can to make sure that this never gets to the president's desk. He can never face this decision. We have to talk to every Senate Democrat, call everyone we can, hold as many press conferences as we can, we can never let this get to the president's desk."

Republicans, Geithner said, some in the Senate and many in the House, did not understand the risk of default. Some of these people talked openly and publicly about how a default was the only way to get Washington to change, and how a downgrade in the nation's credit rating would be good. That wouldn't matter if Boehner and McConnell were stronger leaders, willing to leave those guys behind. But the leaders were trying to have it both ways and extort changes from the president that he would never make. The Republicans thought there was some kind of parachute at the end.

Geithner had to deal with the possibility that the House bill could reach the president's desk. "My recommendation to the president would be, we've got to sign this. If that's what they offer us, we sign it." Because there were no parachutes.

"What's going on?" said Obama, appearing unexpectedly at Daley's door. "What are you guys talking about?"

He knew, of course. They quickly reviewed where they were.

Could I actually veto it? Obama asked, adopting his law professor manner. What would actually happen the day of the veto? The day after?

"It would have massive effects," Geithner said. Treasury had to conduct a bond auction in the open market in about five days, the regular Tuesday auction, with settlement on Thursday. That first auction could be a kind of trip wire, setting off a chain reaction. The federal government couldn't pay its bills. "Why would anyone buy U.S. bonds if it's an open question whether we are going to have the authority to pay for them?"

Another possible outcome, he said, was perhaps worse. "Suppose we have an auction and no one shows up?"

The cascading impact would be unknowable. The world could decide to dump U.S. Treasuries. Prices would plummet, interest rates would skyrocket. The one pillar of stability, the United States, the rock in the global economy, could collapse.

The reality was that if the debt limit wasn't increased, Geithner would have to call off next week's auction. That would surely start a panic.

As he had told them before, the world financial system rested on the foundation of a risk-free asset, and that asset came in only one form: U.S. Treasury securities. They were the only place of safety in a storm. The 2008 financial crisis had been manageable for the United States because the world's confidence that we would solve the problem kept investors buying U.S Treasury debt.

"Every financial asset in the United States, every financial asset in the world, rests on that basic foundation," Geithner said. It would not just be that Social Security checks would not go out, or that the government would not pay businesses on time. Bank deposits, homes, stocks, any investment—anything of monetary value—would be affected.

"So you put that in question, everything comes crashing down and you cannot rebuild it. It's something that will be lasting for generations." Default could trigger a worldwide economic depression worse than the 1930s.

Lew, the most experienced of the group, a veteran of decades of budget wars, had always thought this was scary. Now it was very scary.

The witching hour was much closer than many thought because of these auctions. Treasury would have to sell short-term notes worth about $51 billion next week. Even if signing a short-term debt extension got them past the auction, it was not as if the financial markets would be calm, several noted.

"So," the president said, "if we give $1.2 trillion now in spending cuts"—the amount in the House bill to get the first increase in the debt ceiling for about six to nine months—"what happens next time?" The Republicans would then come back next year, in the middle of the presidential election, and impose more conditions on the next debt ceiling increase. "Are they going to demand the Ryan budget? Are they going to ask us to make massive cuts in Medicare just to fund the government? Just to keep the government from defaulting?" He could not give the Republicans that kind of leverage, that kind of weapon. It was hostage taking. It was blackmail. "This will forever change the relationship between the presidency and the Congress.

"Imagine if, when Nancy Pelosi had become speaker, she had said to George W. Bush, 'End the Iraq War, or I'm going to cause a global financial crisis.' This would forever change the president's authority if Congress can hold a president hostage every time."

So the president said they had to break the Republicans on this. Unless the administration broke them, they would be back whenever it suited them politically.

"We've lived through government shutdowns," Geithner noted. Lew was budget director in 1995 when Newt Gingrich shut down the government during the Clinton presidency. The world had survived. "If you can't get into a national park," Geithner said, that was sad—a large inconvenience.

"It's one thing to have a government shut down," he said. "It's another thing to have an economy shut down. We just don't know what happens." No one knew the mechanics. "No one has ever seen what the economic ramifications would be." It was so far outside anyone's thought process, he said, that the Congressional Budget Office had never done an analysis of what might happen if the U.S. government defaulted. It was beyond the threshold of the conceivable. It was almost like trying to predict what would happen if aliens landed.

What about selling assets? someone asked. Selling government property?

"You can't sell federal property that quickly," Lew assured them.

What about gold? The U.S. government owned about $275 billion worth. Could they sell it? Would that buy time?

No, said Geithner. One reason, it doesn't buy you very much time. The other reason, it'll scare the shit out of everybody. Besides, dumping that much gold on the market would trigger a dramatic drop in price.

They were out of options, Geithner said. The only one might be accepting the House bill, loathsome as it might be, if it passed the Senate. "If the U.S. government can't borrow money," he said, "the 2008 financial crisis will be seen as a minor blip if we default.

"This is uncharted territory of a magnitude that none of us can even imagine," Geithner added, making perhaps his strongest argument. The financial problems in Europe, most immediately in Greece, were much more severe than people realized. He and the president had been focusing on them intensely.

"We are single-handedly propping up the Western financial system right now," he said. "Play with fire, and it might take you past the point of no return."

Greece came up again.

It is one thing for Greece to be Greece, Geithner said. "It's a different thing for us to be Greece. No one would be able to save us."

What about next week? the president asked.

Tax collections only covered about two thirds of what the federal government spent, given the $1.3 trillion annual deficit on a $3.8 trillion budget, Geithner reminded them. That meant $25 billion a week more had to be borrowed; refinancing of the existing debt required another $100 billion a week for a total of $125 billion of new Treasury debt every week.

Some minor arrangements could be made with the Federal Reserve,

Geithner said, but they would not have any real impact. In theory, they would not default until Thursday, when the debt sales cleared, but as soon as it was obvious default was coming, the dam would burst.

"Tim," Nabors chimed in, "is there any way that you can slip this to Friday? Because Congress works towards deadlines. Thursday is not a deadline. They won't get done by Thursday. They'll get done by Friday."

Doesn't this really boil down to two things? the president asked. "If the Republicans believe they can do this to us now, they're going to believe they can do it to us later on. And where are we? Under any scenario we risk a default. That's not my control. The Republicans are forcing the risk of a default on us. I can't stop them from doing that. We can have the fight now, or we can have the fight later on, but the fight is coming to us." What would be gained by delaying the fight until the next summer? And what might be lost?

Discussion turned to the Republicans. Are they really that crazy? The answer around the room was probably yes. Boehner himself understood the consequences, they agreed. But did he have enough control over the Republican conference to get his share of the 218 votes that would be needed for any deal? No. This could spin wildly out of control.

So, no, the president said, he was not going to cave. Period. He said good night, got up and left. He was very agitated.

The others talked some more, reviewed, weighed, but eventually they all went home. There was nothing more to do that night. Not only did they not have a deal, they did not have another option.

Geithner thought there was one other consideration. He did not mention it to anyone, not even the president, but he had thought about it a great deal. It was not just that the president faced an economic choice or a political choice. He faced a moral choice. That was the most difficult decision a leader ever faced. Suppose the Republicans and Democrats banded together and passed a bill so the White House could not keep it from the president's desk? What then? Veto and start a global trauma?

The White House political people said a default would be blamed on the Republicans. Oh, yeah, it would fall on those intransigent, crazy Republicans. But Geithner knew they couldn't be sure. He certainly was not sure. And the president couldn't be either.

The president should not put himself in the position of saying unequivocally that he would veto, Geithner concluded, for one simple reason. No one could be sure how to put the American or the global economy back together again. The impact would be calamitous.

"And the people who would bear the pain of that would be the people less prepared," Geithner told others, "less able to absorb that cost. It would be something you could not cure. It is not something you can come back and say, a week later, oh, we fixed it. It would be indelible, incurable. It would last for generations."

# *37*

---

In several discussions with the president, the question was raised, Do you think Boehner was acting in bad faith?

"No," Obama said. "He wouldn't have exchanged paper with us." The conclusion was that Boehner was just not strong enough or skilled enough to deliver. Perhaps his staff was too inexperienced. Or maybe Cantor, whom Obama said he did not have a feel for, was undermining the whole process.

As in the past, the president's response to Boehner's unwillingness to deal was, "I have some sympathy for him."

Lew, Nabors, Sperling and Bruce Reed, Biden's chief of staff, had finally decided to propose using language from the 1985 Gramm-Rudman-Hollings deficit reduction law as the model for the trigger. It seemed tough enough to apply to the current situation. It would require a sequester with half the cuts from Defense, and the other half from domestic programs. There would be no chance the Republicans would want to pull the trigger and allow the sequester to force massive cuts to Defense.

•　　•　　•

Around noon on Saturday, Nabors went to the Capitol to meet with Jackson. He proposed using a Gramm-Rudman-Hollings sequester as the trigger if Republicans would agree to eliminate the second-step debt limit increase.

We're meeting with Reid and Pelosi later this afternoon to try to get them on board with the sequester, Nabors added.

Appreciate it, said Jackson. This might work.

Jackson and Loper took the White House idea to Boehner, who was amenable. The White House wasn't demanding tax increases, and the sequester would be large enough to guarantee that the savings were greater than the debt limit increase.


Once again, the real negotiation was between Biden and McConnell. As the McConnell whisperer, the vice president's primary task was to move McConnell off the idea of a two-step debt limit extension. They talked early that afternoon.

Biden stated flatly that the extension had to last 18 months, to take them beyond the 2012 election. It was a nonnegotiable demand, he said. As McConnell himself had heard two weeks earlier, the president was not going to give on this even if it brought his presidency down. He was not going to be blackmailed on the debt ceiling every six months.

In effect, the president was saying he could be blackmailed, but only once. They were not going to go through these exhausting, hair-raising negotiations twice a year, Biden insisted.

McConnell had a bottom line also. Of course, it was about taxes. There could be no automatic tax increase in the trigger or sequester. If a joint Senate-House committee could not reach agreement on $1.2 trillion, the trigger could go off but the money would not, under any circumstance, come from a tax increase. It would have to come from spending cuts.

Biden and McConnell, both suffering from severe cases of deal maker's fatigue, finally agreed: a full 18-month debt limit extension and no automatic tax increase in the trigger.

One for you, one for me.

They had staff work out the details. Reed, Lew and Sperling represented the White House. McConnell's chief policy aide, Rohit Kumar, represented McConnell.

But there were lots of other details.

"Is there any way we can have Medicaid on the table?" Kumar inquired in a telephone conference call between the Senate and the White House later that day. "It would be important for us if we could have Medicaid in the trigger."

"We can't do that," replied Sperling, trying to stay calm. "This is a core." Medicaid provided health insurance and services to more than 50 million poor people. "There has never been a low-income program in a trigger before. This would be the first ever. There's no way we can do it."

Lew had been listening carefully. Back in the 1980s he had negotiated the low-income exemptions in the Gramm-Rudman deficit reduction law. In all the discussions with Boehner, McConnell and their staffs it had been clear that low-income programs were not going to be part of any deal. Lew could not believe that this was being raised at the 11th hour.

"Gene," he said to Kumar and Sperling, who were on the speakerphone, "I don't mean to interrupt you, but we're not talking about Medicaid." Suddenly he was shouting into the phone. "You don't have to explain this to him, Gene! No! No! No!"

"Okay," Kumar said. "We're not going to have a conversation where people are yelling. So we will continue." He said good-bye and hung up.


Lew decided to report to the president on the Medicaid dispute. He was deeply offended that the Republicans who had been unable to move an inch on taxing the wealthiest citizens would propose automatic cuts to the poorest. Over the decades, he felt he had learned how to be flexible and cut reasonable deals with Republicans. There was, however, a line that should not be crossed. It wasn't as if the administration had spent the last three months of negotiations proposing some confiscatory tax policy. All they wanted was for the wealthiest to pay the tax rates from the Clinton years, when the United States had had the longest period of economic growth in its history. If everything, including taxes, had been on the table, this would not have been hard to solve.

So here was Rohit suggesting that if Congress couldn't do its job and reach agreement on a second $1.2 trillion in cuts, those who would pay would be the poor, the disabled, the mentally ill? Was that the kind of country they were?

He went to the Oval Office. Mr. President, I just absolutely blew the idea of Medicaid in the sequester out of the water, he said, and provided the details of his explosion, exactly what he had said.

It was the right thing to do, the president said.

Lew and Kumar soon resumed their conversation. Lew would not give on Medicaid, and Kumar finally dropped the idea.

Reid's bill to use $1 trillion in Iraq and Afghanistan "funny money" to fund the debt limit extension still hadn't passed the Senate, but Boehner was already planning a vote in the House. He wanted to demonstrate that Reid's bill couldn't pass. After all, the Senate had already tabled Boehner's bill.

Pelosi called the House Democrats together to review Reid's proposal. Though they were a weak minority, Reid wanted the House Democrats to stick with him, arguing that a strong vote in the House would strengthen his hand.

The first person who would say he didn't like the Harry Reid bill would be Harry Reid, Van Hollen said, but the next piece of legislation, written by House Republicans, would be worse.

As an indication of their distrust of the Senate's Democratic majority and its leader, many of the House Democrats protested that their support would be interpreted by Reid as a license to give more. The Reid bill had no tax increase. They agreed finally to let Reid know the margin for error was very small. A number of the Democrats also said

they would vote for the Reid bill because it would give them an opportunity to vote for lifting the debt ceiling and to demonstrate how
responsibly they were acting. It would be useful political cover if they
wound up voting against the next debt limit bill, which would likely be
worse and have Medicare cuts.

The House defeated the Reid bill at about 3:15 p.m. by a vote of
246–173. No Republicans voted for it, and Reid lost 11 House Democrats. It was, however, one more meaningless exercise. The bill had
been soundly defeated. But Reid, unhappy because he was being left
out of the Biden-McConnell negotiations, was going to soldier on.

McConnell went to the Senate floor that afternoon and, after offering the usual pabulum about "my good friend, the majority leader . . .
there is nobody in the Senate I respect and admire more than my coun-
terpart," said he had just delivered a letter to Reid signed by 43 Republicans saying they would not vote for his bill. Gnawingly, he quoted the
majority leader's own words from 2007: "In the Senate, it has always
been the case, you need 60 votes."

So, dead in the House and dead in the Senate.


Obama invited Reid and Pelosi to the White House.

I'm going to give on the tax trigger, he said. He had concluded that
it was an absolute red line for the Republicans. Reid and Pelosi said
they were not ready to concede.


McConnell knew how to rub it in. He and Boehner were working
closely, and they decided to appear together at a press conference that
afternoon, underscoring Republican unity. Fox News broke into its
regular programming with a "Fox News Alert" as McConnell seemed
to suggest congressional Democrats had been cut entirely out of the
negotiations with the president.

"We are now fully engaged, the speaker and I, with the one person
in America, the one in 307 million, that can sign this bill into law,"
McConnell said.

Later that afternoon, Reid, still furious, went to the Senate floor to say that McConnell's claim was false.

"Members of the Senate, that's not true," Reid said. The White House had talked to McConnell, but "not in any meaningful way."

Standing some 10 feet away from Reid, McConnell responded. "The fact is that the only way we are going to get an agreement before Tuesday is with the president," McConnell said.

Despite the "my good friend" language, the two leaders might as well have been spitting at each other.

"While the Republican leader is holding meaningless press conferences," Reid said, "his members are reaching out to me."

McConnell said they should just vote.

"We are here today," Reid said, "right now, for this reason: It's spelled f-i-l-i-b-u-s-t-e-r. It's unconscionable that the Republicans would filibuster us to default." He continued, "You can put lipstick on it, a nice suit, even a skirt sometimes. It's still a filibuster."

But he had a bill that could not get out of the Senate, and surely, definitely, would not ever pass the House.


The president and Daley were on the patio outside Daley's office with Plouffe, Geithner, Lew and Sperling when they got word that Biden was making progress with McConnell. It looked as if Republicans were ready to agree to a Defense/non-Defense sequester in the trigger.

Plouffe couldn't believe it. These guys are so afraid of increasing revenues that they're willing to put Defense on the chopping block? Republicans' revenue phobia was so intense that they would sell out the Pentagon.

"This is a deal we can probably live with," Obama said, willing to do almost anything to salvage something and prevent catastrophe.

Plouffe thought the president seemed genuinely surprised. Okay, Plouffe said to himself, maybe we're going to avoid default.

•    •    •

At Treasury, Geithner was planning a press conference that afternoon that would outline the payments that would get priority if the U.S. government went into default. The bottom line was that some bills would not be paid. It was going to be alarming to the world, and the press conference could induce a panic all by itself. There was a big debate that included the White House as to whether Geithner should appear before the cameras or do it off-camera. He would be explaining technical issues, but the main message would be that the United States was about to go through a financial typhoon in which the treasury secretary did not have the means to limit the damage. It had the potential to be one of the more memorable moments in American history.

Geithner even considered preemptively leaking out the gruesome details to the media in hopes of pressuring the Republicans.

When it looked like McConnell was making headway, however, Geithner decided not to have the press conference. He was getting increasingly sick of what he called "the extortion game" the Republicans were playing. As the former New York Fed president and current treasury secretary, he had direct pipelines to Wall Street. The current masters of the universe there reported to him that Boehner was making calls to reassure the markets—and the Republicans' growing campaign finance base—that everything was going to be fine.

"Boehner was calling New York," Geithner reported to his senior staff. "They were calling all the guys in New York who were fucking tearing their hair out saying, 'Don't worry, it's just a bunch of politics. We're not going to take it to the edge, and we're not going to default.' "

Geithner said he was trying to tell Boehner, "Don't take it to the edge? We're at the edge." Even the perception that default was close could unleash the catastrophe.

Geithner considered himself a very calm person; he had been through lots of trauma and crisis. Despite the turmoil, he was able to sleep at night. He accepted, but hated, that politics was driving the crisis. He told his staff that in a recent meeting in the Oval Office, Boehner had told the president openly, "Most of my people don't think

I can do this with you because it'll be too good for you. You benefit more than we would."

At 9 p.m. on Saturday night, Boehner's staff got their first real look at the proposal negotiated by Biden and McConnell.

Loper had been in regular contact with Rohit Kumar about the progress of the negotiations, but now he had paper, so he drafted the Republican staff from the House Budget Committee and they pulled an all-nighter trying to understand the plan and to identify its shortcomings.

It was a challenge, because nobody in the office had operated under the Gramm-Rudman-Hollings rules, which dated back to the 1980s. Loper spent the night trying to get his arms around the proposal. What was exempt from cuts? What was the impact on Defense versus non-Defense spending?

At 11 p.m. they held a conference call with staff from Lew's office to walk through the proposal and ask questions about how it would work.

But the basics were still the same as the Rubik's cube that Boehner had negotiated a week earlier—$1.2 trillion in general caps, Reid's supercommittee to find the other $1.2 trillion, and McConnell's complex "disapproval" arrangement.

# 38

By about noon, Sunday, July 31, Biden and McConnell had reached a tentative agreement that the deal would not be linked to a vote on a balanced budget amendment to the Constitution. Many House Republicans still wanted the vote, but Biden pointed out it had no chance of passing the Senate.

Is everybody okay with that? McConnell asked. You need to talk to Boehner about that.

Biden checked. Boehner was okay. Though it was still a big issue with his Tea Partiers, he had a three-part deal that could pass the Senate, and a balanced budget amendment was not part of it.

Nabors, who was closely monitoring Biden's McConnell whispering, thought that it was instructive to watch McConnell. The minority leader loved to be the one doing the negotiating. "But McConnell never wanted to have his hand on the knife," Nabors remarked. "A whole series of books could be written about McConnell."

Biden and McConnell also agreed that none of the cuts in the $1.2 trillion, 10-year cap on general spending would begin in the next 18 months. They would not hit until January 2013. Again, both sides would postpone any real, immediate cuts to federal spending.

.  .  .

In Congress, they had been working on reestablishing regular order. "Let's set the 302s for this year and next," Jackson said. The 302(a) and 302(b) are the legislative allocations for general spending. He was particularly interested in how much would go to Defense in the budgets for the next two years.

Soon Boehner's staff and Jack Lew got in a wrestling match over the Defense numbers. The White House wanted less Defense spending in those two years. It also wanted a so-called firewall between Defense and other budget categories. By stipulating that a specific portion of cuts come from each side of the firewall, this ensured that Defense absorbed what Democrats considered a fair share of the cuts.

Too much, Boehner decided. Not enough for national security, and the House Republicans would never accept such limits on Defense, though it probably only amounted to between $2 and $4 billion. He passed word to McConnell. It fell to Rohit Kumar to call Jack Lew.

"This is bullshit!" Lew said, exploding. "We're not bending."

Nabors, who had known Lew for more than 15 years, had never seen his friend so exercised. "Jack just went nuts," Nabors said. Everyone was exhausted. Nabors found himself yelling at his colleagues in the West Wing, or screaming at an imaginary Boehner or McConnell. "Screw you!" he'd bellow. "You're willing to throw the global economy overboard? We're really going to fight over what amounts to $2 billion? Then fine, let's have this fight."

Nabors was now focusing on the doomsday scenario, and he went to his computer to check on the opening of the Asian markets. Nearly everyone in the West Wing was staring at one computer screen or another, looking at Asia. The markets opened slightly higher and remained in positive territory throughout the day.

When Asia didn't tank, Nabors said, "All right, we've got a couple of hours. We've got a little bit of time to make this work." If the markets had dropped severely, he didn't know what the president would have done.

Bruce Reed, Biden's chief of staff, thought it felt like a modern-day Cuban Missile Crisis. But instead of the fate of the planet being at stake, it was the fate of the economy. It was harrowing. Reed, a Rhodes Scholar, former chief domestic adviser to President Clinton, and executive director of the Simpson-Bowles fiscal commission, was soft-spoken and known for his calmness. But he wasn't calm this day. They didn't dare tell anyone on the outside how bad it looked, he concluded, but it looked pretty bad. He felt they were staring into the abyss with no idea what the outcome might be.

But worse, he had received word from McConnell's inner circle that the Senate minority leader thought it might be to his and the Republicans' long-term advantage to rattle the financial markets. That was why they only wanted a short-term debt limit extension. A shock to the markets, according to this reasoning, would strengthen their hand in the second debt limit negotiation.

Again, it fell to the vice president to speak with McConnell.

The Defense firewall was critical to Pelosi, Biden told McConnell and Rohit Kumar in a call from the West Wing.

"There's got to be some way to resolve the firewall," Kumar said.

"We can't yield," Biden said. "It's like you and revenue."

In a second call, McConnell told the vice president, "I didn't realize this firewall issue was there, frankly."

"Look," Biden said, "we've given up on revenues, we've given on dollar for dollar. All the major things we're interested in we've given up. So basically you've pushed us to the limit."

Biden had gone into the negotiations assuming that the smarter, wiser, cooler heads among the Republicans would not want to do this twice. Now, however, he had to consider that he was being manipulated for just that purpose.

Boehner was facing his own rebellion. The deal would mean real Defense cuts for the next two years. There were no abstractions. People cared about what was going to happen that year. They were not going to live with a specific number coming out of Defense only.

Buck McKeon, California Republican and chairman of the House Armed Services Committee, was raising hell. "You can't do this to Defense," McKeon was saying, and he threatened to bring dozens with him to vote against the deal.

In the afternoon, Boehner finally called the president.

I'm not going to sign off on new lower Defense numbers for 2012 and 2013, he said. I need my Defense guys to vote for this, and I'm going to lose their votes.

Plouffe, who was in the room, was stunned.

"So, we're going to default essentially because a bunch of members of Congress wanted to look after the Defense lobby?" he said. "That is not a defensible place for them to be. God love them, we'll go to town over this."

Plouffe was thinking about how they could frame this in the message wars, but at the same time, he was apprehensive. "So it's all going to fall apart over this?"

"This is insanity!" Geithner could be heard saying as he went out into the hallway outside the Oval Office. These guys are willing to burn the house down over this? He was appalled.

Obama told the others that he had run out of road. The Republicans really wanted to have this argument? No, he said. This was principle. Defense had to play its role, in both the sequester, which had been agreed upon, and the proposed Pentagon cuts for the next two years.

The president called Dan Pfeiffer to the Oval Office. "We think Boehner is not going to take the deal," the president told his communications director. "We're going to need a statement about their rejection."

Pfeiffer went back to his office and pounded out a draft saying that Boehner had walked away again. It was very harsh. He went over the draft with Daley, Plouffe, Lew and Nabors, who all offered suggestions and edits. Everyone was worked up—angry, disbelieving, stunned.

It felt more and more like the Cuban Missile Crisis, only this time, the bombs were going to go off.

The president told Biden to call Boehner.

"The firewall to the Democrats is religion," Biden said to the speaker in a call at about 5:22 p.m. "You can't pass a deal without it."

"On the firewall my Defense guys take a huge hit," Boehner said.

This is absolute political reality, Biden said. "The president and I are being as flexible as we can be without being broken."

"Oh, come on, Joe," Boehner said. "It's all going to come down to plus or minus 2 percent? The president is getting his money" to raise the debt ceiling.

Biden called McConnell.

"There is absolutely no chance of changing a word in the firewall," the vice president said.

McConnell wanted to discuss it further.

No, Biden said.

The vice president then spoke with the president and gave his recommendation. He thought the Republicans could be bluffing. "I'd take it to the brink," he said.

"We can't move on the firewall," the president said. "Now we just wait."


Boehner was still insisting on smaller Defense cuts.

"We can't give there," Biden finally shouted at Boehner. Then he pulled out his trump card. He said he had authority from the president to call off the deal and go to default if the Republicans did not agree on the Defense proposal. The president was now inflexible, Biden claimed. "This has to be the deal."

No, Boehner said. He had decided. His voice came through the speakerphone in a high-pitched whine. To Biden's staff he sounded trapped and unsure.

"You're going to bring the world economy to its knees over this?" Biden shouted.

Boehner said again that he had decided, and that was it.

They hung up.

Was this a bluff? Boehner and his staff immediately wondered. How could the president allow default?

Boehner did not want default under any circumstances. If it happened, the administration would try to blame the Republicans, and they might succeed.

Biden sounded sincere when he claimed that the president had been pushed to his limit. What was Biden up to? And what about the president? Had he really been pushed to the end of the road?


In Boehner's office, they knew they had to find a way out of the Defense spending impasse. The agreement was at a pretty high level of abstraction and it had to be reduced to specifics in writing. Brett Loper, the policy technician, said there was a different way to divide up the spending pie. They could define Defense spending more broadly as "security" so it included money for the State Department, Veterans Affairs and the Department of Homeland Security. If they arranged it right, he figured, they could end up having the other departments absorb most or all of the belt-tightening. Defense itself might even get a little bump in spending.

Loper wanted Boehner's office to stay one step removed from the process, so in a meeting with Boehner, McConnell and their key staff, he suggested that McConnell should recommend to Biden that instead of placing the firewall between Defense and non-Defense spending, it be placed between security and nonsecurity spending.

McConnell had Rohit Kumar call Bruce Reed.

We need to figure out a way to get out of this stalemate, Kumar said. What if instead of considering Defense alone they used a broader "security" category that included State, Veterans Affairs and Homeland Security?

Reed liked the idea. The administration had used the "security/nonsecurity" definition in its own budget.

McConnell signed off quickly. The question was Boehner.

"I can't get it done," McConnell told Biden. "You've got to talk to Boehner directly."


•   •   •

Meanwhile, House and Senate Democrats met. Though there were some who were satisfied, many were intensely chagrined at being forced into another high-stakes game of chicken. They were operating with partial knowledge while the United States sat on the edge of default. They were the lawmakers and they were going to be partners in the final breakdown, igniting God knew what kind of reaction in the national and global financial markets.

Reid, ever suspicious of the minority leader, said he thought McConnell was getting Boehner to stall for time so they could make new demands. The president should give McConnell and Boehner a firm deadline, demand a final answer on deal/no deal.

A sense of alarm engulfed them. It was possible this was getting away from them. Reid and Pelosi called the president.

Was McConnell stalling? they asked. What about a deadline?

No, the president said, he didn't want to do that. "Let the Republicans work it out."

The meeting at the Capitol finally broke up with this lingering question: If the Democrats voted a new agreement down, would they be better off, or worse?

It was going to be a tough sell to the House Democrats, Pelosi knew, and she wanted Lew to meet with them on Monday if there was a deal. Jack was going to have to be out front.


McConnell then spoke with Boehner, who was in his office watching the Greenbrier Classic golf tournament on television. It was time to approach the president.

In the early evening, Boehner called the president.

Would you agree to redefining the firewall as security/nonsecurity? the speaker wanted to know, presenting it as his own idea. Obama said he would get back to him.

Jack Lew examined the security/nonsecurity proposal. Since it was in the administration's own budget, it was a progressive concept. It had come out of the international development community seeking more funding for poor people and for AIDS programs in Africa. The thinking was that they would get more if it was labeled part of the security operations of the U.S. government. Now the question was whether the State Department foreign assistance programs would be more vulnerable to cuts competing with Defense or other federal domestic education and health programs. Foreign assistance was important to Secretary of State Clinton, Lew's former boss. He went to the Oval Office.

"Mr. President," he said, "before we commit to this, I just want to make sure that the numbers that I've done on the back of an envelope have some relationship to the real numbers." It was a clever idea, but he wasn't sure if they should be for it or against it. Just because someone offered you your own idea didn't mean you should immediately and uncritically accept it.

"We're not going to dick around with this?" Geithner asked impatiently. "It'll be okay. We can manage this."

But the president agreed with Lew. "Step back," he said. "Let's think about it." He wanted skepticism. Defense cuts were taking the place of revenue in some perverse way. It was what the Republicans were giving, and the president wanted to make sure they couldn't wiggle out. Making Defense pay its share was critical for the Democrats. No last-minute tricks.

The State Department foreign assistance programs could be eviscerated, Lew worried. It took him more than an hour to check on what precisely had been in the administration's previous proposal, but he finally told the president it looked okay.

The president then phoned Pelosi to say that the Republicans wanted to change the Defense firewall to security/nonsecurity. Reid had signed off, he said, and Boehner was about to start briefing his House Republicans. It was the last thing holding up a deal.

Pelosi checked. No one liked it, but the House Democrats could live with it.

"We're not compromising on the firewall," Biden told Pelosi in a phone call. She then told the president it could be a problem but it would not be a deal breaker.

Pfeiffer, an unnerving presence at this moment, was standing outside the Oval Office holding a final version of the statement announcing the breakdown in talks and blaming Boehner.

At 8:15 p.m. the president phoned the speaker.

"John," the president said, "if this can help you get there, I'm okay with it. But I can't do anything else. It's got to be security/nonsecurity . . ."

The White House team in the Oval Office was listening to the president's end, and it seemed like Boehner had interrupted the president. What now? Hearts sank. Not again. Why had Boehner interrupted?

"Do we have a deal?" Obama asked.

Boehner said they did. "Congratulations," he said.

"Congratulations to you too, John."

Then Obama turned to the staffers in the room. "Let's not do this again," he said. "We're not going to negotiate on the debt limit ever again."


That night the 74-page "Budget Control Act of 2011" was posted on congressional websites. Though it had odd procedural twists, it effectively guaranteed that Obama would get $2.4 trillion added to the debt ceiling. Nearly $1.2 trillion would be cut over 10 years, beginning in 2013, and a new 12-person committee from the Senate and House—the supercommittee—would have until November 23, 2011, to find at least another $1.2 trillion in deficit reduction. If the supercommittee failed, the trigger would go off, sequestering another $1.2 trillion in cuts over 10 years.

Monday on the House floor, Minority Leader Pelosi rose to say she would vote for the bill. "I urge you to consider voting yes, but I completely respect the hesitation that members have about this." She added, "I hear that our Republican colleagues have said they got 98 percent of what they want in the bill. I hope that their votes will reflect that."

The House passed the Rubik's cube by a vote of 269 in favor, with 174 Republicans joined by 95 Democrats. The Senate followed the next day with a vote of 74–26 that included majorities from both parties, and the president signed it.

House Budget Committee Chairman Paul Ryan blasted the deal in *The Wall Street Journal* for its failure to address the "scary, yet simple" math showing that Medicare, Medicaid and Obamacare spending were out of control.

Less expected was former Obama economics czar Larry Summers's attempt to blow a hole in the deal with a *Washington Post* op-ed in which he made the same arguments he had in the White House: "Despite claims of spending reductions, the agreements reached so far are likely to have little impact on actual spending over the next decade." This was, he noted, because "the current Congress cannot effectively constrain" a future Congress, which would do what it wanted.

Summers also noted the failure in the legislation to address whether the Bush tax cuts, especially for the upper brackets, would be extended. As a practical matter, not extending the tax cuts for the wealthy would add nearly $1 trillion to the U.S. Treasury over 10 years, making it easy for the supercommittee to reach $1.2 trillion in deficit reduction.

"But this is an unlikely outcome given the likely composition of the 12-member supercommittee," he wrote.

Lew knew the deal didn't get the whole job done, yet by avoiding default they had done important work. The American economy had been pulled back from disaster. So, there had to be some sense of satisfaction. In his view, it had always been inconceivable that the Republicans would push the economy over the cliff. "After 30 years of this," he told a White House colleague, "high-wire acts get resolved by landing."

The president told me, "In the final three weeks, it was as intense a period as I've had in my presidency."

# 39

Zero. David Plouffe couldn't believe it. The monthly jobs report came out the morning of Friday, September 2, 2011, and there it was, on the very first line: a zero. No jobs had been added to the U.S. economy in the month of August.

Zero, Plouffe repeated to himself. Not 100. Not negative. In a way, negative would have been better. Zero. You couldn't make this up.

Unemployment was stuck at 9.1 percent, meaning 14 million of the 153.6 million Americans in the workforce were unable to find a job. Digging into the numbers only made it worse. The number of people classified as "involuntary part-time workers," meaning they wanted full-time employment but could not find it, was another 8.8 million. Nearly one million people had given up looking for work, meaning they weren't even counted among the 9.1 percent unemployed. In all, 15.4 percent of the workforce was unemployed, underemployed or had given up.

To Plouffe, with his eyes on the 2012 elections, this was terrible news. No president since 1940 had been reelected with unemployment above 7.2 percent.

Plouffe had watched Obama struggle through a brutal August. The debt limit fiasco had driven public opinion of both the president and

Congress to new lows. Inside the Democratic Party, the White House was being blasted for failing to take the lead on the economy.

Within the White House, the senior staff was anxious to begin rebuilding the president's reputation as a strong leader.

On September 8, Obama appeared before a joint session of Congress to push the American Jobs Act, a $447 billion package made up of tax cuts and stimulus spending meant to spur job creation. The speech was delivered in prime time to a national television audience.

The centerpiece of the plan was another year-long extension of the very popular payroll tax cut. Obama was back in the role of tax-cutter-in-chief.

"It will provide a jolt to an economy that has stalled and give companies confidence that if they invest and hire, there will be customers for their products and services," Obama said. "You should pass this jobs plan right away."

Pass this bill. He repeated the demand 17 times in the 32-minute speech.

Eric Cantor was not surprised that the payroll tax cut was back. He had predicted it in 2010. Republicans couldn't oppose it. Raising taxes on working people would be against their economic philosophy, and would get them shredded politically.

"Let's just rip the Band-Aid off," Cantor said in a meeting with Boehner, McConnell and Kyl. Let's just agree with the president and take the issue off the table.

Cantor also had a personal reason for wanting to avoid this fight. He was in the midst of an image improvement project. He had taken a beating during the debt limit battles. He had been seen as inflexible and demanding. His staff was urging him to show at least some visible willingness to work with the administration.

But McConnell had other ideas. He was convinced that the payroll tax cut gave Republicans leverage to get big things.

• • •

The American Jobs Act speech marked the start of an intense media campaign by the president and a shift in strategy. Instead of trying to work with Congress, he would attack. He would take the issues to the American people. He had looked weak, always going back to Boehner, seeking deals. Now it was going to be a new war. In speech after speech, he pushed for Congress to take up the bill, hammering particularly on the issue of the payroll tax cuts.

On September 12 in the White House Rose Garden, Obama surrounded himself with teachers, veterans, firefighters, police officers and others who would be helped by continuing the tax cut.

Stressing the fact that the payroll tax cut would reduce the taxes paid by small business owners, he ridiculed Republican resistance to his jobs plan.

"Instead of just talking about America's job creators, let's actually do something for America's job creators," he said.

Inside the White House, Plouffe was reasonably sure the Republicans wouldn't prolong the fight over the payroll tax cut. The president was scoring points all over the media by slamming Republicans, noting that their unwillingness to extend the payroll tax cut meant they would be raising taxes on all workers.

"They'll be too smart to keep letting us do this," Plouffe told senior White House staff. "They'll agree to it quickly. Take the energy away."

Meanwhile, the other budget issue was still pending. Boehner and Reid continued to voice utter confidence that the new congressional supercommittee would be able to find the additional $1.2 trillion in deficit reduction over 10 years required by the Budget Control Act that passed in August.

In an interview, Boehner said, "The supercommittee is going to work. I've got Reid's and McConnell's commitments the supercommittee is going to work."

It was a sure thing. All Reid and Boehner had to do is appoint the

12-member, bipartisan supercommittee and make sure the committee found the cuts before the November 23 deadline.

If it reached agreement, the supercommittee's plan would be guaranteed a filibuster-free up or down vote without amendments. If there was no agreement, Congress would face a mandatory trigger that would automatically cut or sequester that amount of money.

Boehner told the House Republican leadership and other key members not to worry about the sequester, which would take half the spending cuts from Defense and the other half from domestic programs.

"Guys, this would be devastating to Defense," he said. "This would be devastating, from their perspective, on their domestic priorities. This is never going to happen."

Reid, who had conceived of and pushed for the supercommittee, named Patty Murray, a Washington State Democrat who had been in the Senate 18 years, as the co-chair. She was a Reid loyalist and the fourth-highest-ranking Democrat in the Senate.

For the Republican co-chair, Boehner chose Jeb Hensarling, the 54-year-old Texan who described himself as a movement conservative. The fourth-highest-ranking member of the House Republican leadership, Hensarling was much closer to Cantor than Boehner. He was joined at the hip with Paul Ryan on economic philosophy, and he believed that dramatic structural reform of the entitlement programs was the central governing problem of the day. If Hensarling could get an agreement with the Democrats, it would get the approval of the House Republicans.

Murray reached out to all members of the committee,* including

---

*In addition to the co-chairs, there were 10 other members of the supercommittee. From the Senate, Reid appointed Max Baucus and Massachusetts Senator John Kerry. McConnell appointed Jon Kyl; Senator Rob Portman, of Ohio, who had been OMB director under George W. Bush; and freshman Pennsylvania Senator Pat Toomey, a dedicated deficit hawk, Tea Party favorite and the former president of the ultraconservative Club for Growth. From the House, Boehner appointed Ways and Means Chairman Dave Camp and House Energy and Commerce Chairman Fred Upton, of Michigan. Pelosi appointed the three House Democrats who had served on the Biden group: Xavier Becerra, James Clyburn and Chris Van Hollen.

Jon Kyl, the hard-line Republican whip and one of the group's three Senate Republicans. She phoned him at his home in Arizona.

Oh, Kyl's wife, Caryll, said, Jon is out working in the yard with some rented equipment, so he can't come to the phone. Ever the fiscal conservative, Jon would call back when the machine had been returned and the meter was no longer running. Kyl called Murray the next day. "You know I was renting it by the hour," he explained.

Meetings began in September and by the end of October various proposals and offers were flying around. The vast divide over the size of a deficit reduction deal and its particulars, apparent during the summer in the Obama-Boehner negotiations, still existed.

"I have gone way out on a limb," Reid said in a meeting with Boehner. "We have all made pledges and commitments." Then he offered the standard cliché about such bipartisan deals: "The only way this will work is if we all jump off the bridge together." In order to agree to changes in the cost-of-living adjustments for Social Security and age eligibility in Medicare, he said he had to stick with a proposal made by the Democrats on the supercommittee for a substantial increase in tax revenue. "If you can't agree to it, then no hard feelings. This is hard for both of us."

Soon Reid concluded that the Republican tax phobia was going to prevent any supercommittee agreement. The reason, he said, was not Boehner. "These Tea Party nuts are never going to let him get there."

By November, the supercommittee had made little progress. So Boehner made an end run around Hensarling. He reached out in private to another supercommittee member, Representative Dave Camp, the chairman of the House Ways and Means Committee. Boehner and Camp, two Republican Midwesterners who shared a moderate streak, had both come to Congress in 1991, were on their 11th terms, and had developed a close working relationship and even a friendship.

Boehner told Camp to make a secret offer of $600 billion in revenue over 10 years as part of a broad tax reform package. It had to stay secret. The leaks of his $800 billion revenue offer to Obama had been part of the summer debt ceiling disaster.

That $600 billion seemed right, Camp said. It was half the $1.2 trillion deficit reduction goal and should be achievable.

At noon on Sunday, November 13, Camp made the $600 billion offer to Senator Max Baucus. A member of the supercommittee, Baucus was also chairman of the Senate Finance Committee, making him Camp's tax counterpart.

Thus began a series of seemingly endless discussions between the two tax chiefs. One major obstacle was the Bush tax cuts. In the tax reform, all the income tax rates would supposedly be lowered, Camp argued, so the Bush tax rates would be irrelevant. There would be a whole new tax code. Say you have won, killed the Bush tax cuts forever, Camp said. "You can tell them you ended the Bush tax cuts."

Camp finally suggested they duplicate what Reagan and Tip O'Neill had done in the 1983 Social Security deal. "You say what you need to say to your folks. And I'll say what I need to say to my folks."

Baucus was unconvinced, thought it was gimmicky, and refused to go along.

Boehner told Reid several times that he had no confidence that Baucus had the ability to close a deal.

Several days before the supercommittee approached its November 23 deadline, Murray told Hensarling the Democrats would be willing accept $250 billion in revenue.

We can't do a penny in revenue, Hensarling replied, unless we get the cost-of-living adjustment on Social Security and increase the age of Medicare eligibility. In addition, as he had always said, he had to have serious Medicare structural reform, and he had not seen any detailed plan.

You have to consider this, she pleaded.

He didn't agree.


By Monday, November 21, Hensarling was convinced no deal was possible, and he got on a plane for Texas. Some of the committee members continued, with increasing desperation, to look for a deal, but by the 23rd, there was still no agreement. With Hensarling gone, Murray realized that she alone was going to have to tell the country and world they had failed.

At 4:45, she put out a press release she and Hensarling had previously agreed upon. It was a model of avoidance:

"We end this process united in our belief that the nation's fiscal crisis must be addressed," it said. Left unsaid: Just not by us, just not now.


"Washington's Super Failure," read a *Washington Post* editorial headline the next morning.

"The lesson of the supercommittee is not a happy one," the editorial board wrote. "The committee found itself paralyzed. . . . The gridlock, it turns out, was not a product of procedural failings in the system; it was a result of ideological rigidity."

A *New York Times* headline said, "Failure Is Absorbed with Disgust and Fear, but Little Surprise."

The story's first line asked the question, "Does the American political system even work anymore?"


No one voiced more disappointment in the supercommittee's failure than Minority Leader Mitch McConnell. During a one-hour visit to his second-floor office in the Capitol on July 12, 2012, he repeatedly brought it up and apologized for sounding like a broken record.

He insisted on giving the supercommittee unprecedented authority so an agreement could not be amended and/or filibustered. "My idea to lower it from 60 to 51, that only disadvantaged Senate Republicans. My idea to give up the right to amend, that only disadvantaged Senate Republicans. So I willingly and enthusiastically gave up my party's ability to affect the final vote. Could've been passed with 51 Democrats.

"Divided government would've been the perfect time to solve the biggest problem we have," he said. Get both Democratic and Republican fingerprints on a deal. "So I started with the notion that this is the perfect time to tackle the single biggest problem we have. Most Democrats will tell you privately what we all know, which is that unless you change the eligibility for beneficiaries on the entitlement side, you will never solve the problem. There are not enough health care providers to cut to get there.

"There are just too many people eligible, given the number of people we have, to pay for it. And until you fix that problem, you're on an inexorable path to Greece. And so my view was, I know how strongly the Democrats feel about revenue. We don't think that's the problem. But we're willing to pay some ransom, if that's what it takes, to get the real problem solved."

He insisted that the Republicans would have agreed to limited revenue increases if there was real entitlement reform, and the offers of $250 billion in revenue, or even the $600 billion revenue through tax reform, were genuine.

"I don't think naïveté is one of my shortcomings," he said. "I have many but I don't think that's one of them. I was actually shocked that we didn't finally get an outcome" from the supercommittee.

McConnell knows how to stick to his talking points. He sat patiently in his office with his sphinxlike gaze as I plowed through my questions. He subtly slid by ones he didn't want to address and persisted on those he did. "I know you're going to think I'm repeating myself," he said at the end, repeating himself. "The single biggest threat to the future of this country—there's nothing even close—is the unsustainable path we're on, driven by excessive generosity beyond our ability to pay"—he laughed slightly—"on very popular programs. You cannot straighten this country out until you solve that problem." To solve it, he said, they would need something again like the supercomittee with an expedited, no-amendment, filibuster-free procedure.

"And 2011 was an opportunity lost," he said, blaming the president entirely. "I am mystified. I think it would have made him look good. I think there would have been a very positive response with the markets and with the American people.

"You may think it's to my advantage to blame it on him, but hell, I know what happened. And he was AWOL at the time when we needed a president of the United States to get involved and make a deal."

I noted that Senator Reid insisted he wanted the supercommittee to work.

"The key Democrat is not Harry Reid," McConnell said. "It's Barack Obama. Now obviously I'm partisan, but I know enough about this place to know that when the president wants to make a deal, the members of his party fall in line."

We discussed his famous statement from 2010 that "The single most important thing we want to achieve is for President Obama to be a one-term president." I noted that he had also said in that interview, "I don't want the president to fail. I want him to change" and make deals like Clinton.

"I rest my case," McConnell said, saying that it gets taken out of context all the time and he was talking about a blueprint to get things done, as he and Biden did on the Bush and payroll taxes in the weeks that followed.

I said that the president believed that there were Republicans who wanted any deal on the debt ceiling negotiations to fail because if it succeeded, it would almost guarantee his reelection.

"He should have tested that thesis by making a deal with us," McConnell replied. "Because it's not his responsibility to deliver Republican votes. That'd be my responsibility and Boehner's responsibility. His responsibility is to not lecture us about what our people will or won't do. His responsibility is to act like an adult, a president, willing to tackle the single biggest problem, and let us worry about delivering our side."

•     •     •

Under the law in force, the Budget Control Act, spending cuts of $1.2 trillion over 10 years were scheduled to begin in 2013. With no deal from the supercommittee, the trigger would also go off in 2013 requiring a sequester of another $1.2 trillion in cuts over 10 years. The Bush tax cuts were also set to expire in 2013, meaning another $4 trillion would be taken from taxpayers over the same 10 years.

That could total $6.4 trillion over 10 years, or $640 billion a year, an anti-stimulus package approaching the size of the 2009 Obama stimulus of $787 billion every year for a decade.

By early December, there was still no resolution of the president's payroll tax cut proposal and his media assault was relentless.

"I know many Republicans have sworn an oath never to raise taxes as long as they live," Obama told reporters on December 5. "How could it be that the only time there's a catch is when it comes to raising taxes on middle-class families? How can you fight tooth and nail to protect high-end tax breaks for the wealthiest Americans, and yet barely lift a finger to prevent taxes going up for 160 million Americans who really need the help?"

The president said he would demand that Congress remain in Washington—through Christmas if necessary—until the tax cut was extended.

McConnell and Boehner were still trying to get some offsets, but Cantor saw no point.

We're fooling ourselves, Cantor argued. This is not a winning hand.

At 2:15 p.m. on December 14, Reid went to the White House to meet with the president.

Keep trying for the payroll tax extension, the president said.

If we can't agree to any of this, Reid said, why don't we agree to a six-week extension of the payroll tax?

Why don't you do two months? the president said. Because, six weeks, you come back from the New Year and you're not going to have enough time to get it extended for the full year.


Meanwhile, Cantor ran into Bill Daley and Jack Lew by chance at a holiday reception.

The Senate Republicans are going to do a two-month extension of the payroll tax cut, they told him. You guys are already negotiating.

Cantor was caught off-guard. He didn't know about any negotiations. Had Boehner gone around him again? He had his staff immediately check with Boehner's staff.

No, no, no, that's not true, Boehner's staff insisted. Not accurate.

All right, Cantor's staff replied. Let's kill it in the crib, then. The press is calling about this. Let's say it's a nonstarter. We're not doing two months.

The tone from Boehner's people changed abruptly: Don't publicly criticize the two-month extension.


At 8:30 a.m. on December 16, Cantor headed down to Boehner's office to meet with the speaker and McConnell. I want the two-month extension, McConnell said. Daley and Lew had been right, Cantor realized. McConnell said he was negotiating terms with Reid to get something from the Republican wish list.

The two-month deal was a "nonstarter," Cantor said as forcefully as he could. "I'm already publicly against this on the record. Half of our members are publicly against it on the record. Half of our members aren't even sold on the payroll tax to begin with."

Later, McConnell came back to the House leaders and said, "I can't reach any kind of agreement with Reid. We're back to two months." He wanted Boehner and Cantor to sell two months to House Republicans.

"What you're planning isn't going to work," Steve Stombres told McConnell, not hesitating to challenge him.

The Senate minority leader began to lecture Stombres. The Senate and House are co-equal parts of the legislative branch, he said. "You have to understand that what's good in the House isn't always good in the Senate."

Boehner stepped in. "Let's call it a victory," the speaker said.

McConnell carried the word back to Reid. The speaker was on board.

That Friday night Reid had a meeting with the Senate Democrats to advocate for the two-month extension. On a journey where there are a lot of bad roads open to us, he said, this is the least bad route available. This is the best path and we'll be getting out of here before Christmas.

So the two-month extension sailed through the Senate the next morning, December 17, on a vote of 89–10.

In the afternoon, Boehner and Cantor held a telephone conference call with House Republicans, who had voted for and passed a one-year extension just four days earlier.

I don't love this Senate two-month deal, Boehner said. It's not great. Maybe we should take it and live to fight another day.

It's a terrible deal, Cantor told the conference, taking a stand against the speaker and putting more distance between himself and Boehner than ever before in front of so many Republicans.

Republican Whip Kevin McCarthy got on the line and essentially agreed with Cantor.

When the members themselves were given time to speak, they erupted against the two-month extension. It was madness. People and businesses needed to be able to plan ahead.

"It's a piece of shit," said North Carolina Representative Virginia Foxx.

"It's a sellout to McConnell," said Doc Hastings of Washington.

Even Ohio's Steve LaTourette, considered one of the least conservative members of the Republican conference, couldn't stomach the deal, saying he wanted to come back to Washington to fight it out.

In all, 53 members waited their turn to speak, and 49 were against the deal.

• • •

Joe Biden thought he smelled a rat. Mitch McConnell was one of the wiliest politicians in Washington. Why would he be pushing the idea of a two-month extension? Everyone assumed a full-year extension was inevitable. Nobody could possibly want a second debate on the payroll tax when the two months were up.

McConnell was putting his Republicans on the wrong side of a tax cut debate? No, Biden concluded, McConnell must be up to something.

Biden called his friend, Republican South Carolina Senator Lindsey Graham.

What's going on? Biden asked, reaching Graham at home on Saturday. We can't figure out what you guys are doing, but this looks so dumb it has to be smart.

"No, Joe," said Graham. "I know what you're saying. We just fucked this up. It is as dumb as it looks. You all are in the driver's seat. There is no magic game plan."

"What happened?" Biden asked.

"I don't know, but most of us voted thinking that's the best deal we could get and that the House was okay," Graham said. "Do you think I would have voted for this so quickly if I thought it hadn't been a done deal?"

"Just checking," said Biden.

"I'm not fucking with you," said Graham. "I mean, it's not that I'm beyond fucking with you. I'm just not fucking with you here."

Biden still didn't seem convinced.

"Are you all capable of doing this yourselves? Of fucking something up this bad?" Graham asked.

Biden thought for a moment. "Yeah. I could see our guys doing this."

"Well there's your answer," said Graham. "If you don't stick this up our ass, you all need to fire yourselves."

• • •

The meltdown on Saturday's Republican conference call wasn't yet widely known on Sunday morning, December 18, when Boehner made an appearance on *Meet the Press*.

"Well, it's pretty clear that I and our members oppose the Senate bill—it's only for two months," the speaker said. "How can you do tax policy for two months?"

That Sunday afternoon, the president called Reid at his apartment in the Ritz-Carlton on the edge of Georgetown. Reid was angry and tired. Landra, his wife, was going for chemotherapy treatment the next day.

"What are you going to do?" the president asked about the deal.

"We are done," Reid said. "No force of nature, nothing you say, nothing you can do, we are done." He was sticking with the two-month extension the Senate had already passed.

Shouldn't they think a little bit more on some of this?

"Barack, we are done," Reid said. "We are done."

Reid and Krone, his chief of staff, agreed they were going silent with Boehner. A total lockout. Reid would not talk to Boehner, and Krone would not talk to Barry Jackson, Boehner's chief of staff. But they were nervous. These were high stakes. "The ultimate stare-down," Krone said.

The mood in the White House was now giddy. The speaker of the House had just gone on the record essentially opposing a tax cut, even if for only two months. Obama, however, was worried that taxes would go up on January 1, and Sperling again noted the potentially large negative economic impact.

Obama's family had already left for their traditional Christmas vacation in his home state of Hawaii, and the president was two days late in joining them. "I've told Michelle and the girls I might not be coming," Obama told his economic team. "You should be telling your families the same thing. This is for real. We're not going."

•      •      •

As Christmas approached, Boehner was taking fire from the old-line Republican establishment.

"I think we need to recognize reality," said John McCain in an interview with CNN December 20. "And that is we are not going to see that payroll tax cut expire on the first of January, and we have to accommodate to that reality."

The fight needed to end, McCain said. "It is harming the Republican Party. It is harming the view, if it's possible anymore, of the American people about Congress."

On Wednesday, December 21, *The Wall Street Journal* joined the fray with an editorial headlined "The GOP's Payroll Tax Fiasco." Republicans, the paper's editorial board said, had "thoroughly botched" the politics of the payroll tax cut. "The GOP leaders have somehow managed the remarkable feat of being blamed for opposing a one-year extension of a tax holiday that they are surely going to pass."

For Republican leaders, it is never a good day if *The Wall Street Journal* is calling you idiots.

Boehner reached the president.

Since Harry isn't speaking to me, Boehner said, why don't you send up your guys to sit down with mine to negotiate an agreement?

No, the president said. We're done. Two months. You've got the bill in front of you. You can pass it.

Boehner then summoned the House Republicans for another conference call.

"Speaker's decision," Jeb Hensarling announced.

We lost, Boehner told them. He had struck a deal to approve the two-month extension with the understanding that the full-year extension would be negotiated after the holidays. This time, democracy was suspended—the members were not offered a chance to speak. No one could punch in on the call to complain or disagree.

•      •      •

Because the Senate would not reconsider, Boehner's only option was to pass the two-month extension and get out of town for the holidays.

On December 23, in a speedy House session presided over by Boehner himself, the two-month extension passed by unanimous consent with no individual votes recorded. Despite the procedural camouflage, they could not hide. The two-month extension was now an albatross around the necks of Republicans of the Senate and the House.

Nabors was surprised they had to bring the Republicans kicking and screaming to approve a tax cut. Obviously it was because it had been an Obama proposal. They would injure themselves, even contradict their own anti-tax arguments, in hopes of inflicting greater injury on the president. The Boehner-McConnell agenda was singularly designed to defeat Obama at any cost.

At 1:25, the president delivered a statement in the White House Press Room, congratulating Congress on "ending the stalemate" and passing the payroll tax extension. "This is some good news," the president said. "Just in the nick of time for the holidays." Minutes later, Obama took off for Honolulu.

Media coverage acknowledged the deal was a win for Obama, but the real focus was on the failings of congressional Republicans. "The Humbling of the House GOP," said a headline on Politico.com; "Hate-Filled GOP Suffering from Self-Inflicted Wounds," said *The New York Daily News*; "House GOP Surrenders on Payroll Tax Cut," headlined *The Washington Post*.

But there was more to the story. Not only was there a disastrous lack of coordination between Boehner and McConnell, but the internal politics of the House had become much deeper and more complex. There were now, more than ever, two distinct power centers: one led by Boehner and the other by Cantor.

In early February 2012, the Republicans agreed to extend the payroll tax cut for the full year. The package would add at least $143 billion to the deficit. Six days later, on February 17, the House passed the one-year extension 293–132, and the Senate approved it 60–36.

Obama celebrated the bill's passage on February 21 in the White House's South Court Auditorium. Surrounded by individuals who would benefit from the payroll tax cut, but no members of Congress, he was the champion of tax cuts. "You'll remember," he said, "I called on Congress to pass this middle-class tax cut back in September as part of my broader jobs plan."

Democrats were given no credit but were lumped together with Republicans. The president decried legislative gridlock, and, indicating the taxpayers on the podium, said, "With or without Congress, every day I'm going to be continuing to fight for them."

# 40

In an interview about the debt ceiling negotiations in the summer of 2011, Boehner passed severe judgment on most of the Obama team, except the treasury secretary.

"Geithner was an asset to me in this whole thing. Geithner, Geithner!" Boehner said, as if he had been the lifesaver. "God bless him, but he was the guy running around yelling, Fire! And every day with the president he's screaming, Fire! And you know if it weren't for Geithner, I don't know if the president would have gotten engaged like he did. That's the first thing.

"Second thing is, and I thought about this this morning while I was going over this, and this is probably—hindsight is 20/20—but Bill Daley and I have had a long relationship. We like each other, we trust each other, almost like brothers. I mean we really understand each other. And when he came in as chief of staff I was very hopeful and optimistic. But he wasn't in charge."

Daley at first said he was flattered by Boehner's remark, but that he looked on the speaker as "not quite a brother." He said he would not address the question of who was in charge in the Obama White House.

Who was in charge?

"I have no idea," Boehner said. "Nobody who was in the room was. And I've got Jack Lew and Daley and Rob Nabors and Geithner. But there wasn't anybody in charge. And you know, I look back on this whole thing. The president was trying to get there. But there was nobody steering the ship underneath him."

Had he ever said that to the president?

"No, no," Boehner said. "I don't know that I recognized it until later. Much later. Months.

"Again hindsight. They never had their act together. The president, I think, was ill-served by his team. Nobody in charge, no process. I just don't know how the place works. To this day, I can't tell you how the place works. There's no process for making a decision in this White House. There's nobody in charge."

Isn't the president in charge?

"Yeah, but any good manager, any good leader, has a team around him and a structure around him for making things work and making things happen. I never got the slightest clue that there was a structure there. It's not that they're bad people. But there's no structure."

Yes, Boehner said, the president would talk about a big deal but then send a proposal calling for Medicare cuts of merely $15 billion. However, the conversations between the two of them were good. "He and I never had a disagreement," he said, overlooking or forgetting the heated conversations they had had, especially over the phone.

"I don't think it was clear to me until months later because you know as I reflected on this—and I reflected on it a lot because I've got to tell you, in the year and a half I've been speaker it's the biggest disappointment I've had, not being able to come to an agreement. Especially when we had one. It was right there. It was significant and it would have worked. And the country would be better off today as a result of it."

Many in the White House, I said to him, felt it was hard to get to a deal because Boehner had to prove to his members that he had humiliated the president. That was all that would sell to the Tea Partiers. Compromise was a crime, so a deal that left both sides satisfied was unacceptable. Obama needed to be destroyed. Crushed. A kind of tri-umphalism was necessary.

"No," Boehner said. "It's all about cutting spending. I don't have an evil bone in my body. I'm not capable of it. It's not who I am. You can ask anybody in this whole place," he added, sweeping his hand and his cigarette around the speaker's second-floor office in the Capitol. "My staff think I ought to be tougher. My friends. But I don't have an evil bone in my body. It was all about cutting spending. And they just weren't willing to cut spending. It's as simple as that."

Do you think Obama is willing to cut spending? I asked.

"I don't know. I don't know. Every time you get there, he's got 50 reasons why he can't do that, can't do this, can't do that. Maybe it's the difference between the president and his staff. I don't know."

In the White House, you're seen as a Main Street Republican and Eric Cantor as a Wall Street Republican, I said.

"They are judging style as opposed to substance," Boehner said. "My voting record and Eric's, I wouldn't think there's a dime's worth of difference between them, our voting records historically. I am a con-servative Republican. I have the eighth most conservative voting re-cord in Congress. But I don't wear it on my sleeve. I don't shove it in people's face."*

Boehner also had another complaint about the White House. "There was no outreach when we were in the minority. There is no outreach in a majority. You look at both Bush administrations, Clin-ton's administration, they had a congressional affairs team that was plugged in keeping people up to date. No outreach. Go talk to the Democrats. Because they get treated the same way. There's no out-reach. The place [White House] is dysfunctional.

"I don't know whether it's him or it's him versus his staff or who-ever's calling the shots," Boehner added at one point.

"You've got a bunch of people down there, well-meaning people, who have never done anything. Never run anything. Organizational

---

*In 2010, Boehner had a 94 percent conservative voting record, according to *National Journal* ratings, and Cantor only 82 percent.

structure. When you don't know what you don't know, it gets you in big trouble."


Within the White House, Jack Lew, David Plouffe, Rob Nabors, Gene Sperling and Dan Pfeiffer found Boehner's criticism laughable and untrue. In the president's and their view, Boehner did not come close to steering his own ship. Instead of being a visionary trying to make a grand bargain, Boehner had, almost all alone, crawled out on a limb and watched as Eric Cantor and the Tea Party sawed it off.

The question they asked in the White House was simply, who was in charge in the House of Representatives? And the answer was: Not Boehner.

"I think John wanted to get a deal," the president said to me in an interview. "And I think that, had he had more control of his caucus, we could have gotten a deal done a month earlier.

"John was in a tough spot. He couldn't get it done. I'm sympathetic to that. I think that him trying to spin it is understandable. But ultimately the test of leadership has to be, when the stakes are highest, being willing to set politics aside to do what's best for the American people. And I felt that that was not done in this situation. And I think a big opportunity was missed."

It would have been easier in the 1990s, he said, during the period when Republicans held the majority in the Congress with Bob Dole as Senate leader and Newt Gingrich House speaker. They had more control. "I could have done a deal with Bob Dole," the president said as we walked out of the Oval Office. "I could have even done a deal with Newt Gingrich."

There was one last question. He had faced an economic choice and a political choice, but hadn't it also been a moral choice about what a president should do in a genuine national crisis?

"Mm-hmm," he replied. "Well, what I realized was essentially that we were doing enormous damage to the economy and the psyche of the American people, and that this was not the way government was supposed to work. And at this point, during these last few days of the

process, [I] was absolutely convinced that if there was a way to resolve this that would be good for the American people and good for
the economy, that the political fallout for me had to be secondary. And
that I would willingly lose an election if I was able to actually resolve
this in a way that was right. So this was one of those times where,
similar to the decision to go after bin Laden, where you have to get out
from above your individual self-interests and your political concerns.
And that is a tough place to be, but that's ultimately your job as president of the United States."

The debt limit crisis was a time of peril for the United States, its economy and its place in the global financial order. When you examine
the record in depth, you cannot help but conclude that neither President Obama nor Speaker Boehner handled it particularly well. Despite
their evolving personal relationship, neither was able to transcend
their fixed partisan convictions and dogmas. Rather than fixing the
problem, they postponed it.

Though there were brief interludes when the president and the
speaker considered real entitlement cuts and tax increases, at least
through tax reform, too much got muddled. I believe their discussions
about a grand bargain were sincere. But when they met resistance from
other leaders in their parties, they did not stand their ground.

Obama and Boehner met privately a number of times in the negotiations in early July—the Merlot-and-Nicorette summits—but then
they let the bargaining on key spending and tax issues take place at the
staff level. The result was an exchange of mind-numbing written offers and counteroffers, the details of which readers have been spared.
I know from my interviews with the president and the speaker that
neither of them fully understood the details or the ramifications for
budgets and people.

Most extraordinary was the repeated use of the telephone for critical exchanges. Especially baffling was President Obama's decision to
make his critical request for $400 billion more in revenue in a spur-
of-the-moment phone call. The result was a monumental commu-

nications lapse between the president and the speaker at a critical juncture. They still disagree vehemently about what was said and what it meant.

It is a fact that President Obama was handed a miserable, faltering economy and faced a recalcitrant Republican opposition.

But presidents work their will—or should work their will—on the important matters of national business. There is occasional discussion in this book about Presidents Reagan and Clinton, what they did or would have done. Open as both are to serious criticism, they nonetheless largely worked their will.

Obama has not. The mission of stabilizing and improving the economy is incomplete. First, the short-term federal fiscal problem has not been solved. Instead it has been pushed off to the future, leaving the United States facing what is now called the fiscal cliff: By law, some $2.4 trillion in spending cuts must begin in 2013, along with an increase in income and payroll taxes. Just the cuts in the first year would amount to $240 billion, or nearly 25 percent of general discretionary spending—a staggering, unprecedented amount.

Second, the long-term problem of unsustainable entitlement spending on Medicare, Medicaid and Social Security, highlighted by Republican House Budget Chairman Paul Ryan and familiar to all informed politicians and economists, including the president and Boehner, has been left largely unaddressed. The combined cost of the three programs in 2012 is about $1.6 trillion. The Congressional Budget Office projects that will nearly double in 10 years to $3 trillion.

Boehner also was responsible. The federal debt issue, he told me, bothered him before he got to Congress 22 years ago. "And I'm sure as hell going to do something about it," he said, adding that the cause was more important than the job. "I need this job like a hole in the head," he said, adding he would have been willing, even happy, to risk his speakership for that cause. But he never closed the deal with the House Republicans and established firm leadership. He could have called Eric Cantor in and had the conversation of a lifetime, put it on the line with the man he thought was working against him. He could have said something along the lines of "You or me." Instead, he tried to sneak a debt ceiling deal past Cantor, the other Republican leaders in the House, and Senate Minority Leader McConnell.

The monster federal debt and annual deficits come from two problems: continued spending increases and no cuts; and too little tax revenue.

In three and one half years, Obama, the Republicans and the Democrats never really cut any significant spending. Instead, they passed laws agreeing to cut spending in the future beginning in 2013. They also never raised taxes.

These Washington leaders were risk averse. There was so much effort, most of it sincere, but so little result. Americans are now left with a still struggling economy in the midst of a presidential election. It is a world of the status quo, only worse.

# AFTERWORD

## WHAT IS REALLY HAPPENING IN WASHINGTON'S ECONOMIC WARS

During the election year of 2012, there was no progress on the budget and fiscal issues. "We weren't talking to each other," said chief White House economic coordinator Gene Sperling.

So in November, after President Obama's reelection, he and the Congress were facing the dramatic fiscal cliff that would suck billions of dollars out of the still struggling economy. In seven weeks, on January 1, 2013, all the Bush tax cuts would expire and the automatic spending cuts known as the sequester would kick in immediately.

Obama and his White House team realized they had some initial leverage. If no action was taken, income taxes would go up across the board, potentially providing $4 trillion in new revenue and deficit reduction over 10 years.

The president just wanted to raise the taxes on the two upper-income brackets—this meant anyone making more than $250,000 a year. It would affect only the top 2 percent of earners, and would yield about $800 billion over 10 years. Republicans, the party of tax cuts, didn't want any taxes to go up, but with the Bush tax cuts automatically expiring, they would face tremendous political pressure to support any proposal to maintain the tax cuts for the other 98 percent. Obama was going to get his way with the rich, a longtime policy goal and campaign promise.

Brett Loper, the top policy aide to Republican House Speaker John Boehner, admitted, "We knew we were going to blink."

At the same time, Obama was willing to go further on deficit reduction with entitlement reforms, spending cuts, and tax reform, a package that would trim about $2 trillion more from the deficit over the next 10 years.

The president summoned the congressional leaders for a 10:15 a.m. meeting in the Roosevelt Room on November 16, 2012. In the press, it was described afterward by all sides as a chummy gathering infused with goodwill. All promised to put the campaign behind them, roll up their sleeves, and come up with a sensible balanced plan. *The New York Times* called it "a rare show of bipartisan bonhomie" on its front page the next day.

In the spirit of conviviality, Obama gave the Merlot-loving Boehner, his primary adversary, a bottle of Italian wine for his 61st birthday, which was the next day.

But as so often is the case, the participants' public pronouncements did not reflect the deep divide between them. Note-takers for both Democrats and Republicans recorded the meeting's unpleasant end. In the closing moments, the president placed a new demand on the table. He said that he would not sign any legislation that did not include a debt ceiling increase. The memory of the 2011 struggle to find $2.4 trillion in spending cuts—so the Republicans would vote to extend federal borrowing authority by that amount—was too painful. The Republicans had seized the leverage in those negotiations by threatening not to extend the debt ceiling at all, which could have triggered a global economic meltdown.

"That episode from 2011 was the worst," Obama said. "I will not sign anything that does not have a debt limit increase."

"Everything comes at a price," Boehner replied. "And I'm going to use the debt limit to extract things out of you that I would not otherwise get."

"Well, that's my price," Obama retorted sharply. He would not permit a replay of the previous year.

The giant accumulated U.S. debt of more than $16 trillion was the problem, Boehner said, "not the discussion of the debt."

"Last time the debate over the debt ceiling cost us one percent of GDP [Gross Domestic Product]," Obama replied. "We can't continue to do this. I'm not going to agree to a deal and then have the same fights in February and March."

Talks began at a slow pace. Several days later Rob Nabors, the White House congressional relations chief, met with the top staffers to the House Republican leaders and key committee chairmen. He brought the outline of a plan.

"I could give you this piece of paper, but it's not really worth it because you'll laugh at it," Nabors said, acknowledging the distance between the two sides.

A week later, November 29, Treasury Secretary Timothy Geithner presented Boehner and House Republicans with a proposal calling for $1.6 trillion in new revenue over 10 years—twice what Boehner was currently offering. Half the revenue would come from allowing rates to rise on the top 2 percent, and the other half from eliminating tax deductions and loopholes. The speaker was surprised, though the $1.6 trillion figure had been in Obama's budget proposal released the previous February.

You've got to be kidding me, Boehner said to House Republican Majority Leader Eric Cantor after the meeting. This isn't a serious offer. They shared an uneasy laugh.

Republicans soon trashed the offer in public. "I'm disappointed in where we are, and disappointed in what's happened over the last couple weeks," Boehner was quoted in *The Washington Post*. "Going over the fiscal cliff is serious business. And I'm here seriously trying to resolve it. And I would hope the White House would get serious as well."

•    •    •

Obama called Boehner to the White House 10 days later on Sunday, December 9, at 1 p.m. Boehner reiterated his position: The problem was excessive federal spending.

No, the president said, it was not a spending problem but a health care spending problem. After talking for 45 minutes, they summoned Nabors and Mike Sommers, a Boehner aide for 15 years who was now the speaker's chief of staff, to the Oval Office.

"We had a very good meeting," Obama said, "we're close to an agreement."

"We agreed we're going to raise rates on millionaires," Boehner told them. He saw it as a huge concession. Republicans had always insisted they would not go along with an increase in any income tax rates. But given the president's enormous leverage, this was Boehner's blink.

Boehner had decided to try to limit the tax increase to those who made $1 million or more. This was about 400,000 families, or just 0.2 percent of all taxpayers. It would raise about $460 billion over 10 years, less than a third of what Obama was seeking.

The president also seemed to make a concession. Instead of the $1.6 trillion in revenue, he said, "I need more than $1 trillion in revenue."

"I'm thinking more like $1 trillion revenue," Boehner replied. That would include revenue from tax reform. This too was an apparent concession, up from his previous offer of $800 billion achieved through tax reform.

"We'll let these guys work out the details," Obama said, referring to Nabors and Sommers. "You guys need to get together and discuss this as soon as possible. All right. Excellent." They seemed to be headed in the right direction—the middle.

In his SUV, Boehner told Sommers that he also expected to get significant entitlement and tax reforms.

That afternoon, Nabors went to see Loper, Boehner's chief policy adviser, to outline the president's requests. He said Obama now wanted more than $1.2 trillion in revenue.

Afterward, Loper called the speaker. "I don't know what the disconnect is," Loper said, "but the two of you are not anywhere near each other."

The next day, December 10, at 11:12 a.m., Nabors sent an email to Senate Majority Leader Harry Reid's chief of staff, David Krone, to report on the president's proposal. Again, it was a different story: "Deficit reduction equal to $2 trillion: $1.4 trillion in revenue . . . and $600 billion in spending reductions."

As usual, the numbers were shifting. What was Obama's revenue number?

On December 13, at 5:15 p.m., the president and Boehner met in the Oval Office again. Geithner, Nabors, Sommers, and Loper were present.

"So I see two paths, John," the president said. Door number one: If they did not reach a deal, he would use his upcoming inaugural address and State of the Union speech to blame Boehner and Republicans.

Loper was shocked. Obama was not treating the speaker as a partner. He was acting like an adult threatening a child.

"Or," Obama continued, "you can do the balanced approach through door number two. We can come up with $2 trillion in savings." They would all be heroes and the vast majority of the public would be with them.

The president added that he was going to ignore the debt ceiling. Extending the Treasury's borrowing authority was nonnegotiable. "You might as well go talk to Pelosi," he added, referring to Nancy Pelosi, the House minority leader. "Figure out what you can work out with her, because I'm not engaging on it."

If they did not reach a deal, Obama said, he would never cut spending again in the next four years.

Boehner accused the president of backpedaling on the spending cuts and entitlement reform he had offered in July 2011.

Now is a different time, Obama said, and we have had an election.

Boehner considered it a status quo election because the Republicans had held their majority in the House.

Obama said he was going to get the $800 billion in revenue from the two upper-income tax brackets no matter what because all tax cuts were expiring and there was no way the Republicans could let taxes go up for the other 98 percent. "I'm still going to get an $800 billion tax increase," he said.

"Well," Boehner said, "what do I get for $800 billion?"

Basically nothing, Obama told him. It's baked into the reality of the expiration of the Bush tax cuts. If the speaker did not think a grand bargain would come together, he added, he better start thinking about a Plan B—a fallback position. And let me know what it is, Obama said, because any Plan B would require his support.

Sommers and Loper left the meeting outraged. By their calculation the president had talked—lectured—for nearly 45 of the meeting's 50 minutes. Afterward, Loper summarized the president's message: "I'm going to bring down on your head fire and brimstone and torture until you just cry in agony and misery."


On Friday, December 14, Boehner was back at his home in Ohio. He had gone over a new proposal with Eric Cantor, the majority leader, who was closer to the more extreme Tea Party wing of the House Republican majority. About 5 p.m., Boehner called Obama with a detailed offer: Income tax rates go up on those making more than $1 million a year; total revenue $1 trillion; $1.2 trillion in spending cuts; and a debt limit increase for one year. As part of the deal, the sequester would be replaced.

Obama thanked the speaker and said he thought this was a serious offer from which they could work. The offer of $1 trillion in revenue, however, was a bit short, he said, and the $1.2 trillion in spending cuts too high. However, he said, he would go along with a change favored by Republicans in how the Consumer Price Index (CPI) was used to calculate cost-of-living increases in Social Security. That would lower annual cost-of-living increases for Social Security by a mere 0.1 to 0.3 percent a year but save billions in the long run. Obama said he did not want to raise the age for Medicare eligibility to 67 and insisted that he had to have an extension of unemployment insurance, increased infrastructure spending, and payroll tax cuts.

For the first time in a month, it seemed there was a small hope for an agreement.

By the next night, Boehner's concessions had leaked to the media, which reported accurately that Boehner had given in on the two key matters—extending the debt limit for a year and agreeing to raise taxes on those who made over $1 million. There was widespread angst among Republican House members who had not been told in advance that the speaker was going to make these concessions. Many were disappointed, even furious, to learn about it through the media.

"We're getting crushed," Loper said.

On Saturday, Loper and Nabors met to work on a paper that would precisely define and isolate the differences between the administration and the House. After an exchange of emails that day and the next, they agreed on a half-page summary: "Revenue target? Administration: $1.2 trillion. House: $940 billion. . . . Spending target? Administration $760 billion. House $1.04 trillion."

They printed this out on a single sheet of paper.

The size of the differences between them depended on what was being measured. One way to measure this was as a difference of more than $500 billion, seemingly large. The biggest single variance was in the treatment of savings from interest payments that would not have to be made because of reduced federal borrowing. By common practice, this was calculated to be roughly 20 percent of the savings, since they would not have to spend to service more debt. Republicans didn't want to count interest savings; the White House wanted to count it for the whole $1.2 trillion in proposed cuts, which would save roughly $280 to $290 billion in interest by the Obama administration's calculation.

However, if the debate over interest savings were set aside, the difference was only $200 billion over 10 years—just $20 billion a year, a minuscule number compared to the annual federal deficit of about $1 trillion. The difference was 1/50 of the deficit.

On the surface, they looked close.

•     •     •

Monday, December 17, was a pivotal day. Obama met with Boehner in the Oval Office in the morning. The president's team included Geithner and Nabors. Boehner brought Sommers and Loper. There were high expectations for this pre-Christmas meeting. It was as if the fever of discord was about to break.

"I was pleased you moved on Friday," Obama said as they sat down at 11.

Boehner complained directly, and somewhat bitterly, that the concessions he had made had leaked to the press. It was unsettling to his members who had not been informed. Negotiation by leak was not effective, and eroded the necessary trust.

The president said he had nothing to do with the leaks.

Ignoring the Nabors-Loper paper, Obama presented a new written proposal. The single sheet of paper had 22 bullet points. It called for $1.2 trillion in revenue from allowing the rates on high-income taxpayers to rise and eliminating some loopholes and deductions. He had made a concession and would only require tax increases from those families who made more than $400,000 a year (up from $250,000). Another $95 billion in revenue would come from small adjustments to tax brackets that would happen automatically when the measurement of the Consumer Price Index was changed. The rest would come from raising the capital gains and dividend rates for top-bracket taxpayers.

I can't go that high in revenue, Boehner said. I am already beyond what I am comfortable doing.

An incident from 2011 had left a mark on the speaker but he did not mention it to the president. During the debt ceiling negotiations, Obama had proposed jacking up the revenue number from $800 billion to $1.2 trillion. When Boehner floated the idea to Cantor and Steve Stombres, Cantor's chief of staff, he ran into a buzz saw. They told Boehner that he might get a mere 50 votes from House Republicans for such a high revenue number. Little had changed, and $1.2 trillion was out of the question.

I'll tell you exactly what I can do, Boehner told Obama. I can do

$1 trillion total revenue. The only way I can sell it to my members is if it is balanced, dollar for dollar, with real spending cuts in programs. He wondered if they could eliminate some of the federal programs entirely, rather than just cutting their spending. Even small but dramatic cuts in the federal government would have huge symbolic value for his Republicans. He dismissed the $290 billion in interest savings as not a real cut in government spending. He noted that the revenue number was his chief concern, and that of the House Republicans.

I can't move off $1.2 trillion in revenue, the president said, noting again that taxes would go up for everyone if the Congress did nothing. Insisting that the top brackets pay more was inevitable. If he didn't get more, Obama argued, the Democrats would say he was a terrible negotiator. What's wrong with you? they would ask. You gave up. Why would you ever go below $1.2 trillion?

The president's proposed spending reductions would be $1.22 trillion, including $400 billion in health care and another $400 billion in other unspecified programs, plus $290 billion in interest savings and $130 billion from the Consumer Price Index changes. Sperling wanted $200 billion of unspecified savings to be a partial replacement for the sequester.

Boehner wanted the president to eliminate the alleged interest savings and was skeptical of the $400 billion in unspecified savings. They were, however, not that far apart, he told Obama. Though he counted the other savings a little differently, he saw that they were close. "If you can move up another $130 billion or $150 billion on the spending side, we can get there."

Health care costs were the big issue. They were out of control, especially the spending on Medicare. On health care cuts, Boehner suggested, you're at $400 billion, I'm at $600 billion. "Can we split the difference here? Can we land at $500 billion?"

"I have to look at not just the numbers on a piece of paper," Obama said, "but what's behind the numbers." The impact on elderly Medicare beneficiaries could be dramatic if they went too far on cuts. "Four hundred billion is it. I just can't see how we go any further on that."

Obama asked Nabors what he thought.

"I don't think we're that close," the congressional relations chief said, especially on the $290 billion in interest. That was the major catch. The savings would be real but would not involve cuts to government programs.

"We can sit here and stare at each other for a while longer," Boehner said, "or I can go back and visit with my guys and see if we have any ideas for what to do next." He stood up. "I'll let you know," he said, and began to walk out.

Well, okay, the president said. "You're going to call me right?"

Boehner promised to call within a couple of hours.

In his SUV, the speaker told his aides, "He wasn't moving so I figured it was time to leave and let him stew on it for a while."

Boehner thought Obama was using his enormous political capital as a reelected president to break the Republicans and force them to accept what would be unacceptable under any other circumstances.


Obama didn't stew. He called Boehner at 2:30 p.m.

"We got a deal?" he asked.

Let's take the Medicare age increase off the table, Boehner replied, but insisted they stick to $1 trillion in revenue and $1 trillion in spending cuts.

Obama said he appreciated the offer. "I will talk to my folks. I will call you back in an hour." The revenue is going to have to stay the same at $1.2 trillion, he repeated. "You should anticipate that I will move on spending. I'm going to give you a counter that gets us closer, so close that it would be silly for us not to get an agreement."

Just before 4 p.m., Obama called Boehner again and made good, adding another $50 billion in spending cuts. By his calculation that would get them to spending cuts of nearly $1 trillion, the speaker's goal, without counting anything from interest savings. If interest was counted, which made sense to him, it would total more than $1.2 trillion in spending cuts.

The president said he still needed Boehner to agree to $1.2 trillion in revenue. He offered to add another $70 billion in small business expensing, which would be a tax cut. That would take the revenue down to $1.13 trillion. "We're getting closer. I can't go any further down."

In a third call, Boehner spoke from talking points his staff had prepared. The Tea Party would not go along, and he felt there was no trust with the president. It was a bailout message.

"Mr. President, as I said earlier today, we've worked hard and in good faith. Your revenue number is still just too high. I hope that you can get to parity . . . to a balanced approach. And my door is going to stay open for you to do that. For now, the best we may be able to do is address the immediate question of taxes for next year. I haven't given up hope for an agreement, and that's what I'm going to be telling people, publicly and privately. But I need to give my members a plan tomorrow. The cliff is right around the corner"—the tax increases and automatic spending cuts.

The House, the speaker said, needed to start moving on the proposal to allow tax rates to go up only on those making more than $1 million a year. He called it his own Plan B. He, Cantor, and Mitch McConnell, the Republican Senate leader, had been discussing a Plan B with the $1 million threshold for weeks. The idea was to be realistic and give some on taxes—to blink, but in such a way that it meant tax increases for only the smallest number of taxpayers.

"But even as we do that," Boehner continued, "I'm going to make clear that everything we've discussed is still on the table. We need to continue to find a way to a broader solution. It may not happen immediately, but it has to happen. I'm not crazy about this Plan B, but frankly, I think as we go forward with it, it might help make the case on both sides of the aisle for the framework you and I have been talking about. So again, as I said earlier today, this is not an ultimatum. We have to move ahead, but I'm not shutting the door on a potential agreement."

"Essentially," Obama replied, almost pleading now, "I've proposed parity." We are $100 billion to $130 billion apart on revenue, he said. An agreement "would be huge for the country. What I'm

asking for would be meaningless for the people who would pay. If
you walk away now, there's going to be hardening on both sides. It's
not going to be easy to come to an agreement. It's going to be harder
to come to an agreement." He knew the Democrats were in no mood
for entitlement cuts. "If you need me to, I can get Republican supporters [from the Business Roundtable] to put pressure on your caucus." Obama added, "On a $2.4 trillion deal, we decided to blow it
up over 5 percent of a deal?" He was incredulous. "Both sides will
harden again."

"We need to get there," Boehner replied, "but Plan B might get us
people who look at it the right way."

"I've given you a lot of concessions," Obama said. "I've given you
parity. Our folks will start going in the wrong direction, and we won't
be able to get them back. You will be able to say that you have more
cuts than revenue under any scenario."

That was not accurate by Boehner's math, because he would not
count the $290 billion in interest savings.

"But I can't go any further than this," the president continued. "It's
a good deal and the country wants it. There's no stomach for crazy
shit. If we can get a deal, I can get Nancy and Harry to get there. People are going to say that we're bad leaders and that we're crazy."

"This is difficult for everybody," Boehner said. "I'm going to lay out
Plan B, and I'm going to continue to work with you on Plan A. We need
to take the tax issue off the table. My guys will be in a different place"
once that happens.

"Democrats will be in a bad place," the president said. "Don't hang
up on me. . . . Be honest with me, why can't we get it done? Is it Cantor? Is it McCarthy?" Obama asked, referring to Republican House
whip and chief vote counter Kevin McCarthy. "Their supporters want
to get it done. What's the thought process? It's getting harder, not
easier."

"This is the risk we have to take," Boehner said. "I can't do the revenue number." He felt that Obama was underestimating the amount
of revenue his plan would produce and overestimating the spending cuts. The gap was too wide to close. Brett Loper felt even more

strongly about the difference. The numbers did the negotiators a dis-
service, in Loper's view, by making them appear closer to a deal than
they were.

"What is it about the politics?" Obama pleaded.

"My guys just aren't there," Boehner said.

There was a long, uncomfortable pause.

"We'll keep working," Boehner said.

"Describe the scenario in which it gets done," Obama asked. "We
are $150 billion off, man. I don't get it. There's something I don't get."
I'm going to have to take it to the public, he said.

Boehner said he was going ahead with Plan B, and they hung up.

The president appealed for an agreement at a December 19 press conference two days later. "What separates us is probably a few hundred
billion dollars," he revealed, but did not provide details, and no one in
the media seemed to focus on how close that statement showed they
were. "If you kind of peel off the partisan war paint, then we should
be able to get something done."

Boehner conducted a meeting of all the House Republicans to discuss alternatives. Afterward he held a one-minute press conference to
announce Plan B—tax increases for only those making more than $1
million a year.

"Tomorrow," he said with what sounded like absolute confidence,
"the House will pass legislation to make permanent tax relief for nearly
every American—99.81 percent of the American people."

"Oh, my God!" Representative Kevin McCarthy, the House whip,
said to himself. He was standing nearby and almost gasped.

Within the House majority he had a doctrine called "the McCarthy Rule," intended to prevent embarrassing defeats. In accordance
with the McCarthy Rule, House leadership was supposed to educate
the members and count the votes before announcing a date for a vote.
Boehner's Plan B—though technically only a tax increase for 0.19 percent of taxpayers—was a violation of Republican antitax orthodoxy.
McCarthy knew they would never get the votes.

After the press conference, McCarthy told Boehner, "This is a heavy lift."

Boehner said passing the tax increase just for millionaires would give him a stronger hand in the negotiations with Obama.

As whip, McCarthy was closer to the rank-and-file Republicans than anyone else in the leadership. He and his vote counters took a confidential poll. The initial inquiry was simple: Vote your conscience, vote your district, but don't surprise me. It was better to get bad news than bad data. Members who had said they would always be there when the leadership needed them now said no. There was no way, especially with no spending cuts. McCarthy told Boehner that Plan B was doomed.

Boehner's staff calculated that about 230 members wanted Plan B to pass—12 more than the necessary majority of 218. The problem was only 200 were willing to get out in front publicly to vote for it. The remaining 30 indicated there was no way they would declare support for even a small tax increase in a public vote. Period. That was the measure of courage in the House majority.

In what was a giant public embarrassment for the speaker and House Republicans, especially after numerous public declarations by him and Cantor that Plan B would pass, Boehner canceled the vote.

*The Washington Post* reported that Mike Kelly, a congressman from Pennsylvania, took the microphone after the announcement was made and yelled to his fellow Republicans, "Really, we can't support our speaker?"

Sommers gathered the speaker's senior staff in his small office. They smoked cigars and had a couple of glasses of wine. It was depressing and difficult—the deep divisions among House Republicans, especially Boehner and the rank and file, had once again been exposed.

Later Sommers went to see Boehner. "Are you all right?" the chief of staff inquired.

"I don't want anybody stressing about this," the speaker replied.

Are you kidding me? Sommers thought to himself. How could they not be stressing about this? They were just about to go off the fiscal cliff. They had failed to execute a major legislative priority. Who could be stressing? Apparently not Boehner, who seemed as laid-back as ever.

Two days after Christmas, December 27, Boehner was at his home beside a golf course in a suburb of Cincinnati. His wife, Debbie, had gone to Florida. The temperature was barely above freezing, too cold for golf, and the speaker had too much time on his hands. He had already made several trips to the local building supply store to get the material to rebuild the drainpipe on a humidifier.

On the television, there was a clip of Harry Reid on the Senate floor saying, "The House of Representatives is . . . being operated by a dictatorship of the speaker."

Boehner began a slow burn. If anything, the embarrassing rejection of Plan B demonstrated the precise opposite. "It's not the outcome that I wanted," he had said at a press conference, "but that was the will of the House."

In Washington the next day, December 28, the speaker prepared for a 3 p.m. meeting with Obama and the other congressional leaders at the White House. At a briefing with staff, he predicted, "Nothing good can come from this meeting."

White House security insisted that all the Senate aides attending the meeting such as David Krone, Reid's chief of staff, and Rohit Kumar, McConnell's top policy adviser, go through metal detectors. This was an unusual breach of protocol. Congressional leaders and their senior aides expected to be exempt from these procedures.

Security also insisted that Boehner's aides go through the screening. That's not protocol, Boehner's security chief said. That's not how it works with the speaker's senior staff.

No, White House security insisted.

If you want the speaker at the meeting, they're not going through the metal detectors, Boehner's security chief said.

Boehner's aides were waved through.

Reid and McConnell were sitting on a sofa and chair in the reception area of the West Wing when Boehner walked up the stairs.

"Fuck you," the speaker said, glaring at Reid.

"What did I do?" Reid asked.

You know what you did, Boehner said. Go fuck yourself. Go fuck yourself.

I'm at a loss, Reid replied.

What you said on the floor about me being a dictator, Boehner said. All that shit. Do you even listen to the stuff that comes out of your mouth?

Reid slowly stood up. McConnell stood too, looking very uncomfortable.

David must have written that for me, Reid said, throwing his chief of staff, who had just arrived, under the bus.

But Krone was having none of it. Whenever I see the speaker's name in something, I cross it out, he said.

So Reid tried again. I've had far worse things said to me just today, he told Boehner.

It was an awkward moment, but the Senate majority leader was used to extricating himself from tense situations of his own making. On his tendency to shoot from the hip, Reid had once told Krone, "My mouth works faster than my brain. And it just comes out."


By 3 p.m. they gathered in the Oval Office.

"The big offer is still on the table," Obama said. If the $250,000 tax threshold proposed for income taxes was presented to the House, it would pass, he claimed. This was because it would continue the Bush lower rates for 98 percent of the taxpayers. The question was, what would the Republican leaders permit to come for a vote?

Boehner was sitting deep in one of the sofas with his arms crossed. "The House will only act after the Senate acts," he said. Once the Senate's acted, we'll act. If you do something, we're not going to ignore it. We'll either accept it or amend it. The more bipartisan it is in the Senate, the better chance it has of passing in the House.

We all know you offered a threshold of $400,000, Senate Minority Leader McConnell said to Obama. We know Senate Democrats are at least at $500,000. We know that there are 55 to 60 votes (in the Senate) for the current policy on estate tax with the higher exemption and lower rates. We'd like to be able to get something where you, Mr. President, will say I'll sign it, and I and the speaker each can say I can support it. I think I can get you 30 Senate Republicans for that, but you need to sweeten the pot compared to what you just laid out, Mr. President.

We need to at least do something, Reid said. It may be imperfect, but we need to act. Someday history may look back, and look at us meeting and kind of snicker. But we're all we've got. We've got to come to an agreement. We're here, this is it.

Pelosi asked how much it would cost to set the rate increase threshold at $500,000.

Geithner said the reduced revenue over 10 years would be about $100 billion to go to a $400,000 threshold, and another $60 billion to go to $500,000. But it would depend on deduction limitations on the top brackets.

Obama said that the Kyl-Lincoln estate tax with only a 35 percent tax rate and generous $5 million exemption was a problem for Democrats.

Kyl-Lincoln has majority support in the Senate, McConnell reminded them.

Obama said he was not comfortable with Kyl-Lincoln and a $400,000 to $500,000 deal on the rate side. We lose too much revenue. I'm open to either $250,000 and current 2012 estate level ($5 million and 35 percent tax), or $400,000 and the 2009 estate tax level ($3.5 million and 45 percent tax).

Pelosi said they should discuss how immoral it was not to tax people's estates and not get that $120 billion from the rich.

It's their money, Boehner objected.

Obama cautioned that they weren't going to persuade each other on philosophy. Let's not get into a debate about the morality of the death tax, he said.

Even if we get this done, he added, next year we're going to have to start over on deficit reduction. We need one and a half trillion dollars to stabilize the annual deficit and debt. My $400,000 offer was in a larger context. I'm not going to argue about that again. On the death tax, I think it's fair that you don't want to go back to 2001 ($675,000 exemption and 55 percent tax), but the Kyl-Lincoln approach is an obstacle for me.

I've got 55 or 60 votes for Kyl-Lincoln, McConnell said. If you only get a handful of Republicans for this deal, it's not going to pass the House.

Obama said he thought he had 56 or 57 Senate votes for his proposal at the $250,000 threshold—tax cuts for 98 percent of the people.

I'm not sure that's true, McConnell said.

If we don't get significant revenue here, Obama said, then we're going to have three to four months of trench warfare, three months to the next crisis. The spending cuts and entitlement reforms you'll get will be less next year versus my last offer to the speaker. You prefer tax cuts to deficit reduction. We prefer to protect entitlements against deficit reduction. So this is going to be hard. I'm not comfortable with Kyl-Lincoln and a $500,000 threshold. I'll do '09 levels, maybe come up from that a little bit.

Boehner said the two Senate leaders, Reid and McConnell, should do a deal, and the House would react.

They turned to the farm bill, another pending issue with economic consequences. If milk goes to 10 bucks a gallon, the president said, I'm going to blame you people. If you think people are going to be upset about the tax rates, wait till milk's 10 bucks a gallon.

How about we use the money from not fighting the Iraq and Afghanistan wars in the future? Reid asked. Called the Overseas Contingency Operations (OCO) fund, this was a favorite of the majority leader's and had been in past Republican budget proposals for a savings of $1 trillion.

No, Boehner said.

"Oh," Reid said, "you can have your gimmicks, but we can't have ours."

Jack Lew, the White House chief of staff and former budget director who was soon to be confirmed as treasury secretary, reminded everyone that they faced automatic spending cuts of $1.2 trillion over 10 years in the sequester, which was scheduled by law to go into effect in three days. He reiterated that the supercommittee, which had failed, was originally meant to find the $1.2 trillion from both revenue and cuts.

How about we come up with a mix to at least put off the sequester for the first year? Lew proposed. How about $60 billion in revenue and finding $60 billion in cuts that turn off the sequester for a year?

The problem is spending, Boehner said.

You keep saying that, the president noted.

You're going to keep hearing that, the speaker replied.

"At some point," Obama said sharply, "you are going to have to say what you are for."

"Our members won't accept revenue for sequester replacement," Boehner said. The 2011 deal had been clear to him and the Republicans. They'd agreed on no revenue in the sequester in exchange for extending the debt ceiling in one step, a huge concession to Obama in Boehner's mind. This meant the president had not needed to go through contentious debt ceiling negotiations during the election year.

Obama and his team disagreed vehemently. The sequester made no sense, and it had to be replaced. Any replacement, in their view, had to be balanced with spending cuts and revenue. They had until January 1, only a few days off, to do just that. It was not too late to replace the onerous sequester.

McConnell repeated that they should start with the premise that, on any deal, the more Republican senators voting for it, the better chance it had of passing the House.

"There aren't going to be 218 votes in John Boehner's caucus," Obama said. They would need House Democrats as well.

Okay, John, Reid asked, if we pass something, are you going to tell me you're going to bring it up?

Boehner said the House would consider it, maybe amend it.

I want to hear you say it, Reid pressed. Are you going to bring it to the floor for a vote?

"I'm not trying to be coy," Boehner said. The House would consider it, amend it, or pass it. I'm being honest, he said.

Obama turned to Boehner and quietly said that the speaker was playing a word game. Harry's asking you a specific question and you're not giving him a specific answer.

"I love Harry," Boehner said to everyone. "I love Mitch, but I'm not going to put the faith of the whole House in their hands." He said he would not commit right now to passing whatever they came up with without knowing what it was.

All right, the president said, Mitch and Harry, you guys work out a deal.

They returned to the sequester. What if we apply the tax increases to the sequester? Reid asked.

"We are not going to use tax increases to turn off the sequester," Boehner reiterated. In his view this was changing the agreement. The sequester consisted of only spending cuts. Any replacement had to be the same.

Obama's team heatedly disagreed. There was nothing from the 2011 agreement binding them to cuts only. But they soon realized the Republicans would not accept their position.

Obama returned to the numbers. He summarized: You can have $400,000 and the 2009 estate tax levels, or you can have $250,000 and the 2012 estate tax levels. Guys, I keep coming to you and I keep putting things on the table, and you guys keep rejecting it, thinking there's going to be a better deal. And every time, it gets worse.

Reid asked if there was a room that McConnell and he could use to start talking.

Nabors went to see if the Cabinet Room was available.

With the meeting breaking up, Obama asked Reid and Krone to stay behind. They agreed that their formulation—$400,000 and the 2009 estate level or $250,000 and the 2012 estate tax level—should be their offer to McConnell.

Reid and Krone went to the Cabinet Room to meet with McConnell and Kumar.

The Senate could pass something, Kumar said, but Boehner could amend it in the House and send it back. "Then we're screwed, because it's after January 1."

"With all due respect to the speaker," Krone responded, "until he can prove that he can pass anything, he has no say." He just told my boss, "Fuck you," he reminded them, and as they all could see from the Oval Office meeting, Boehner had little to say, insisting that the ball was with the Senate. "He's no longer a participant," Krone continued. "We'll pass what we agree to and if he doesn't like it then that's his problem."


"It's clear the president wants us to get a deal," Reid told Krone as they drove up Pennsylvania Avenue back to the Senate. Obama was forward-leaning, putting lots of proposals and compromises out there.

Krone read it differently. If they went off the cliff with tax increases for everyone, there would be an uproar to restore the cuts for most—at least 98 percent—and the tax-cutting Republicans would lead the charge. That might give Obama more leverage. "He's willing to go off the cliff," Krone said.

Reid called Jack Lew from the car.

Lew wasn't there but Obama himself called back.

On his note cards stamped "David Krone, Chief of Staff," Krone wrote: "Ask him if he fully accepts we may get NO deal."

Reid asked the question.

Absolutely, Obama said. He realized they might not be able to get a deal despite how close they were.

Both the president and the speaker were playing a dangerous game of chicken over perhaps $150 billion to $200 billion. No one would pull back or say let's split the difference.


About four hours after leaving the White House, McConnell and his policy chief, Rohit Kumar, sent an offer to Reid and David Krone. It was titled "Plan C (Compromise)."

"Attached is our first crack at advancing the ball," Kumar said in a 9:33 p.m. email to Krone. "As promised, it's underwhelming but designed to get the ball rolling."

Obama wanted to add spending for infrastructure and unemployment insurance totaling $83 billion. Kumar said this was a problem and outlined the Republican thinking: "It's important that we limit this effort to the tax issue because it's already going to be seen as a tax hike bill so adding spending makes it both a tax hike and spending increase bill, which is double unhappiness for our side."

McConnell's strategy was threefold: He would give Obama as little tax revenue as possible; he would not agree to replace the sequester with tax increases; and if faced with a choice between a tax increase or the sequester, he would take the sequester.

McConnell's priority, and Boehner's, was to chip away at the amount of tax revenue Obama would get from a final deal. So the Senate Republican leader proposed what he considered a middle ground on the all-important tax rate threshold. Instead of the $250,000 sought by Obama and the $1 million Boehner had tried but failed to get through the House, McConnell suggested thresholds of $500,000 or $750,000 for a married couple. This would reduce the total new tax revenue take by about $150 billion over 10 years. On the estate tax, McConnell proposed the current policy with its generous $5 million exemption, and some other standard Republican ideas.

Reid and Krone agreed to have a sit-down with McConnell and Kumar at 3 p.m. the next day, Saturday, and promised to produce a counteroffer before they met.

Ten minutes before the scheduled 3 p.m. meeting, Reid canceled. However, he sent a counteroffer moving the threshold ever so slightly, to $275,000 for individuals and $350,000 for those filing jointly. In addition, he proposed raising the estate tax rate to 45 percent and lowering the exemption to $3.5 million.

What the hell took them so long to come up with this? McConnell wondered.

An hour later, McConnell sent a counteroffer, setting the income tax threshold at $500,000. He also proposed replacing only one year of the 10-year sequester with spending cuts by using savings from the changes to the Consumer Price Index.

Reid countered with a proposal to move the tax rate threshold to $360,000 and $450,000.

Kumar thought it was a little bit of progress. For the first time he saw a path forward, though Reid was also asking to replace the sequester spending cuts with tax increases. Democrats were trying to use the sequester to raise taxes.

So an hour and a half later, McConnell sent another counter, proposing income tax threshold levels at $450,000 and $550,000.

Krone answered half an hour later. "We are getting very close," he told Kumar. "I'm going to send my staff home, because I've got to talk to Senator Reid in person." He also said he needed to confer with the administration, and he would get back to McConnell by 10 a.m. the next day, Sunday.

"We shouldn't go home," Kumar objected. The stakes were too high. "It's only 7:30. We should continue to meet through the night. We should try to reach an agreement tonight so that we have Sunday and Monday to draft them and act and all that."

Krone stuck to his plan. He wanted to talk to Reid.

Sunday morning brought a series of delays as Reid went over the details with the White House and Senator Chuck Schumer, the New York Democrat who was third in the party leadership in the Senate. There was a lot of resistance. Nabors presented a typed summary which Reid threw in the fireplace—his way of disposing of evidence he didn't want left behind.

By 1 p.m., Krone sent word to McConnell's office: "Our offer stands," referring to Reid's Saturday offer. Nothing more would be coming. That was it.

McConnell and Kumar concluded that Reid wasn't negotiating in good faith anymore and wasn't interested in getting a deal. They believed he was willing to go over the cliff with the tax increases and automatic sequester spending cuts, thinking the resulting political pressure would allow him to get a deal closer to the president's original $250,000 threshold. A deal that would yield, according to the latest study from the Joint Committee on Taxation, $829 billion in additional revenue over 10 years.

•     •     •

It was the endgame now, two days before they would go off the cliff.

McConnell went to the Senate floor on Sunday, December 30, at 2 p.m. and announced that he'd just placed a call to the vice president "to see if he could help jump-start the negotiations on his side." Referring to the 2010 and 2011 deals he had struck with Joe Biden, McConnell said, "the vice president and I have worked together on solutions before, and I believe we can again."

"Does anyone down there know how to cut a deal?" McConnell asked Biden in a 2:15 p.m. phone call. "Can you please get up to speed on this and call me back?"

At 3:30, Biden told McConnell, "I'm only the vice president. You and I can get a deal, but it'll have to be sold to Harry. When you came down to the floor and said you'd called me, Harry reacted poorly because he thinks I've already cut the deal with you and I'm screwing Senate Democrats yet again."

On the looming automatic spending cuts in the sequester, Biden said, "I know that you won't use the tax increases from rates going up to pay for the sequester." The 2011 Biden-McConnell deal from 18 months earlier had no relevance. Of course, since Republicans were about to swallow a tax increase deal with no entitlement and spending cuts, they would not want tax increases used for the sequester.

Biden said, however, the sequester had to be replaced with both spending cuts and tax increases—the balanced approach. "The president thinks it should be turned off with revenue and spending."

Though that was contrary to what McConnell firmly believed the terms of the 2011 deal had been, he did not respond.

Biden continued, "Maybe we should just instruct the [congressional] committees to find $60 billion in new spending cuts" and "$60 billion in new revenue from tax reform," rather than rate increases to pay for a whole year of sequester, estimated at $120 billion. Income tax reform, a process that would take a year or more, was the key. Democrats and Republicans all seemed to favor it. Ideally, tax reform would cut loopholes and deductions. The result would be lower—not higher—income tax rates.

The president would not agree to raise the threshold on income tax rates very much from his initial offer of $250,000, Biden said. Maybe he'd move enough to cut the revenue take by $100 billion over 10 years.

But, he added, "sequester is the most difficult."

"How do we actually make this happen?" McConnell asked.

"If you and I agree," Biden said, "then I'll go to the president and advocate it. If he agrees, then the president will call Harry and say, this is what I'm willing to do, since [Reid] never countered. And then you can accept it, and the history books will say whatever they want. But it can't be me doing the deal, at least not for the next 24 hours. I'm worried that with so little time, if someone gets a hair up their ass, we'll be screwed."

Shortly after 6 p.m., McConnell called Biden. He said Rohit Kumar would present the Republican offer orally to the vice president.

Let's do $400,000 individual, $550,000 married, Kumar said. If you can come up a little, that would be helpful. We just need some nominal movement. I'm not going to give you a number because I don't want to piss you off, but I'm just telling you, this is too low.

"I don't think we can do sequester here," Kumar continued. It looked like they could not agree on how to replace it. "You guys want it to be revenue and spending, our guys want it to be all spending. It's now six on [Sunday] the 30th, and I don't think we have time to do that."

"I'm sure he [Obama] won't do that," Biden said. They had to do something on the sequester.

"Just let the sequester hit for a few weeks," Kumar responded, "so that members will see the pain when their staff get their salaries whacked." Congressional office budgets would be cut by 8.2 percent, which could include reductions to staffers' salaries.

Got to do something on the sequester, Biden insisted, but he ended the conversation by saying, "We understand each other's sensitivities." He said he'd call back between 7:15 and 7:45.

He spoke with Obama and called McConnell back at 9:45 p.m. "We can do permanent rates at $400,000 [single], $450,000 [married]," Biden said, giving some on the rate threshold.

He said that on some subsidiary issues that were not major parts of the negotiation, the administration wanted some low-income pro-grams extended for one year. And the sequester would have to be de-layed for a year.

At 11:10, McConnell called Biden back.

Instead of $400,000 and $450,000, let's do $450,000 and $500,000, McConnell said, proposing several other small changes. "Let's do a one-month delay in the sequester."

Jack Lew was on the line on the vice president's side and proposed limiting any changes to the estate tax to five years.

Kumar responded that this suggested that Obama was not inter-ested in getting a deal because the other tax changes were going to be permanent.

"Okay, let's keep talking," Biden said, returning to the sequester. He suggested delaying it for perhaps three to six months.

One day left. It was now 12:15 a.m. on December 31 and Biden told McConnell, "The only issue we have left is the sequester. We could shoot for three months on the sequester." That, he noted, would mean $15 billion in revenue and $15 billion from spending cuts.

At 12:40, McConnell called Biden back. The minority leader con-cluded they had a deal on tax rate thresholds. He had squeezed as much out for his side as possible.

"We're only talking about the sequester now," McConnell said. Even though Biden wanted half spending cuts and half revenue, Mc-Connell wanted just spending cuts. For him it was 100 percent clear that their 2011 deal had been an outright trade—a spending-cut-only sequester in exchange for raising the debt ceiling the full amount of $2.4 trillion in one step.

As a way out, Biden proposed that each side would have an oppor-tunity to offer an amendment on the sequester. They could battle it out on the Senate floor.

That's a reasonably elegant solution, Kumar said of the amendment idea. Whoever came up with it should be commended.

It was actually the president's idea, Biden said.

Oh, well, good for him, Kumar said.

So sometime after midnight Biden went home. He had talked with the president, who insisted that they delay the sequester for two months. That would get him past his inauguration and the State of the Union address.

Biden was back in the office at 6:40 a.m.

"Even though I said yes last night, I can't do the amendment deal on sequester," he told McConnell. "I have to have a two-month delay on sequester as part of the package."

McConnell agreed, but only if they found offsets. Even though he wanted spending cuts only, he was willing to consider something that would look like a tax increase.

Between 7 a.m. and 2 p.m., Nabors and Kumar went back and forth by email, trading ideas to offset two months of the sequester. Kumar listed some $130 billion in proposed offsets to take care of the two months on the sequester such as cuts in Medicare for the wealthy that could save $30 billion.

At 11 a.m., Biden and McConnell spoke on the phone.

Using Kumar's first name, Biden complained, "Rohit is being a little bit of a jerk and hardheaded on offsets."


At 1:45 p.m. the president delivered televised remarks before a group of middle-class supporters.

Kumar emailed Nabors: Is he going to call a code on the negotiations? Was Obama going to pronounce the negotiations dead?

Nabors emailed back: No, it was a previously scheduled event.

In his remarks, Obama said, "For the last few days, leaders in both parties have been working toward an agreement that will prevent a middle-class tax hike from hitting 98 percent of all Americans, starting tomorrow. Preventing that tax hike has been my top priority. . . . Middle-class families can't afford it. Businesses can't afford it. Our economy can't afford it."

He added confidently, "Keep in mind that just last month Republicans in Congress said they would never agree to raise taxes on the wealthiest Americans. Obviously, the agreement that's currently being discussed would raise those rates and raise them permanently."

McConnell was appalled that Obama so misunderstood the psychology of the Republicans and of the negotiating process. Taunting, even ridiculing, Republicans in the middle of a serious, high-stakes negotiation was a mistake. Obama was making a bad call and undermining any sense of trust.

McConnell went to the Senate floor to speak. He decided to address the practical problems.

"As the president just said, the most important piece, the piece that has to be done NOW, is preventing the tax hikes," McConnell said. "[Obama] suggested that action on the sequester is something we can continue to work on in the coming months. So I agree, let's pass the tax relief portion now. Let's take what's been agreed to and get moving."

Biden told Bruce Reed, his chief of staff, who was participating in and taking notes on all the phone calls, that the worst thing about congressional gridlock was the lack of personal trust between the two sides. It was hard to split the difference and come to a deal if you didn't know whether the other side had its fingers crossed behind their backs when they spoke.

As the so-called McConnell whisperer, Biden could be persuasive. But there were limits, so Biden next suggested that McConnell call the president directly.

I think we're getting close, Obama said when McConnell called. I understand you can't do a year on the sequester. This is a modest attempt to buy a couple of months. If you think about how this is perceived, you and I are both involved deeply in a last-ditch effort to avoid the cliff. If we only do a deal with a half of it [tax increases], tomorrow there's a big fuss over the automatic spending cuts [the sequester]. The story will be we dealt with half of it. That will hurt us in the public. The risk of doing a sequester amendment is we both want something done, but it might not happen, because they might fail. He wanted two months and then they could deal with other issues, such as a debt ceiling extension. "I know that you're going to fight me on all these things."

Even though it's only two months, McConnell replied, we're having difficulty finding agreement. We've sent you a bunch of stuff.

Rohit's always picking offsets that seem to stick it to our guys, Obama complained. We need to lock in something neutral but real. By his calculation, they were only six or seven billion dollars away.

McConnell said he saw the difference as $20 billion, but added, Surely we can find it.

I wanted to have a deal at 9 a.m., Obama told him. Now we're getting close to failing. You're looking plenty good in this thing. News stories are appearing that say I'm caving in. Your base thinks you've outfoxed me.

McConnell said that his dilemma was that Obama was now offering zero spending reductions. The negotiations were about taxes.

That was because they were not getting a big deal, the grand bargain of more than $2 trillion in deficit reduction, Obama said. And that's why I really put myself out there with this $1 trillion in spending cut proposals. All of that was real. I was just as specific as the speaker. I said I could do large spending cuts now if we do large revenue now.

The final tax increase deal was only going to get about $625 billion. There would be no spending cuts.

The Democrats think in 13 hours they'll have revenue and can work backward, Obama continued. That's the strong view within Harry's caucus. They think they're getting revenue regardless. The simple solution is to identify two months on the sequester. Nothing should be controversial. It should be neutral.

I'm in favor of that, McConnell said, but you have to identify replacements for two months of the sequester that are real but aren't toxic.

Everything Rohit offers is something that only hurts Democratic priorities, Obama said, that's how it seems to us. This included targeting entitlements. It becomes toxic on our side. We should be able to do this.

Okay, McConnell agreed, let's take one more run at this. Let's look for a bipartisan, nontoxic way.

Obama told McConnell that the Democrats and Reid were just as unhappy as Republicans with a two-month sequester postponement. They want the tax increases to count for the sequester, Obama said. He knew that the Republicans would not go along. "I agree that doing that would be too much . . . given how you guys saw the deal." But we need to do two months just to buy time. We need some space. Let's take one more run. Even if there are things you're not totally happy with, as long as they're genuine. Let's get it out of the way. I'll be hurt by this more than anyone else. Let's take another run.

Biden called McConnell at 3:50 p.m. "We're almost there," he said. Look, Democrats are insisting I come up and sell the package tonight. Less than two months won't work. We have to have two months on the sequester.

Yeah, McConnell said, my folks are getting impatient too. We're down to the last few billion. They say, let's get there.

At 6 p.m. Nabors asked Kumar where the revenue for a two-month deal would come from. Kumar had been sitting on a proposal for some time and explained it to McConnell. It was deep in the tax weeds. It would look on the surface like a tax *increase* and be scored that way, but it would really be a tax *cut* that benefited the rich.

Kumar proposed that taxpayers be allowed to convert their 401(k) retirement plans to Roth Individual Retirement Accounts (IRAs). In doing so the taxpayers would have to pay an immediate tax, but future earnings from the new IRAs would not be taxed. The revenue gain would be $12 billion over 10 years, but the taxpayers would save more over the long run.

McConnell liked the idea. He thought the plan could be sold to Republicans because the federal government would actually, in the long run, get less money.

But when Kumar emailed the plan to the White House, one Biden aide realized it was "fake revenue."

Two hours later, Nabors emailed to say the revenue side wouldn't work. It was gimmicky in the extreme. The only people who would pay this tax would be the wealthy, and their net tax liability would be reduced in the long run. Did they have anything else?

No, Kumar answered. It's eight o'clock. He realized it was too late to litigate. I don't have anything else for you.

Nabors replied, I don't think this is going to work for us, especially not in the context of everything else. We're taking grief from the left for this whole thing. This is just a tax cut for the rich. Because the only people who are going to do this are people who have financial planners who say, pay the tax now because you'll pay less tax later.

Biden felt Rohit had run out the clock to pull a fast one with a tax increase that wasn't really a tax increase.

McConnell called Biden. I hear you don't like our Roth IRA proposal, he said. Just seems to me that we're not going to get there. Let's just do the tax deal.

"No, no, no, no," Biden said. He had to get two months on the sequester. "We have to do this. Let's just get this done. I've got to come up there and sell this package tonight" to the Senate Democrats. "We've got to do this now. I'll take your Roth IRA offset. We shouldn't index"—meaning increase the exemption for inflation on the estate tax—"for the first five years. We'll agree to index it after that."

No, I can't sell that, McConnell said.

Biden gave in on the estate tax, knowing that McConnell had more than 60 votes because a number of Democrats supported it. I know we're fighting you on the taxable income versus adjusted gross income ($10 billion), Biden went on about a technical issue. We'll give you that. Let's just do the deal. "We should all just swallow hard and get this done. No sudden moves."

McConnell agreed. They had a deal.

That evening around nine or ten, Biden went up to speak to the Senate Democrats. The caucus could sometimes be raucous and unruly, but now there was a festive, supportive atmosphere. The senators had been trapped there all day, waiting for white smoke. Reid wouldn't allow anyone to raise technical issues or objections to forestall a vote.

The final agreement dealt with issues such as unemployment insurance, tax credits for college tuition, increased taxes on capital gains and dividends, a limitation of deductions and increased payments to Medicare doctors. It was far from a grand bargain to stabilize the deficit. The real bottom line was simple. Tax revenue would go up by $625 billion over 10 years, raising rates on singles earning over $400,000 and couples earning over $450,000. The only spending cut was $12 billion in general cuts, with half in Defense. The only revenue was the $12 billion in fake revenue on the retirement account conversion.

In the early-morning hours of January 1, 2013, the Senate approved it 89–8, with three Democrats and five Republicans voting against.

At a full House Republican leadership team meeting at 3:30 p.m. on January 1, Boehner outlined the options: amend it or pass it. The Senate would almost certainly ignore an amended bill. If his conference wanted to take that route, he would go along and even vote for it, he said. But after the Plan B fiasco, they would have to line up 218 votes in advance. If they couldn't, they would have to pass the Senate bill— House Republicans could not go out and take the heat for the across-the-board tax hike that would occur if they went over the fiscal cliff. There was political risk in either course.

At a second meeting of the Republican conference, a number of members stood up to note that the Senate bill was not that bad. Though it was a tax increase for the top one percent, it was a permanent tax cut for the other 99 percent. In addition, the estate tax and capital gains rates were not that bad.

The mood had shifted from fight, fight, fight to let's postpone the fight to another day.

Whip Kevin McCarthy had his deputies take the count and it was clear there weren't 218 votes for an amended bill. So Boehner put the Senate bill on the floor for a vote. He was one of the first to vote for it, but he was joined by only 84 other Republicans. Although 151 Republicans, including Cantor and McCarthy, voted no, it passed the House 257 to 167 because 172 Democrats joined the 85 Republicans to vote in favor.

Boehner was deeply disappointed. He had hoped the year 2013

would be the time for serious tax and entitlement reform, along with significant spending cuts. They had made the top-bracket tax increases permanent, a longtime Obama goal, and now getting tax reform, which always aimed for lower rates, would be much more difficult, if not impossible.

Mike Sommers, Boehner's chief of staff, told some of the speaker's senior staff: "I think this is one of the things that our members have had to realize, that our leadership team has had to realize, that the conservative movement as a whole has had to realize. There is a limit to what you can do with a majority in one half of one branch of Congress."

Instead of pursuing the reform and government-shrinking programs that the House Republicans deemed necessary, the House was now going to have to be negative and focus on stopping further tax increases and new spending and legislation that Obama wanted.

Sommers summarized the essential condition of the House Republicans in 2013: "We are primarily a blocking majority."


At the State of the Union on February 12, McConnell walked with Biden.

"No more deals," McConnell told the vice president.

Nearly two months passed and as March 1 approached, the White House and the Congress reached no agreement on a replacement for the sequester's automatic spending cuts. There was much public hand-wringing by the White House, which said the sequester would be a full-scale disaster.

"These cuts are not smart," Obama said in a February 19 press conference, forecasting disaster. "They will hurt our economy. They will add hundreds of thousands of Americans to the unemployment rolls." Congress must act, he said.

But Congress did not act.


What had happened during the prolonged, tense wrangling of 2011 and 2012? Examine the outcomes, which are what matter, and from one perspective, it seems both sets of negotiations left the House Republicans in a better position than the administration. In both cases—from positions of both strength and weakness—the Republican House of Representatives coaxed the White House into accepting far less than the president wanted in revenue and far more than he wanted in spending cuts.

In 2011, the Republicans seized the leverage in the debt ceiling negotiations with a naked threat to wreck the U.S. economy by allowing the Treasury to default on the country's obligations unless massive spending cuts were enacted. In the end, $2.4 trillion in cuts were approved and tax rates remained unchanged.

Democrats could console themselves with the fact that a (wholly man-made) debt ceiling catastrophe had been averted, and could claim a small victory, in that entitlement programs were not slashed.

But in the end, there was no grand bargain, there were none of the sweeping entitlement reforms the president had called for, and the tax code remained untouched. And to make matters worse, the $800 billion in revenue Boehner had offered from tax reform was left on the table.

What did the Republicans give up? They raised the debt ceiling for a year and a half—something that even Boehner conceded they would eventually have done anyway.

"When you look at this final agreement that we came to with the White House, I got 98 percent of what I wanted," the speaker boasted publicly after the 2011 deal. "I'm pretty happy."

At the end of 2012, the tables seemed to have turned. The looming expiration of the Bush tax cuts gave the White House an apparent advantage. But that would include tax increases for the middle class.

In his very first offer to Republicans, in late 2012, Obama proposed to raise tax rates only on individuals and families making $250,000 or more. In addition, he wanted to cut deductions and loopholes for the top brackets. This could conceivably have raised $1.6 trillion in revenue. He also demanded a debt ceiling increase, and the elimination of the sequester.

In exchange, he offered Republicans spending cuts of what he said was $1.22 trillion.

What Obama got was $625 billion in new revenue—less than half of his original offer. The debt ceiling was untouched, and the sequester—which leaders from both parties had long insisted was bad policy and bad economics—was offset by only $24 billion in spending cuts and "fake revenue." Available evidence shows that the majority of time and energy spent on the negotiations by both sides was driven by a near-obsession with income tax rates. The sequester, treated by negotiators as an afterthought, remained the law of the land.

In an appearance in the White House Briefing Room at 11:20 p.m. on January 1, Obama's assessment of the bill was decidedly lukewarm.

He applauded the increase in taxes on high earners. But he added, "Speaker Boehner and I originally tried to negotiate a larger agreement that would put this country on a path to paying down its debt while also putting Americans back to work rebuilding our roads and bridges, and providing investments in areas like education and job training. Unfortunately, there just wasn't enough support or time for that kind of large agreement."

In his assessment of the fiscal cliff deal, it was hard not to hear an echo of the president's lament, from 2011, that "a big opportunity was missed."

Taken as a whole, the results appeared to favor the Republicans. In the space of 18 months, Republicans in Congress wrested $2.4 trillion in spending cuts from the White House, while Obama came away with a comparatively paltry $625 billion in increased revenue—$4 in spending cuts for every $1 in revenue.

On May 14, the Congressional Budget Office released a bombshell, declaring that "the budget deficit will shrink this year to $642 billion." That was $200 billion below the estimate they had produced just three months earlier in February 2013. This dramatic reduction was because of "higher-than-expected revenues and an increase in payments to the Treasury by Fannie Mae and Freddie Mac." In a single year the deficit had gone down $200 billion, at a time when the president and Boehner had been haggling over a $150 billion difference *over 10 years*. I recalled one of the most vivid lines from the negotiations: "We are $150 billion off, man," Obama had said to Boehner. "I don't get it. There's something I don't get."

There are some things the president and Boehner may not get, but there is more they would not do. They would not compromise, perhaps split the difference. You can't read that and not think, why doesn't one of them or both say, "Let's split the difference." The number was insignificant. But neither would.

What they did not get was that they had larger obligations than the ones to their party or their doctrines. They did not get that a genuine deal would send multiple messages to the world. First it would stabilize the annual deficit and cumulative debt. Second it could lay the conditions for a burst of economic growth as businesses would have some certainty. Some $1.45 trillion in cash hoarded by businesses might be freed up to expand and hire. There would be evidence, sorely lacking for years, that Democrats and Republicans could work together. There would be at least short-term proof that Washington could work once again for the common good, instead of ducking the hard decisions. The White House and Republicans responded only when a gun was held to their heads.

One of the key players recently emailed, "Sadly, I don't see anything coming together anytime soon. And that's what has me depressed."

Others directly involved say they are frightened because there are too few conversations between the White House and the Republicans, and there is insufficient framework or history to suggest how they might succeed in the next round, which is sure to come by the end of 2013.

# CHAPTER NOTES

**PROLOGUE**

The information in this chapter comes primarily from author's notes and rec-ollections of the 2006 and 1981 Gridiron dinners.

2 *"This is a true story"*: Lynn Sweet, "Best of Gridiron: Obama, Lynne Cheney and Bush," *Chicago Sun-Times* blog, March 12, 2006, http://blogs.suntimes.com/sweet2006/03/best_of_gridiron_obama_lynne_c.html.

**CHAPTER ONE**

The information in this chapter comes primarily from background interviews with six firsthand sources and contemporaneous notes by a participant.

9 *After the meeting, Senator McConnell told reporters:* Jeff Zeleny and David M. Herszenhorn, "Obama Seeks Wide Support in Congress for Stimulus," *The New York Times*, January 6, 2009, p. A15; Jim Puzzanghera and Christi Parsons, "Obama Sweetens Stimulus for GOP," *Los Angeles Times*, January 6, 2009.

9 *Pelosi announced that it was "a new day":* Jon Ward and S. A. Miller, "Obama Pushes Stimulus Plan on Capitol Hill; GOP Open to $800 Billion Relief," *The Washington Times*, January 6, 2009, p. A1.

13 *It listed five unambiguously conservative proposals:* Author obtained copy of document entitled "House Republican Economic Recovery Plan."

## CHAPTER TWO

The information in this chapter comes primarily from background interviews with five firsthand sources.

18  *According to Cao, Emanuel "insinuated":* On the record author interview with former Representative Joseph Cao, November 30, 2011.

19  *On the phone with Emanuel, Hill said:* Rob Garver on the record interview with former Representative Baron Hill, March 7, 2012.

21  *The House vote was 244–188:* Jackie Calmes, "House Passes Stimulus Plan with No G.O.P. Votes," *The New York Times*, January 29, 2009.

## CHAPTER THREE

The information in this chapter comes primarily from background interviews with six firsthand sources.

25  *It took days more:* David Rogers, "Senate Passes $787 Billion Stimulus Bill," *Politico*, February 13, 2009, http://www.politico.com.

25  *At a signing ceremony in Denver:* Compilation of Presidential Documents, "Remarks on Signing the American Recovery and Reinvestment Act of 2009 in Denver, Colorado," February 17, 2009, http://www.gpo.gov/fdsys/browse/collection.action?collectionCode=CPD; "Obama's Remarks at Stimulus Signing," *The New York Times*, February 17, 2009, http://www.nytimes.com/2009/02/17/world/americas/17iht-17textobama.20261060.html.

25  *"Absolutely, we need earmark reform":* CNN transcript of the first presidential debate, September 26, 2008, http://www.cnn.com.

26  *At the same time, he issued a statement:* Compilation of Presidential Documents, "Statement on Signing the Omnibus Appropriations Act, 2009," http://www.gpo.gov/fdsys/browse/collection.action?collectionCode=CPD.

26  *House Majority Leader Steny Hoyer:* Alex Isenstadt, "Hoyer to W.H.: Hands off Our Earmarks," *Politico*, March 3, 2009, http://www.politico.com.

27  *But the 61-year-old North Dakotan:* "Kent Conrad: The Statistician," *Time*, April 14, 2006, http://www.time.com/time/nation/article/0,8599,1183973,00.html.

## CHAPTER FOUR

The information in this chapter comes primarily from background interviews with two firsthand sources.

30 *Republicans were beating hard on the administration:* Email compilation of 27 media references to author from the office of the speaker, April 23, 2012; see also Michael O'Brien, "Pelosi: 'Where Are the Jobs?' Was Effective in Bringing Dems Down," *The Hill*, November 6, 2010, http://thehill.com/blogs/blog-briefing-room/news/127997-pelosi-where-are-the-jobs-was-effective.

31 *In a memo to the president dated December 20, 2009:* Author's review of the December 20, 2009, memo.

34 *Given his three minutes to question the treasury secretary:* "RYAN TO GEITHNER: Why Propose a Budget You Admit Is Not Credible, Not Sustainable?," Video/audio podcast, February 3, 2010, http://www.house.gov/apps/list/hearing/wi01_ryan/2310RtG.html.

## CHAPTER FIVE

The information in this chapter comes primarily from background interviews with six firsthand sources.

38 *In a flurry of nine terse emails:* Author's review of emails.

38 *But the Conrad issues:* Author's review of emails.

38 *He emailed Orszag, "Conrad is intending":* Author's review of emails.

40 *On January 19, 2010, he won:* Michael Cooper, "G.O.P. Senate Victory Stuns Democrats," *The New York Times*, January 20, 2010.

40 *Brown was sworn in:* Janet Hook, "Republican Scott Brown of Massachusetts Sworn In to Senate," *Los Angeles Times*, February 4, 2010.

41 *It needed 60 votes to overcome:* Senate Roll Call Votes, 111th Congress, 2nd Session, "On the Amendment (Conrad Amdt. No. 3302)," http://www.senate.gov.

41 *In an interview, President Obama later recalled:* On the record author interview with President Barack Obama, July 11, 2012.

41 *Obama unveiled his budget proposal:* Compilation of Presidential Documents, "Remarks on the Federal Budget," February 1, 2010, http://www.gpo.gov/fdsys/browse/collection.action?collectionCode=CPD.

42 *Senator Orrin Hatch:* Press release, "Hatch Calls Administration's Budget 'Toy Fire Truck to Put Out a Five Alarm Fire' of Unsustainable Debt," Office of Senator Orrin Hatch, February 1, 2010, http://hatch.senate.gov.

44  *He emailed Summers and others:* Author's review of emails.

45  *Later, in the public signing ceremony:* Compilation of Presidential Documents, "Remarks on Signing an Executive Order Establishing the National Commission on Fiscal Responsibility and Reform and an Exchange with Reporters," February 18, 2010, http://www.gpo.gov/fdsys/browse/collection.action?collectionCode=CPD.

## CHAPTER SIX

The information in this chapter comes primarily from background interviews with four firsthand sources.

46  *At a ceremony in the East Room:* Carol E. Lee, "Obama Signs Historic Health Care Bill," *Politico*, March 23, 2010, http://www.politico.com.

48  *On May 4, 2010, Obama addressed the Business Council:* Eamon Javers, "Obama Lays Out Defense of Record," *Politico*, May 5, 2010, http://www.politico.com.

48  *The Business Roundtable and the Business Council:* Ivan G. Seidenberg and James W. Owens, "Letter to Director Orszag on Policy Burdens Inhibiting Economic Growth," http://businessroundtable.org/news-center/business-roundtable-letter-to-the-white-house-on-policy-burdens-inhibi/.

49  *"Fat-cat bankers":* Brian Montopoli, "Obama Versus the 'Fat Cats,' " *60 Minutes*, CBS, December 13, 2009.

51  *On December 8, 2010, Ivan Seidenberg released:* "Business Roundtable's Roadmap for Growth," December 8, 2010, http://businessroundtable.org/studies-and-reports/roadmap-for-growth/.

52  *Seidenberg said publicly:* Mark Drajem, "Seidenberg Turns from Obama Critic to Advocate on Taxes, Trade," *Bloomberg*, December 8, 2010, http://www.bloomberg.com/news/2010-12-08/business-roundtable-urges-cuts-in-u-s-spending-revamped-taxes.html.

53  *Orszag delivered his final speech:* Peter Orszag, "Fiscal Accomplishments and Budget Update," The Brookings Institution, July 28, 2010, http://www.bloomberg.com/news/2010-12-08/business-roundtable-urges-cuts-in-u-s-spending-revamped-taxes.html.

54  *He took parts of the Obama memo:* Peter Orszag, "One Nation, Two Deficits," *The New York Times*, September 6, 2010.

54  *At his press briefing:* White House press briefing by press secretary Robert Gibbs, September 7, 2010, http://www.whitehouse.gov.

55  *Orszag continued his star turn:* Peter Orszag, "Malpractice Methodology," *The New York Times*, October 20, 2010.

## CHAPTER SEVEN

The information in this chapter comes primarily from background interviews with six firsthand sources and contemporaneous notes by a participant.

57  *On election night, November 2, 2010:* Steve Peoples, "Final House Race Decided; GOP Net Gain: 63 Seats," *Roll Call,* December 8, 2010, http://www.rollcall.com/news/-201279-1.html.

60  *"Simply unacceptable":* Press release, "Pelosi Statement on Proposal Released by Co-Chairs of the Fiscal Commission," Office of House Minority Leader Nancy Pelosi, November 10, 2010, http://pelosi .house.gov.

61  *The Democrats got "shellacked":* William Branigin, "Obama Reflections on 'Shellacking' in Midterm Elections," *The Washington Post,* November 3, 2010.

61  *Polls showed an approval rating of Congress:* Gallup poll, "Congressional Approval at 17% After Elections," November 11, 2010, http:// www.gallup.com/poll/144419/congressional-approval-elections .aspx.

62  *"Thank you for the pay freeze":* Peter Baker and Jackie Calmes, "Amid Deficit Fears, Obama Freezes Pay," *The New York Times,* November 29, 2010.

65  *Six weeks earlier he had published the book:* Eric Cantor, Paul Ryan and Kevin McCarthy, *Young Guns: A New Generation of Conservative Leaders* (New York: Threshold Editions, 2010).

67  *"The Fiscal Commission has been a success":* "Statement for the Record from Congressman Paul Ryan," Member Statements for Final Commission Report, December 3, 2010, p. 27, http://www.fiscal commission.gov/sites/fiscalcommission.gov/files/documents/ MemberStatements.pdf.

67  *"The commission's majority report includes":* Press release, "Statement by the President on the Work of the National Commission on Fiscal Responsibility and Reform," December 3, 2010, http:// www.whitehouse.gov.

67  *In an interview on July 11, 2012:* On the record author interview with President Barack Obama, July 11, 2012.

68  *In his State of the Union address:* Compilation of Presidential Documents, "Address Before a Joint Session of the Congress on the State of the Union," January 25, 2011, http://www.gpo.gov/fdsys/browse/ collection.action?collectionCode=CPD.

68  *His proposed budget, released in February:* Jackie Calmes, "Obama's
    Budget Focuses on Path to Rein in Deficit," *The New York Times*,
    February 14, 2011.

## CHAPTER EIGHT

The information in this chapter comes primarily from background interviews
with six firsthand sources and contemporaneous notes by a participant.

69  *On Thursday, December 2, Nancy Pelosi:* Brian Beutler, "House Dems Pass
    Only Middle Class Tax Cut Bill," *Talking Points Memo*, December 2,
    2010, http://tpmdc.talkingpointsmemo.com/2010/12/house-dems
    -pass-middle-income-only-tax-cut-bill.php.

69  *"I'm trying to catch my breath":* Jake Sherman, "Boehner: Dem Tax Bill
    'Chicken Crap,' " *Politico*, December 2, 2010, http://www.politico.com.

70  *In an October 2010 interview:* Major Garrett, "Top GOP Priority: Make
    Obama a One-Term President," *National Journal*, October 23, 2010.

76  *When Obama entered the Roosevelt Room:* Compilation of Presidential
    Documents, "Remarks at Forsyth Technical Community College in
    Winston-Salem, North Carolina," December 6, 2010, http://
    www.gpo.gov/fdsys/browse/collection.action?collectionCode=CPD.

77  *He had personally engaged the tax issue:* Abby Phillip, "Schumer: Raise
    the Tax Cut Limit to $1 Million," *Politico*, November 14, 2010, http://
    www.politico.com.

78  *At 6:30 that night Obama announced:* Compilation of Presidential
    Documents, "Remarks on Tax Reform and the Extension of
    Unemployment Insurance Benefits," December 6, 2010, http://
    www.gpo.gov/fdsys/browse/collection.action?collectionCode=CPD.

78  *"There are things in here that I don't like":* Ibid.

78  *Ohio Senator Sherrod Brown accused the president:* Press release,
    "Sen. Brown Outlines Efforts to Maintain Unemployment Insurance
    and Middle Class Tax Cuts," Office of Senator Sherrod Brown,
    December 1, 2010, http://www.brown.senate.gov.

78  *It was in this atmosphere that Obama appeared:* Compilation of
    Presidential Documents, "The President's News Conference,"
    December 7, 2010, http://www.gpo.gov/fdsys/browse/collection
    .action?collectionCode=CPD.

79  *Looking back on the negotiation, the president later told me:* On the record
    author interview with President Barack Obama, July 11, 2012.

79  *On Wednesday, December 15, the Senate voted 81–19:* Lori Montgomery
    and Shailagh Murray, "Congress Votes to Extend Bush-Era Tax Cuts
    Until '12," *The Washington Post*, December 17, 2010, p. A01.

79 *Bruce Reed, who had been the staff director:* David M. Herszenhorn, "Congress Sends $801 Billion Tax Cut Bill to Obama," *The New York Times*, December 16, 2010.

79 *On December 15, Don't Ask, Don't Tell repeal passed:* Lisa Mascaro and Michael Muskal, "Senate Votes to Repeal 'Don't Ask, Don't Tell,' " *Los Angeles Times*, December 18, 2010.

79 *On December 22, the START treaty was ratified:* Mary Beth Sheridan and William Branigin, "Senate Ratifies New U.S.-Russia Nuclear Weapons Treaty," *The Washington Post*, December 22, 2010.

80 *On February 11, Biden spoke:* "Country's Best Days Are Ahead, Biden Tells UofL," February 11, 2011, https://louisville.edu/mcconnellcenter/ events/past/2011/biden/countrys-best-days-are-ahead-biden-tells -uofl-audience.

80 *"We saw coming that this debt ceiling could end up being":* On the record author interview with President Barack Obama, July 11, 2012.

## CHAPTER NINE

The information in this chapter comes primarily from background interviews with four firsthand sources.

81 *Summers resigned as head of the National Economic Council:* Sheryl Gay Stolberg, "Obama's Economics Chief Is Set to Leave," *The New York Times*, September 21, 2010.

81 *One day, he said, the president would decry:* Brian Montopoli, "Obama Versus the 'Fat Cats,' " *60 Minutes*, CBS, December 13, 2009; Julianna Goldman and Ian Katz, "Obama Doesn't 'Begrudge' Bonuses for Blankfein, Dimon," *Bloomberg*, February 10, 2010, http://www .bloomberg.com/apps/news?pid=newsarchive&sid=aKGZkktzkAlA.

84 *In 2010, still in the minority, Ryan released:* "A Roadmap for America's Future," http://roadmap.republicans.budget.house.gov.

84 *In a hearing on February 2, 2010:* Walter Alarkon, "Budget Chief Attacks Ryan's Blueprint," *The Hill*, February 2, 2010, http://thehill.com/ homenews/house/79421.

84 *Ryan posted a clip from the event:* YouTube video uploaded by Rep. Paul Ryan, "President Obama Highlights Paul Ryan's Efforts to Save Medicare & Social Security," January 29, 2010, http://www.youtube .com/watch?v=ZBT5wnDK7L0&feature; for a transcript of highlights of the exchange, see http://paulryan.house.gov/news/DocumentPrint .aspx?DocumentID=190545.

86 *On April 5, 2011, Ryan, now chairman:* "The Path to Prosperity," http:// budget.house.gov/fy2012budget/.

86 *The CBO largely confirmed Ryan's claims:* CBO Report, "Long-Term Analysis of a Budget Proposal by Chairman Ryan," April 5, 2011, http://www.cbo.gov/publication/25159.

88 *In a January 6 letter to Harry Reid:* Press release, "Secretary Geithner Sends Debt Limit Letter to Congress," U.S. Department of the Treasury, January 6, 2011, http://www.treasury.gov/connect/blog/Documents/Letter.pdf.

88 *He was replaced by former Clinton Commerce Secretary William Daley:* Christi Parsons and Rick Pearson, "Obama Names William Daley as Chief of Staff," *Chicago Tribune,* January 6, 2011.

89 *Jack Lew was now head of OMB:* White House press release, "President Obama Announces a New OMB Director: Jacob Lew," July 13, 2010, http://www.whitehouse.gov.

89 *After two years of struggling, Gene Sperling:* Lori Montgomery and Brady Dennis, "Obama Names Sperling to Head National Economic Council," *The Washington Post,* January 7, 2011.

89 *Obama appointed Rob Nabors, 39, director:* Mike Allen, "Who Is Rob Nabors?" *Politico,* January 28, 2011, http://www.politico.com.

## CHAPTER TEN

The information in this chapter comes primarily from background interviews with five firsthand sources.

91 *Plouffe, 44, replaced David Axelrod:* Aamer Madhani and James A. Barnes, "Axelrod Says Plouffe to Replace Him at White House Next Year," November 14, 2010, http://www.nationaljournal.com/congress/axelrod-says-plouffe-to-replace-him-at-white-house-next-year-20101114.

92 *His 2009 campaign book:* David Plouffe, *The Audacity to Win: The Inside Story and Lessons of Barack Obama's Historic Victory* (New York: Viking, 2009).

92 *"We had just elected":* Ibid., p. 1.

92 *"I've been impressed by your judgment":* Ibid., p. 24.

92 *"Very observant, Plouffe":* Ibid., p. 386.

93 *Finally, on April 9, Congress passed:* Anne McGinn, "Obama Signs Continuing Resolution; Administration Says Divided Government Works," Fox News, April 9, 2011, http://politics.blogs.foxnews.com/2011/04/09/obama-signs-continuing-resolution-administration-says-divided-government-works.

94 *In an internally circulated six-page chronology:* Author obtained copy of document.

94  *The Congressional Budget office, which produces:* David A. Fahrenthold, "Budget Deal: CBO Analysis Shows Initial Spending Cuts Less Than Expected," *The Washington Post*, April 14, 2011; Naftali Bendavid, "U.S. Budget Analysis Shows Smaller Savings," *The Wall Street Journal*, April 14, 2011.

94  *The battle over the continuing resolution, Obama later recalled:* On the record author interview with President Barack Obama, July 11, 2012.

96  *Failure to raise the debt limit in a timely manner:* U.S. Government Printing Office, "Federal Reserve's First Monetary Policy Report for 2011," hearing transcript, http://www.gpo.gov/fdsys/pkg/ CHRG-112shrg65824/html/CHRG-112shrg65824.htm.

96  *It would be "catastrophic and unpredictable":* Victoria McGrane and Damian Paletta, "Dimon: Hitting Debt Ceiling Would Be 'Catastrophic,'" *The Wall Street Journal*, March 30, 2011.

### CHAPTER ELEVEN

The information in this chapter comes primarily from background interviews with six firsthand sources and contemporaneous notes by a participant.

104  *"We're all connected":* Compilation of Presidential Documents, "Remarks at George Washington University," April 13, 2011, http:// www.gpo.gov/fdsys/browse/collection.action?collectionCode=CPD.

105  *Ryan took out his BlackBerry:* Press release, "Paul Ryan Responds to President's Disappointing, Partisan Speech," Office of Representative Paul Ryan, April 13, 2011, http://paulryan.house.gov.

106  *Ryan's presence at the George Washington University speech:* Lori Montgomery, "Obama Address Was Surprise Attack, GOP Lawmakers Say," *The Washington Post*, April 14, 2011; Mark Landler and Michael D. Shear, "Obama's Debt Plan Sets Stage for Long Battle over Spending," *The New York Times*, April 13, 2011; editorial, "The Presidential Divider," *The Wall Street Journal*, April 14, 2011; see also Jackie Calmes, "Obama's Deficit Dilemma," *The New York Times*, February 27, 2012.

106  *"I was not aware when I gave":* On the record author interview with President Barack Obama, July 11, 2012.

108  *The three free trade agreements:* Binyamin Appelbaum and Jennifer Steinhauer, "Congress Ends 5-Year Standoff on Trade Deals in Rare Accord," *The New York Times*.

109  *Two days later, on October 14, Obama traveled:* Compilation of Presidential Documents, "Remarks at General Motors Orion Assembly

Plant in Lake Orion, Michigan," October 14, 2011, http://www.gpo
.gov/fdsys/browse/collection.action?collectionCode=CPD.

## CHAPTER TWELVE

The information in this chapter comes primarily from background interviews
with eight firsthand sources and contemporaneous notes by six participants.

## CHAPTER THIRTEEN

The information in this chapter comes primarily from background interviews
with six firsthand sources and contemporaneous notes by two participants.

## CHAPTER FOURTEEN

The information in this chapter comes primarily from background interviews
with five firsthand sources and contemporaneous notes by two participants.

## CHAPTER FIFTEEN

The information in this chapter comes primarily from background interviews
with five firsthand sources and contemporaneous notes by two participants.

134 *On Saturday morning, June 18:* On the record author interview with
   Speaker John Boehner, June 7, 2012.
134 *"The president and I whupped 'em pretty good":* Excerpt of a Playbook
   Breakfast video interview between Mike Allen and Speaker Boehner,
   December 14, 2011, http://www.politico.com/playbook-breakfast/.
134 *Later, the president recalled the conversation:* On the record author
   interview with President Barack Obama, July 11, 2012.
136 *He noted that McConnell had said:* Corbett B. Daly, "Schumer Questions
   GOP Sincerity on Job Creation," *Face the Nation*, CBS, June 19, 2011,
   http://www.cbsnews.com/2100-3460_162-20072389.html.
137 *"REVENUE" was the dreaded word:* Author obtained copy of document.

## CHAPTER SIXTEEN

The information in this chapter comes primarily from background interviews
with six firsthand sources and contemporaneous notes by a participant.

143 *"I came in through the South Entrance":* On the record author interview
   with Speaker John Boehner, June 7, 2012.
145 *Asked about the conversation with Boehner:* On the record author
   interview with President Barack Obama, July 11, 2012.
147 *A few hours later, the president appeared:* Compilation of Presidential
   Documents, "Address to the Nation on the Drawdown of United

States Military Personnel in Afghanistan," June 22, 2011, http://www.gpo.gov/fdsys/browse/collection.action?collectionCode=CPD.

## CHAPTER SEVENTEEN

The information in this chapter comes primarily from background interviews with eight firsthand sources and contemporaneous notes by a participant.

150 *Early on the morning of Thursday, June 23, Cantor gave:* Janet Hook and Corey Boles, "Tax Dispute Stalls Debt Talks," *The Wall Street Journal*, June 24, 2011.

153 *"I can't," Cantor said:* see Ibid.

153 *"Deficit talks in danger":* David Rogers, "Deficit Talks in Danger as Eric Cantor Bails," *Politico*, June 23, 2001, http://www.politico.com.

153 *The next day, the* New York Times *editorial board:* Editorial, "Their Temper Tantrum," *The New York Times*, June 23, 2011, p. A24.

154 *"I understand his frustration":* Benjy Sarlin, "With Ball in Speaker's Court, Boehner Doubles Down on Anti-Tax Rhetoric," *Talking Points Memo*, June 23, 2011, http://tpmdc.talkingpointsmemo.com/2011/06/with-ball-in-speakers-court-boehner-doubles-down-on-anti-tax-rhetoric.php.

154 *In a press conference, he laid out:* Felicia Sonmez, "Boehner: Tax Hikes in a Debt Deal Proposal 'Cannot Pass' House," 2chambers blog, *The Washington Post*, June 24, 2011, http://www.washingtonpost.com/blogs/2chambers/post/boehner-tax-hikes-in-debt-deal-cannot-pass-house/2011/06/24/AGtLj8iH_blog.html.

154 *On June 29, 2011, President Obama appeared:* Compilation of Presidential Documents, "The President's News Conference," June 29, 2011, http://www.gpo.gov/fdsys/browse/collection.action?collectionCode=CPD.

155 *A statement released by the speaker's office:* Press release, "Speaker Boehner Statement in Response to Remarks by President Obama," office of Speaker John Boehner, June 28 [*sic*], 2012, http://www.speaker.gov.

155 *At the White House, Nabors, Lew and Sperling:* Author obtained document.

156 *On July 1, the White House sent:* Ibid.

157 *In bold type on the first line:* Ibid.

158 *On Sunday, July 3, Boehner had a bunch:* On the record author interview with Speaker John Boehner, June 7, 2012.

158 *It was a brutally hot summer evening:* Historical weather for Washington, D.C., Farmers' Almanac, http://www.farmersalmanac.com/weather-history/20052/2011/07/03/.

159  *"The more I got into this":* On the record author interview with Speaker John Boehner, June 7, 2012.

160  *That's exactly right:* On the record author interview with President Barack Obama, July 11, 2012.

### CHAPTER EIGHTEEN

The information in this chapter comes primarily from background interviews with nine firsthand sources and contemporaneous notes by two participants.

161  *On Tuesday, July 5, the president made a short statement:* Compilation of Presidential Documents, "Remarks Prior to White House Press Secretary James 'Jay' Carney's Briefing," July 5, 2011, http://www.gpo .gov/fdsys/browse/collection.action?collectionCode=CPD.

162  *In a statement released later, Boehner said:* Press release, "Speaker Boehner on President Obama's Comments Regarding His Request for a Debt Limit Increase," Office of Speaker John Boehner, July 4 [*sic*], 2011, http://www.speaker.gov.

162  *Loper handed them Boehner's counterproposal:* Author obtained document.

166  *"Listen, $788 billion was real simple":* On the record author interview with Speaker John Boehner, June 7, 2012.

166  *On the morning of Thursday, July 7:* Carl Hulse and Mark La Landler, "President Looks to Broader Deal in Deficit Talks," *The New York Times*, July 7, 2011, p. A1.

168  *"Okay, so, he wants to get reelected":* On the record author interview with Speaker John Boehner, June 7, 2012.

169  *The president spoke to the media at about 1 p.m.:* Lori Montgomery and Paul Kane, "Obama Calls Debt Talks 'Constructive,' Invites Parties to Reconvene Sunday," *The Washington Post*, July 7, 2011.

169  *Afterward, Pelosi expressed concern:* David Rogers, "Debt Talks Turn to Tax Reform," *Politico*, July 7, 2011, http://www.politico.com.

169  *"Oh, hell yeah!":* On the record author interview with Speaker John Boehner, June 7, 2012.

170  *"Don't insult us," Pelosi retorted:* Jonathan Allen, "Nancy Pelosi's Back at the Negotiating Table on Debt Ceiling," *Politico*, July 8, 2011, http:// www.politico.com.

### CHAPTER NINETEEN

The information in this chapter comes primarily from background interviews with six firsthand sources and contemporaneous notes by a participant.

171  *At 8:30 a.m. on July 8, the Labor Department announced:* Annalyn Censky, "June Jobs Report: Hiring Slows, Unemployment Rises," CNN Money,

July 8, 2011, http://money.cnn.com/2011/07/08/news/economy/june
_jobs_report_unemployment/index.htm; see also Employment
Situation News Release, "The Employment Situation—June 2010,"
U.S. Bureau of Labor Statistics, July 2, 2010, http://www.bls.gov/
schedule/archives/empsit_nr.htm.

171 *"After hearing this morning's jobs report":* Press release, "Speaker
Boehner: Tax Hikes on Job Creators Would Make Things Worse,"
Office of Speaker John Boehner, July 8, 2011, http://www.speaker.gov.

171 *Asked about the prospects:* On the record author interview with Speaker
John Boehner, June 7, 2012 and Ibid.

172 *Though Conrad had been the impetus:* Conrad's letter to author, April 26,
2012.

172 *Most of them had signed a pledge:* See "What Is the Taxpayer Protection
Pledge?" Americans for Tax Reform, http://www.atr.org/taxpayer
-protection-pledge.

173 *While serving on the Simpson-Bowles commission:* "Conrad Remarks at
Hearing on President's FY 2012 Defense and International Affairs
Budgets," March 10, 2011, http://budget.senate.gov/democratic/index
.cfm/speeches-and-remarks?ContentRecord_id=61ce0ef9-6f41-4dee
-9a8e-3bf1b0f60aa2.

174 *He handed Sperling one sheet of paper:* Author obtained document
entitled "Individual Income Tax Reform," dated July 8, 2011.

175 *He decided to leave no doubt:* Author obtained two-page document dated
July 9, 2011.

175 *In an interview, the president recalled:* On the record author interview
with President Barack Obama, July 11, 2012.

176 *They began drafting a pessimistic memo for Boehner:* Author obtained document entitled "Tax Reform Principles: Key Areas of Disagreement."

## CHAPTER TWENTY

The information in this chapter comes primarily from background interviews
with seven firsthand sources and contemporaneous notes by a participant.

179 *That same morning, Cantor read:* Editorial, "Boehner's Obama Gamble,"
*The Wall Street Journal,* July 9, 2011.

180 *The* New York Times *story on $1 trillion in revenue:* Carl Hulse and Mark
La Landler, "President Looks to Broader Deal in Deficit Talks," *The
New York Times,* July 7, 2011, p. A1.

180 *The memo was titled:* Author obtained memo.

182 *In an interview, the president recalled:* On the record author interview
with President Barack Obama, July 11, 2012.

184 *"Despite good-faith efforts"*: Press release, "Statement by Speaker Boehner on Debt Limit Discussions," Office of Speaker John Boehner, July 9, 2011, http://www.speaker.gov.

186 *In an interview later, Boehner described his decision*: On the record author interview with Speaker John Boehner, June 7, 2012.

186 *Asked about Boehner's explanation for pulling out*: On the record author interview with President Barack Obama, July 11, 2012.

### CHAPTER TWENTY-ONE

The information in this chapter comes primarily from background interviews with six firsthand sources and contemporaneous notes by a participant.

189 *In an interview, Obama later recalled using*: On the record author interview with President Barack Obama, July 11, 2012.

### CHAPTER TWENTY-TWO

The information in this chapter comes primarily from background interviews with four firsthand sources.

200 *"The things I will not consider"*: Compilation of Presidential Documents, "The President's News Conference," July 11, 2011, http://www.gpo .gov/fdsys/browse/collection.action?collectionCode=CPD.

200 *Later that morning at the Capitol*: Press release, "Speaker Boehner Remarks on Ongoing Debt Limit Discussions," Office of Speaker John Boehner, July 11, 2011, http://www.speaker.gov.

201 *Cantor handed out copies*: Author review of notes from PowerPoint presentation.

207 *That evening by 8:30*, Politico: Jonathan Allen and Jake Sherman, "With John Boehner Bailing, Eric Cantor Ascends as GOP Voice," *Politico*, July 11, 2011, http://www.politico.com.

### CHAPTER TWENTY-THREE

The information in this chapter comes primarily from background interviews with four firsthand sources and contemporaneous notes by a participant.

208 *"Republicans have a plan"*: John Bresnahan, Jake Sherman and Jonathan Allen, "Angry John Boehner Rallies GOP Troops on Debt Limit," *Politico*, July 12, 2011, http://www.politico.com; see also press release, "Speaker Boehner: GOP Has Been Clear: Real Spending Cuts & Reforms, No Tax Hikes," Office of Speaker John Boehner, July 12, 2011, http://www.speaker.gov.

208 *McConnell pulled no punches*: Floor updates, "Reid, McConnell," July 12,

2011, http://www.republican.senate.gov/public/index.cfm/floor
-updates?Date=12-Jul-11.

209 *In response to a question about what would happen:* Corbett B. Daly,
"Obama Says He Cannot Guarantee Social Security Checks Will Go
Out on August 3," CBS News, July 12, 2011, http://www.cbsnews
.com/8301-503544_162-20078789-503544.html.

209 *Asked about his relationship with the speaker:* Scott Pelley, "Obama:
Boehner 'Would Like to Do the Right Thing,' " CBS News, July 12,
2011, http://www.cbsnews.com/stories/2011/07/12/eveningnews/
main20078935.shtml.

209 *"Well, then, he's going to have to explain":* Ibid.

209 *"John," Obama began, "you said this was my problem":* John Bresnahan,
Jake Sherman and Jonathan Allen, "Angry John Boehner Rallies GOP
Troops on Debt Limit," *Politico,* July 12, 2011, http://www.politico
.com; press release, "Speaker Boehner: GOP Has Been Clear: Real
Spending Cuts & Reforms, No Tax Hikes," Office of Speaker John
Boehner, July 12, 2011, http://www.speaker.gov.

210 *Neither he nor Obama addressed McConnell's assertion:* Floor updates,
"Reid, McConnell," July 12, 2011, http://www.republican.senate.gov/
public/index.cfm/floor-updates?Date=12-Jul-11.

211 *For his part, McConnell was direct:* On the record author interview
with Senate Minority Leader Mitch McConnell, July 12, 2011.

217 *"We both agree on entitlements":* Jake Sherman and Jonathan Allen,
"House GOP Not Ready to Blink on Debt Negotiations," *Politico,*
July 12, 2011, http://www.politico.com.

217 *In an interview later, Boehner said:* On the record author interview with
Speaker John Boehner, June 7, 2012.

## CHAPTER TWENTY-FOUR

The information in this chapter comes primarily from background interviews with six firsthand sources and contemporaneous notes by a participant.

219 *In an interview, the president said:* On the record author interview with
President Barack Obama, July 11, 2012.

220 *The Moody's report stated:* Abby Phillip, "Moody's Puts Debt Rating on
Review," *Politico,* July 13, 2011, http://www.politico.com.

225 *Cantor described Obama as "abruptly walking out":* Russell Berman and
Sam Youngman, "Obama Warns Cantor: 'Don't Call My Bluff,' "
*The Hill,* July 13, 2011, http://thehill.com/homenews/administration/

171403-obama-warns-cantor-dont-call-my-bluff-in-debt-talks; blog
post, "The Leader's Ledger," Office of Majority Leader Eric Cantor,
July 13, 2011, http://majorityleader.gov.

226 *The president later recalled the confrontation:* On the record author
interview with President Barack Obama, July 11, 2012.

## CHAPTER TWENTY-FIVE

The information in this chapter comes primarily from background interviews
with six firsthand sources and contemporaneous notes by a participant.

228 *"With so much at stake":* Congressional Record, Vol. 157, No. 105,
July 14, 2011, http://www.gpo.gov/fdsys/pkg/CREC-2011-07-14/html/
CREC-2011-07-14-pt1-PgS4568.htm.

229 *"I just went up and put my arm around Eric":* On the record interview
with Speaker John Boehner, June 7, 2012.

229 *"Let me just say we have been in this fight".* Felicia Sonmez, "Boehner
Defends Cantor from Democratic Criticism in Debt Limit Talks,"
2chambers blog, *The Washington Post,* July 14, 2011, http://www
.washingtonpost.com/blogs/2chambers/post/boehner-defends-cantor
-from-democratic-criticism-in-debt-limit-talks/2011/07/14/
gIQAzjfTEI_blog.html.

229 *Afterward, when Boehner and Cantor were waiting together:* On the record
author interview with Speaker John Boehner, June 7, 2012.

230 *"S&P is going to issue a statement":* Press release, "S&P Places U.S.
'AAA/A-1+' Rtgs on CreditWatch Negative," Standard & Poor's,
July 14, 2011, 7:46 p.m., http://www.reuters.com/article/2011/07/14/
market-ratings-creditwatch-us-idUSWNA372820110714.

234 *That evening, there was the congressional baseball game:* "Congress at
the Bat," *Talking Points Memo,* July 14, 2011, http://media
.talkingpointsmemo.com/slideshow/congress-at-the-bat-50th-annual
-congressional-baseball-game.

235 *Reid had, that day, expressed support:* Paul M. Krawzak, "Backup Debt
Plan in the Works," *Congressional Quarterly,* July 14, 2011, http://public
.cq.com/docs/news/news-000003908298.html.

## CHAPTER TWENTY-SIX

The information in this chapter comes primarily from background interviews
with four firsthand sources.

237 *In an interview a year later:* On the record author interview with Speaker
John Boehner, June 7, 2012.

237 *Boehner handed Daley and Geithner a two-page offer:* Two-page document obtained by author entitled "Deficit Reduction Package," dated July 15, 2011.

239 *"There was one point before this":* On the record author interview with Speaker John Boehner, June 7, 2012.

### CHAPTER TWENTY-SEVEN

The information in this chapter comes primarily from background interviews with six firsthand sources and contemporaneous notes by a participant.

240 *The second was a four-page counteroffer:* Author obtained document entitled "Deficit Reduction Package," dated July 17, 2011.

243 *The president would later recall that he was pleased:* On the record author interview with President Barack Obama, July 11, 2012.

245 *In an interview later, Boehner said:* On the record author interview with Speaker John Boehner, June 7, 2012.

246 *In an interview, the president recalled:* On the record author interview with President Barack Obama, July 11, 2012.

248 *At 7 p.m., Loper sent a three-page offer:* Author obtained document, titled "Deficit Reduction Package," dated July 17, 2011.

250 *In an interview he recalled a discussion with the president:* On the record author interview with Speaker John Boehner, June 7, 2012.

250 *Asked about this the president said:* On the record author interview with President Barack Obama, July 11, 2012.

250 *It was really about votes? I asked:* On the record author interview with Speaker John Boehner, June 7, 2012.

### CHAPTER TWENTY-EIGHT

The information in this chapter comes primarily from background interviews with six firsthand sources.

252 *But in a meeting with fellow senators that morning:* Gang of Six, Executive Summary on Talking Points Memo, http://talkingpointsmemo.com/documents/2011/07/executive-summary-of-gang-of-six-deficit-reduction-plan.php.

252 *Because it was bipartisan:* Jannifer Haberkorn and Matt DoBias, "Gang of Six Plan Looks to Health for Savings," *Politico,* July 19, 2011, http://www.politico.com; Manu Raju, "Gang of Six Back from the Brink," *Politico,* July 19, 2011, http://www.politico.com.

253 *"Some progress was made":* Compilation of Presidential Documents, "Remarks Prior to White House Press Secretary James 'Jay' Carney's

Briefing and an Exchange with Reporters," July 19, 2011, http:// www.gpo.gov/fdsys/browse/collection.action?collectionCode=CPD.

254 *Asked about his reaction to the Gang of Six:* On the record author interview with President Barack Obama, July 11, 2012.

255 *So Cantor put out a statement praising:* Russell Berman, "Cantor Gives 'Gang of Six' Plan Mixed Review," *The Hill*, July 19, 2011, http:// thehill.com/homenews/house/172423-cantor-gives-gang-of-six -plan-mixed-review.

255 *Through a spokesman, Boehner said:* Andy Sullivan, "Senate Budget Plan Falls Short: Boehner Aide," Reuters, July 19, 2011, http://in.reuters .com/article/2011/07/19/usa-debt-boehner-gangofsix-idINWEN 564220110719.

256 *He later told* The Washington Post: Peter Wallsten, Lori Montgomery and Scott Wilson, "He Promised Change in Washington. Then the Debt Deal Collapsed. So Obama Changed Course," *The Washington Post*, March 18, 2012, p. A9.

257 *When he was done he had a three-page offer:* Author review of document entitled "Deficit Reduction Package—Nabors Draft 7/19/2011 6:27 PM."

259 *It was panned by the American Enterprise Institute:* Marc A. Thiessen, "The Gang of Six's $3 Trillion Tax Hike," *The Washington Post*, July 21, 2011; Mark Steyn, "Gang of Six Bag of Tricks," The Corner blog, *National Review*, July 19, 2011, http://www.nationalreview.com/ corner/272254/gang-six-bag-tricks-mark-steyn; James C. Capretta, "The Gang of Six Disaster: The Worst Plan So Far," ibid., July 20, 2011, http://www.nationalreview.com/corner/272311/gang-six -disaster-worst-plan-so-far-james-c-capretta; editorial, "The Gang of Six Play," *The Wall Street Journal*, July 21, 2011.

### CHAPTER TWENTY-NINE

The information in this chapter comes primarily from background interviews with eight firsthand sources and contemporaneous notes by a participant.

### CHAPTER THIRTY

The information in this chapter comes primarily from background interviews with 10 firsthand sources and contemporaneous notes by a participant.

272 *A band of angry Democratic senators:* Alexander Bolton, "Reid: 'I'm the Senate Majority Leader. Why Don't I Know About This Deal?' " *The Hill*, July 21, 2011, http://thehill.com/homenews/senate/

172895-reid-confronts-obama-budget-director-on-possible-debt
-ceiling-deal; Meredith Shiner, "Silence on Obama Meeting Follows
Uproar over Debt Deal," *Roll Call*, July 21, 2011, http://www.rollcall
.com/news/senate_democrats_volcanic_over_deal_rumors-207575-1
.html.

273   *Headlined "Push Intensifies":* Carl Hulse and Jackie Calmes, "Push
      Intensifies for Larger Deal on Debt Impasse," *The New York Times*,
      July 20, 2011, http://www.nytimes.com/2011/07/21/us/
      politics/21fiscal.html.

273   *When Lew was done, Senator Barbara Mikulski:* Paul Kane, "Debt
      Talks Bring Tensions Between Democrats, Obama to Surface,"
      *The Washington Post*, July 21, 2011.

273   *Reid was so angry that he talked to reporters:* Manu Raju, "Harry Reid:
      Deal Must Have Revenues," *Politico*, July 21, 2011, http://
      www.politico.com.

275   *"Geithner has two concerns," the president later recalled:* On the record
      author interview with President Barack Obama, July 11, 2012.

277   *In an interview, Boehner, who was consulting notes:* On the record author
      interview with Speaker John Boehner, June 7, 2012.

278   *Obama later told me that he presented the speaker:* On the record author
      interview with President Barack Obama, July 11, 2012.

281   *Asked in an interview whether the Gang of Six releasing their plan:* Ibid.

### CHAPTER THIRTY-ONE

The information in this chapter comes primarily from background interviews
with eight firsthand sources.

285   *The president later recalled the meeting with Reid and Pelosi:* On the record
      author interview with President Barack Obama, July 11, 2012.

287   *The draft proposal Nabors sent:* Author obtained copy of document.

### CHAPTER THIRTY-TWO

The information in this chapter comes primarily from background interviews
with seven firsthand sources.

295   *Boehner told me later, "Harry and I":* On the record author interview with
      Speaker John Boehner, June 7, 2012.

296   *"What happened to common courtesy?":* Author review of emails.

297   *One reporter joked:* David A. Fahrenthold and Lori Montgomery, "Death
      of 'Grand Bargain' Boils Down to Two Men, Divided and Distrustful,"
      *The Washington Post*, July 23, 2011, p. A11.

299 *"He was spewing coals"*: On the record author interview with Speaker John Boehner, June 7, 2012.

299 *Boehner later recalled, "He wasn't going"*: Ibid.

299 *"I was pretty angry," Obama told me*: On the record author interview with President Barack Obama, July 11, 2012.

301 *"I just got a call about a half hour ago"*: Compilation of Presidential Documents, "Remarks on the Federal Budget and an Exchange with Reporters," July 22, 2011, http://www.gpo.gov/fdsys/browse/collection.action?collectionCode=CPD.

301 *"I'd sat here and watched his performance"*: On the record author interview with Speaker John Boehner, June 7, 2012.

302 *"There was an agreement with the White House"*: "Rep. John A. Boehner, R-Ohio, Holds a News Conference," CQ Transcriptions, July 22, 2011.

302 *Later Boehner told me that he realized the importance*: On the record author interview with Speaker John Boehner, June 7, 2012.

### CHAPTER THIRTY-THREE

The information in this chapter comes primarily from background interviews with six firsthand sources and contemporaneous notes by a participant.

304 *Leader Pelosi will not be able to join the call*: Author review of email.

307 *How did the president feel*: On the record author interview with President Barack Obama, July 11, 2012.

308 *Boehner arranged an afternoon conference call*: Author review of an internal readout of the conference call.

310 *At 5:21 p.m., Michael Steel, Boehner's press secretary*: Author review of email.

311 *"I will not support any short-term agreement"*: Press release, "Reid Statement Reaffirming Opposition to Short-Term Debt Ceiling Increase," Office of Senate Majority Leader Harry Reid, July 23, 2011, http://www.reid.senate.gov.

311 *"Listen," Boehner recalled telling the president*: On the record author interview with Speaker John Boehner, June 7, 2012.

312 *Boehner recalled, "He was moaning and groaning"*: Ibid.

312 *In a statement to the press, Boehner's spokesman*: Jamie Klatell, "Reid: I Hope GOP Leaders Will Reconsider Their Intransigence in Negotiations," *The Hill*, July 24, 2011, http://thehill.com/homenews/senate/173135-reid-hopes-gop-leaders-will-reconsider-their-intransigence.

312 *Asked about Boehner's description*: On the record author interview with President Barack Obama, July 11, 2012.

## CHAPTER THIRTY-FOUR

The information in this chapter comes primarily from background interviews with six firsthand sources.

314 *On Sunday morning, July 24, Boehner appeared:* Chris Wallace, "Treasury Secretary Tim Geithner, Speaker of the House Boehner Talk Debt Ceiling Deadline," *Fox News Sunday*, Fox, July 24, 2011, http://www.foxnews.com/on-air/fox-news-sunday/2011/07/24/treasury-secretary-tim-geithner-speaker-house-john-boehner-talk-debt-ceiling-deadline.

315 *In an interview nearly a year later:* On the record author interview with Speaker John Boehner, June 7, 2012.

315 *Did someone hang up on the other?:* Ibid.

320 *Reid and Pelosi left the White House:* Jennifer Steinhauer and Helene Cooper, "Rival Debt Plans Being Assembled by Party Leaders," *The New York Times*, July 25, 2011, p. A1.

320 *Asked about the meeting with Reid and Krone:* On the record author interview with President Barack Obama, July 11, 2012.

320 *Late that night, the majority leader released a $2.7 trillion deficit reduction plan:* Jake Sherman, Manu Raju and John Bresnahan, "Stalemated, Parties Go Separate Ways," *Politico*, July 24, 2011, http://www.politico.com.

321 *"It will include enough spending cuts":* Press release, Office of Senate Majority Leader Harry Reid, July 23, 2011, http://www.reid.senate.gov/newsroom/pr_072411_ceiling.cfm.

321 *Using OCO, Boehner later told me:* On the record author interview with Speaker John Boehner, June 7, 2012.

## CHAPTER THIRTY-FIVE

The information in this chapter comes primarily from background interviews with six firsthand sources and contemporaneous notes by a participant.

322 *The White House publicly endorsed Reid's plan:* White House press release, "Statement by the Press Secretary," July 25, 2011, http://www.whitehouse.gov/the-press-office/2011/07/25/statement-press-secretary.

323 *In an interview later, McConnell said:* On the record author interview with Senate Minority Leader Mitch McConnell, July 12, 2011.

324 *"Interest rates would skyrocket":* Compilation of Presidential Documents, "Address to the Nation on the Federal Budget," July 25, 2011, http://www.gpo.gov/fdsys/browse/collection.action?collectionCode=CPD.

324  *"This isn't a game of chicken"*: Scott Wong and Manu Raju, "Harry Reid's Debt Ceiling Plan Faces Tough Odds," *Politico*, July 25, 2011, http://www.politico.com.

324  *"The debt limit vote sucks"*: Robert Draper, *Do Not Ask What Good We Do: Inside the U.S. House of Representatives* (New York: Free Press, 2012), pp. 246–247.

325  *Later that day, the White House issued a warning:* Statement of Administration Policy on S.627—Budget Control Act of 2011, Office of Management and Budget, July 26, 2011, http://www.whitehouse .gov/sites/default/files/omb/legislative/sap/112/saps627r_20110726 .pdf.

325  *His job became more difficult that afternoon:* Letter to Speaker John Boehner, Analysis of the Impact on the Deficit of the Budget Control Act of 2011 as Proposed in the House, Congressional Budget Office, July 26, 2011, http://www.cbo.gov/sites/default/files/cbofiles/ ftpdocs/123xx/doc12336/housebudgetcontrolact.pdf.

328  *In an interview, Obama later said he had recognized:* On the record author interview with President Barack Obama, July 11, 2012.

329  *We're going to the chapel to pray:* Lisa Mascaro and Kathleen Hennessey, "Boehner, Hitting Another Wall on Debt Limit Plan, Calls Off Vote," *Los Angeles Times*, July 28, 2011.

## CHAPTER THIRTY-SIX

The information in this chapter comes primarily from background interviews with seven firsthand sources.

330  *It finally passed 218–210:* Carl Hulse and Robert Pear, "Senate Quickly Kills Boehner Deal," *The New York Times*, July 30, 2011, p. A1.

330  *A clearly frustrated Boehner said after the vote:* Press release, "Congressman Boehner Remarks on the House Floor re: the GOP Budget," Office of Speaker John Boehner, http://boehner.house.gov/ news/documentprint.aspx?DocumentID=254536.

## CHAPTER THIRTY-SEVEN

The information in this chapter comes primarily from background interviews with eight firsthand sources and contemporaneous notes by a participant.

343  *The House defeated the Reid bill at about 3:15 p.m.:* Carl Hulse, "House Rejects Reid Debt Ceiling Proposal," Caucus blog, *The New York Times*, July 30, 2011, http://thecaucus.blogs.nytimes.com/2011/07/30/ house-rejects-reid-debt-ceiling-proposal/.

343 *McConnell went to the Senate floor:* Congressional Record—Senate, July 30, 2011, p. S5090, http://www.gpo.gov/fdsys/pkg/CREC-2011-07-30/pdf/CREC-2011-07-30-pt1-PgS5090-2.pdf.

343 *"We are now fully engaged, the speaker and I":* "Rep. John A. Boehner, R-OHIO, Speaker of the House, Holds a News Conference," CQ Transcriptions, July 30, 2011.

344 *"Members of the Senate, that's not true":* Congressional Record—Senate, July 30, 2011, p. S5120, http://www.gpo.gov/fdsys/pkg/CREC-2011-07-30/pdf/CREC-2011-07-30-senate.pdf.

344 *"The fact is that the only way":* Ibid.

344 *"While the Republican leader is holding":* Ibid.

344 *"We are here today," Reid said:* Ibid.

## CHAPTER THIRTY-EIGHT

The information in this chapter comes primarily from background interviews with eight firsthand sources and contemporaneous notes by a participant.

348 *When Asia didn't tank:* See historical prices, Nikkei 225, July 25, 2011, http://finance.yahoo.com.

355 *Monday on the House floor:* Press release, "Pelosi Floor Speech on Budget Control Act of 2011," Office of House Minority Leader Nancy Pelosi, August 1, 2001, http://pelosi.house.gov/.

355 *The House passed the Rubik's cube:* Carl Hulse, "Long Battle on Debt Ending as Senate Set for Final Vote," *The New York Times*, August 1, 2011, p. A1.

355 *The Senate followed the next day with a vote:* Jennifer Steinhauer, "Debt Bill Is Signed, Ending a Fractious Battle," *The New York Times*, August 2, 2011, p. A1.

356 *House Budget Committee Chairman Paul Ryan blasted:* Paul Ryan, "Where's Your Budget, Mr. President?" *The Wall Street Journal*, August 3, 2011.

356 *Less expected was former Obama economics czar:* Lawrence Summers, "Moving Forward After the Debt Deal," *The Washington Post*, August 2, 2011.

## CHAPTER THIRTY-NINE

The information in this chapter comes primarily from background interviews with 12 firsthand sources and contemporaneous notes by two participants.

357 *The monthly jobs report came out:* Employment Situation News Release, "The Employment Situation—August 2011," U.S. Bureau of Labor

Statistics, September 2, 2011, http://www.bls.gov/schedule/archives/empsit_nr.htm.

358 *On September 8, Obama appeared:* Compilation of Presidential Documents, "Address Before a Joint Session of the Congress on Job Growth," September 8, 2011, http://www.gpo.gov/fdsys/browse/collection.action?collectionCode=CPD.

359 *On September 12 in the White House Rose Garden:* Compilation of Presidential Documents, "Remarks on Job Growth Legislation," September 12, 2011, http://www.gpo.gov/fdsys/browse/collection.action?collectionCode=CPD.

359 *In an interview, Boehner said:* On the record author interview with Speaker John Boehner, June 7, 2012.

361 *"I have gone way out on a limb":* Author obtained memo, dated October 26, 2011.

363 *At 4:45, she put out a press release:* Press release, "Statement from Co-Chairs of the Joint Select Committee on Deficit Reduction," Office of Senator Patty Murray, November 21, 2011, http://www.murray.senate.gov.

363 *"Washington's Super Failure," read a* Washington Post *editorial:* Editorial, "Washington's Super Failure," *The Washington Post*, November 22, 2011, p. A18.

363 *A New York Times headline said:* Michael Cooper, "A Failure Is Absorbed with Disgust and Fear, but Little Surprise," *The New York Times*, November 22, 2011, p. A19.

363 *During a one-hour visit to his second-floor office:* On the record author interview with Senate Minority Leader Mitch McConnell, July 12, 2011.

366 *"I know many Republicans have sworn":* Compilation of Presidential Documents, "Remarks on Payroll Tax Cuts and Unemployment Insurance," December 5, 2011, http://www.gpo.gov/fdsys/browse/collection.action?collectionCode=CPD.

368 *In the afternoon Boehner and Cantor held a telephone conference call:* Author review of notes of the conference call.

370 *"Well, it's pretty clear that I and our members":* Meet the Press transcript, NBC, December 18, 2011.

371 *"I think we need to recognize reality":* Ashley Killough, "McCain: Payroll Tax Cut Showdown 'Harming' the GOP," CNN Politics blog post, December 20, 2011, http://politicalticker.blogs.cnn.com/2011/12/20/mccain-payroll-tax-cut-showdown-harming-the-gop/.

371 *On Wednesday, December 21,* The Wall Street Journal: Editorial, "The GOP's Payroll Tax Fiasco," *The Wall Street Journal,* December 22, 2011.

372 *On December 23, in a speedy House session:* Jennifer Steinhauer, "For Payroll Tax Cut, Next Step Is Obama's Signature," The Caucus blog, *The New York Times,* December 23, 2011, http://thecaucus.blogs .nytimes.com/2011/12/23/for-payroll-tax-cut-next-step-is-obamas -desk/.

372 *At 1:25, the president delivered:* Compilation of Presidential Documents, "Remarks on Congressional Action on Payroll Tax Cut and Unemployment Insurance Legislation," December 23, 2011, http:// www.gpo.gov/fdsys/browse/collection.action?collectionCode=CPD.

372 *"The Humbling of the House GOP," said a headline:* Carrie Budoff Brown and Jonathan Allen, "The Humbling of the House GOP," *Politico,* December 23, 2011, http://www.politico.com.

372 *"Hate-Filled GOP Suffering from Self-Inflicted Wounds":* Thomas M. DeFrank, "Hate-Filled GOP Suffering from Self-Inflicted Wounds," *Daily News* (New York), December 23, 2011, p. 4.

372 *"House GOP Surrenders on Payroll Tax Cut":* Rosalind S. Helderman, "House GOP Surrenders on Payroll Tax Cut," *The Washington Post,* December 23, 2011, p. A1.

372 *Six days later, on February 17:* Steven Sloan, Richard Rubin and Kathleen Hunter, "Congress Passes Extension of Payroll Tax Cut," *Bloomberg,* February 18, 2012, http://www.bloomberg.com/news/print/ 2012-02-17/house-passes-extension-of-payroll-tax-cut-through -2012-by-vote-of-293-132.html.

373 *"You'll remember," he said, "I called on Congress":* Compilation of Presidential Documents, "Remarks on the Payroll Tax Cut and Unemployment Insurance Legislation," February 21, 2012, http:// www.gpo.gov/fdsys/browse/collection.action?collectionCode =CPD.

## CHAPTER FORTY

374 *In an interview about the debt ceiling:* On the record author interview with Speaker John Boehner, June 7, 2012.

374 *Daley at first said he was flattered:* Author phone interview with William Daley, June 2012.

375 *"I have no idea," Boehner said:* On the record author interview with Speaker John Boehner, June 7, 2012.

376 *In 2010, Boehner had a 94 percent:* Michael Barone and Chuck

McCutcheon, *Almanac of American Politics 2012* (Chicago: University of Chicago Press, 2011).

376 *"I don't know whether it's him":* On the record author interview with Speaker John Boehner, June 7, 2012.

377 *"I think John wanted to get a deal" the president said to me:* On the record author interview with President Barack Obama, July 11, 2012.

379 *"And I'm sure as hell going to do something about it":* On the record author interview with Speaker John Boehner, June 7, 2012.

# ACKNOWLEDGMENTS

This book is based almost entirely on my own reporting, interviews and review of documents and meeting notes.

My thanks go to all sources, named and unnamed, for their time, their willingness to provide me recollections of their experiences, their assessment and context, and in some cases backup notes and documentation.

This is my 17th book with my editor Alice Mayhew, book lover and idea machine, at Simon & Schuster. I am grateful for her expertise, her swift and sure editing, and her invaluable advice. My thanks, too, to Jonathan Karp, publisher, for his hands-on management at each crucial stage; and Carolyn K. Reidy, CEO, for her steadfast support.

At Simon & Schuster, I am also grateful to Michael Selleck, Executive Vice President, Sales and Marketing; Irene Kheradi, Vice President and Executive Managing Editor; Jackie Seow, Vice President and Art Director; Tracey Guest, Director of Publicity; Elisa Rivlin, S&S Counsel; Twisne Fan, Senior Director of Production; Nancy Singer, Director of Interior Design; Joy O'Meara, Design Director; Lisa Healy, Senior Production Editor; Jonathan Cox, Editorial Assistant; Martin Karlow, proofreader; and Susan Gamer, cold reader.

My thanks to Fred Chase, copy editor extraordinaire and counselor to the author and his assistants. He spent 10 days in Washington working with us. Fred's steady presence, wisdom, sharp eye, and ability to roll with the punches helped make this, our seventh book together, a genuine pleasure.

My friend Christian Williams spent more than a week in Washington reviewing the manuscript at an early stage. I'm grateful for his input and insights, which proved most valuable.

As always, Carl Bernstein, my former colleague and co-author on the Nixon Watergate story, provided sound advice and many ideas. I thank him for his assists and friendship. Special thanks as well to my friends Rick Atkinson and David Maraniss.

Many thanks to Kate Mertes and Richard Shrout for their indexing expertise.

My continuing admiration and many thanks go to Marcus Brauchli, Katharine Weymouth, Don Graham and Steve Luxenberg at *The Washington Post*.

I'd like to extend a note of special appreciation to MaryAnne Golon, Wendy Galietta and Marlon Correa at the *Post* for their swift and invaluable assistance supplying many of the photographs used in this book.

No project like this starts in a vacuum. In this case, it was filled by reporting and analysis done by countless reporters at *The Washington Post*, *The New York Times*, *The Wall Street Journal*, *Politico*, *Roll Call*, *The Hill*, the *Los Angeles Times*, the Associated Press, and many other news organizations. The contours and, at times, details of this story appeared in these publications.

Of particular relevance were a March 18, 2012, piece in *The Washington Post*, "He Promised Change in Washington. Then the Debt Deal Collapsed. So Obama Changed Course," by Peter Wallsten, Lori Montgomery and Scott Wilson, and an April 1, 2012, *New York Times Sunday Magazine* piece, "The Game Is Called Chicken," by Matt Bai.

Robert B. Barnett—agent, attorney, friend—provided invaluable help, as always. He is a unique presence and force in Washington, D.C. Because he represents President Obama and other political figures, he did not see this book until it was printed, nor was he consulted on its contents.

Rob, Evelyn and I share a deep gratitude for the kindnesses done and cares taken by Rosa Criollo and Jackie Crowe.

Tali, my eldest daughter, was not able to help edit this book because of the rushed production schedule. She, her husband Gabe, and their daughter, Zadie, my first and only granddaughter, are in our thoughts daily.

My daughter Diana, who is in her sophomore year of high school, matures daily and shows a remarkable love of learning and books.

This is the 14th book my wife, Elsa, has guided me through in our three decades together. All that makes sense in life, she provides— devotion, friendship and love.

# PHOTOGRAPHY CREDITS

# INDEX

# ABOUT THE AUTHOR

Bob Woodward is an associate editor at *The Washington Post,* where he has worked for 41 years. He has shared in two Pulitzer Prizes, first for the *Post's* coverage of the Watergate scandal, and later for coverage of the 9/11 terrorist attacks. He has authored or coauthored twelve #1 national nonfiction bestsellers.

He has two daughters, Tali and Diana, and lives in Washington, D.C., with his wife, writer Elsa Walsh.